Contents

Unit 1: Principles of Computer Science

Unit 2: Fundamentals of Computer Systems

Unit 3: Planning and Managing of Computing Projects

Unit 4: Software Design and Development Project

A small bit of small print

Pearson publishes Sample Assessment Material and the Specification on its website. This is the official content and this book should be used in conjunction with it. The questions in *Now try this* have been written to help you test your knowledge and skills. Remember: the real assessment may not look like this.

REVISE BTEC NATIONAL Computing

REVISION GUIDE

Series Consultant: Harry Smith

Authors: Steve Farrell, Mark Fishpool, Christine Gate and Richard McGill

While the publishers have made every attempt to ensure that advice on the qualification and its assessment is accurate, the official specification and associated assessment guidance materials are the only authoritative source of information and should always be referred to for definitive guidance.

This qualification is reviewed on a regular basis and may be updated in the future. Any such updates that affect the content of this Revision Guide will be outlined at **www.pearsonfe.co.uk/BTECchanges**. The eBook version of this Revision Guide will also be updated to reflect the latest guidance as soon as possible.

A note from the publisher

In order to ensure that this resource offers high-quality support for the associated Pearson qualification, it has been through a review process by the awarding body. This process confirms that this resource fully covers the teaching and learning content of the specification or part of a specification at which it is aimed. It also confirms that it demonstrates an appropriate balance between the development of subject skills, knowledge and understanding, in addition to preparation for assessment.

Endorsement does not cover any guidance on assessment activities or processes (e.g. practice questions or advice on how to answer assessment questions), included in the resource nor does it prescribe any particular approach to the teaching or delivery of a related course.

Pearson examiners have not contributed to any sections in this resource relevant to examination papers for which they had prior responsibility.

Examiners will not use endorsed resources as a source of material for any assessment set by Pearson.

Endorsement of a resource does not mean that the resource is required to achieve this Pearson qualification, nor does it mean that it is the only suitable material available to support the qualification, and any resource lists produced by the awarding body shall include this and other appropriate resources.

Introduction

Which units should you revise?

This Revision Guide has been designed to support you in preparing for the externally assessed units of your course. Remember that you won't necessarily be studying all the units included here – it will depend on the qualification you are taking.

BTEC National Qualification	Externally assessed units
For both: Extended Certificate Foundation Diploma	1 Principles of Computer Science 2 Fundamentals of Computer Systems
Extended Diploma	1 Principles of Computer Science 2 Fundamentals of Computer Systems 3 Planning and Management of Computing Projects 4 Software Design and Development Project

Your Revision Guide

Each unit in this Revision Guide contains two types of pages, shown below.

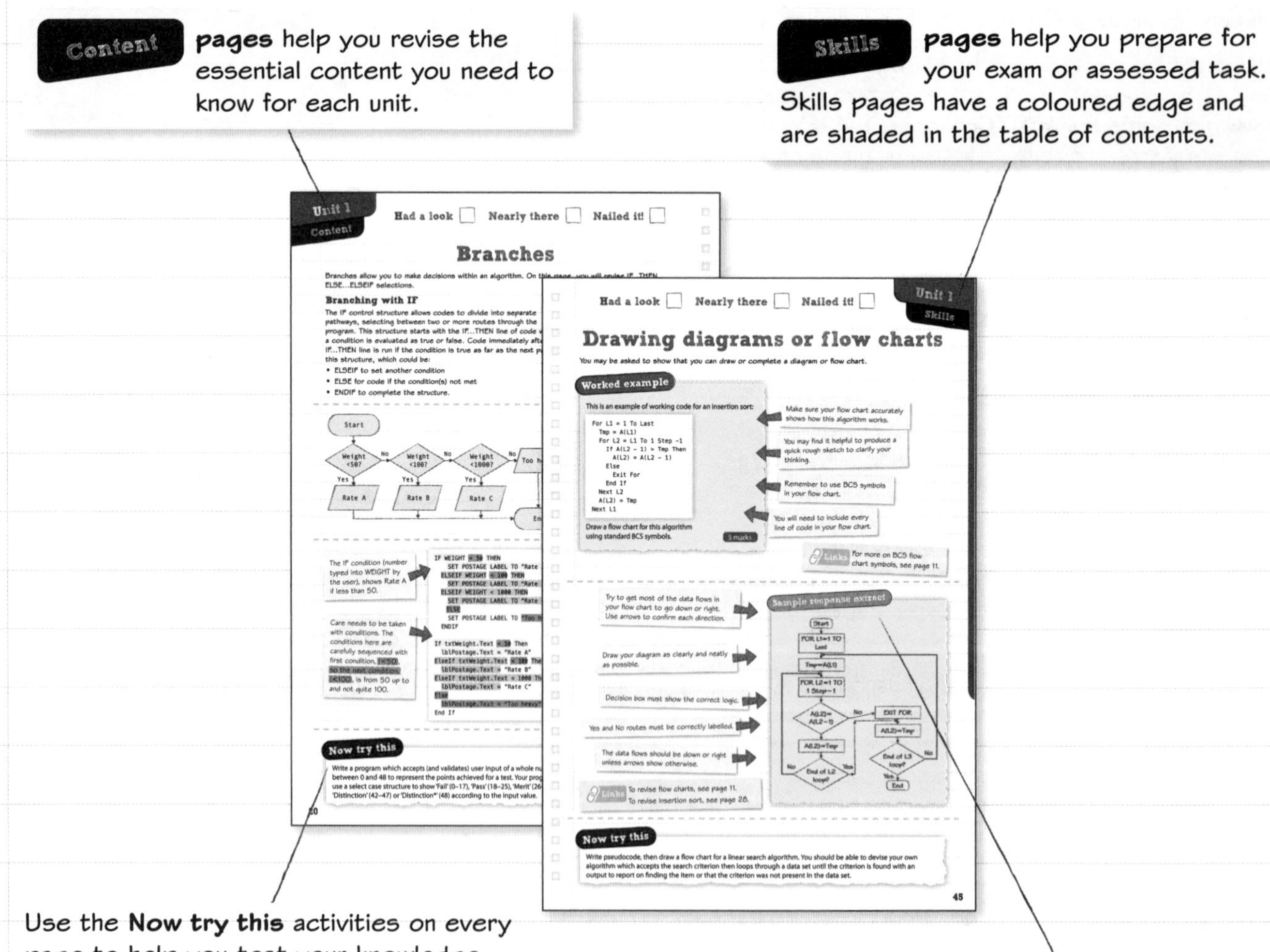

Content **pages** help you revise the essential content you need to know for each unit.

Skills **pages** help you prepare for your exam or assessed task. Skills pages have a coloured edge and are shaded in the table of contents.

Use the **Now try this** activities on every page to help you test your knowledge and practise the relevant skills.

Look out for the **sample response extracts** to revision questions or tasks on the skills pages. Post-its will explain their strengths and weaknesses.

Identifying problems and processes

Computational thinking enables you to analyse a problem, break it down into smaller parts, recognise patterns within the problem and finally identify a strategy to solve it. Over the next few pages, you will revise the first stage of computational thinking – decomposition.

Decomposition – step 1

Every computer program is made up of a number of processes or actions. Before an app can be written, the problem to be solved and the processes (actions) inside the app need to be identified. The first step in decomposition involves identifying and describing the problem and the processes required to solve it.

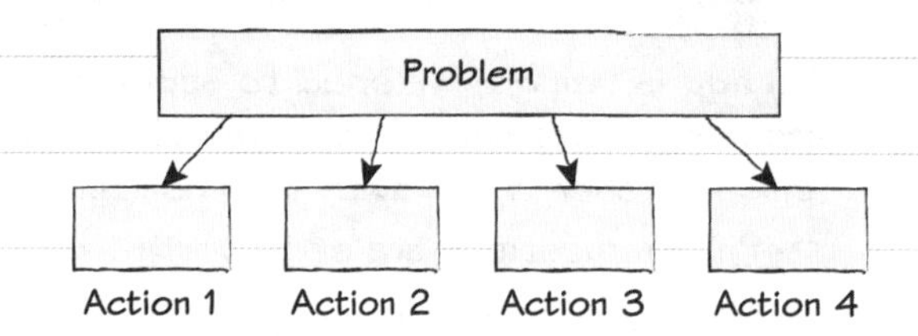

Case study: App to collate spreadsheets

An app is being developed to bring together several spreadsheets from different members of a team into one workbook which can then be used for a mail merge.

The mail merge is to be from a worksheet in the workbook using data which is selected and copied from member worksheets.

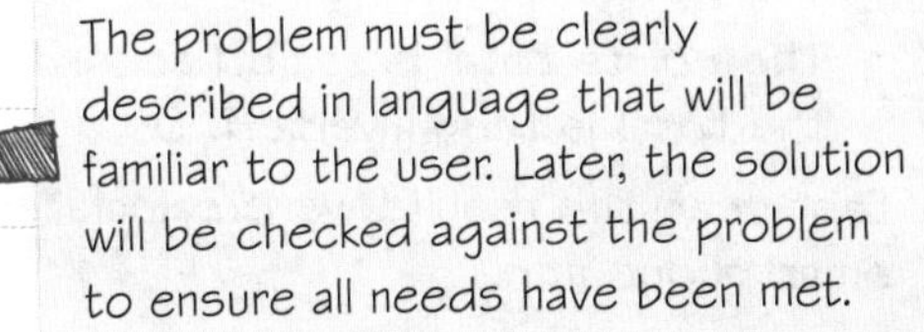

u Photography	-------	-------	E
-------	Animal Management	Photography	G
-------	Computer Games Develop	Electrical	C
-------	Fashion& Textile design	Animal Management	N
English Literatu	-------	-------	P
-------	Beauty therapy	Hairdressing	P
-------	Hairdressing	Animal Management	C
-------	Beauty therapy	Hairdressing	E
Photography	-------	-------	P
Biology	-------	-------	P
-------	Sport	Fitness	E
u Psychology	-------	-------	P
-------	Sport	Fitness	T
-------	Computer Games Develop	Wood	P
-------	Sport	Fitness	P
Art	-------	-------	N
-------	Theatrical & media makeup	Photography	E
-------	Hairdressing	Public Services	B
-------	Engineering	Computer Games Deve	C
-------	Fitness	Sport	N
-------	-------	-------	P
Art	-------	-------	H
-------	Theatrical & media makeup	Photography	C

1. Copy and paste member worksheets into designated worksheets in the master workbook.
2. Run macro code to loop into each of the designated worksheets. Loop down each row of data and loop along the columns in each row.
3. Select every data item that is not dashes and copy.
4. Move to appropriate cell in merge worksheet, then paste special as value.
5. Complete loops when blank cells are found.
6. Save workbook.

Once the problem has been described, the processes needed to program the solution can be identified. These become the framework of the solution, with the detailed steps needed to implement each process added at the next stage.

Only data which are names of courses are to be copied to the worksheets for mail merges. The cells with dashes in them are to be ignored.

Now try this

You are designing an app to allow builders to price jobs.

(a) Write down a list of outputs needed for this app.
(b) Write down a list of inputs needed for this app.
(c) Choose one input and describe the actions needed to test it for validity.

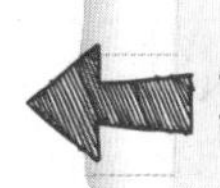

Think about what data is actually needed and don't include more than that.

Had a look ☐ Nearly there ☐ Nailed it! ☐

Breaking down problems and processes

Once the problem and processes have been identified, the next stage of decomposition is to break down the problem and processes into a sequence of steps.

App to support a competition

An app is being developed to support a charity treasure hunt. There will be four teams of up to six people. Each team will be given photographs of various places within the treasure hunt boundary and clues on sheets of paper. When calculating the scores, the following rules must be applied:

- Photo questions are each worth 1 point.
- Other questions are each worth 2 points.
- Deduct 1 point for a wrong answer.
- Blank answers are each worth 0 points.
- The points total is scaled according to how many are in the team: each member is worth 25%, and the total is then inverted. So a team of four has a scaling of 100% and a team of two has 200%.

Last year, the results were calculated in a spreadsheet. This year the organisers plan to use a smartphone app.

Steps in calculating points using app

1. Enter the team name with number of members in the team.
2. Enter number of correct photo questions.
3. Enter number of correct other questions.
4. Enter number of wrong questions.
5. Calculate points for correct other questions by multiplying number correct by 2.
6. Calculate subtotal by adding adjusted other questions to correct photo questions, then subtracting number of wrong questions.
7. Calculate team scaling.
8. Multiply subtotal by team scaling.
9. Repeat steps 1 to 8 for all teams.
10. Sort by totals to show winning team.

Team	Subtotal	Scaling	Total
A (2)	49	200%	98
B (3)	58	133%	77
C (6)	90	67%	60
D (4)	37	100%	37

Now try this

A local independent corner store would like to check its stock using a mobile phone app.

(a) What do you think would be needed to make this practical?

(b) What steps are needed to make the app work using the phone's camera to scan barcodes on stock items?

Think specifically about how barcodes can be used.

Communicating problems and processes

On this page, you will revise the final stage of decomposition – how to describe and communicate the key features of problems and processes to clients and other programmers.

Communicating algorithms

Describing problems and processes as a set of structured steps – an algorithm – will enable clients and programmers to understand how a proposed solution will work. At this stage, mistakes in the understanding of the problem or design flaws may become apparent before the project moves to the coding phase.

Revise algorithm design on page 8.

Restaurant tablet

A restaurant is planning to use a tablet for each table so diners can browse the menu using video footage of the ingredients and dishes, and read reviews from other diners before choosing their meal. The tablet will display the final bill, at which point diners can log into their PayPal account or make a payment using card or cash to the waiter. Clients may then enter feedback about their meal.

Using pseudocode

Pseudocode can be used to explain to clients and other programmers how code will work. This pseudocode shows the process by which a customer pays and is given an option to rate their experience at the restaurant.

```
If PayPal
  Enter tip amount
  Log in to PayPal
If not PayPal
  Waiter takes payment
User selects whether they want to leave feedback
If yes
  Enter star rating
  Write comments
Show thank you screen on the tablet
```

Revise how to produce, apply and interpret pseudocode on pages 9–10.

Using a flowchart

You could also use a flowchart to show the algorithms required to demonstrate the processes.

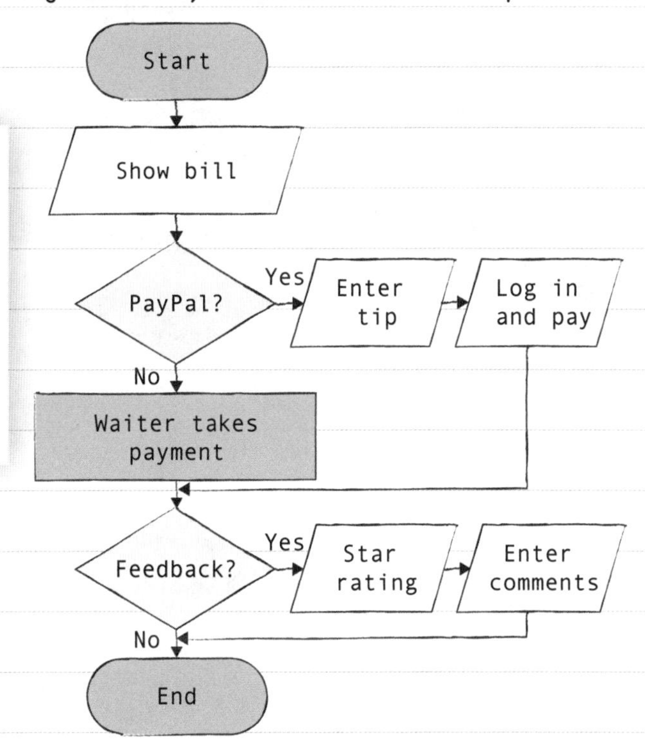

Now try this

An independent jeweller is setting up a website as a retail outlet. It would like to offer a loyalty discount for customers who purchased within the last year as well as giving a reduction of 10% on the sale for more than one item and a choice of postage rates of next day or economy. The jeweller is VAT registered, so VAT needs to be added to the sale after any discounts and postage.

Describe the processes that would be needed to calculate a quote for a customer visiting the website.

What actions are needed to produce the quote? Each action will be a process.

Had a look ☐ Nearly there ☐ Nailed it! ☐

Pattern recognition

Once the problem and processes have been described, the next step involves pattern recognition where you look for repeating features within problems and between problems. This will enable you to create code that can be reused in other apps.

Common elements and individual differences

- Identifying common elements or features in problems needing coded solutions or within systems requiring maintenance can result in producing program code that can be re-used in other apps.
- Identifying any differences and individual elements within problems that can utilise common code need interpreting so library code can be adapted by using appropriate parameters or branching within subroutines.

Code libraries

Code libraries are used by many organisations to improve the effectiveness of programming teams by keeping copies of program segments that are easy to find and to re-use.

Documentation is an essential element of a code library as this is needed to clearly identify code segments with how they can be used as reliable building blocks for new apps.

Debugging time can be reduced by using library code as these program segments will have already been extensively tested and signed off as fit for purpose.

Parameters

Parameters are vital for much re-usable code to control the values that can be passed into a subroutine and so make the workings of this code reliable and predictable.

This code uses 0, 99, 2, 5 as fixed numbers, making it very inflexible as the code would need editing to be used elsewhere.

```
Sub ColumnSort(ByRef SA (,))
Dim Z, FirstRow, Passes, Item As Integer
Dim Temp As String
FirstRow = 0
Passes = FirstRow
While Passes <= 99
  Item = FirstRow
  While Item <= 99
    If SA(2, Item) > SA(2, Item + 1) Then
      For Z = 0 To 5
        Temp = SA(Z, Item)
        SA(Z, Item) = SA(Z, Item + 1)
        SA(Z, Item + 1) = Temp
      Next Z
    End If
    Item = Item + 1
  End While
  Passes = Passes + 1
End While
End Sub
```

An example of code that is hard to re-use.

This code uses parameters NoCols, FirstRow, LastRow, Col instead of fixed numbers, making the code much more re-usable.

```
Sub ColumnSort(ByRef SA(,), NoCols, FirstRow,
LastRow, Col)
Dim Z, Passes, Item As Integer
Dim Temp As String
Passes = FirstRow
While Passes <= LastRow - 1
  Item = FirstRow
  While Item <= LastRow - 1
    If SA(Col, Item) > SA(Col, Item + 1) Then
      For Z = 0 To NoCols
        Temp = SA(Z, Item)
        SA(Z, Item) = SA(Z, Item + 1)
        SA(Z, Item + 1) = Temp
      Next Z
    End If
    Item = Item + 1
  End While
  Passes = Passes + 1
End While
End Sub
```

An example of the same code tweaked to make it re-usable.

Now try this

Write down all the benefits and disadvantages of reusing code within an organisation. Do the positives outweigh the negatives?

Use a single line for each item so it's easy to see whether the positives outweigh the negatives.

Describing patterns and making predictions

Once you have identified repeating features, you will need to describe the patterns. You can then make predictions based on these patterns which will enable you to design program algorithms.

Cleaning dates data

Research was carried out to find computer games titles that had been on sale during the last three decades. Over 10 000 items of data were downloaded from the internet. Some dates were not recognised as such by the spreadsheet. The number of these entries made manual editing a poor option due to the time it would take and the errors that might be introduced into the data set by so much repetitive work.

000000002016-06-21-0000Jun 21, 2016
000000002016-08-23-0000Aug 23, 2016
000000002016-08-23-0000August 23, 2016
000000002016-09-10-0000Sep 10, 2016
1994-12-09JP
1994-12-22JP
1995-01
1995-01-27JP
1995NA
1995NA

Each date was in one of these forms:
- 00000000 then date (yyyy-mm-dd) then -0000 then the date as text
- date (yyyy-mm-dd) then two letters
- date (yyyy-mm)
- date (yyyy) then two letters.

Cleaning the dates data

Search and replace could be used to clean some of the data (for example, removing 00000000). Code could edit the data into a consistent yyyy-mm-dd format, which could then be used as dates in the spreadsheet.

Code was written to loop down the data, copying each item into a variable that was then edited into the yyyy-mm-dd form, according to the type of form it started with.

Pseudocode 1

```
Select top cell of the dates column
Start loop
Copy the cell into a variable, CellContent
If left 8 characters of CellContent = 00000000
  CellContent = mid(CellContent, 9,10)
If length of CellContent =12
CellContent = left(CellContent, 10)
```

```
If length of CellContent =7
  CellContent = CellContent + "-01"
If length of CellContent =6
  CellContent = left(CellContent,4) + "-01-01"
Set active cell to CellContent
Move down a cell
Loop if active cell not empty
```

Pseudocode 2

Loops

Loops are used to repeat code that uses patterns in the data for processing, such as deleting parts of data items that are not wanted.

For more on loops, see page 19.

Now try this

1. Create a spreadsheet to generate the first 20 numbers in the Fibonacci sequence.
2. Produce an algorithm that calculates the *n*th term of the Fibonacci sequence.

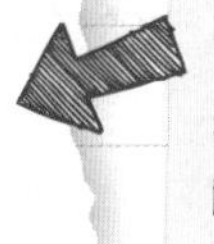

Each term in the Fibonacci sequence is the sum of the previous two terms: 1, 1, 2, 3, 5, 8, 13.

Had a look ☐ Nearly there ☐ Nailed it! ☐

Pattern generalisation and abstraction

After pattern recognition, the next step is to generalise and abstract these patterns to identify all the information necessary to solve a problem. To help you do this, you need to revise variables, constants, key and repeated processes, inputs and outputs.

Representing a problem as code

Identifying information that is necessary to solve an identified problem is an essential part of the programming life cycle. Parts of a problem or system can be represented in code as variables, constants, key processes, repeated processes, inputs and outputs.

	Definition
Variables	Values in a problem or system that may change Usually input by the user or may result from calculation
Constants	Values in a problem or system that remain fixed while the code runs
Key processes	Processes that are essential to understanding of a problem or how a system works
Repeated processes	Processes that occur multiple times within a problem
Inputs	Values read or entered into the system
Outputs	Information presented to the user

Workout app

You recently saw a television programme which suggested that every opportunity to exercise should be taken as 'every little helps!'

As you spend a lot of time using a computer, you think that an app to help encourage a work out whilst using a computer might be useful.

The mouse could be moved to the corners of the screen and clicked, exercising the lower arm, wrists and fingers. These actions could be repeated with the other side of the body.

Even the toes and feet could be exercised by placing the keyboard on the floor and alternatively tapping the space bar and numeric keypad to ensure the foot has some movement.

Key and repeated processes

Mouse inputs are to click onto one of 4 target images placed at the four corners of the form. Clicking on the correct target image will increment (add 1) to the variable, TapCount.

Keyboard inputs are to tap the spacebar or one of the number keys. Tapping any of these will increment (add 1) to the variable, TapCount.

```
Start button mouse click
  Initialise TapCount, StartTime to 0
  Initialise Target, to random between 1-4
  Set image(Target) to active
Target image mouse click
  IF Target matches image
    Increment TapCount
    Play success sound
  ELSE
    Play fail sound
  Call Update statistics
Key press event
  IF space or number pressed
    Increment TapCount
    Play success sound
  ELSE
    Play fail sound
  Call Update statistics
Update statistics subroutine
OUTPUT TapCount
  FOR Countdown = 5 TO 1 STEP -1
    Display Countdown
```

A start button can start the workout by clearing the variables, TapCount, StartTime, to zero.

The screen will show the target images and workout statistics. Target images can have three variants for active, inactive and correct click. Workout statistics can show time taken, number of correct taps/clicks, number of incorrect taps/clicks, average speed and accuracy percentage.

Speakers can make a sound each time a correct click or key press is made or a different sound if a wrong click or key press is made.

Now try this

Write down two key processes and two repeated processes for a website shopping cart.

Think about the actions that take place in the website shopping cart.

Representing the new system

The last element of pattern generalisation and abstraction is to represent the new system using variables, constants, key processes, repeated processes, inputs and outputs. Filtering and ignoring any information not needed to solve the problem will enable you to focus on the actual problem.

For more information on variables, constants, key processes, repeated processes, inputs and outputs, see page 6.

Filtering information

Before writing a program, think carefully about what is actually needed to help solve the problems you are asked to code.

In a database, for example, it is very easy to add fields to a table so there is a place for every possible aspect of the data subject. A better approach is to look at the information that is required from the system, which can then be matched to the data needed to populate the reports and screens outputting from the system.

Case study: Health club members list

A system is being written to handle the members list for a health club. It will hold all the information needed for the club's day-to-day operations.

The system should be quick and easy to use as well as using validation techniques to reduce errors typed into the system.

Members could be issued cards which allow scanning into the system by barcode, swiping or NFC (contactless near-field communication).

Reports can be used to extract data from the system onto paper and data can be exported for use in mail merges.

Printed outputs

Reports from the health club members database could include:

- schedule showing the activities booked for that day, week or month
- members list summary
- member details with all the information about an individual member
- members activity log detailing the activities undertaken over a period of time
- members payments due statement with what is currently owed to the club
- booking receipt to confirm an activity has been reserved.

Tables

The database could include the following tables:

- members
- activities
- bookings
- payments.

Forms

These forms will allow easy navigation of the database to make it more user friendly:

- main menu to click buttons navigating to other parts of the system
- members to add, edit or delete a member
- bookings to add, edit or delete a booking
- payments to record a payment
- reports to choose a report for printing.

Now try this

Create a data dictionary identifying the fields needed for the tables in a database to keep track of a health club members list.

The tables are listed in bullets on this page. What fields would each table need?

Had a look ☐ Nearly there ☐ Nailed it! ☐

Algorithm design

The final stage in computational thinking is to design the algorithm using a step-by-step strategy to solve the problem. This will enable you to clearly understand how the program will work.

Designing an algorithm

Define the overall purpose of the program.

Divide into the processes needed.

Plan the steps needed for each process.

Check the algorithm against the original need to confirm it will be fit for purpose.

Algorithm design

There are often many algorithms in a program which can be at different levels of detail. Designing a program can start with an overall algorithm to summarise how the system works, with other algorithms providing detail needed to design smaller sections of code.

For more information on standard algorithms, see pages 26–29.

Case study: Stock control system

The owner of a second-hand furniture shop is considering writing a stock control program because she quite enjoys coding and wants to have control over how the app looks and behaves.

The app is to run on a PC in the shop as a restricted version so customers can find out if there is anything in the back stock room that interests them.

New item pseudocode

This algorithm enters a new item of stock, checks all the data present and then saves to a stock data file.

```
If any field has not been completed
  Display message
  Show * next to every field not completed
  Place cursor in first field not completed
When all fields completed
  Generate stock number
  Copy fields to Stock file
  Save Stock file
Clear fields on the New item form
```

Stock search pseudocode

This algorithm searches for an item in a stock data file and shows the results on-screen.

```
Click on search button
  If search textbox is empty and furniture checked
    Loop around stock array
      Display all furniture
  If search not empty and furniture checked
    Loop around stock array
      Display all furniture matching textbox
  If search empty and other checked
    Loop around stock array
      Display all non-furniture items
  If search not empty and other checked
    Loop around stock array
      Display other items matching textbox
Place cursor into search textbox
```

Sale pseudocode

This algorithm allows the user to record details of the sale of an item and then save to the data file.

```
Select item sold
Select customer
If customer not known
  Open New customer form
  Enter new customer
  Click on Confirm button
  Copy fields to Customer array
  Save Customer file
  Close form
Show customer information
Click confirm sale
Save Stock, Customer and Sales files
Print receipt
Clear fields on the Sales form
```

Now try this

A car electronic cruise control keeps the vehicle at a constant speed by using the accelerator, gear change and brake, until the driver cancels cruise control by using the brake.

Write pseudocode to design a cruise control system that also links into the sat-nav to prevent the vehicle from exceeding speed limits.

What inputs and outputs are needed for the control device?

Had a look ☐ Nearly there ☐ Nailed it! ☐

Structured English (pseudocode)

There are two main methods you can use to plan program algorithms – pseudocode (structured English) and flow charts. On this page, you will revise commonly used pseudocode terms and how to apply them. Pseudocode can be converted to a programming language to implement:

```
REPEAT UNTIL the end of file
  READ into Sectors(Y)
  Increment Y
Set LastSector to Y – 1
Close the data file
```

```
Do
  Input(1, Sectors(Y))
  Y = Y + 1
Loop Until EOF(1)
Lastsector = Y – 1
FileClose(1)
```

Representing operations

- **BEGIN…END** can be used for any code which you want to keep separate or simply to show where your algorithm starts and finishes.
- **INPUT/OUTPUT** are for any part of the algorithm that allows data in or out such as typing into a textbox or displaying a result.
- **PRINT** is used when a hard copy is produced.
- **READ/WRITE** are for when data are read into the algorithm from a file or written out to a file.

Representing decisions

- **IF…THEN…ELSE…ELSEIF (ELIF)** are used for branches in the algorithm.
- Simple branches use **IF…THEN** to define a test condition and action for condition is met which are usually indented or you could use BEGIN…END for them.
- **ELSE** is used when actions are required when an IF…THEN condition is not met.
- **ELSEIF (or ELIF in some programming languages)** is for actions to be carried out if the previous IF…THEN condition is not met and a further test needs to be made.
- **WHEN** is used to represent select case structures with several branches possible based upon the contents of a variable.

Representing repetition

Each of these are written as a single pseudocode line to define the loop followed by the repeated code indented in the code.

- **FOR** is the unconditional FOR…NEXT loop with the pseudocode line showing how many times the loop iterates.
- **REPEAT UNTIL** is a conditional loop with the pseudocode line defining what ends the loop.
- **WHILE/WHILE NOT** are conditional loops with code defining what allows the iteration.

Dos and don'ts

👍 Use program command words to identify branch and loop structures.

👍 Use indents to show what's included in a structure.

👍 Summarise sections of code.

👎 Don't write actual code which is ready to run.

👎 Don't produce pseudocode in your program editor.

👎 Don't include too much detail about how code will do an action such as swapping items.

Now try this

Produce pseudocode for spreadsheet code to copy rows in a worksheet to one of three other worksheets based upon contents of first cell in each row. A fourth worksheet is used for copies of rows where first cell does not match. This needs to be able to handle any number of rows, starting in a cell named 'FirstCell'.

Read the requirement carefully then consider how you would explain the algorithm in simple words.

Had a look ☐ Nearly there ☐ Nailed it! ☐

Interpreting pseudocode

Pseudocode is used to plan program algorithms. It enables the programmer to visualise how a program will work and to see improvements to the logical structures and processes after reading it. On this page, you will revise how to interpret and develop pseudocode.

Zilch

Zilch is a game played with six dice where the players each take turns throwing the dice to earn points. A target score is set.

The game is won by the player who goes over the target score after the same number of turns as the other players.

When a player has a turn they keep on throwing until either they 'stick' to keep their points or throw a non-scoring combination of dice – 'Zilch' – when their points for the turn are zero.

Zilch dice points rules

There are six dice with several possible points schemes in use. We shall use the scoring below:

1, 2, 3, 4, 5, 6	3000 pts
Three pairs	1500 pts
Three the same	dice number × 100 pts
Dice showing 5	50 pts
Dice showing 1	100 pts

Interpreting and developing code

The process calculating the outcomes of each stage of the game will produce points earned and dice left for the next throw. This will be large and complex, so needs to be broken down into sub-processes, making them easier to focus on and write.

How would you do this if playing with real dice? The first process is to find out if the highest score is thrown, then next highest and so on. Each of these algorithms will be a section of pseudocode.

Preparation for identifying the highest score can take place inside this loop by counting how many of each number has been thrown in the Totals() array. This loop can also show the dice number on the screen.

The structure of this pseudocode can be evaluated against the requirement to identify a throw of 1, 2, 3, 4, 5, 6 using dry runs.

The code here is reasonably effective. Less effective code could use another FOR loop to count how many of each number was thrown. Less effective code might test for a number being thrown more than once, rather than 0.

The highest score is 1, 2, 3, 4, 5, 6 with the method shown here using an array, Totals(), to find out if each number has been used once. Before the check, each item in Totals() is set to 0 using a FOR loop.

A FOR loop throws the dice using the variable, Throw, to hold the number for each dice.

```
Set Score to 0
FOR X = 1 TO 6
  Set Totals(X) to 0
FOR X = 1 TO 6
  Set Throw to random number between 1-6
  Set Dice(X) to Throw
  Increment Totals(Throw)
  Show Dice(X) on the form with its number
Set Winner to True
FOR X = 1 TO 6
  IF Totals(X) = 0 THEN set Winner to False
IF Winner
  Add 3000 to Score
  Show Score on the form
  END subroutine
```

The variable, Winner, is set to true then a FOR loop iterates through the Totals() array, changing Winner to false if any of the numbers were not thrown.

Now try this

Produce a description of how this pseudocode calculates a score in Zilch:

```
FOR X = 1 TO 6
  IF Dice(X) = 1
    Add 100 to Score
    Decrement DiceLeft
  IF Dice(X) = 5
    Add 50 to Score
    Decrement DiceLeft
Show Score on the form
```

The sequence is important. Start with the first line of the pseudocode and interpret the meaning. Remember, indents show how much code is inside a structure such as a FOR loop.

Flow charts

Flow charts provide a pictorial complement to pseudocode, helping you to plan algorithms. British Computer Society (BCS) symbols are commonly used in flow charts.

Flow chart shape	Description
(rectangle)	**Process** used for anything in code that cannot be represented by any of the other symbols.
(diamond)	**Decision** shows where there is a choice of two paths with the condition that needs to be met written inside the symbol.
(parallelogram)	**Input/output** shows every place where data or events come into or leave the algorithm.
(arrow)	**Connectors** are used to reduce the need to draw lines across the flow chart.
(rounded rectangle)	**Start/end** symbols show the entry and exit points in the algorithm.

Alarm flow chart

This flow chart illustrates how an alarm works on a mobile phone.

The flow chart has to begin and finish with start/end symbols. The rest of it needs to show the routes that are possible in the code.

The alarm is set with an input from the user.

A decision is used to show how the system regularly checks the actual time to the alarm. When they match, the yes branch is taken so the alarm is sounded.

The user can now input into the system to either turn the alarm off or snooze.

If snooze, the app enters a process to wait a short time before the alarm sounds again.

If the user turns the alarm off, a process disables the alarm and the app ends.

Waiting is shown in this flow chart both as a process (wait 2 minutes) and as a loop (time = alarm?). These are both valid techniques for showing the delay with the author of the flow chart able to choose the method they prefer to show this delay.

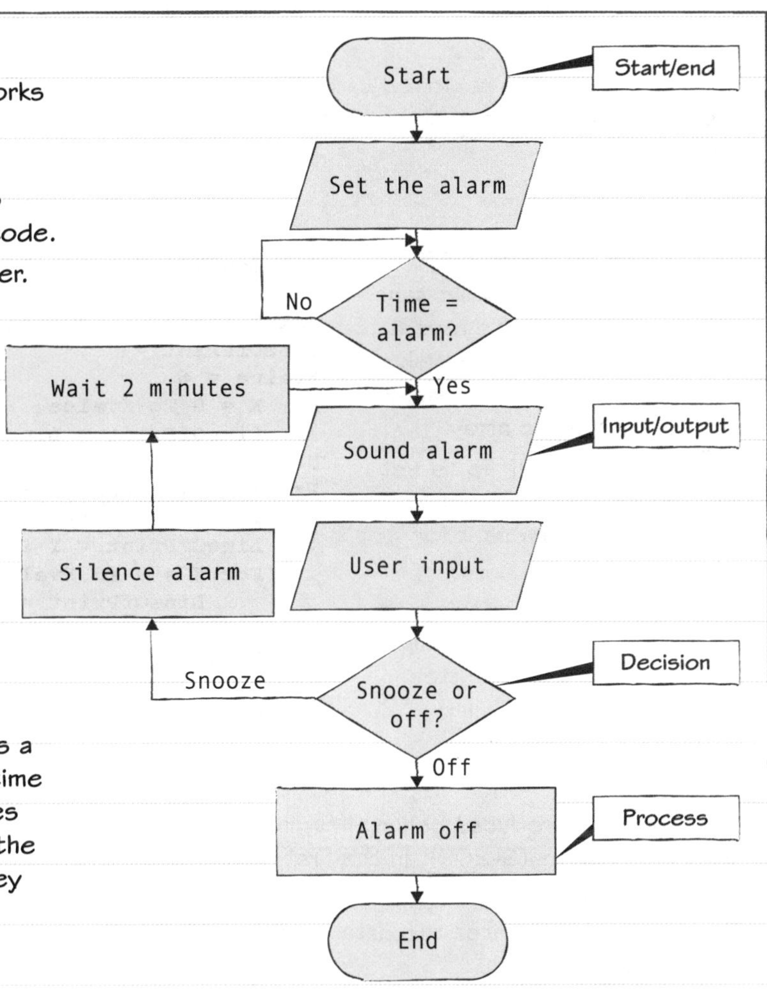

Now try this

An independent jeweller is setting up a website as a retail outlet. It would like to offer a loyalty discount for customers who purchased within the last year as well as giving a reduction of 10% on the sale for more than one item and a choice of postage rates of next day or economy. The jeweller is VAT registered, so VAT needs to be added to the sale after any discounts and postage.

Produce a flow chart to illustrate this algorithm.

There should be a symbol in the flow chart for each line of your pseudocode.

Make sure you use the correct symbols.

Had a look ☐ Nearly there ☐ Nailed it! ☐

Handling data within a program

Programming paradigms can be used to build computer code to handle data within a program. On this page, you will revise common data-handling techniques and structures provided within programming languages to process data.

Reading a data file

```
FileOpen(1, EmployersFile, OpenMode.Input)
Y = 0
Do
    Y = Y + 1
    For X = 0 To 9
        Input(1, Employers(X, Y))
        TempEmployers(X, Y) = UCase(TempEmployers(X, Y))
    Next X
Loop Until (EOF(1))
FileClose(1)
LastEmployer = Y
```

Code to read a data file usually needs an indefinite loop to repeat reading each line from the disk until it reaches the end of file.

A variable, EmployersFile, has been set to name the data file before the code here opens it for input. A variable, Y, is set to zero before the Do loop to keep track of each line read in from the EmployersFile and which item in the array, Employers(), is used to store the input data.

A nested loop uses the variable, X, to keep track of the data for each employee and which item in the array is used to store the input data. This loop uses a UCase() function to force each data item to upper case.

After EmployersFile is closed variable, Y, is used to set variable, LastEmployer, so the program knows the subscript number of the last employee record in the array, Employers().

Writing a data file

```
FileOpen(2, NameOfFile, OpenMode.Output)
LineOfPrint = "Allocations(6-200)"
PrintLine(2, LineOfPrint)
LineOfPrint = " ,"
Xvalue = 6
For X = 0 To Xvalue
    LineOfPrint = LineOfPrint & X & ","
Next X
PrintLine(2, LineOfPrint)
For Y = 0 To LastAllocation
    LineOfPrint = Y & ","
    For X = 0 To Xvalue
        LineOfPrint = LineOfPrint & Allocations(X, Y) & ","
    Next
    PrintLine(2, LineOfPrint)
Next Y
FileClose(2)
```

Code to write a data file can use a definite loop to repeat writing each line to the disk as the code knows how many records are in the array.

A variable, NameOfFile, is set to name the data file before the code here opens it for output.

This code uses a variable, LineOfPrint, which is built up into each line to be written to the disk with a comma between each data item.

Two FOR...NEXT loops are used to write to disk.

The first loop produces column headings for when the data file is opened into Excel with the name of the array, Allocations(6-200), in the first column and numbers from the loop variable, X, for which array item is in the other columns.

The second loop writes the data to disk. After this loop, the data file is closed.

Now try this

Produce a program to read in a data file, make changes to the data and write it back to the disk. The data file can be created using Excel and saved as CSV (comma separated variables). Use a calculation in the spreadsheet to produce a reference number in the first column. The program you write can add 'REF' to these numbers before writing them back to disk. You can open the new data file in Excel to confirm the reference numbers have been set by your code.

Include a comma between each item when writing to disk.

Constants and variables

On this page, you will revise the data types you can use to define constants and variables.

Constants and variables

Constants and variables are very similar, with both naming a place in memory where data can be held. A constant does not change when code runs, the contents of a variable is usually changed by calculations or user input.

Arrays

An array is a variable which can contain many different values, each of these identified by the subscript (number) inside brackets at the end of the array name. A lot of code uses arrays to hold data records for the program.

Links For more on arrays, see page 23.

Text variables and constants

These can be combined (concatenated), searched or part of the string can be selected and used, such as the first three characters.

- **Alphanumeric strings** are used to hold combinations of letters from the alphabet and numbers, such as AB3076.
- A **character** is a single letter or number such as A, B, 6. A string is one or more characters. In a program, these variables can be used for any combination of words, spaces or numbers such as an address or a name.
- **Strings** can hold alphanumeric characters as well as other characters including escape codes such as CrLf (carriage return/line feed).

Numeric variables and constants

- **Floating point (real)** variables are used to contain numbers which may have a fractional part. These variables can hold a range of values which depends upon the type used. A single has a range of -3.4028235E+38 to 3.4028235E+38, using 4 bytes of memory. A double is ±1.79769313486231570E+308 and uses 8 bytes of memory.
- **Integer** variables and constants are used to contain whole numbers. These variables can hold a range of values, which depends upon the type of integer used. A short integer has a range of –32768 to 32767, using 2 bytes of memory. A long integer has a range of –2147483648 to 2147483647 and uses 4 bytes of memory.

Date/time

Declaring a variable as a date can save the programmer a lot of effort as there are functions available to calculate dates, such as DateAdd, and these variables can show the date in whatever format is required for the app.

A date variable can also be used for time. The actual content of date variable is a number with the whole part the date (number of days since 1 January 1900) and the fractional part the time, e.g. 6am is .25, midday is .5 and so on.

Boolean

A Boolean variable has only two possible values – true or false.

It is a good data type for use in a conditional statement, such as IF Found THEN, where Found is the Boolean variable.

Boolean variables can also be used to represent **objects**, such as option buttons in code.

Now try this

Write code which uses six different data types to hold information entered by the user. Process each of the entries using a method appropriate to the data type, for example, Boolean, to make a decision, using appropriate output to show the results of your processing.

Decide upon the data types with what you'll do with them before you start coding.

Had a look ☐ Nearly there ☐ Nailed it! ☐

Managing variables

You need to revise the difference between local and global variables and when to use them, as well as the use of naming conventions to give meaningful names to objects in your code.

Managing variables

Managing variables helps to get the best performance from an app in terms of reliability, although there can be a very small reduction in speed due to the creations and releasings of **local variables**.

The minor speed hit is more than compensated for by the extra reliability due to much more control over where variables exists in the code.

Good program design is very clear on where a variable is used or changed and so if another part of the code tries to use such a variable an error is generated to alert the programmer.

Parameters

A parameter is an argument in brackets after the name of a subroutine or function code passing a value into this code.

A parameter is a local variable to the subroutine or function unless it is defined by reference, in which case it is the same variable as was used by the code calling the subroutine or function.

The default for a parameter is by value, which means that what's inside a variable is passed into the subroutine or function and so does not affect this variable elsewhere.

Global and local variables

The scope of a variable defines which parts of the code can see or use it.

A global variable exists everywhere in the code and only ceases when the app closes.

A local variable exists inside a subroutine or function subprogram whilst that code is running then ceases when the subprogram ends.

If a subroutine calls another subroutine, any local variables in the calling subprogram would not be seen by the called subroutine unless passed in as a parameter.

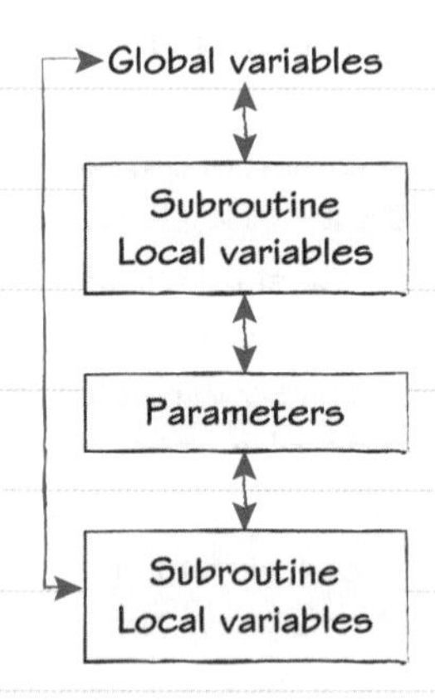

Global can be used anywhere; local and parameters are private to the subroutine.

Naming conventions

The programmer has a lot of choice of the names of variables used in code, although there are a number of reserved words, such as open, which cannot be used as variables because they are part of the programming language.

A good variable name helps to document the code because it describes what the variable contains. Capitalisation can be used to help see words used in a variable name, e.g. CarColour.

Bad names are anything meaningless or which mislead about the use of the variable.

Variable names – dos and don'ts

- 👍 OKtoGo
- 👍 VATdue
- 👍 NameOfFile
- 👎 oktogo (poor capitalisation)
- 👎 Var1 (meaningless)
- 👎 Axx (meaningless)

Now try this

Create a poster showing how the scope of variables affects where they can be used in a program.

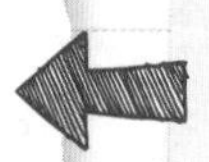

You can use circles to show each scope.

Arithmetic operations

Programming paradigms can be used to implement arithmetic operations, which include mathematical functions such as + and *, relational operators such as = and <, Boolean operators such as NOT, as well as date and time.

Mathematical operators

Mathematical operators are plus (+), minus (-), divide (/ or DIV) and multiply (*). Remember that the computer will always use BIDMAS (brackets, indices, divide, multiply, add, subtract) for the order in which a calculation is worked out.

The following calculation needs to set Pay by working out the HourRate + Supplement before multiplying by Hours, but gives a wrong result:

Pay = HourRate + Supplement * Hours

This is because brackets should be used to calculate the addition before multiplying:

Pay = (HourRate + Supplement) * Hours

Relational operators

Relational operators are frequently used in code, especially for conditions which control a branch into a choice of coding routes.

In these examples:

Pay has been set to 3.9

Cost has been set to 4

Equals	Pay = Cost	False
Less than	Pay < Cost	True
More than	Pay > Cost	False
Not equal to	Pay <> Cost	True
Less than or equal to	Pay <= Cost	True
More than or equal to	Pay >= Cost	False

Modulo

When a number is divided into another, the remainder (rem) is called the modulo or modulus, (MOD), which is often useful in calculations carried out by code needing the number remaining after division.

Modulo operator examples

10 % 3 returns 1 in Python code.

7 mod 4 returns 3 in VB.NET code.

= MOD(4, 3) returns 1 in an Excel cell.

23 rem 4 returns 3 in Prolog code.

Boolean operators

Boolean operators can be complex calculations but always end with a result of True or False.

In these examples:

Car has been set to True

Diesel has been set to False

Opposite (NOT)	NOT Diesel	True
All of them (AND)	Car AND Diesel	False
Any of them (OR)	Car OR Diesel	True

Date/time operators

Usually a date in program code is held internally as a whole number (the day count from 1/1/1900) and time as the fractional part of a number, e.g. .75 is 6pm, so 6pm on 17 October 2017 is held as 43025.75, so simple arithmetic can often be used. Excel® has a known bug which calculates 1900 as a leap year.

Other programming languages make it very difficult for the programmer to reach the underlying numbers. It is much easier and practical to use the date and time functions provided.

Now try this

Create an Excel spreadsheet to show expressions illustrating mathematical, relational, Boolean and date/time operators. Copy and paste another version of each of your examples so a printed copy shows both the calculation workings and the result.

Use a single quote (') at the start of each of the copied examples so the workings print.

Had a look ☐ Nearly there ☐ Nailed it! ☐

Arithmetic functions

Arithmetic functions enable you to code arithmetical operations – random, range, round, truncation – in a program. The Excel spreadsheet is used to demonstrate these arithmetic functions on this page.

Arithmetic functions

random()	Generates a random number.
range()	Creates an array of elements using the range of values in the brackets.
round()	Rounds a number up or down to the nearest whole number.
truncation()	Rounds a number down to the number of decimal places in the brackets.

Using the range() function

One argument will create a range of integer numbers from 0 to one before the argument, e.g. range(5) creates 0, 1, 2, 3, 4.

Two arguments create a range of integer numbers from first argument to one before the last, e.g. range(2,6) creates 2, 3, 4, 5.

Three arguments create a range of integer numbers with the last argument defining how much each item increments, e.g. range(1,12,3) creates 1, 4, 7, 10.

In code, **10 in range(1,4)** will return false.

ROUND() and TRUNCATE() functions

These are both used to specify the number of decimal places showing for a number.

The round() function will adjust a number to fit with the least significant digit rounded up or down.

The truncate() function simply removes any digits that do not fit.

Round and Trunc

	A	B
1	17.256	
2	17.26	17.25
3	=ROUND(A1,2)	=TRUNC(A1,2)

RAND and RANDBETWEEN

	A	B
1	0.322574	=RAND()
2	88	=RANDBETWEEN(1,100)

Using the random() function

The random() function will usually generate a random number larger than 0 and less than 1.

Some programming languages accept an argument inside the brackets to define the largest random number that can be produced.

Excel offers the RANDBETWEEN() function which accepts two arguments to define the scope of random numbers that are generated.

Now try this

Create an Excel spreadsheet to generate test data where the A column contains random numbers between 3 and 50, the B column a random date up to a year before today (assuming 365 days in the year) and the C column a random letter between A and Z.

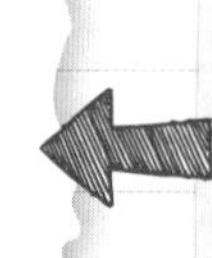

Use the NOW() function as part of your calculation for the date.

Use the CHAR() function as part of your calculation for the letter.

String handling and general functions

String handling and other built-in general functions convert between different types of number and strings and perform general operations such as dealing with data files and printing.

String conversions

Converting to numeric allows code to use numbers stored as strings in calculations. CInt() converts to integer, CDbl() to double data type for floating point (float) numbers. CStr() can convert a number into string if there is need for searching or extracting part of the number.

String ← calculations

Search for matching characters → **Number** Carry out

Manipulating strings

- **Concatenation** is joining together two or more strings. The '+' character is used for concatenantion by C, Java, Python, VB.NET among others whilst the '&' character is unique to Visual Basic. With numbers, '+' performs addition, but it concatenates strings.
- **Length** is how many characters are in a string. Many languages have a len() function to return this number.
- **Position** is where a character or group of characters are in a string. VB.NET uses the IndexOf method, Python the find method.

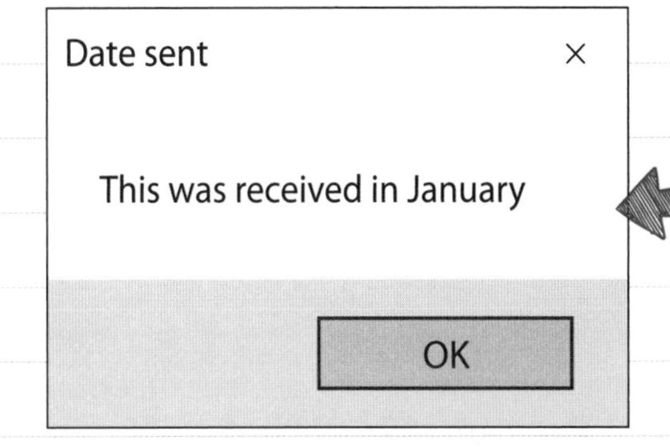

Making it work

The VB.NET code below uses concatenation to join text with month name extracted from date variable, DoR, after converting into a string variable, strDoR. DoR is formatted to "09 January 2017" (long date) before conversion, so number of characters in the month can be calculated as length of date string minus 8 (2 digits day, 4 year, 2 spaces around month).

Month position is calculated from 1 more than index of first space plus 2 (index starts at 0).

When this code runs, MsgText will contain "This was received in January"

```
DoR = "9/1/2017"
strDoR = CStr(Format(DoR, "long date"))
MonthLen = Len(strDoR) - 8
DoRpos = strDoR.IndexOf(" ") + 2
DoRmonth = Mid(strDoR, DoRpos, MonthLen)
MsgText = "This was received in "
MsgText = MsgText & DoRmonth
```

Input and open functions

Input lets users enter into a variable. This Python code shows a prompt of 'How many?', storing the response in Quantity:

```
Quantity = input("How many?")
```

Open connects code to a data file with an argument defining type of access, e.g. read, write. This Python example shows a file, Data.csv, being opened to read the data:

```
DataFile = open("Data.csv","r" )
```

Range and print

Range is a function to return a range object. This Excel code example shows a calculation, =Rand(), being entered into a range of cells:

```
Range("A2:D12").Formula = "=Rand()"
```

Print sends text to screen or other output such as a data file. This Python code writes the contents of a variable, DataVar to a file, data.txt, opened in write mode as DataFile:

```
DataFile = open("data.txt","w")
print(DataVar, file=DataFile)
```

Now try this

Create code to extract and use part of a date converted to string in a short sentence as described in the Making it work box above.

Use some form of console or message box output to check what is in the variables as you develop this code.

Validating data

Programming paradigms can be used to build effective validation techniques into code, improving the validity of inputs with post-check actions aiding further accuracy.

Validation check techniques

Checking data as it is entered for validity is a basic technique used in many ways to check the **data type** and **range** with any **constraints** before the code attempts to process the entry.

This screening helps to reduce errors and gives the user the opportunity to correct mistyping at the time of entering the data.

Data types and boolean

- Checking for the correct data type is basic validation preventing a lot of data entry errors, e.g. by rejecting text when a number is needed.
- Boolean logic can be applied to a data entry where an input could use a choice of validation rules, e.g. a vehicle registration could be in the form of XX99XXX or X999XXX.

Range

Many validation checks ensure inputs are within a range of values, such as age to make sure someone is not too young.

An age can be entered into a textbox with simple validation to ensure a number has been entered within an acceptable range, such as between 18 and 25.

A date of birth is much better data as this would still be useful for years after the data entry as an up-to-date age can be calculated from the current date obtained from the computer clock.

11 February 1998

February 1998

Mon	Tue	Wed	Thu	Fri	Sat	Sun
26	27	28	29	30	31	1
2	3	4	5	6	7	8
9	10	11	12	13	14	15
16	17	18	19	20	21	22
23	24	25	26	27	28	1
2	3	4	5	6	7	8

Constraints

Validation using constraints is essential for data entry such as a reference number with a clear structure. A reference number should be fixed with a set number and combination of letters and digits, e.g. STR00234, which are very straightforward to check. In this example the first three characters would be letters, the next five characters constrained to numbers and the overall number of characters must be eight.

Post-check actions

An app should include post-check actions which provide feedback to the user on why a validation check has failed and what the user needs to do to correct their entry:

- **Enforcement action** usually clears the bad data from the screen.
- **Advisory action** usually keeps the data but also sends a warning message.
- **Verification action** asks the user to confirm their data is correct.

Now try this

What validation can be applied to a data entry requiring a UK postcode?

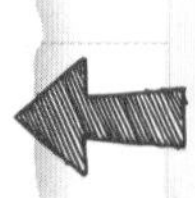

What positions do the letters and numbers occupy in a postcode? Are there any further techniques available?

Loops

Control structures include loops, also known as iterations, which repeat code as many times as needed. This page revises how to improve the effectiveness of code iterations by appropriate use of REPEAT, FOR, WHILE structures and any mechanisms needed to break out of them.

Unconditional loops

The classic unconditional loop is FOR...NEXT where a loop variable is used to keep count of the number of iterations with the NEXT line in this structure used to determine when the loop is complete.

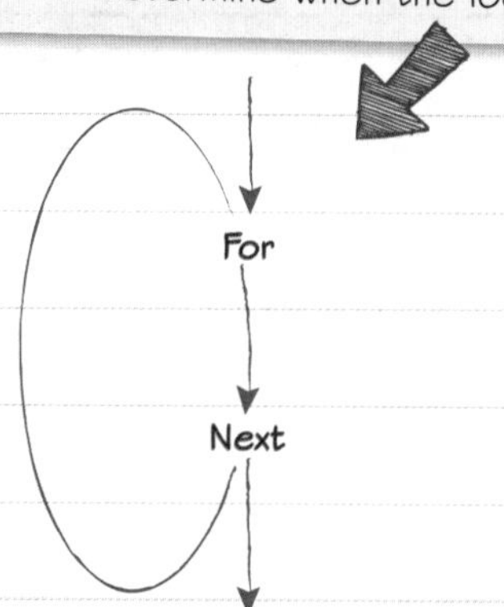

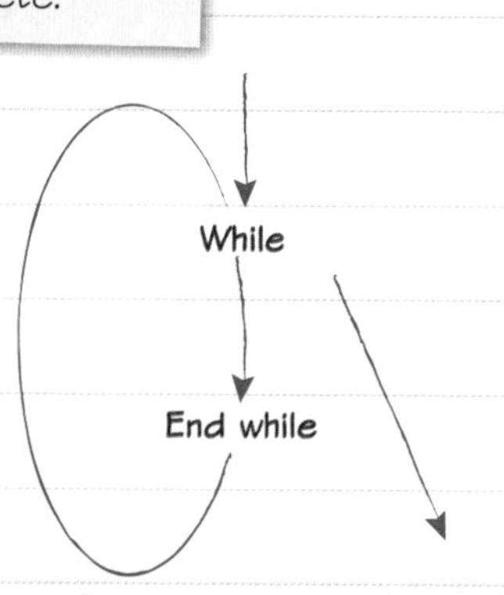

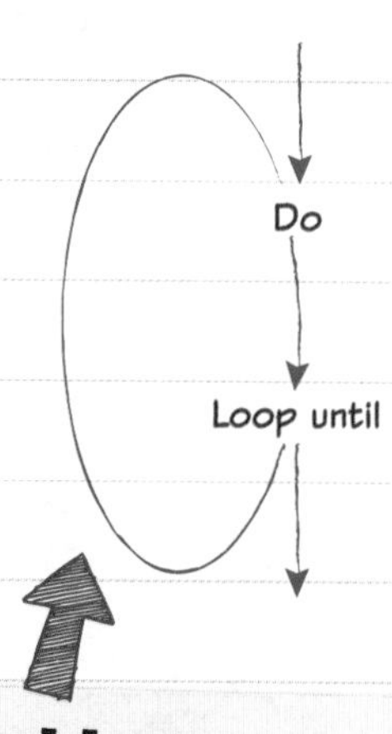

Pre-conditional loops

Conditional loops will continue until an event occurs or a condition is met.

The condition can be at the start, e.g. WHILE, which is known as a pre-conditioned loop, so the code inside the loop will not be run at all if the condition is not met when this structure is executed.

Post-conditional loops

If the condition is at the end, e.g. REPEAT UNTIL or LOOP UNTIL, it is a post-conditional loop so code inside the loop will run at least once, even if the condition is not met as the test is after the body of the loop.

These structures offer the programmer more control over how the loop will work.

Using loops

FOR...NEXT	✓ looping through arrays ✓ generating test data
WHILE REPEAT UNTIL	✓ reading in data files ✓ checking for user attempts, e.g. passwords

Breaking out of a loop

When running a loop, the programming environment creates a structure which needs to end properly or there might be problems if the code runs for a long time.

Programming languages include commands such as BREAK, EXIT FOR or EXIT DO to finish a loop early.

Most code should not need to exit, as a conditional loop should respond to such situations. An unconditional loop requiring an early exit should probably be conditional.

Now try this

Produce a guide on appropriate uses for each loop type. Include examples of how the condition test for a conditional loop can best be used at the start or at the end of the loop.

Think of a situation where iteration code should not be run if a condition is not met.

Had a look ☐ Nearly there ☐ Nailed it! ☐

Branches

Branches allow you to make decisions within an algorithm. On this page, you will revise IF...THEN... ELSE...ELSEIF selections.

Branching with IF

The IF control structure allows codes to divide into separate pathways, selecting between two or more routes through the program. This structure starts with the IF...THEN line of code where a condition is evaluated as true or false. Code immediately after the IF...THEN line is run if the condition is true as far as the next part of this structure, which could be:

- ELSEIF to set another condition
- ELSE for code if the condition(s) not met
- ENDIF to complete the structure.

Case study **Postage rates**

An app could be written to allocate a postage rate according to the weight of a shipment:

Weight	Rate
Below 50 g	A
50 g or more and below 100 g	B
100 g or more and below 1000 g	C
1000 g or more	Too heavy

The app will allow the user to type a weight into a text box, txtWeight, then show the appropriate rate on-screen.

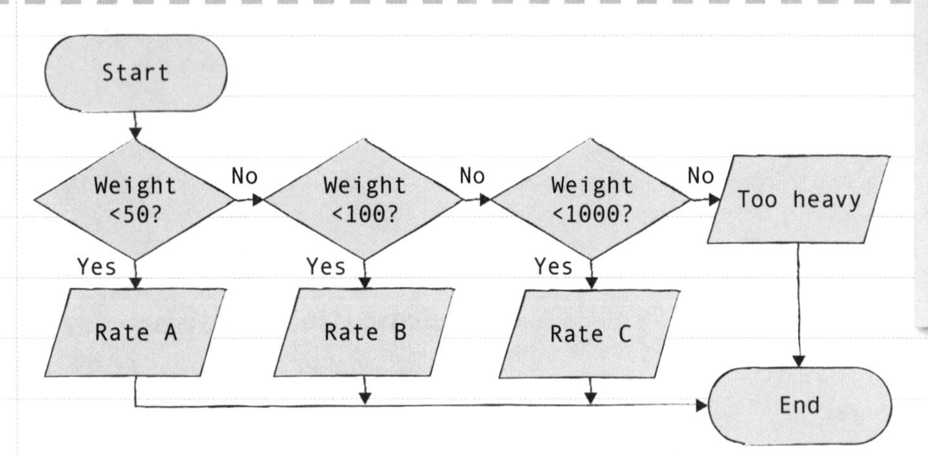

The IF condition (number typed into WEIGHT by the user), shows Rate A if less than 50.

```
IF WEIGHT < 50 THEN
    SET POSTAGE LABEL TO "Rate A"
  ELSEIF WEIGHT < 100 THEN
    SET POSTAGE LABEL TO "Rate B"
  ELSEIF WEIGHT < 1000 THEN
    SET POSTAGE LABEL TO "Rate C"
   ELSE
    SET POSTAGE LABEL TO "Too heavy"
  ENDIF

If txtWeight.Text < 50 Then
  lblPostage.Text = "Rate A"
ElseIf txtWeight.Text < 100 Then
  lblPostage.Text = "Rate B"
ElseIf txtWeight.Text < 1000 Then
  lblPostage.Text = "Rate C"
Else
  lblPostage.Text = "Too heavy"
End If
```

ELSEIF statements respond to other weights with ELSE line running code not met by any other condition showing "Too heavy".

Care needs to be taken with conditions. The conditions here are carefully sequenced with first condition, (<50), so the next condition, (<100), is from 50 up to and not quite 100.

Now try this

Write a program which accepts (and validates) user input of a whole number between 0 and 48 to represent the points achieved for a test. Your program will use a select case structure to show 'Fail' (0–17), 'Pass' (18–25), 'Merit' (26–41), 'Distinction' (42–47) or 'Distinction*' (48) according to the input value.

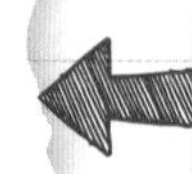

Be very careful to code for the grade boundaries and use test data to ensure they are met.

Function calls

Programming paradigm control structures include function calls. A function is a sub-program that returns a value when it is called. This page revises how to define a function and declare any arguments, as well as how to call the function.

Functions

The **definition** needs the keyword **FUNCTION** followed by its name. **Arguments** can be used in a similar way to sub-routines as parameters inside brackets after the function name.

There needs to be a line of code inside the function where the return value is defined.

To call a function, either a variable is set to the function or the function name is used in a place where the value it returns can be used.

Function example code

The function code below takes parameters and processes them into a reference number from the first two characters of FirstName, Surname, DoB followed by last two characters of FirstName, Surname (DoB needs to be converted into a string before the first two numbers can be used). RefNo is converted into upper case before being returned by this function.

```
Function RefNo(ByVal FirstName, ByVal Surname, ByVal DoB)
  RefNo = FirstName.substring(0, 2)
  RefNo = RefNo + Surname.substring(0, 2)
  RefNo = RefNo + CStr(DoB).Substring(0, 2)
  RefNo = RefNo + FirstName.substring(Len(FirstName) -2, 2)
  RefNo = RefNo + Surname.substring(Len(Surname) -2, 2)
  RefNo = UCase(RefNo)
End Function
```

These parameters are ByVal meaning that their values can be used inside the function as local variables and will not change anything else in the program.

The following line of code calls this function:

```
Reference = RefNo(txtFname.Text, txtSurname.Text, dtpDoB.Text)
```

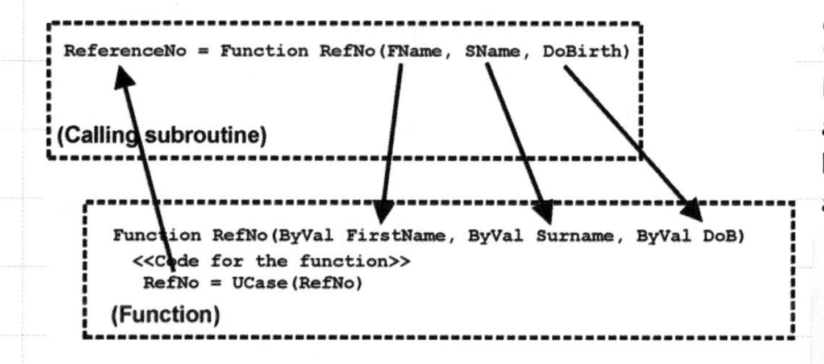

Parameters

In the code above, FirstName, Surname and DoB are all parameters passed in by the values of text boxes and a date picker on the form. These are all used as local variables by the function.

This shows how the parameters are passed into the function which then returns the value in RefNo.

Now try this

Write a program or create a spreadsheet which has a function that creates a reference number from first name, last name and date of birth entered into a form or spreadsheet cells.

Prepare some test data to confirm your function works as expected.

Had a look ☐ Nearly there ☐ Nailed it! ☐

Lists

Data structures enable you to store and process data in a computer program. A linked list is a data structure using pointers to link to the next item. A data set can have several lists.

Linked lists

These are used where a program needs to be able to follow a sequence between items of data which may be of different types.

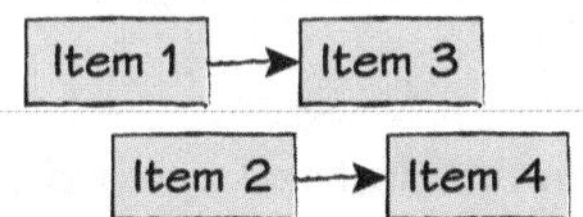

Linked lists

The example below has two pointers before each item, first location, second job role.
The end of each list is −1 (11111111 in binary).

	0	1	2	3	4	5	6	7	8	9	A	B	C	D	E	F
0	07	08	D	A	V	I	D	OE	1E	H	E	L	E	N	2A	16
1	A	B	D	I	L	1D	24	T	A	N	G	E	L	32	2B	M
2	U	I	N	44	3E	S	T	E	V	E	3D	33	J	O	S	H
3	U	A	49	4A	E	L	I	Z	A	B	E	T	H	-1	45	H
4	A	R	R	Y	-1	-1	J	O	E	-1	-1	B	R	I	A	N

Location start pointers are 00 (Bristol), 15 (London), 23 (York) with these teams: Bristol (David, Helen, Abdil, Joshua, Harry), London (Tangel, Muin, Elizabeth, Brian), York (Steve, Joe).

Job role start pointers are 01 (Sales), OF (Support) with Sales (David, Helen, Muin, Joshua, Elizabeth, Brian), Support (Abdil, Tangel, Steve, Harry, Joe).

Code to define a list

This code creates a list, adds some items then loops through the list to show the items.

```
Dim lstNames As New List(Of String)
lstNames.Add("Mo")
lstNames.Add("Sarah")
lstNames.Add("Sam")

lstNames.Sort()

For Each item In lstNames
  MsgBox(item)
Next
```

The variable, lstNames, is defined as a list of the string data type. Three items are added to the list, "Mo", "Sarah", "Sam".

How the code works

The code uses the sort method to change the order of data items inside the list into an alphabetical sequence.

An iteration loops through the items In the list, using a message box to show each.

Now try this

Create some test data consisting of six sales people, each working from one of two offices and whether they have a driving licence. Copy this data onto squared paper using pointers for the office and driving licence.

You can print squared paper from Excel using borders and row/widths adjusted to create square cells.

Arrays

The array is a data structure widely used in code as a variable containing several data items.

Variables and arrays

A variable is a place in memory used by code to hold an item of data. Variables are named (declared) in code by the programmer, usually defined for a particular type of data.

An array is a variable with many places for data so different items can be held. Brackets at end of the array name enclose subscript(s), used to identify the current item in the array.

1D array

97
79
68
11
39
7
70
51

ArrayItem(4)

2D array

22	44	41	63
35	11	20	6
96	13	61	90
49		31	36
99			59
26			85
17	59	20	50
77	49	1	88

ArrayItem(1,2)

One-dimensional (1D) arrays

A one-dimensional array has a single subscript inside the brackets and can be thought of as a single list of items.

An array can store only one type of data but the data can be of any type including integers, characters and strings.

Arrays can work very well with loops. A loop variable can be used as the subscript so each item in the array can be used in comparisons or other operations.

TestData(0)	23.8739745010
TestData(1)	24.0826482235
TestData(2)	24.6732391543
TestData(3)	25.0122885583
TestData(4)	25.3637706381
TestData(5)	25.8537892214
TestData(6)	25.8946307915
TestData(7)	26.7077571746

The data above shows an example of how an array could be used to hold data streamed into the computer from a test device.

Two-dimensional (2D) arrays

A two-dimensional array is multi-dimensional as it has two subscripts inside the brackets and can be thought of as able to hold a table of data. The example data, right, shows how an array could be used to look up postage rates.

PostageRate(2,1) holds £7.45, the rate for 100 g with £1000 compensation (cover). The subscript used for rows and subscript used for columns is the choice of the programmer and makes no difference as long as the program code is consistent in how these are used.

```
Cover = 2
Weight = 4
lblRate.Text = PostageRate(Cover, Weight)
```

The 0 subscript in both dimensions is used to hold a title for that set of data, e.g. row 3 holds the rates for up to 1 kg.

Postage rates

	0	1	2	3
0		£500	£1000	£2500
1	100 g	£6.45	£7.45	£9.45
2	500 g	£7.25	£8.25	£10.25
3	1 kg	£8.55	£9.55	£11.55
4	2 kg	£11.00	£12.00	£14.00
5	10 kg	£26.60	£27.60	£29.60
6	20 kg	£41.20	£42.20	£44.20

Now try this

Produce code that uses a 2D array to hold a set of postage rates for different weight ranges and insured amounts. The user should be able to enter a weight, select the insurance and see the postage cost.

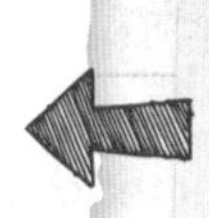

Use the data shown on this page to populate your array.

Had a look ☐ Nearly there ☐ Nailed it! ☐

Records

A record is a data structure used to hold an item such as a product or person, often in a database table. The record is made from fields, each of which is defined to an appropriate data type. For example, a product description would be text, quantity as number and so on.

Fields

Fields are columns in a table object shown in the datasheet view, with each holding an item of data such as a date for each record.

These fields are set up in the design view of a database. The screenshot, right, shows some of the data types available for fields including AutoNumber to increment an integer with each new record, Date/Time to show a date-picker and hold dates, Short Text for most data entries and Yes/No.

tblLoans

LRef	Date out	Date in	GameRef	MemberRef	Returned?
1	08/11/2016	17/11/2016	PC0287	BE02	☑
2	09/11/2016		PC1945	NE03	☐
3	09/11/2016		WI0452	MO12	☐

tblLoans

Field Name	Data Type
LRef	AutoNumber
Date out	Date/Time
Date in	Date/Time
GameRef	Short Text
MemberRef	Short Text
Returned?	Yes/No

Case study: Console games club objects

A club has been formed by a group of friends to loan each other games for their consoles. The number in the group has expanded to the point where it has been agreed to create a database to keep track of who has what. The diagram below represents how the various tables of a database and their fields can be linked using a query.

Using records in a computer program

A database query can join tables together into a data set which consists of any mix of the table fields and can contain records selected by criteria to be used by forms and reports.

A computer program can carry out similar operations on data using arrays or data objects to hold the data using XML (eXtensible Markup Language) as data source document formats.

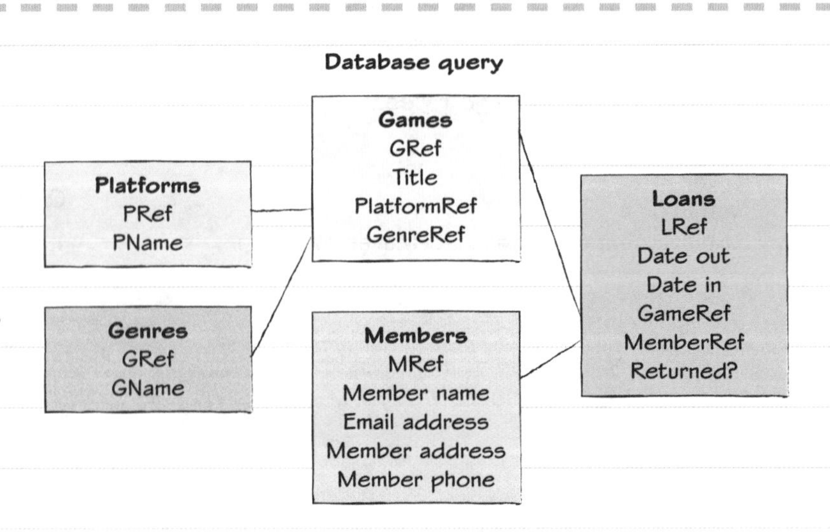

Now try this

Create a database for the console games club described on this page.

Use the table and field names shown in the ERD on this page.

Sets

A set is a collection of records in a database or other data source that could be made from some of a table, filtering or a query data set.

Sets of data

A set consists of some data that has been brought in from a structure such as a table in a database, an array in a program or records that match a criterion.

The set will meet a particular need, such as clients with a policy due for renewal, students who failed to submit work on time or any other useful collection of data.

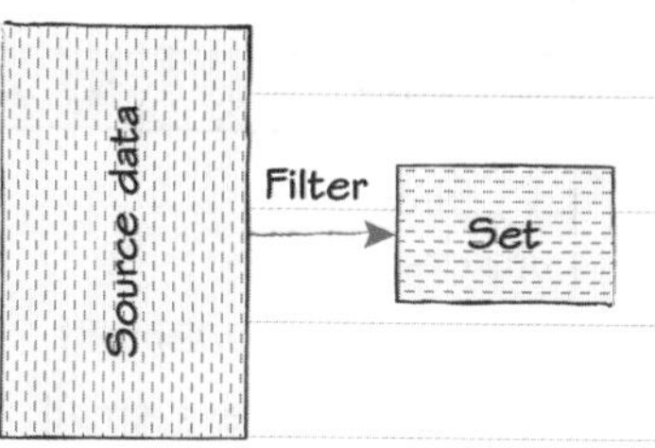

Queries and data sets

A database uses queries to produce data sets. A data set is often temporary and used for a purpose such as providing the data for a report.

If a query is used for a report, the data set is generated when the report runs but not kept, so if the same report is run again the query will generate a fresh data set based on data currently held in the records.

Database queries can bring in data from several tables and apply criteria to these records to produce a data set that exactly matches what is required for a report.

Data sets like this exist on many car trading websites, with the website users being able to filter results by such categories 'make' and 'price'. A visitor to the website would be able to see which vehicles are within their budget.

Set of cars selected by brand, sorted by price

Bugatti EB110 Dauer				**£894,950**
2002	11,200 miles	Manual	Petrol	
Bugatti Veyron 8.0 2dr				**£935,000**
2008	15,000 miles	Automatic	Petrol	
Bugatti EB110 Dauer				**£950,000**
2003	2,500 miles	Manual	Petrol	
Bugatti Veyron 8.0 2dr				**£975,000**
2010	13,500 miles	Automatic	Petrol	
Bugatti Veyron 8.0 2dr				**£1,200,000**
2011	22,750 miles	Manual	Petrol	
Bugatti Veyron 8.0 2dr				**£1,275,000**
2012	11,000 miles	Automatic	Petrol	

Examples of data sets

Title	Genre	Developer(s)
Afro Samurai	Action	Namco Bandai Games
Air Conflicts: Secret Wars	Action	Games Farm
Air Conflicts: Vietnam	Action	Kalypso Media
Amazing Island	Action	Ancient
Anarcute	Action	AnarTeam
Animaniacs: The Great Edgar Hunt	Action	Warthog Games
Aquaman: Battle for Atlantis	Action	Lucky Chicken Games
Arslan: The Warriors of Legend	Action	Koei Tecmo
Arslan: The Warriors of Legend	Action	Koei Tecmo
Asterix & Obelix XXLPAL	Action	Étranges Libellules
Attack on Titan	Action	Omega Force
Avatar: The Last Airbender	Action	THQ

Sets of data can be produced by databases and by apps processing some or all the data present into just that which is wanted.

This data set is from a database of games available for consoles and computers, selecting the data for action games. This would be useful for a customer looking to purchase such a product.

Now try this

What examples of sets can you identify in the learner data held by your centre?

Consider the information that is kept about you and your achievements.

Had a look ☐ Nearly there ☐ Nailed it! ☐

Bubble sort

Sorting can be an essential technique when processing data into information. The most commonly used sorting algorithms used to sequence data are the bubble sort, quick sort and insertion sort. On this page, you will revise the bubble sort, which is a simple, basic algorithm.

Benefits	Limitations
Simple to understand Easy to implement Only needs a small amount of RAM Stable and reliable	Slow Very poor with large data sets Old algorithm

How it works

The bubble sort works by starting with the first item which is passed up the data set by swapping with the next item, until a larger item is met, then the larger item is passed up and so on. At the end of the first pass, the highest item will be at the end.

This process keeps on repeating until all the data is sorted into sequence.

Case study: Bubble sort algorithm

DO...LOOP WHILE repeats the code until there is nothing left to sort using Switch which is set to false at the start of the iteration and to true when an item is sorted into a new position.

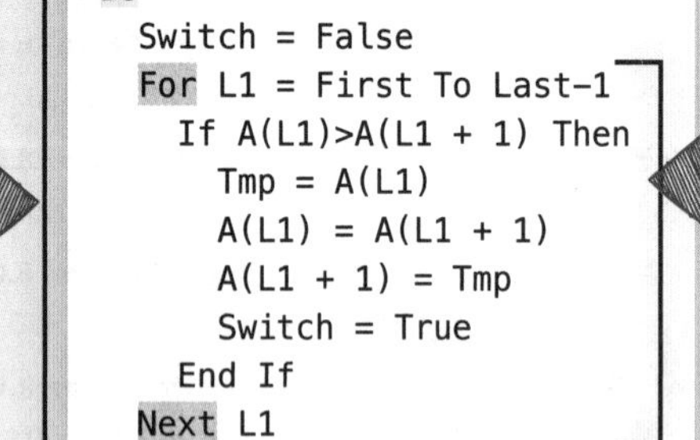

```
Do
  Switch = False
  For L1 = First To Last-1
    If A(L1)>A(L1 + 1) Then
      Tmp = A(L1)
      A(L1) = A(L1 + 1)
      A(L1 + 1) = Tmp
      Switch = True
    End If
  Next L1
Loop While Switch
```

The FOR...NEXT loop starts at the beginning of the data, ending at the item before last. Each time through this loop the current item is compared to the next and if the current item is larger, they swap. During the first iteration the largest item, 75 below, is moved to the end, like a bubble rising to the top in a glass. Further repeats of the FOR...NEXT loop inside the DO...LOOP WHILE structure bubble each next highest items, 27, 16, to their correct places.

A(1)	A(2)	A(3)	A(4)	A(5)	A(6)
27	16	75	12	31	32
16	27	75	12	31	32
16	27	12	75	31	32
16	27	12	31	75	32
16	27	12	31	32	75
16	12	27	31	32	75
12	16	27	31	32	75

Now try this

(a) Enter six values in the first row of a spreadsheet.

(b) Copy this data into the second row and reorder it to show one pass of the bubble sort algorithm.

(c) Repeat this process until all the values are sorted.

Use the pseudocode for guidance.

Quick sort

The quick sort is a popular sorting algorithm used to sequence data.

Benefits	Limitations
Good at sorting large data sets Good at mostly sorting data Widely used and popular Concise code using sophisticated recursions Does not need much temporary memory Can work well with parallel processing	Not efficient at sorting very jumbled data sets Difficult to write Not perfectly stable because equal items might not stay in same sequence

How it works

The algorithm selects a pivot in the data, then loops until items from left of the data set are all below the pivot and items from right all above the pivot. The pivot item can then be copied to its place before recursing the sort subroutine to do it all again for another pivot.

This is like sorting a pile of paper into two heaps, one heap less than an arbitrary value (pivot), the other more. Each of these heaps can then be further divided and sorted then put back together into a sorted whole.

Case study: Quick sort algorithm

Low is the lowest item in the array, High the highest item.

The WHILE High>Low loop iterates until the sort is completed.

WHILE L1<L2 AND A(L1)<=Pivot loop finds where from the left of the data set Pivot should be. The item here is copied to the low place and replaced by the Pivot.

```
Sub QuickSort(Low, High)
While High > Low
  L1 = Low
  L2 = High
  Pivot = A(Low)
  While L1<L2
    While A(L2)>Pivot
      L2 = L2 - 1
    End While
    A(L1) = A(L2)
    While L1<L2 And A(L1)<=Pivot
      L1 = L1 + 1
    End While
    A(L2) = A(L1)
  End While
  A(L1) = Pivot
  Call QuickSort(Low, L1 - 1)
  Low = L1 + 1
End While
End Sub
```

Pivot is set to a point in the data.

The WHILE A(L2)>Pivot loop finds where from the right of the data set Pivot should be. The low item is copied to this place.

The WHILE L1<L2 loop is used to iterate until the sort is completed.

A(1)	A(2)	A(3)	A(4)	A(5)	A(6)	Pivot
93	18	55	13	21	42	93
42	18	55	13	21	93	42
21	18	55	13	21	93	42
21	18	55	13	55	93	42
21	18	13	13	55	93	42
21	18	13	42	55	93	21
13	18	21	42	55	93	21

The recursion takes place with the quicksort sub-routine called from itself to sort what is left in the data set. The data examples shown here highlight in green the range of the data set that are sorted with each quicksort recursion with the Pivot value for each recursion in the right-most column of this data.

The first pivot, 93, is placed at the end as there are no greater values. When 42 is the pivot, 55 is moved next to 93 ready for 42 to copied to its place. When 21 is pivot, 13 is moved so 21 can be copied to its place completing the sort.

Now try this

(a) Enter six values in the first row of a spreadsheet.

(b) Copy this data into the second row and re-order it to show one pass of the quick sort.

(c) Repeat this process until all the values are sorted.

Use the pseudocode for guidance.

Insertion sort

One of the most common algorithms used to sequence data is the insertion sort.

Benefits	Limitations
Algorithm well understood Simple to code Sort stable so existing matches kept in same sequence Memory efficient Good with sequential data Good when data almost completely sorted	Can have performance issues when used with slow backing storage Poor performance with large lists

How it works

The insertion sort has been known and understood for decades, modestly improving the bubble sort with better performance.

Code starts from the low end, checking each pair of items to ensure the later item is larger than the previous one.

When an item is found to be out of place, all the items after the low end are moved back so the found item can be inserted at the beginning of this data set.

The process then re-starts to find the next item that is in the wrong place so it can be inserted into its correct position.

Case study: Insertion sort algorithm

The FOR...NEXT using L1 as loop variable iterates for each item in the data set with Tmp holding the current item.

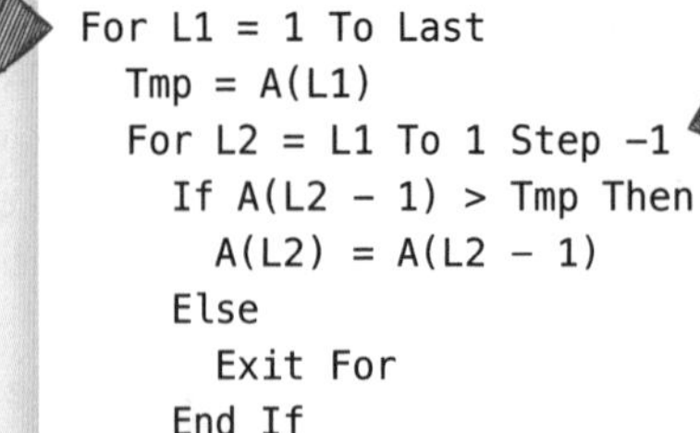

```
For L1 = 1 To Last
  Tmp = A(L1)
  For L2 = L1 To 1 Step -1
    If A(L2 - 1) > Tmp Then
      A(L2) = A(L2 - 1)
    Else
      Exit For
    End If
  Next L2
  A(L2) = Tmp
Next L1
```

The FOR...NEXT using L2 as loop variable starts with an IF statement to find when an item in the array is larger than the next item at which point it iterates from the current L1 item to the start moving data items back one place then Tmp is put into where the lowest of the data items was moved.

The lowest item of each iteration is inserted into the correct place with items shuffled up to make space for the sorted item. In the example below, 8 is inserted into the first position with items after moved to their next place up to where the 8 was. The other insertions were 39 then 40.

A(1)	A(2)	A(3)	A(4)	A(5)	A(6)
9	16	68	8	39	40
8	9	16	68	39	40
8	9	16	39	68	40
8	9	16	39	40	68

Now try this

(a) Enter six values in the first row of a spreadsheet.

(b) Copy this data into the second row and re-order it to show one pass of the insertion sort algorithm.

(c) Repeat this process until all the values are sorted.

Use the pseudocode for guidance.

Searching

Searching is a typical use for a computer system holding massive amounts of data which can be accurately checked for any items that match the search criteria. There are two basic types of searching algorithm: serial/linear and binary. On this page, you will also revise two other common algorithms, to count occurrences and for input validation.

Serial/linear search

This is a very simple algorithm, which starts at the beginning of the data, then looks at each item until a match is found. This is a good way to **count the occurrences** that match criteria in a data set as well as the best search option for data that has not been sorted into a sequence.

- ✓ best for unstructured data
- ✓ very simple to program
- ✓ works with any data set
- ✓ easily counts number of occurrences
- ✓ works with any combination of criteria

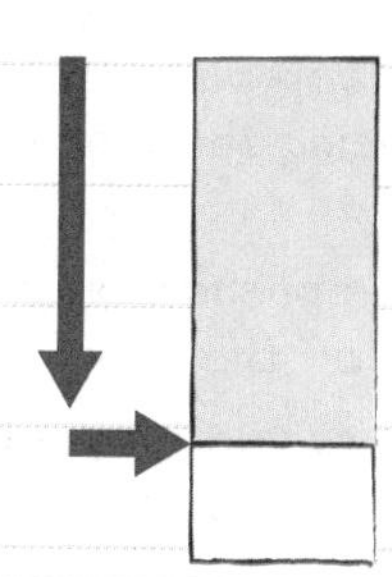

Serial searches each item until found.

Binary search

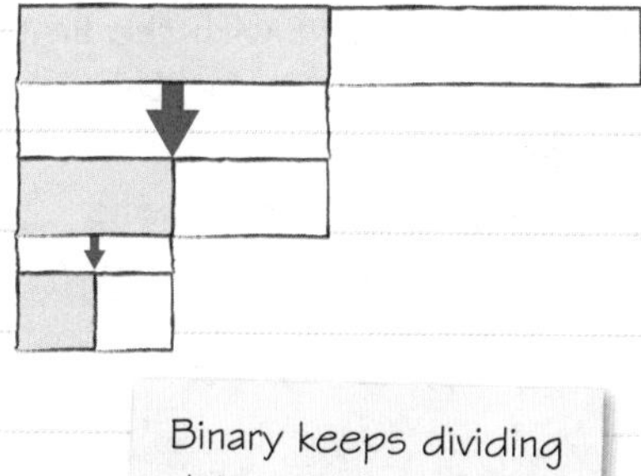

Binary keeps dividing data until found.

This algorithm can be used with data which has a sequenced order. The code starts by looking at the mid-point of the data to decide if the item matching the search criteria is before or after this item. The mid-point of the half of data containing the item is then looked at to decide if the item matching the search criteria is before or after. This is repeated until the item matching the search criteria is found.

- ✓ best algorithm for sorted data set
- ✓ very quick
- ✓ works with very large data sets
- ✓ programming algorithms are well known

Count occurrences

This is almost the same algorithm as for a linear search, except that it counts how many are found, rather than returning items matching search criteria.

Input validation

Validation of search criteria is essential to reduce wasted search time from bad data entries.

Now try this

1 (a) Create a spreadsheet model to calculate the lowest and highest number of comparisons needed to find an item using a linear and also using a binary search.

(b) How many comparisons are needed for 100/10 000/1 000 000-sized data sets using these methods?

2 Is there an obvious choice of algorithm for these searches? Why?

Remember the binary search starts half way through the data set, then keeps on halving until only the search item remains.

Had a look ☐ Nearly there ☐ Nailed it! ☐

Using stacks and queues

Stacks and queues are different techniques used to keep data items temporarily when a program is running. A stack brings back the last item (LIFO) whereas a queue retrieves the first item (FIFO).

Stacks

A stack is a last in first out (**LIFO**) structure, rather like a pile of plates which are stacked with the top plate (the last one added to the stack) being the first to be removed from the stack.

Items are pushed onto the stack to store and popped off the stack when retrieved.

Stacks are used many thousands of times every second when code runs on a computer for subroutine return addresses.

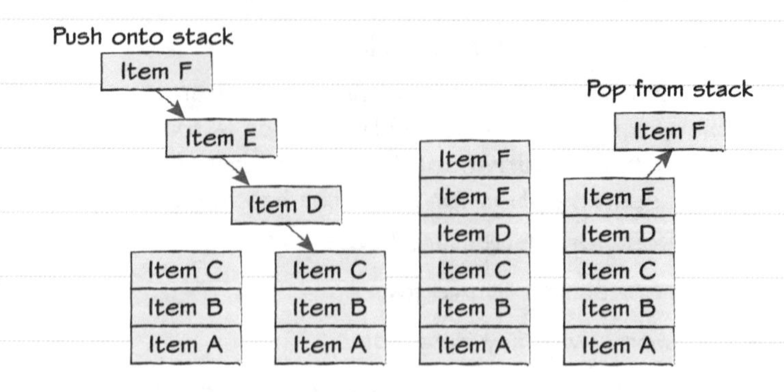

Queues

A queue is a first in first out (**FIFO**) structure, similar to a tunnel or conveyor belt with the first item written (added) to the queue being the first to be read from the queue.

Queues are used in many places where items are buffered on a computer system to wait for processing.

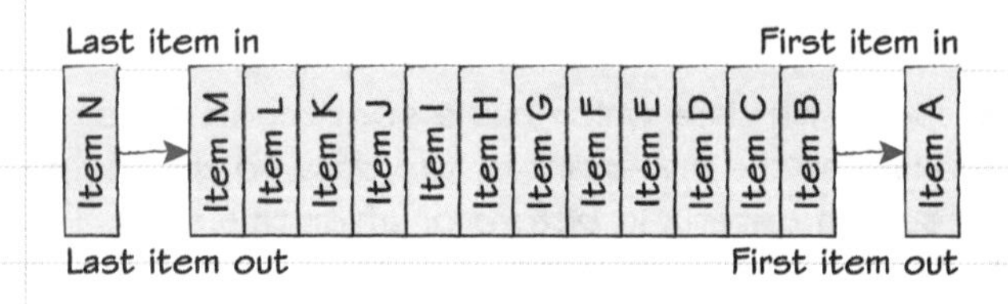

Examples of stacks

- Subroutines and functions use a stack to remember the address of the line of code that called them, which is used as the return address for when the subroutine or function completes.
- Spreadsheets use a stack to keep the part answers when calculations are worked out following BIDMAS. For example, a multiplication part answer would be pushed onto the stack before being popped off to add to another part answer.

Examples of queues

- Operating systems use queues for printing, with the first sent to the printer being the first to get printed.
- Computers use a keyboard buffer between the keyboard and the operating system so if the keyboard is used very quickly, the keys are read into the computer in the order they were typed.

Now try this

Create a paper-based story board and/or an animation to illustrate how program sub-routines use stacks for their return addresses.

You can use an example of a subroutine calling another subroutine.

Procedural programming structure

Procedural programming is the traditional type of programming language used to produce code that starts from one point then follows routes through the code, calling procedures and functions as needed, to help structure the code.

Procedural programming structures

Structure	Definition
Statement	Line of code
Block	Collection of statements
Procedure (sub-routine)	Named sub-program that can be called from other places in the code that returns when completed to where it was called from
Function	A procedure that returns a value

Using procedural programming structure

Good practice	Poor practice
👍 Use sensible procedure and function names making self-documenting code. 👍 Use arguments to pass values into procedures and functions.	👎 Copy and paste the same code into several places in the program. 👎 Use procedures to work out values that are returned in global variables.

Evaluating code

The code shown below has examples of both good and bad programming practice.

```
For Y = 0 To 20
  SB(Y) = ""
Next Y

'Read Dfile into P() array
  lblProgress.Text="Reading data"
FileOpen(1,Dfile,OpenMode.Input)
Y = 1
Do
  Input(1, S(0, Y))
  P(0, Y) = UCase(S(0, Y))
  If Not (EOF(1)) Then
    Input(1, P(1, Y))
  End If
  Y = Y + 1
Loop Until EOF(1)
```

- The FOR Y loop used to set initial values for array is good. Poor practice would be 21 lines of code to do this instead of the loop structure.
- SB(), P() are poor naming, as they are meaningless. Better practice would be names such as ShoppingBasket(), Products().
- Y is a good name for the loop variable as it is used to loop around the array Y subscript.
- The comment ('Read Dfile...) is good practice as this helps to document the code.
- Setting label, lblProgress.Text, to let the user know what the code is doing is good practice.
- Using a variable, Dfile, for the data file is good practice as this an appropriate name. Using a variable makes the code much more readable than the full file and folder names.
- Using the Ucase() function is good practice to make the data consistent in the program.
- IF NOT branch is poor practice as it handles an unexpected end of data file showing the data structures have not been fully planned.

Now try this

Interpret the code given and explain the product of this function. Suggest ways in which it could be improved.

```
Function Letters(ByVal Word1)
  Dim X As Integer
  Dim Word2 As String
  Word2 = ""
  For X = 1 To Len(Word1)
    Word2= Mid(Word1, X, 1) & Word2
  Next
  Letters = Word2
End Function
```

You can use a FOR loop to iterate the number of characters (LEN) in the word.

Had a look ☐ Nearly there ☐ Nailed it! ☐

Procedural programming control structures

Within procedural programming, control structures define the sequences and routes available to run through code with branching to respond to when the conditions are met and iteration to repeat sections of code.

Control structure	When to use it
Sequence	Everywhere apart from lines of code used to define part of a different control structure
Condition	Wherever a decision needs to be made on which path is to be taken through the code
Iteration	When a section of code needs to be re-run

Sequential code

```
Call InitialiseVariables()
StudentD    File =
"Choices    tch_D.csv"
Employe    le =
"Emplo    atch_D.csv"
Sessions    lot = PMslots
BatchLett r = "D"
Call ReadData()
```

This is the default structure, simply lines of code which follow each other. The code starts to run with the first line in the program, then the second line and so on.

Conditional code

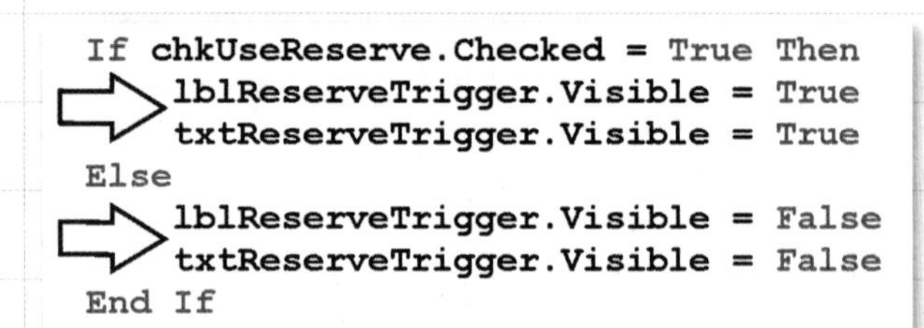

```
If chkUseReserve.Checked = True Then
    lblReserveTrigger.Visible = True
    txtReserveTrigger.Visible = True
Else
    lblReserveTrigger.Visible = False
    txtReserveTrigger.Visible = False
End If
```

Conditional code takes one of two routes through the code with the condition used to determine which of the routes is taken.

A condition is anything that works out as true or false. In the code example here, the condition is whether the checkbox object, chkUseReserve, has been selected.

Iterative code

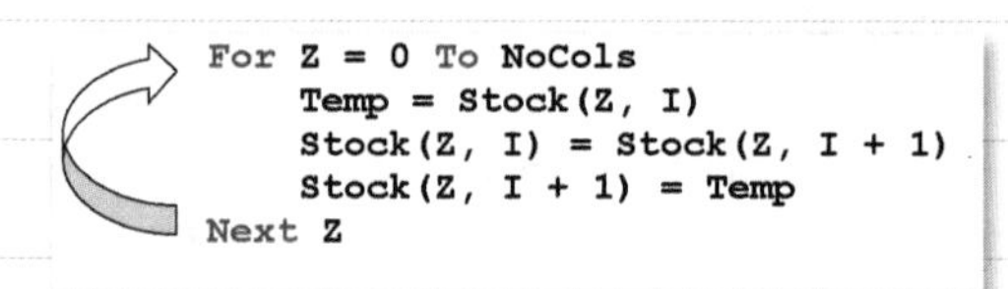

```
For Z = 0 To NoCols
    Temp = Stock(Z, I)
    Stock(Z, I) = Stock(Z, I + 1)
    Stock(Z, I + 1) = Temp
Next Z
```

Iterative code is often called a loop as it repeats a section of code by looping around it.

The code example here shows a FOR...NEXT loop which starts at 0 and continues for as many times as are in the variable, NoCols.

The loop variable, Z, starts at 0 and increments with each loop, so Z will contain 1 on the next iteration, then 2 and so on until Z reaches the value held in NoCols when the loop completes.

Types of conditional code

- IF...THEN...ELSE is a simple structure which offers two routes, according to whether the condition between IF...THEN is true or false.
- SELECT CASE is a more complex structure offering as many branches as the program needs. This structure lists as many conditions as needed with the code to be run for each.

Types of iterative code

- Definite loops have a set number of iterations, such as FOR...NEXT where the number of loops is defined in the FOR line.
- Indefinite loops repeat until a condition is met, such as DO...LOOP UNTIL. The condition can be at the end of the structure so the loop code runs at least once. If the condition is at the start the loop code will not run at all if the condition is false when the program runs.

Now try this

Produce code using appropriate procedural structures to accept ten numbers, loop through to add them together, find the mean average and to then find further averages of those values above or below the mean. Step through your code to see variable contents as the averages are calculated.

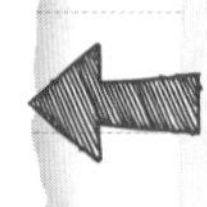

Put a breakpoint in your code to pause so you can see how they change using an appropriate tool, such as a watch window or hovering pointer over variables in the code.

Object-oriented programming structure

Object-oriented programming is a type of programming language using objects with properties to define what they are and methods to define what can be done with them.

Classes

A class is the starting point for any object, giving the object its characteristics. You can think of a class as the template defining the methods and properties for a new object.

- Methods are the actions that can be carried out on the object such as changing a property.
- Properties, such as a salary, individualise the object.

An example of object-orientated programming structure.

Instances

A new object will be an instance of a class. There can be many instances of a class, each of which is an object. In the example on this page the employee class can be used to create several instances, each of which is an employee object.

Objects

The objects can be used in your code according to their methods and properties.

Objects such as buttons and text boxes are also available in modern visual languages that you can use to construct the interface. Dragging a new button from a toolbox onto a form creates a new instance of the button class.

Now try this

Complete the code or produce your own code to define an invoice class to be used by a form including a method definition for output and data for Name, Amount, Date, Customer.

```
class Invoice
{
public:
}
```

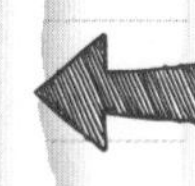

You will need to create a new instance of the class.

Had a look ☐ Nearly there ☐ Nailed it! ☐

Object-oriented programming features

Object-oriented programming can be used with a range of techniques – inheritance, encapsulation, polymorphism and overloading, data hiding and reusability – to provide a lot of flexibility on how an object can behave.

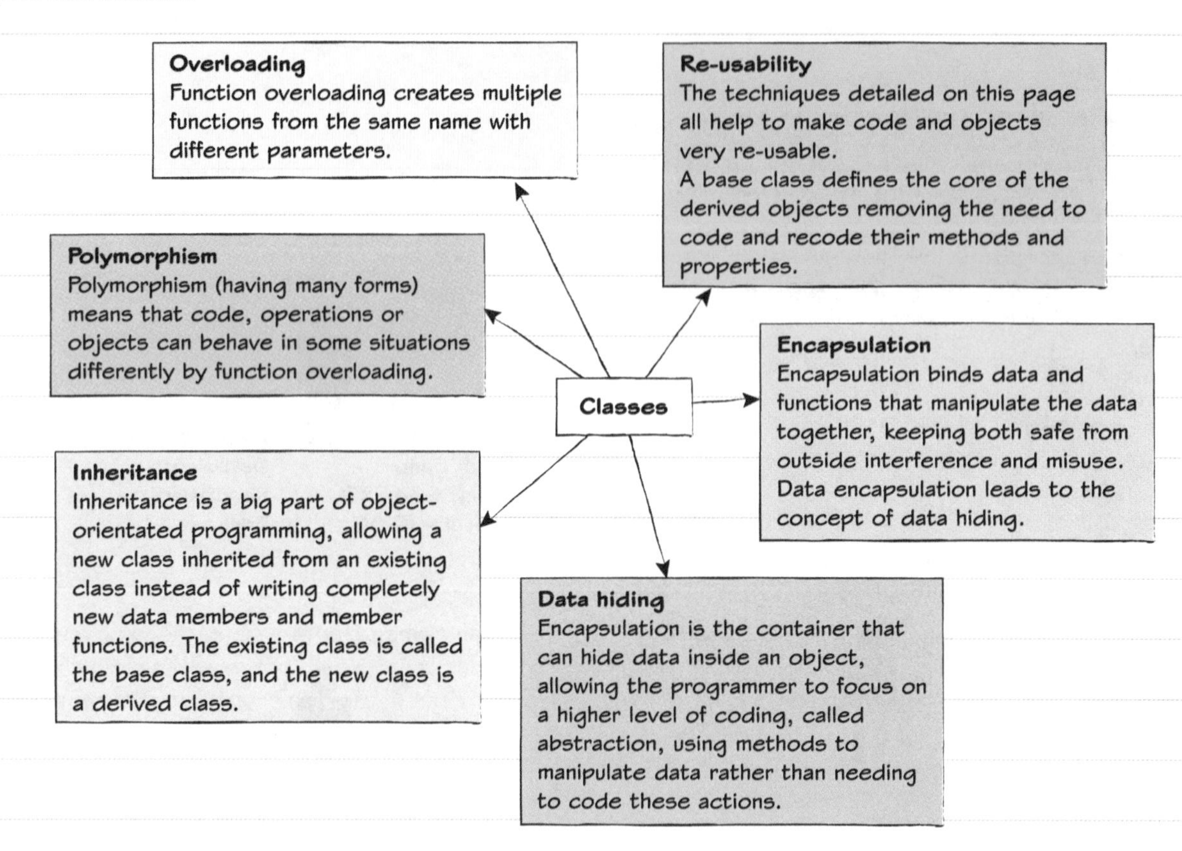

Common object-oriented programming languages include:

- C++
- Microsoft® C#
- Oracle® JavaScript
- PHP
- Ada.

Now try this

Modify the DrawSquare method to enable a rectangle to be drawn if two parameters are provided. Overload this class to accept just one length.

```
Public Class DrawShape
  Public Sub Shape(sender, X, Y, ShL, ShH)
    Dim myBrush As New System.Drawing.SolidBrush(System.Drawing.Color.Red)
    Dim formGraphics As System.Drawing.Graphics
    formGraphics = sender.CreateGraphics()
    formGraphics.FillRectangle(myBrush, New Rectangle(X, Y, ShL, ShH))
    myBrush.Dispose()
    formGraphics.Dispose()
  End Sub
End Class
```

Event-driven programming structure

Event-driven programming produces code that responds to events such as a mouse being clicked on a button or another object.

Event-driven programs and sub-routines

- Modern event-driven programs mostly use forms for the user interface, with objects on the forms such as buttons which generate events that start code in the sub-routine which responds to the event.
- Sub-routines can be written as code modules by the programmer to structure their code. Sub-routine modules are also generated for responding to each event a programmer needs to code, usually by clicking on an object then selecting the appropriate event.

Main loop

Programmers do not usually code for the main loop, as this is provided by the programming environment to continuously look for an event to occur, at which point the event handler sub-routine code is called to respond to the event. This loop recognises which event to call the appropriate code, for example the mouse click event handler for a button which has just received a click from the user.

Event-driven programming offers a wide and varied choice of events so the coder can choose the exact event that is required.

Callback functions

The purpose of a callback function is to carry out a task in the background and then to report back to the program when the task is completed.

This could be compared with shopping. A normal function is like going to the supermarket, filling the trolley and paying at the checkout, which needs your full attention. A callback function can be likened to online shopping where the order can be quickly placed and you can do other tasks until the order arrives.

Event handler code

The sub-routine below is code to handle the CheckedChanged event of a checkbox object, chkUseReserve. This code would usually be triggered when the mouse clicks on the object to check or uncheck, but would also be invoked if the object checked property was changed from another sub-routine.

The code uses an IF selection structure to branch through one of two different routes according to whether this checkbox has changed to checked or unchecked.

```
Private Sub chkUseReserve_CheckedChanged(ByVal sender As_ System.Object, ByVal e As System.EventArgs)
Handles_ chkUseReserve.CheckedChanged

  If chkUseReserve.Checked = True Then
    lblReserveTrigger.Visible = True
    txtReserveTrigger.Visible = True
  Else
    lblReserveTrigger.Visible = False
    txtReserveTrigger.Visible = False
  End If
End Sub
```

This code responds to the CheckedChanged event, so it runs when the checkbox is set or cleared.

Now try this

Write code for appropriate events to show a 'Rollover' effect on an object on a form, by changing the background colour and counting how many times the mouse moves over the object.

Create your objects first then select the events you want to code.

Had a look ☐ Nearly there ☐ Nailed it! ☐

Event-driven programming features

Event-driven programs are used extensively in modern apps, which depend upon mouse clicks or a touch screen. Events can also be triggered by objects such as a timer to produce regular events that occur alongside other events such as a mouse click.

Service-orientated processing

Service-orientated processing is the breaking down of complex problems into a collection of separate (but potentially linked) processes, each providing a specific service for client applications.

These programs often work in the background. For example, a database can run as a service on a server listening for requests and providing responses.

Service-orientated processes can establish connections with each other using messages passing across a network.

These processes respond to events to produce the actions needed to provide the required service.

Events, handlers and loops

An event can be almost anything that happens to an app when it runs. As well as obvious events such as a mouse click, there can be subtle events such as key down, key up, key press to offer the programmer a lot of control over which trigger function to use to start the event handler running.

Event loops keep spinning around, waiting for an event to occur so they can call the appropriate **event handler** to run code.

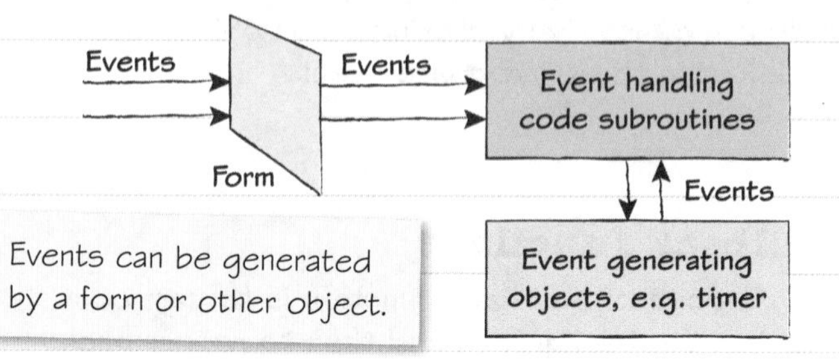

Events can be generated by a form or other object.

Time-driven events

A timer object can be used to generate time-driven events which occur at regular intervals.

The coding behind a clock, stopwatch or similar will use a timer object to generate the regular events needed to update the display.

A timer object can be defined in code with how long between the events it generates.

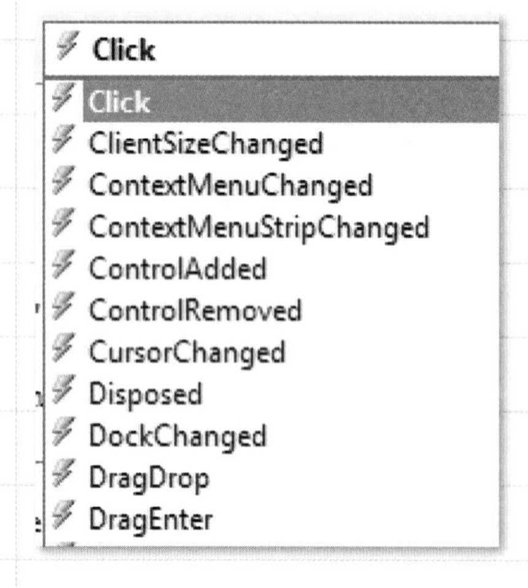

Trigger functions

A trigger function is there to respond to events which the code encounters, triggering an event handler code sub-routine.

The programmer has a wide choice of which of these to select from inside the programming environment.

The screenshot, left, shows just a few of the trigger events available for an object on a form in a VB.NET program. When the programmer clicks on one of these triggers, the programming environment starts up a new sub-routine to handle that event.

The coder can then enter the code they want to run for this event trigger.

Now try this

Use a timer object and code to demonstrate time-driven events and trigger functions by showing labels on a form counting seconds and minutes.

Use meaningful names for your objects.

Coding for the web: Characteristics

Mark-up and web languages are used to create websites and to provide extra functionality such as live calculations. HTML is the mark-up standard.

Web mark-up languages

There is a choice of web mark-up languages to produce code for a website to run in your browser, each with its own characteristics, features, **performance** and power.

A modern web mark-up language needs to meet the standards of HTML5 as this is the expected environment a browser will use to display and run the webpage.

Platform independence and security

A web mark-up language needs to be stable and to run on:

- different browsers such as Safari, Chrome
- different hardware such as mobile phones, tablets, computers and smart televisions.

Web mark-up languages should be able handle secure transactions such as payments.

Web language popularities

The IEEE Spectrum Survey recently completed a survey using the following sources to rank the popularity of web programming languages:

- search results in Google
- data from Google Trends
- tweets sent on Twitter
- GitHub repositories
- StackOverflow questions
- Reddit posts
- Hacker News posts
- demand for jobs on the Career Builder job site
- demand for jobs on the Dice job site
- IEEE Xplore journal articles.

Popular programming languages

- Definite loops have a set number of iterations, such as FOR...NEXT where the number of loops is defined in the FOR line.
- Java
- C
- C++
- Python
- C#
- PHP
- JavaScript.

Power

The power of HTML has increased with each revision as more features are added to improve what can be done inside the browser and to help performance and platform independence.

HTML5 provides improvements including:

- editable content on a webpage
- validation for email addresses
- better form features
- better audio support.

Protocols

HTTP (hyper text transfer protocol) has been one of the major enablers of web browsing, providing a request/response relationship between the webpage in the browser and the website providing the page.

HTTP carries overheads such as the need for HTTP to poll the server to get new updated data, which slows the communications.

Newer technologies such as WebSocket offer a persistent connection where the client and server can send data to each other at any time.

Now try this

Research a web language to produce a summary of your choice.

You could use Java for this exercise.

Had a look ☐ Nearly there ☐ Nailed it! ☐

Coding for the web: Uses

Code can be written using web languages to respond to the user in ways such as calculating a shopping cart total. Such code can utilise client-side processing and **scripting** to run on the user computer or can be **server-side** with a request to the server for data.

Client-side processing

This code can run in the browser to show whether the user has visited the website before by opening a cookie then showing a prompt for the user to enter their name if the cookie is not present, setting the cookie after the user name is entered so it is there for the next visit.

```
function Visitor(info){
  var vName = GetCookie('vName')
  if (vName == null) {
    vName = prompt("Please enter your name");
    SetCookie ('vName', vName, exp);
}
return vName;
}
```

```
var vSQL = opDB.createStatement();
vSQL.executeQuery("SELECT * FROM dbTable;");
var SQLresult = vSQL.getResultSet();
while (SQLresult.next()) {
    results.push(new DataModel({
      Ref: SQLresult.getInt("Ref"),
      Username: SQLresult.getString("Username"),
      Description: SQLresult.getString("Description")
    }));
}
```

Server-side processing

The code fragment to the left can run on a server to select all the records from a MySQL database table named dbTable, then loop around them to display in the browser screen.

The main web platform choice for the hosting severs is between Linux and Windows. These are both good and reliable systems, so most of the issues and implications of implementing are down to how the server-side code is set up, programmed and tested.

Server-side and client-side advantages

Server side	Client side
Good for: ✓ MySQL queries to retrieve data ✓ saving user data ✓ validating users.	✓ interacts directly with objects, for example buttons on user browser window ✓ fast response times

Implementing code on a web platform

Most of the **issues** around code on a web platform are about compatibility with the browser and that security settings may prevent code from running on the user computer.

The main **implication** is that a reliable internet connection needs to be present for the browser to connect to the web.

Now try this

Produce an example each of where client-side and server-side processing are used, with the implications of implementing such code on these web platforms.

eBay could be used for the server-side processing example.

Translation issues

Translating code between programming languages is sometimes needed when implementing a new system. The implications and impacts on users, organisations and developers need to be anticipated and planned for to minimise disruption.

Translating between languages

Writing code always needs the programming language to translate this high-level code into low-level code the computer can understand.

Translating a high-level language into another high-level language needs a program called a translator (source-to-source compiler). These are mostly used to move code from old to newer hardware between languages such as FORTRAN-to-Ada.

Reasons for translating code

- Replacement of old with new hardware which will not support legacy code.
- New software environment used with the organisation.
- Need to keep to new standards brought in by the organisation.

The drawbacks of translating code outweigh the benefits.

Benefits
Can save time
Can save cost from not needing much programmer involvement
May be able to use a lot of the original documentation from the original app
May be able to re-use previous test plan and data

Drawbacks
Time to test the new translations work correctly
Distancing of translated version from original program design and implementation
Readability of code reduced because humans write code that makes sense using names of variables
Translated code may need a lot of editing to make it understandable for future maintenance
Original code results from a lot of thinking and planning, may use structures too subtle for software utility to recognise, leading to errors
Will need thorough testing to ensure that everything still works as intended and that no logic or processing errors have occurred

Implications for users, organisation and developers		
Users	**Organisation**	**Developers**
Users familiar with the older version of an app may find that a new version changes the user interface in subtle and annoying ways, such as order of selected objects on a form using tab, keyboard shortcuts not working, or forms not holding the focus as expected.	There will be a cost and time required to test the translated app. There might be a knock-on impact if subtle errors in output data are not detected during testing and go live.	Developers will almost certainly find the new code less comprehensible than the old and harder to maintain.

Now try this

Explain why an organisation might need to translate code between programming languages.

What change in the systems would bring about this need?

Had a look ☐ Nearly there ☐ Nailed it! ☐

Translation alternatives

On this page, you will revise alternative methods of translating code.

Translating code

There are many problems in producing a utility to convert code from one language to another. Each language has a large collection of low-level code used to make the program source code written by programmers into the machine code that can actually run on the computer. This makes it very difficult for conversion software to move code that both runs and can be maintained by programmers.

Google Web Toolkit (GWT) and Hiphop

- The GWT utility generates JavaScript from Java and features a test browser where you can test how the Java code executes with a step-through debugger.
- Facebook produced its HipHop Virtual Machine (HHVM) to compile PHP into C++ to improve how quickly webpages can run code.

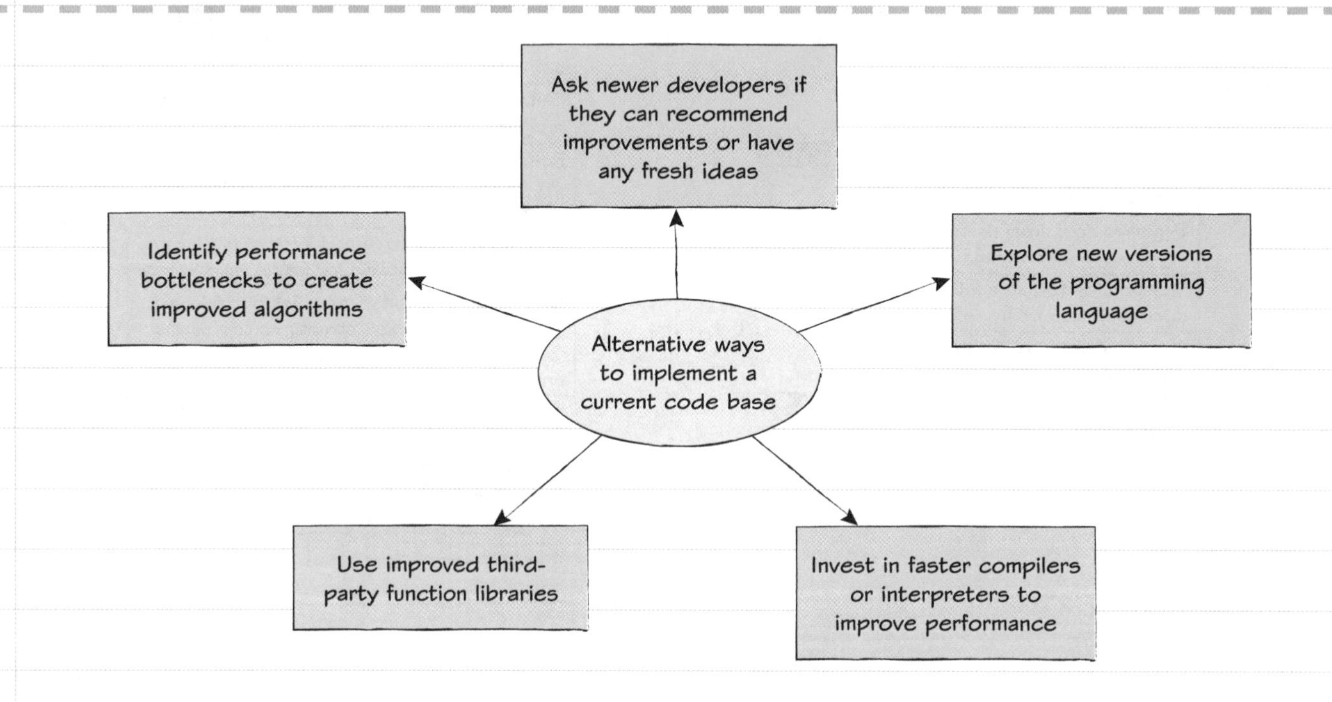

Implications of translating code

Whatever programming paradigm being used, the ability to debug programs, identify errors and fix them remains essential. Finding errors in computer-generated code can be very difficult.

The short-term gain from moving the code can easily be lost if the new solution is difficult to understand and edit. Any problems that are encountered will need to be resolved by editing code and testing the modified solution.

Now try this

Produce an advert for a named translation tool.

Try to find some webpages reviewing the tool.

Your Unit 1 exam

Your Unit 1 exam will be set by Pearson and could cover any of the essential content in the unit. You can revise the unit content in this Revision Guide. This skills section is designed to **revise skills** that might be needed in your exam. The section uses selected content and outcomes to provide examples of ways of applying your skills.

Exam skills

These are some of the exam skills you'll need:

- ✓ Understanding the question
  Revise this on page 42
- ✓ Short-answer questions
  Revise this on page 43
- ✓ Performing calculations
  Revise this on page 44
- ✓ Drawing diagrams or flow charts
  Revise this on page 45
- ✓ Longer-answer questions
  Revise this on page 46
- ✓ Analyse data and information
  Revise this on page 47
- ✓ Predicting outcomes
  Revise this on page 48
- ✓ Evaluate questions
  Revise this on page 49

Question types

Command words are the key terms used in questions, for example 'identify', 'explain', 'draw'. They identify the approach you should take to answering the question.

Question types

Command words are the key terms used in questions, for example 'identify', 'explain', 'draw'. They identify the approach you should take to answering the question.

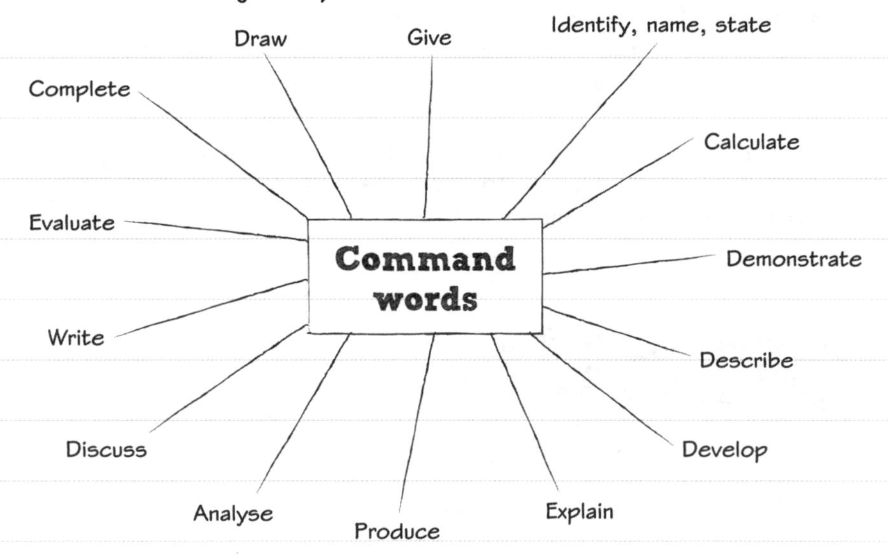

Exam checklist

Before the exam, make sure you have

- ✓ a black pen you like and a spare
- ✓ a pencil, sharpener and eraser for drawing diagrams and flow charts
- ✓ a calculator in case you are asked to perform calculations
- ✓ double checked the time and date of your exam.

Check the Pearson website

The questions and sample response extracts in this section are provided to help you to revise content and skills. Ask your tutor or check the Pearson website for the most up-to-date **Sample Assessment Material** and **Mark Scheme** to get an indication of the structure of your actual paper and what this requires of you. The details of the actual exam may change so always make sure you are up to date.

Now try this

Create a revision timetable around your exam schedule.

Had a look ☐ Nearly there ☐ Nailed it! ☐

Understanding the question

Understanding what a question is asking you to do will help you to take the right approach to your answer. Here are some skills you could use to enable you to focus on the purpose of the question.

Worked example

Building For Excellence (BFE) is a group of local builders wanting a mobile phone app to give an instant price for a job, which can then be texted to the client. The app should be simple and easy to use.

The client requirements for the app are given in the information.

Describe the problem, inputs, processing and outputs for the BFE app. **4 marks**

Read the scenario and tasks very carefully to help you understand the type of answer you are expected to write.

Identify and highlight the command word in the question. This indicates the skills you will need to demonstrate in your answer. In this revision question, **describe** indicates you will need to outline the key features of four items.

Look at the marks available for a question which should help you to understand the level of detail required. Questions that ask you to demonstrate or apply your knowledge and understanding will have fewer marks than an **evaluate** question which will require a longer answer and may have a maximum of 12 marks.

Sample response extract

The app is to run on mobile phones, be easy to use and allow BFE builders to give instant prices for jobs. The details of the price can then be sent to the client as a text. Inputs will be name of client, mobile number of client, hours needed and materials. Processing to multiply hours by hourly rate, multiply distance by travel rate, add costs. Output to show costs of hours, travel, total cost, text to client.

If you have time, re-read your answers to check they make sense and answer the question.

Worked example

Draw a screen design for the app and label the main features. **4 marks**

The command word **draw** asks you to show your understanding through a diagram or flow chart. In this revision question, the task also requires you to label the diagram, so be sure you include annotations.

Sample response extract

Pricing App — App name
Client name: [ ]
Client mobile: [ ]
Materials: [ ]
Hours: [ ]
Job price: £320 — Price
[Calculate] [TXT prices] — Action buttons

Make sure you carefully read the client requirements to include inputs for all the data that will be required for the app.

Make sure every output identified in the client requirements is included in your design.

Links Revise pages 1, 2 and 3 on decomposition

Now try this

Write pseudocode for the calculations needed by this app.

Short-answer questions

Short-answer questions, with command words such as explain, identify, state, want you to provide factual information. The answers normally only require one or two words or short sentences.

Worked example

State two reasons why flow charts are used. **2 marks**

This is a **state** question, so your answer will not need much detail.

Sample response extract

1 To explain how an algorithm works
2 To help in identifying errors in code

Worked example

This is an **explain** question, so your answer should communicate the usage of each symbol.

Explain how each of these flow chart symbols is used. **3 marks**

Describe each symbol.

(a) ____________

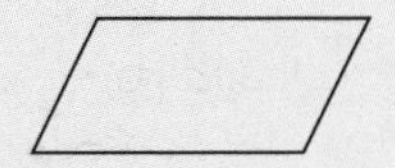

(b) ____________

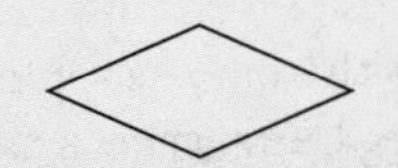

(c) ____________

Sample response extract

(a) A terminator used to show each place where the program starts or ends
(b) Input/output used to show points in the algorithm where data is input or output
(c) Decision used to show the places in the algorithm where the program takes one of two branches according to the decision shown in this symbol

The learner has clearly explained each of the three flow chart symbols. This answer includes enough detail and keeps to the point.

This question is simply asking you to **identify** the items. Don't worry about the pros and cons.

Worked example

Identify an appropriate item of information that could be held in each of these types of variable:

(a) Alphanumeric string
(b) Character
(c) Floating point (real) **4 marks**

Sample response extract

(a) Anything which could be a mix of letters, numbers, spaces and general typing such as an address, e.g. 12 Station Road
(b) Similar to alphanumeric string, but can only be a single character such as a variable used to hold gender, e.g. M
(c) Numbers with fractional parts such as a variable used to hold the average value of a data set, e.g. 23.453

Make sure you include an example for each.

Links To revise types of data, see page 13.

Now try this

Identify appropriate items of information that could be held in each of these types of variable:

(a) date/time (b) integer (c) Boolean.

Had a look ☐ Nearly there ☐ Nailed it! ☐

Performing calculations

You may need to show you have the skills to perform calculations involving either numbers or string handling.

Worked example

A program calculates cost of paint to decorate a room. Paint is available in 5-litre cans (£10), 2.5-litre cans (£6) and 1-litre cans (£3). A litre of paint covers 2 m^2. Variables are; Cans1l, Cans25l, Cans5l, Cost, Coverage, PaintCost, PaintNeeded, WallArea, WallHeight, WallLength.

(a) What will WallArea hold if WallLength=12, WallHeight=3 (metres)?

(b) What will PaintNeeded hold?

(c) What will Cans1l, Cans25l, Cans5l hold?

(d) What will be the cost of paint for this job?

8 marks

Sample response extract

(a) WallArea = WallLength * WallHeight, so will hold 36

(b) PaintNeeded = WallArea / Coverage so will hold 18

(c) Cans5l = integer of PaintNeeded/5 so will hold 3
PaintNeeded = PaintNeeded – (Cans5l * 5)
Cans25l = integer of PaintNeeded/2.5 so will hold 1
PaintNeeded = PaintNeeded – (Cans25l * 2.5)
Cans1l = round up of PaintNeeded so will hold 1

(d) Cost = (Cans5l * 10) + (Cans25l * 6) + (Cans1l * 3) so will hold 39

Each part of the answer covers two points. The learner has also shown their workings.

Worked example

A game uses variables to hold strength (as a percentage), time (seconds), kills (integer) about the player with the score calculated as 1000 * strength * kills / time.

(a) How does time affect the score?

(b) Identify three combinations scoring 40.

8 marks

Use a pencil and paper to define how the score is calculated; strength * kills / time with some example numbers. Use numbers that are easy to multiply and divide to get a 'feel' for how the calculation works.

Sample response extract

(a) A shorter time results in a higher score. This is because the time is divided into the other variables.

(b) Three combinations scoring 40:
Strength=50% Kills=8 Time=100
50%*8=4, 4/100=0.04, 1000*0.04=40
Strength=50% Kills=16 Time=200
50%*16=8, 8/200=0.04, 1000*0.04=40
Strength=100% Kills=8 Time=200
100%*8=8, 8/200=0.04, 1000*0.04=40

When answering a **calculate** question, remember to show your workings as part of your answer. Even if your answer is not correct, you may get credit for your method.

Now try this

A multi-level game is being developed with the score calculated from the number of steps taken in each level added to a bonus awarded for completing the level. The points for each step in level 1 is 10, each subsequent level has 5 added to the previous step points so level 2 has 15 points per step, level 3 has 20 points per step and so on. The bonus for completing level 1 is 50, with the bonus doubling for subsequent levels, so level 2 has a bonus of 100 points, level 3 has 200 and so on.

What will be the score from 50 steps in level 1, 48 steps in level 2, 58 steps in level 3, 52 steps in level 4 and 12 steps in level 5?

Include the bonus for each level.

Drawing diagrams or flow charts

You may be asked to show that you can draw or complete a diagram or flow chart.

Worked example

This is an example of working code for an insertion sort:

```
For L1 = 1 To Last
  Tmp = A(L1)
  For L2 = L1 To 1 Step -1
    If A(L2 - 1) > Tmp Then
      A(L2) = A(L2 - 1)
    Else
      Exit For
    End If
  Next L2
  A(L2) = Tmp
Next L1
```

Draw a flow chart for this algorithm using standard BCS symbols.

5 marks

Make sure your flow chart accurately shows how this algorithm works.

You may find it helpful to produce a quick rough sketch to clarify your thinking.

Remember to use BCS symbols in your flow chart.

You will need to include every line of code in your flow chart.

Links For more on BCS flow chart symbols, see page 11.

Try to get most of the data flows in your flow chart to go down or right. Use arrows to confirm each direction.

Draw your diagram as clearly and neatly as possible.

Decision box must show the correct logic.

Yes and No routes must be correctly labelled.

The data flows should be down or right unless arrows show otherwise.

Sample response extract

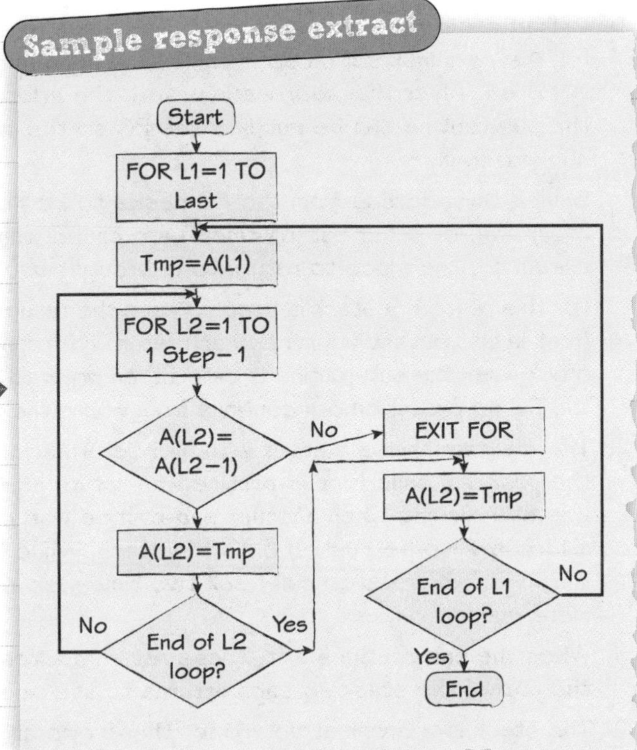

Links To revise flow charts, see page 11.
To revise insertion sort, see page 28.

Now try this

Write pseudocode, then draw a flow chart for a linear search algorithm. You should be able to devise your own algorithm which accepts the search criterion then loops through a data set until the criterion is found with an output to report on finding the item or that the criterion was not present in the data set.

Had a look ☐ Nearly there ☐ Nailed it! ☐

Longer-answer questions

Some questions may require longer, more in-depth answers. You will need to take a slightly different approach to these questions.

Worked example

Programming languages use stacks to remember return addresses from sub-routine calls.

Analyse with reference to a diagram how a programming environment passes program execution to a sub-routine and the data structure used to return to the point in the code where the sub-routine was called when the sub-routine completes. **10 marks**

> Take a little time to make sure you fully understand what the question is asking you to do. Note down the points you want to cover on a piece of paper.

> For this **analyse** question you need to be clear on:
> - program execution, including sub-routines and data structures
> - the uses of stack-based memory allocation.

Sample response extract

Program execution simply runs through the code line by line unless a control structure causes a different route through the code. A sub-routine is a named sub-program that can be called from anywhere (within scope) of the program so the execution jumps to the sub-routine then returns to the next line of code after the call.

> Start your answer with a clear introduction which makes reference to the question. Here the learner explains what happens when code is executed and defines a sub-routine.

When program code is executed a specialised register (program counter, PC) inside the CPU holds the address of the next instruction in memory. When an instruction is brought into the CPU, usually, the length of the instruction is added to the PC so it now points to the next code to be run from memory.

Calling a sub-routine needs the PC to 'save' the address that is there for the next instruction so it can be brought back when the sub-routine is exited. After this address is saved, the address of the first line of the sub-routine can be put into the PC so the program can execute this sub-program.

Saving the address from the PC needs to be flexible, so if there is recursion, or other sub-routine(s) are called whilst the sub-routine is executed, the place to return to is brought back in the correct order.

> Try to plan the structure of your answer in a logical way rather than just adding points as you remember them.

For this reason, a stack is used to save the return addresses. This is a FILO (first in last out) structure so each return address can be pushed onto the stack when the sub-routine is called then popped off when completed to the PC so execution can continue from where the last call was.

> Use accurate technical language wherever possible.

The diagram shows a stack with four return addresses. The first time the program called a sub-routine was return address 1. This sub-routine was still running when another sub-routine was called, causing return address 2 to be pushed onto the stack. While this sub-routine was running it recursed to call itself two times, so return addresses 3 and 4 were pushed on.

> Your diagram might look like this:

Return 4
Return 3
Return 2
Return 1

When the sub-routines exit, these return addresses can be popped off the top of the stack so each returns to the point where it was called.

The stack is a great structure for these operations as the sub-routines can return in reverse order.

Links To revise data structures, see page 22.

Now try this

Discuss how a function can be written by a coder into their program. Include what is needed to define the function, declare arguments, return the value and call the function.

Analyse data and information

Analyse questions want you to examine a topic in detail and look at the relationship between the parts. This might involve discussing the advantages and disadvantages of possible solutions and predicting outcomes, but you may not be expected to give a conclusion.

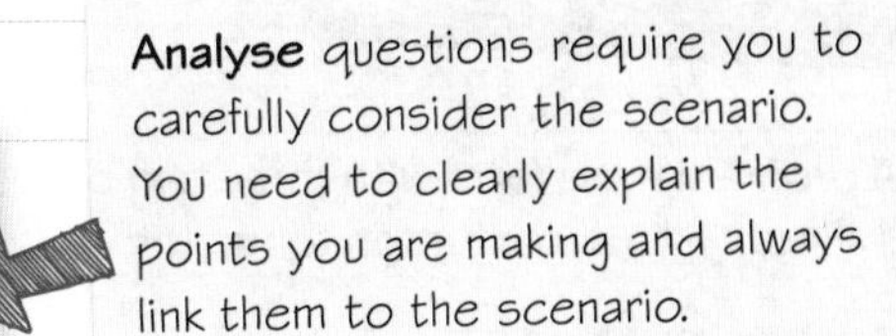

Worked example

Restique Relics (RR), a successful restoration and reclaimed building antiques retailer, is considering raising its online presence. It already advertises selected individual items on online market places. RR plans to set up a website so potential clients can see all of their current products with a shopping cart and checkout.

For this question, you need to be clear on the uses of both:
- server-side scripting
- client-side scripting.

Discuss the ways that client-side and server-side scripting could be used to implement a website for Restique Relics. **6 marks**

Try to write answers that use fluent and accurate technical vocabulary.

Sample response extract

When you visit a website there are many ways that scripting can be used to enhance the experience. [1] Server-side scripting runs on the server computer that you are visiting and client-side scripting runs in the browser of the computer you are using. [1]

Start your answer with a short introductory sentence, linked to the question and scenario.

Remember to Include a clear definition of what you are going to be writing about, in this case server-side scripting and client-side scripting.

The main use for server-side scripting is to search the data sets held on the server and to return the results to you. [1] RR would use MySQL to allow visitors to its website to see the products and to search for specific items or features.

Explain the main uses of server-side scripting and client-side scripting.

The shopping cart will be controlled by scripting. This could be on the server or the client, but the better choice would be the server. [1] This is so the information about products selected, client, payments, etc. can be kept safely under the control of the website. This would provide a more reliable solution, e.g. two people would not be able to buy the same product.

Your answer should consider the advantages/disadvantages of the solution.

Client-side scripting would be good to respond to the browser to make best use of the features provided. [1] Cookies can be used to record visits and to welcome clients back.

This is a balanced consideration of the issues, using logical chains of reasoning showing a full awareness of their relative importance to the scenario.

The best websites use a mix of server- and client-side scripting to produce a quick and accurate browsing experience. [1]

The elements of the question are carefully considered with arguments clearly linked to the given scenario.

Links To revise how websites use code, see pages 37 and 38.

Now try this

Discuss the benefits and drawbacks of translating code between programming languages.

Start by defining what is meant by translating code between programming languages in your answer and why this might be needed. Remember to identify and explain both benefits and drawbacks.

Links To revise translating code between programming languages, see pages 39–40.

Had a look ☐ Nearly there ☐ Nailed it! ☐

Predicting outcomes

Here are some examples of skills which will help you to predict outcomes from a given computing solution.

Worked example

A program has a form with three text boxes, txtNumber1-#3, six labels, lblResult1-#6 and a button to run the code shown below:

```
Dim tNumber1
Dim tNumber2
Dim tNumber3

tNumber1 = CSng(txtNumber1.Text)
tNumber2 = CSng(txtNumber2.Text)
tNumber3 = CSng(txtNumber3.Text)

<#1>lblResult1.Text = tNumber1 + tNumber2 * tNumber3
lblResult2.Text = (tNumber1 + tNumber2) * tNumber3
lblResult3.Text = tNumber2 / tNumber3
lblResult4.Text = tNumber1 + tNumber2 Mod tNumber3
lblResult5.Text = tNumber1 <#2>< tNumber3 Mod tNumber2
lblResult6.Text = tNumber2 <2>> tNumber1 * tNumber3
```

For this question, you will need to follow the program execution and predict the outcome. Write down the input numbers, carefully read each line of code and perform the calculation described.

Complete the table with the outcomes you predict for the six labels for each row of inputs into the text boxes. **8 marks**

Remember the BIDMAS rule for calculations.

Sample response extract

	lblResult1	lblResult2	lblResult3	lblResult4	lblResult5	lblResult6
txtNumber1 2 txtNumber2 5 txtNumber3 4	22	28	1.25	3	TRUE	FALSE
txtNumber1 4 txtNumber2 1 txtNumber3 3	7	15	0.33333	5	FALSE	FALSE
txtNumber1 3 txtNumber2 5 txtNumber3 8	43	64	0.625	8	FALSE	FALSE
txtNumber1 3 txtNumber2 8 txtNumber3 2	19	22	4	3	FALSE	TRUE

Notice logical operators. These will produce true or false values.

You may find it helpful to write out your calculations when working out the answer. However, this revision question requires you only to note down what would be displayed on the labels – so you should show only what will appear as a result of running the program.

Now try this

Create a spreadsheet or write a program with these calculations. Add another four calculations of your choice using any combination of mathematical (+-*/), relational (= < > <> <= >=) and Boolean (NOT, AND, OR) operators. Work out the answers for some test data and check them with the results from the app you've produced.

'Evaluate' questions

Questions that ask you to evaluate want you to show you can consider all sides of an argument in order to provide a well-supported judgement on a topic or problem. This may include writing a supported conclusion or a recommendation for the technologies, procedures and outcomes of a computerised solution.

Worked example

A dedicated computer system uses memory to hold numerical data.

Evaluate integer and floating point (real) data types usage by program code and how they are held in memory. **8 marks**

For this **evaluate** question, you need to be clear on the concepts of:

- binary
- floating point numbers
- integers.

Sample response extract

Computers use a range of structures to hold data inside memory using just two digits, 0 or 1, which are only good for yes/no, but when 8 of these BITs are grouped into a byte, 256 combinations are available.

Remember to start your answer with an introduction, linked to the question and scenario.

Integers are whole numbers, held in memory as simple binary numbers occupying 2 or 4 bytes. This choice of short (range of −32768 to 32767) or long integer (−2147483648 to 2147483647) allows less memory for whole numbers expected to be in the short range.

Floating point numbers resolve issues integers have with numbers which are very large or have a fractional part. These are also known as real because they are the closest to numbers in the real world.

Use your technical knowledge of the area and combine it with examples to help support your explanations and evaluations.

Floating point uses the same principles as standard form with a mantissa and an exponent. The mantissa is the high part of a number normalised with the decimal point moved to the largest digit and the rest of the number rounded to a set number of places, for example, in denary 24457892.25 becomes 2.45, with the exponent holding how many places the point moved, so this standard form is 2.45×10^7 or 2.45E07.

If possible, use a calculator to help get your number work correct.

There is a rounding issue as the number is lost when the mantissa is formed. The original number cannot be fully recalculated. In this example, 2.45×10^7 could only be brought back as 24500000.

Both standard form and floating point are very space-efficient techniques for holding very large numbers.

Floating point works in the same way, except that it is all in binary. 24457892.25 is a large binary number, 01011101010011001010100111.01, which in floating point would have 0.1011101 as an 8 bit mantissa and an exponent of 00011001 as binary point moves 25 times from the low end of the original binary number.

Try to give good examples with accurate workings. Here there are examples of the ranges of different data types and binary representations of numbers.

Integers are best for whole numbers in a known range, with floating point for very large or small numbers and those which have fractional parts.

Now try this

Evaluate the uses of one- and multi-dimensional arrays with examples. Plan your answer using bullet points.

Types of computer system

Computer systems include smartphones, tablets, notebooks, laptops, desktop pcs and massive server-based systems.

Components

A computer system can comprise many elements.

Other components might include:

- video camera
- microphone
- software
- speakers
- hard discs
- memory
- processor
- scanner
- printer.

A typical computer system comprising hardware and software.

Examples of computer systems

Mobile devices are portable and easily carried in a pocket or bag, mostly suited to deal with small amounts of data. PCs are larger, general purpose computers with only a small number of users. Servers are large computers that interact with many computers and users.

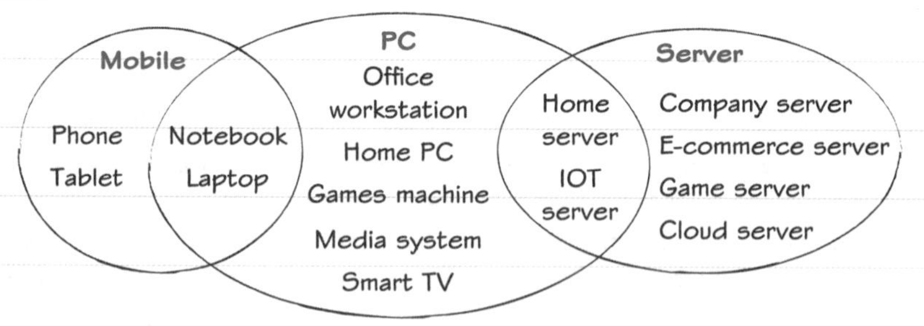

Computer systems as multi-functional devices

Multi-functional devices (MFDs) are those that serve more than one purpose. These are commonly combined printers and scanners, which may also include other functions such as the capability to fax/copy. It might also be the case that a PDA with built in scanner can be viewed as an MFD, combining the functions of a data entry device, barcode scanner and communications device into one.

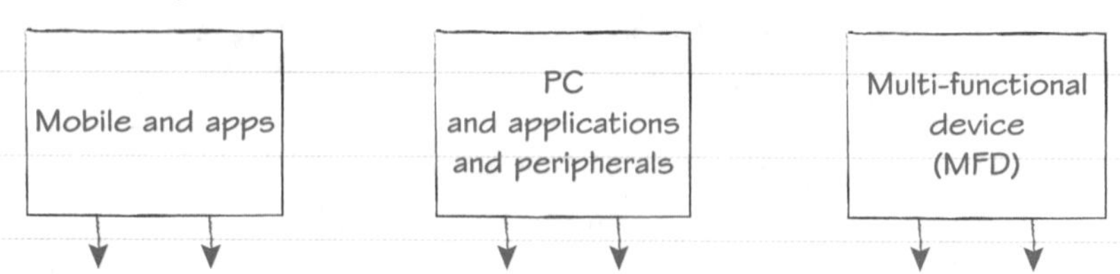

Tasks involving mobility

General purpose computing and communication tasks

Printing, copying, scanning, faxing, stapling and emailing.

Health logging, sat nav/compass, remote data entry, mobile communications

Social communications, office tasks, email client, video player, media controller, browser, diary, editor

Web server, email server, SOHO server and security, database manager

Network server, network security, network policies, cloud server, communications server, dbms

Now try this

Briefly describe the differences between mobile devices, personal computers and servers.

Internal components

Each internal component of a computer has a purpose, a set of features and a specific use.

Internal components of a computer

If you open up a computer you will see the following components.

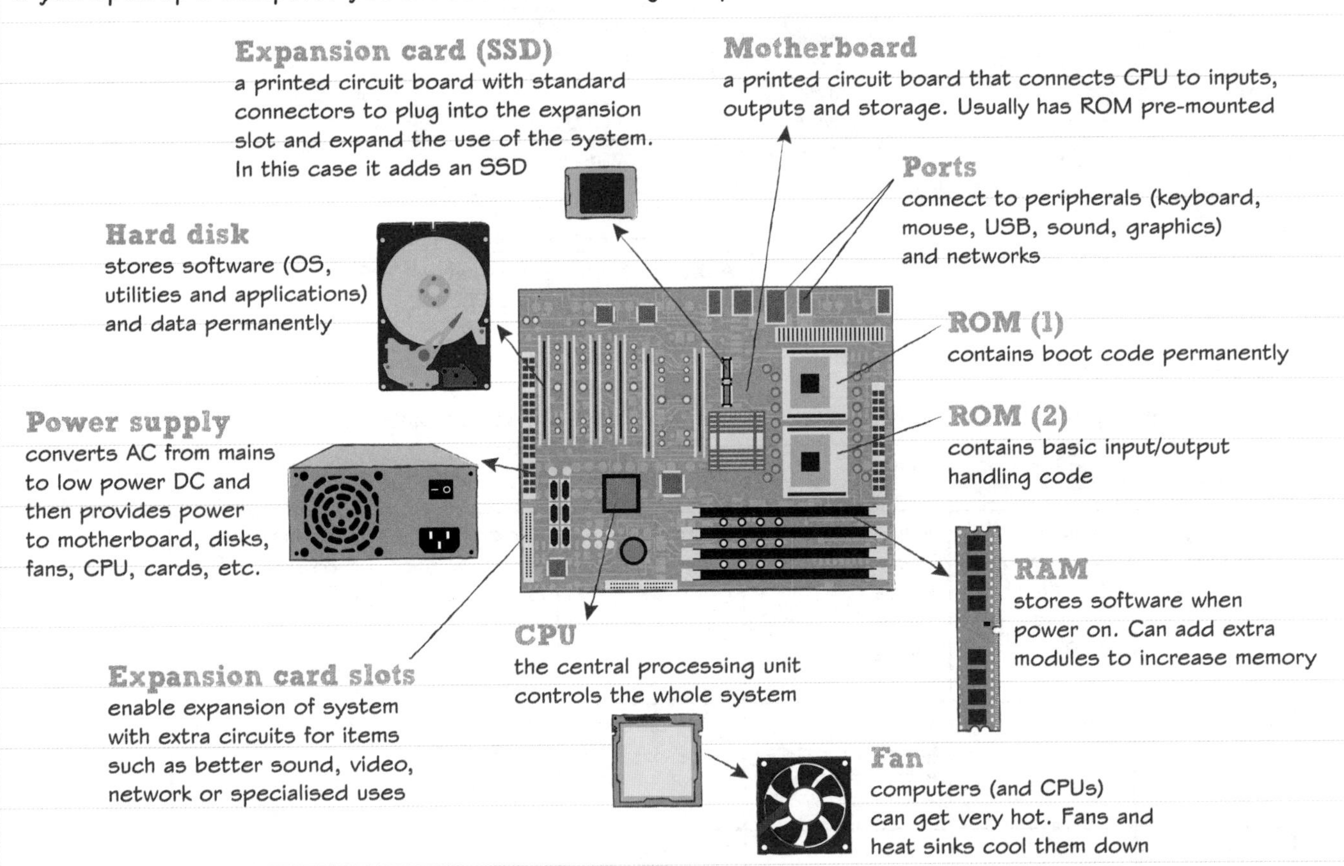

Factors affecting choice of components

When selecting components to include in the computer there are a number of factors to consider.

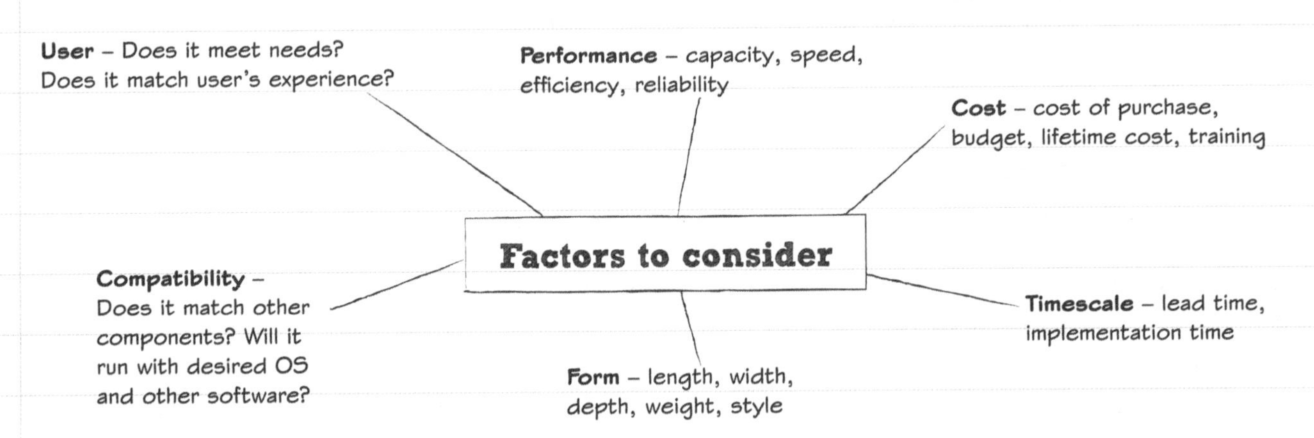

Now try this

Cover the image above and try to recall from memory five internal components of a computer and their purpose.

Had a look ☐ Nearly there ☐ Nailed it! ☐

Input and output devices (1)

All computer systems process input to create useful outputs. They do this using input and output devices, but the features of these devices affect their performance.

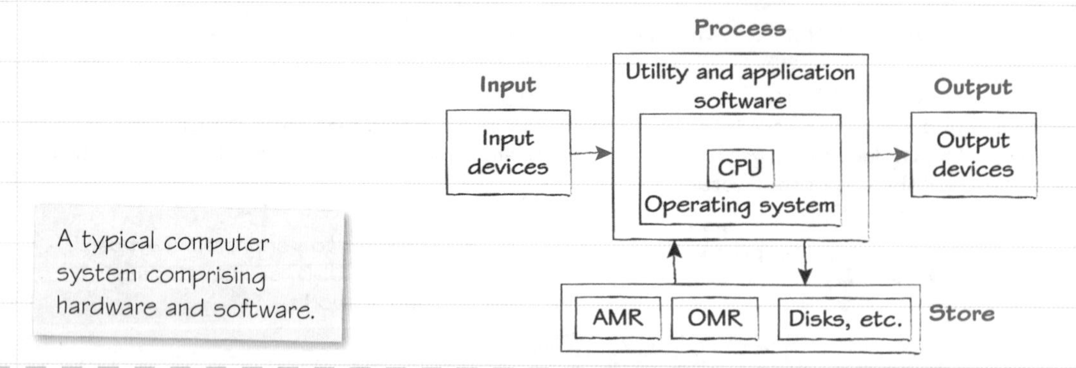

A typical computer system comprising hardware and software.

Input devices

Input devices operate in several ways, e.g. via a direct keypress, a pointer or audio.

	Direct key press	Pointers	Audio	Visual	Sensors	Electronic Magnetic
Input hardware (examples)	Keyboards Specialised keypads Discrete buttons	Mouse Trackpad Stylus Tablet Touchscreen	Microphone Telephone handset	Camera Motion sensor Object sensor Gaze sensor Scanner: biometric	Environmental Biometric GPS	Receivers Readers
Specialist uses (examples)	ATM EPOS	Mobile device screens for data entry and control	Voice control Voice data entry	OMR, OCR, ANPR, EPOS Barcode scanning	Security, alarms IOT Satellite navigation	Security Payments MICR
Technologies	A button selects a particular operation in context. This is converted to a digital (binary) code.	Combines detecting relative positions on-screen with a button-type press to invoke a command at the selected range or (x,y) position.	Analogue audio is converted to digital using an ADC and then processed and/or stored.	Light is captured by an array of light sensors. These are converted into binary patterns for processing or storage.	A sensor captures analogue data and converts it into digital (using a specialised ADC) to process and store as binary data.	Data is received in a known format and translated into the required format for the application.

How input features affect performance

Input features can improve performance of the computer by targeting and to some extent trading off between:

- a faster speed of response
- a more accurate response/resolution
- more controllability/smoothness
- more feedback/feel
- automation/accuracy
- improved ease of use through ergonomics/form factor
- making it configurable
- using the most appropriate interface/connector.

Now try this

Car manufacturers face very critical decisions regarding input devices for even apparently simple user systems, such as audio, which is commonly a microprocessor based system. Consider how each of the input features above could positively affect the system's performance and thus the car user's safety.

Input and output devices (2)

Computers output information to a user via output devices.

Examples of output devices

Output can take four major forms: display devices, devices that produce a physical object (such as a printer), devices that produce audio and devices that control something else, for example, switches and motors.

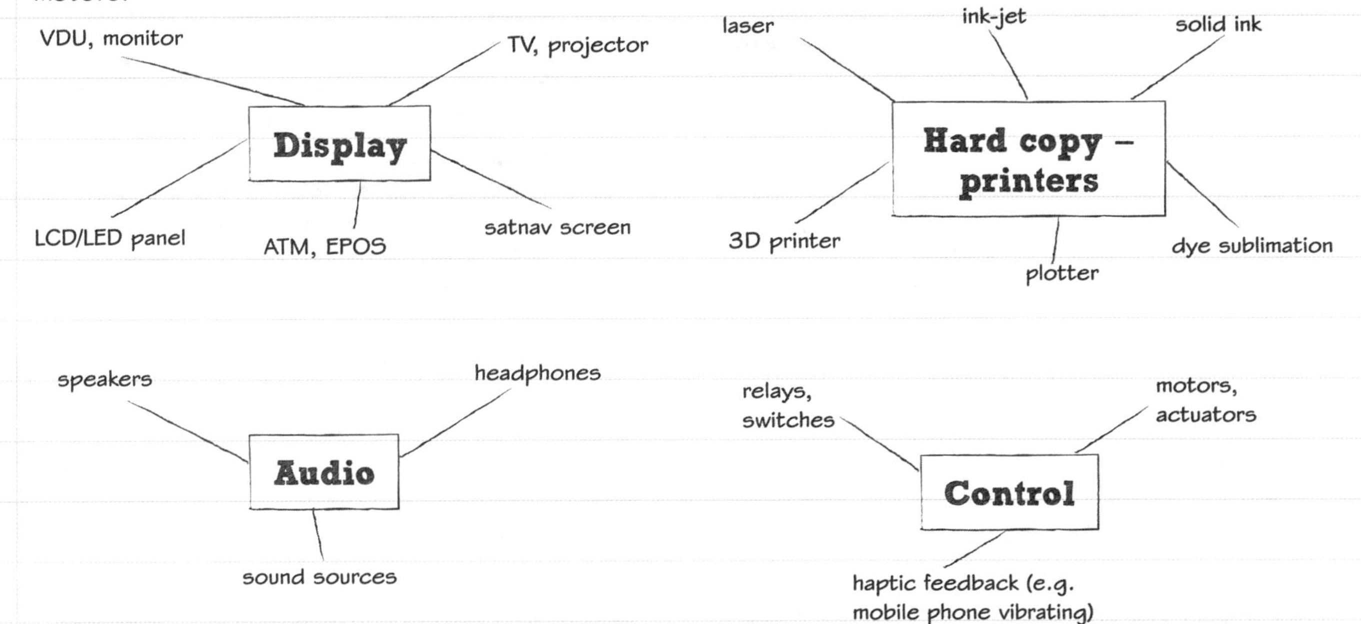

How output features affect performance

- **Clarity and accuracy** of output (resolution, sample rate, frame rate, colour depth, contrast, etc.) – the more detail that the device can output, the clearer and more accurate an image or sound or finer the control will be.
- **Noise** – the less unwanted noise or random signals generated by a device, the more fit for purpose it will be.
- **Speed** of output – the higher the volume of printing required the more speed of output becomes essential.
- A **display, sound source or control system** that updates quickly causing fewer drop-outs or obvious buffering is very desirable.
- **Automation** – the more a device can be automated to deal with what it is processing the better it will be. Some modern sound systems can automatically adapt the sound output to the room they are contained in; some smart TVs can adapt the sound and colour depending on whether a movie, talk show or music is being played, etc.
- **Configurable** – for even more control it is useful to have configurable output so that, for example, the sound output can be really finely tuned in a car audio system, a networked music system, etc. or a printer can be configured, for example to default to double-sided printing with a 12 mm border.
- **Form factor and connectivity** – it is vital that the output device is compatible with the target computer system.

Now try this

A maternity hospital is considering upgrading its obstetric ultrasound output facilities (for scanning women in pregnancy). They currently use a standard 2D monochrome monitor with a small photo printer which prints directly from the screen.

Write short notes on desirable features of an upgraded output system.

Had a look ☐ Nearly there ☐ Nailed it! ☐

Storage

The features of storage devices affect their performance and the performance of a computer system.

Hierarchy of storage

Larger secondary storage devices are generally slower, while smaller main memory devices, on a processor, are faster.

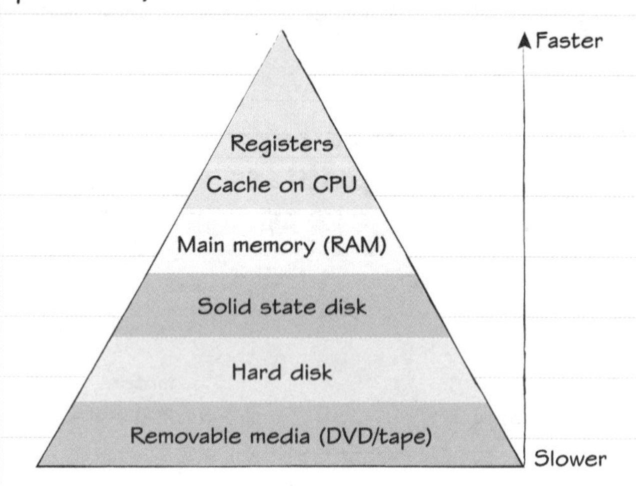

How features affect performance

Performance depends on a number of factors:

- **Rotational latency**: depends on spin speed.
- **Seek time**: depends on density of tracks and some command processing overhead.
- **Data transfer**: internal disk transfer rate is the speed at which data is transferred from the disk surface to the controller while external data transfer rate is the speed at which data is moved between disk controller and the memory.
- **Fragmentation**: the transfer rate is also dependent on file fragmentation. The more the physical file is fragmented across the disk the slower the access time will be.

How a hard disk works

The disk spins at very high speed, rotating round the tracks. The arm moves in and out very quickly to different parts of a sector. It reads or writes from the track sector to the disk controller. The controller then interrupts the CPU which moves the data to main memory.

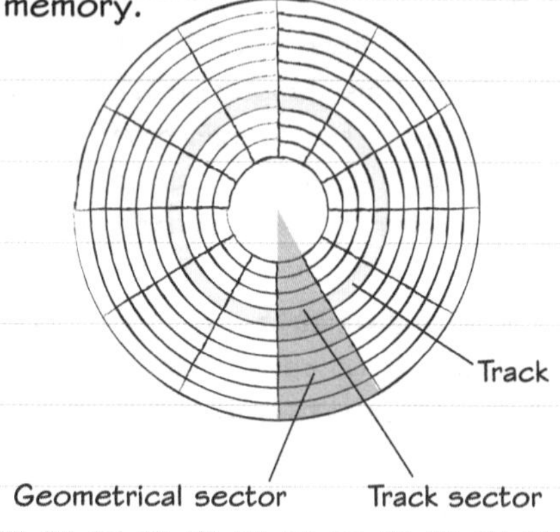

Disk cache

A disk cache is a memory buffer with the disk system or part of RAM which ideally holds data likely to be needed next (for example, next block of data, frequently used data or data to be written back to disk) to greatly speed up data transfer.

- **Read ahead/behind**: the disk head reads data ahead of and behind the requested track sector and stores these just in case.
- **Speed matching**: the buffer is used to deal with speed differences between I/O interface (SATA, Pata, SCSII, etc.) and r/w speed from the platter.
- **Write acceleration**: a write back cache can cache write data so the CPU can carry on even though the data has not been written to disk.

Solid state drives

Solid state drives are made from integrated circuits (ICs). Solid state drives:

- ✓ are like a disk logically but like a memory physically
- ✓ do not require mechanical operation
- ✓ have no moving parts
- ✓ consume very little power
- ✓ do not overheat
- ✓ operate while moving
- ✓ are shockproof
- ✓ are small and light
- ✓ are mobile
- ✓ have fast access – no physical latency.

Now try this

Fenton Cycles is designing a Satellite Navigation System for cyclists.

What storage device should it use for its system, and why?

Data storage and recovery

Data storage and recovery are commonly provided by network attached storage (NAS).

Network attached storage (NAS)

A NAS:

- is a server operating solely to serve files to network clients
- is seen by clients as a disk on the net
- can automate backup or offer more configurable backup and archiving
- is usually a plug-and-play device
- was originally conceived for large systems but now is often used for media servers or similar for home systems.

Advantages of a NAS are that it offers:

- shared mass storage facilities
- fault tolerance
- backup
- manageable on-site 'cloud storage'.

RAID

RAID is a redundant array of independent disks, that is, a bunch of cheaper, smaller disks to operate like a very large, expensive disk system.

You can combine all the disks to create:

- a very large storage area
- or very fast storage
- or very fault-tolerant storage
- or some combination of these.

Many RAID variants exist for these different objectives, though some are now obsolete.

NAS with RAID

A basic computer system with a cut-down OS and network connection(s) could be:

- an old system with open source NAS software
- an embedded system using a RISC chip
- a hardware-based system with an ASIC chipset running file protocols.

It usually has a large disk or RAID system for file storage, but can share files from any medium, including USB. It often has facilities for backup to removable media such as CD/DVD or tape.

RAID Variants

RAID 0, 1 and 5 are the most common, along with hybrids such as RAID 1-0.

- **RAID 0** is very fast but if one disk fails the system breaks.
- **RAID 1** is great for fault tolerance, but takes 2 GB of space to store 1 GB of data as it creates a mirror drive of the original as it saves.
- **RAID 3** stripes data across drives and has a dedicated parity drive to rebuild the system should a data drive fail.
- **RAID 5** is fast, economical and fault tolerant. Any disk can be swapped and rebuilt automatically if it fails but if another goes whilst being rebuilt then the system will break.

RAID variants for different purposes

The diagram shows how each RAID variant uses striping (data written across disks) and mirroring (data copied bit for bit on different disks and parity (error check and correction)).

Key
Data (1, 2, 3...)
Parity (p1, p2...)
Data stripe
Disk

RAID 0 — Striping, no mirroring, no parity. Effectively makes one very large storage volume

Disk 1	Disk 2	Disk 3
1	2	3
4	5	6

RAID 1 — Mirroring, no striping, no parity. Can write to both at same time

Disk 1	Disk 2
1	1
2	2
3	3
4	4

RAID 5 — Striping, distributed parity (p). In this 5-disk system there is parity information for every 4 items of data

Disk 1	Disk 2	Disk 3	Disk 4	Disk 5
1	2	3	4	P1(1–4)
5	6	7	P2(5–8)	8
9	10	p3(9–12)	11	12

Now try this

CJ Jones Services runs a local cloud-based backup service for businesses located in its office block using a NAS with a RAID 1 system. One of its clients has suggested that a RAID 5 system is better.

Discuss this view for this particular business.

Had a look ☐ Nearly there ☐ Nailed it! ☐

Operating systems (1)

An operating system is the vital software that makes a computer system a functional device.

Types of operating system

Single-user single-tasking

On early computers a task had to be shut down before another could run.

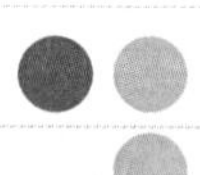

Single-user multi-tasking

Most PCs and devices running **Windows**, **OSX**, **IOS** and **Android** allow one user to have a spreadsheet running whilst watching a video on the same processor.

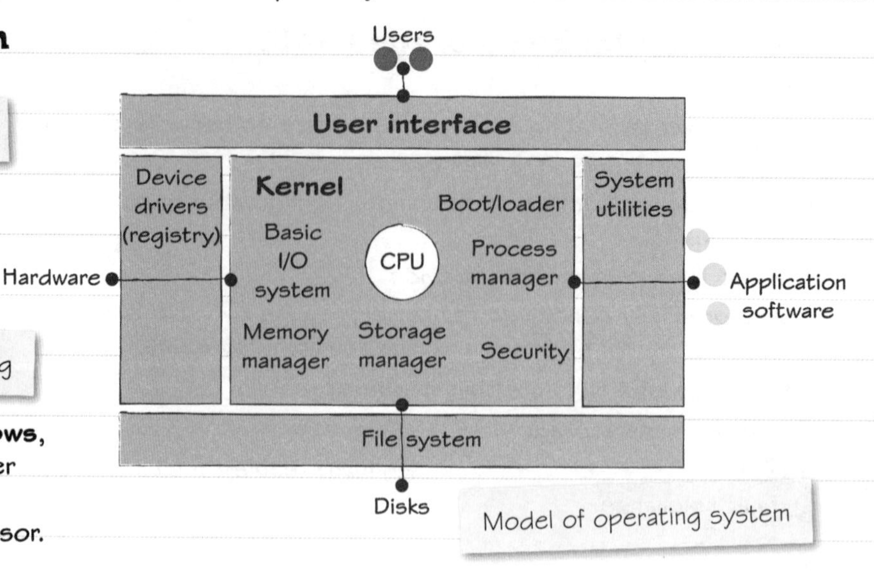

Model of operating system

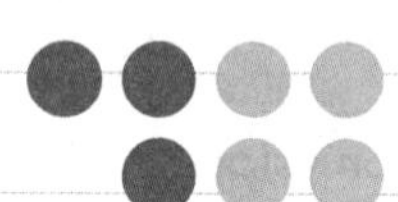

Multi-user multi-tasking

Large systems such as those used by the Met Office run OS like **Unix** and **MVS** and share processing power amongst a number of users.

4 Real time

Very fast processing with totally predictable response to inputs is essential. Embedded systems, for example, in medicine, robotics, planes, cars (e.g. ABS, satnav), and NAS devices run on a RTOS.

Device drivers

Device drivers **extend** the **kernel** of the OS to allow it to work with any device from any manufacturer.

To work with a particular OS the device designer will **map** the particular OS calls (**interrupts**) to the **individual hardware commands** of the device.

The basic operating system may know how to control a number of devices (e.g. keyboard, mouse) at a basic level, but device drivers add extra functionality (e.g. mouse gestures).

Network operating systems

Network operating systems (NOS) such as Windows and Netware are usually **single-user multi-tasking** OSs.

The administrator is the **user** who manages security and client access.

Each client system has its own OS, though access to this can be controlled by the NOS.

Managing networks and security

The job of a NOS is to manage resource sharing and scheduling and security for a network by:

- managing log-on security so each client will log on to the network and the level of access allowed is determined by the NOS
- sharing I/O resources such as printers, scanners, etc. using queues and buffers
- managing storage by presenting network storage as normal volumes
- managing network access (LAN, WAN).

Now try this

SuperMouse has introduced a mouse that allows touch ID and haptic feedback as well as all the normal mouse functionality. It wants it to be used on Windows and Apple equipment.

What operating system component will it create to do this and how will it work?

Operating systems (2)

The kernel is the central core of the operating system. Its job is to control and manage all the system hardware, software and the running of tasks on the system.

The heart of the operating system

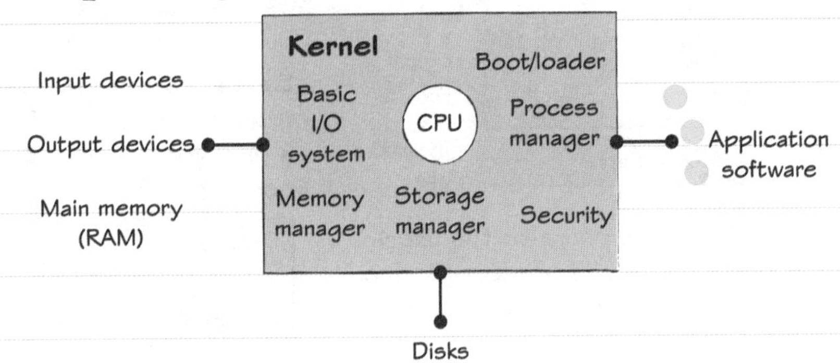

Booting

Parts of the kernel are on ROM chips which are loaded into running memory immediately after the system is turned on and the Power On Self Test (POST) is passed. The BIOS (basic input output system) and the boot system are loaded and executed to pull in the rest of the kernel and the device drivers, user interface and system utilities.

Executing

After 'booting', the OS can now operate fully by responding to events generated by the CPU, software or devices, handled as interrupts.

Interrupts

Devices	CPU	Software
Interrupt request – IRQ	Exception/trap	Software interrupt

Scheduling and multi-tasking

S	A	B	S	A	B	C	S	A	B	S	A

S=scheduler

A,B,C: processes taking turns

CPU time

The kernel schedules tasks (from one or more users to the CPU). A hardware interrupt (e.g. the clock or an I/O transfer being completed) calls the scheduler (S), which decides which process to allocate next. It will choose from those waiting according to the scheduling algorithm being used. Note: the scheduler itself (S) also takes CPU time.

Processes flow diagram

Processes can be in three states: waiting to be scheduled, running or blocked (waiting, for example, for a slow I/O operation to complete).

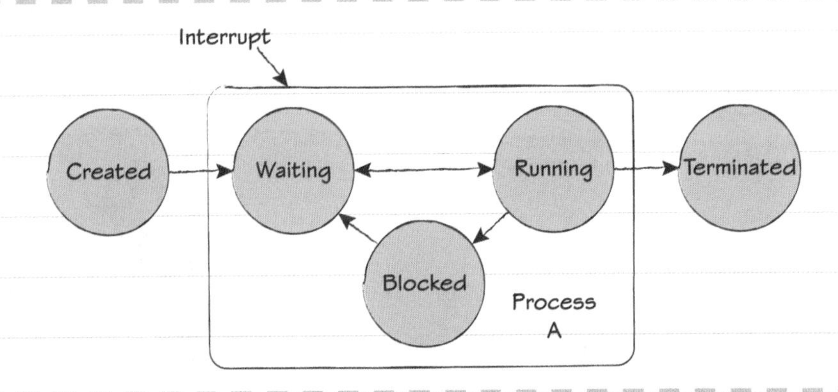

Now try this

Jane is using a CAD program to draw a machine tool.

By following the flow diagram above explain what happens if Jane chooses to print the document she is working on.

Had a look ☐ Nearly there ☐ Nailed it! ☐

The kernel: Managing the system

File system and file handling

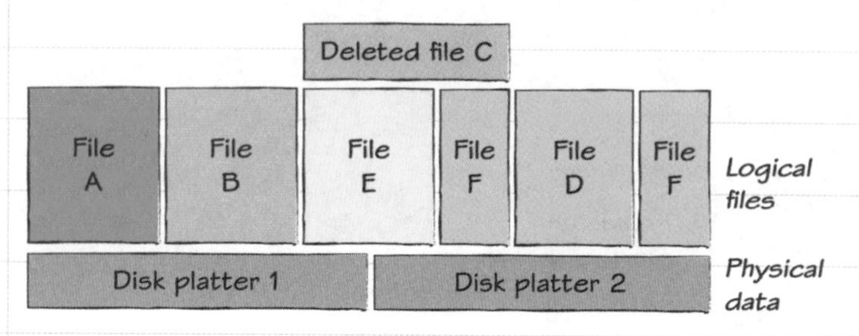

An OS presents a **logical** (how it appears to the user) file system to hide the **physical** details of storage. The OS will decide where to put the data on a device, a platter, a sector and block, and how.

For example, it can fragment the data into different gaps on the disk but it will appear as one contiguous file to the user on a volume (which could be a hard disk, an SSD, a CDRW or in the cloud).

I/O handling

The kernel provides communication facilities between peripherals and the processes and data structures to facilitate this, such as buffers, queues, lists and tables.

Each I/O device will issue an interrupt request (IRQ) when invoked. A mouse move, a print job finished, a key press, etc. all send an IRQ.

Schedules	Process list	Priority
Buffers	Buffer	Device speeds not equal
Spools	Print queues, etc.	Ensuring data sent is in order
Calls	IRQ table	IRQ calls

Memory management

All software (the OS, utilities and applications) has to be loaded into the memory to run. All applications used by the user (or users on a multi-user system) must share the memory without clashing.

The kernel's memory manager allocates memory space in order to do this.

Virtual memory

If RAM gets too full the OS can swap a fixed portion of it (page) to secondary memory rather than stop operating.

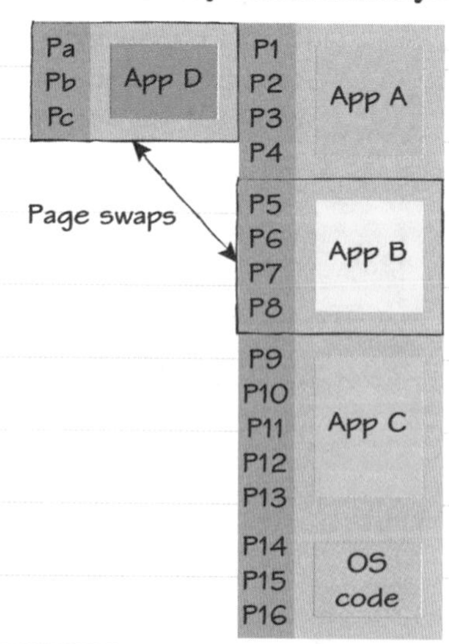

System modes

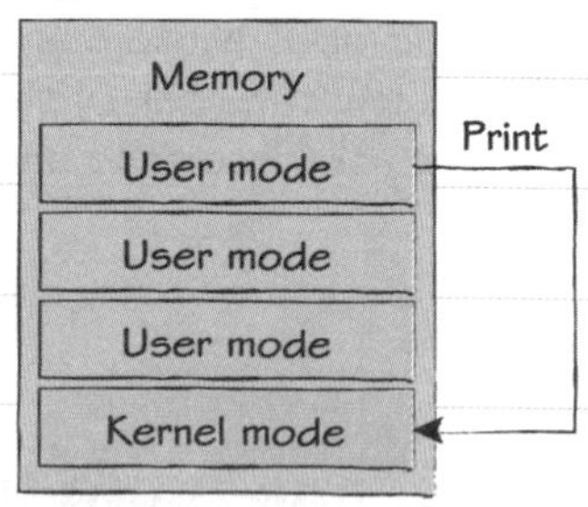

System (kernel) processes like process loading, handling I/O or storage need to access all of the RAM. **Kernel mode** is therefore dangerous. It can crash the whole system.

This privilege is not granted in modern OS to applications.

They are put into **User mode**, each with its own workspace, so that if the code corrupts it will only crash that one application. To access system resources (to print, store, display, etc.) they must issue a system call (using a system interrupt) which the OS makes available for this purpose rather than access the device memory directly.

Now try this

What advantages derive from the operating system presenting the file system in a logical manner rather than showing the exact manner in which the data is stored?

Operating systems (3)

The user interface provides a consistent way for a user to interact with the computer system; the most common forms are graphical (GUI), text (command line) and menu based.

GUI

Graphical user interfaces, such as those used by Apple Macintosh, Windows, Unix shells (including X-Windows, Gnome, etc.), are now the most common interface provided on systems.

Features of GUI

- WIMP: windows, icons, menus, pointers
- Visual metaphors: desktop, apps, file cabinets, trash can, clock, calendar, etc.
- Visual and audio feedback: dragging, dropping, opening (zooming), ringing
- Action metaphors: pointing at, touching, dragging, dropping

Why select a GUI?

👍 Ease of use: very easy to learn and use

👍 Control: easy to control with good feedback

👍 Multi-tasking: visual through windows

👍 Speed: smooth and fast on modern CPUs, but GUI does require extra processing

👎 Complex or batched tasks: not suitable!

Menu-based systems

Menu-based systems are still very common in practice for:

- TV menus
- ATMs
- CNC machines
- running configuration applications
- some mobile OS apps.

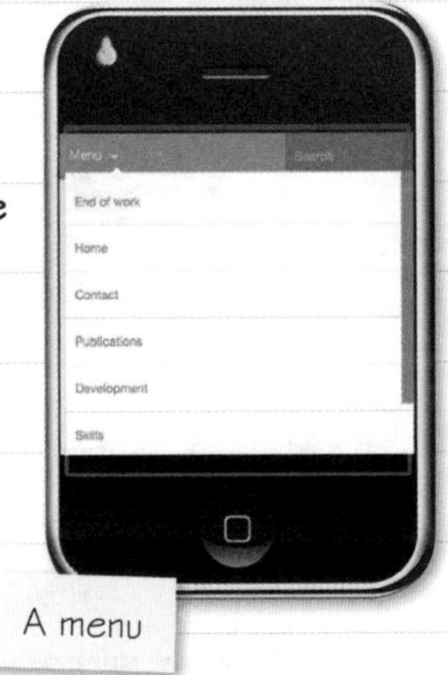

A menu

Features of menu-based systems

- Lists of options
- Often in multiple levels
- Scrolled through and selected using key or pointer or voice command

Why select a menu-based system?

👍 They are easy to program provided that only simple choice-based functionality is required.

👎 Tedious when having to select from multiple levels of menu

👎 Not suitable for multi-tasking or complex tasks

Command line interface (CLI)

Most modern OS including Windows and Unix-based systems (such as Mac OSX and Linux) offer a CLI alternative to the GUI.

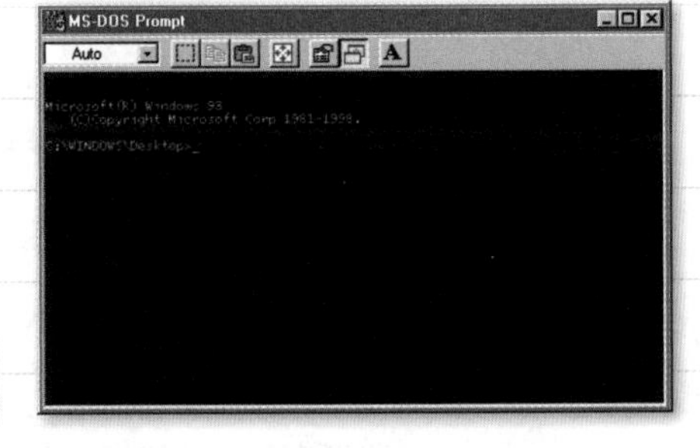

DOS prompt CLI

Early operating system user interfaces were text-based, command line interfaces. They were relatively difficult to learn and slow to use. Although not offered often as a default OS, a CLI is still a useful alternative to GUIs for direct control of the OS, or to run batches of operations to achieve more complex tasks or automate routine tasks.

Now try this

Gibber Amps is building a new electronic guitar effects box for its amplifiers, which simulates six famous amplifiers, adds 20 audio effects, equalisation and volume. It will have a guitar lead input socket and output socket to the amp. It will have a small colour touchscreen to control the I/O and effects.

Discuss which type of user interface would be most suitable for a guitarist during a gig.

Utility and application software

Software comprises the instructions that make the hardware work and do something useful.

Utility software

Utility software is a type of system software that performs a specific task to extend or aid the operating system. It may provide a service that the OS lacks or may improve on the version in the OS, or it may add some functionality that is useful, but is not a central part of the OS. Many OSs over time incorporate the best of the utility software that is written for them.

Application software

Application software (or an app) is software that performs tasks that give a direct benefit for a user (entertainment, production, clerical, communication, management, logging, etc.). These may be bundled applications such as the office applications, games and media software that are given away with operating systems such as Mac OSX. They may be proprietary apps (either paid for or free) or may be open source.

Examples of utility software by purpose

Computer security	Housekeeping
Anti-virus Encoders Cryptographic Firewall Network monitoring and analysis	Backup and restore System monitors System profiles Registry cleaners Memory checkers
File management	**Disk handling**
File managers Fast copy Batch delete Data compression	Disk checkers Disk cleaners Disk defragmenters Disk space analysers partition managers
GUI extensions	**System health**
Theme handlers	Screensavers

Smartphone showing a number of installed applications

Good software

Good software has the following features:

- a quality interface appropriate to purpose (rich media for web or video games, voice control, forms input with touch display and voice control for car media centre)
- efficient algorithms or fast processing
- compatible file structures
- enriches the user's life or makes it simpler
- takes full advantage of available hardware and OS
- tried and tested, easy to use.

Types of software

- **General purpose**, e.g. spreadsheet
- **Integrated**, e.g. office software with same GUI
- **Customisable**, e.g. DBMS with processes, macros, VBA, etc.
- **Specific**, e.g. game, satnav
- **Bespoke**, e.g. controlling new smart warehouse, very large e-commerce solution, international banking system, woodcutting program for timber sash production factory

Now try this

ITForA is a charity that collects old PCs and rebuilds them to be sent to Africa.

Justify three applications that the charity could use to help administer the business and three utilities that they could use whilst rebuilding and testing the PCs.

Open source software

Open source software is often thought of as 'free software', but actually it embodies a series of principles about the way software projects should be run, managed and shared that underlies the development and distribution of the software.

The principles of open source software

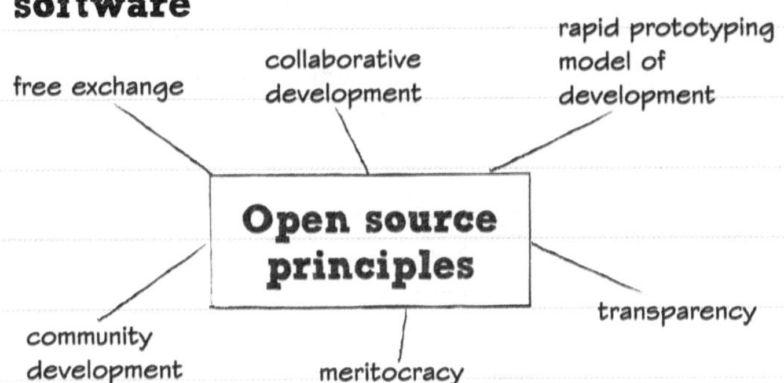

Open source licences

- Licence usually asserts copyright to original writers.
- Allows freedom to use the copyright material, modify it, copy it and indeed redistribute it without restriction.
- Often modelled on GNU, General Public Licence (GPL), but actually there are well over a thousand different open source licences.

Open source operating systems

Operating systems are complex and critical components of the computer system and thus most current OS are open source (e.g. Linux) or build on open source OS (e.g. Macintosh OSX, Android, Chromium) or include open source components (Windows) to reap the advantages of OSS development.

Open source applications

There are a very wide range of well-established and supported applications available to be used as they are or modified to be exactly to the requirements of the user, including web servers (e.g. Apache), web clients (Mozilla Firefox), office software (OpenOffice, LibreOffice), databases (MySql), graphics (GIMP) and many more.

Benefits for users

- Cost of buying is zero or very low – though may still need to pay for installation, training etc.
- Affordable upgrading for the lifetime of the software.
- Software will not be dropped for commercial reasons.
- Transparent bugs are openly acknowledged and dealt with.
- Interoperable with other OSS and much commercial software.
- Flexible – can be adapted to suit exact needs rather than having to be used as is.

Implications of open source software

- May not work with existing systems, or may require a complete changeover
- Installation, customisation, support and training costs may be high
- Help from user community may not be as fast nor as tailored
- Can evolve to suit developers' needs, rather than users' needs.

Software cost benefits

- Lower costs of marketing and distribution
- Lower costs of developer teams
- Lower cost of management
- Commercial companies are able to build on solid, reliable code.

Software development benefits

- More rapid development
- Loyal teams – sense of ownership
- Build team skills – all code assessed transparently by peers
- Flexible, quality, modular development – individuals with better skills can work on what they are best at
- Innovative – focus on technical rather than commercial objectives.

Now try this

A design studio intends to update the computer systems in the office, which currently run on a proprietary operating system with illustration and design software and standard office software. Its software house has suggested it uses Linux with OSS which it will install and maintain.

State two reasons why the studio should consider this.

Choosing hardware and software

There are a number of factors affecting choice of hardware, utility and application software.

Spec and price

When considering choices you have to weigh up several factors.

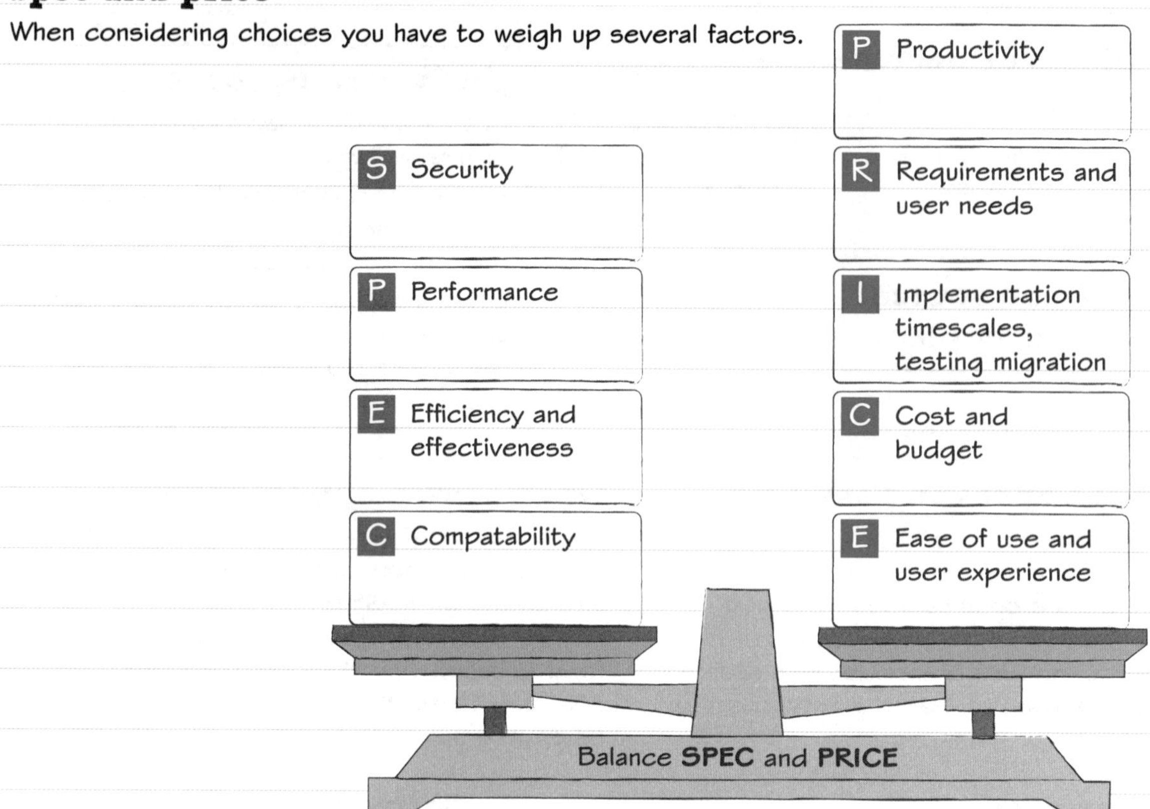

Spec

The spec of the product, whether hardware or software, is clearly important and must be weighed up. The spec will include ensuring the product does not cause any **security** issues; that the **performance** of the product is what is required (e.g. a hard disk has sufficient capacity and speed for dealing with 100 000 sales a day); that the CPU is sufficiently fast for games playing; that the product is **efficient** and effective (e.g. that the OS is capable of handling 20 users on five tasks each simultaneously; that the webserver can handle 100 000 simultaneous connections without failing); and perhaps most crucially that the product is **compatible** with the system.

Price

The price or value (cost versus benefit) of a product and of implementing it is also crucial. Consider all of the value factors: Will it make users more **productive**? Does it meet all of the user **requirements**? What are the costs and timescales for the **implementation** or integration of the product? What is the **cost** compared to the the budget? Is it **easy** to use and/or within the users' experience or will there be training needs?

Remembering 'spec v price' will be useful when answering questions which ask you to discuss or evaluate any choice of hardware or software. The technical details you will discuss may be different but the concepts to work through will be the same.

Now try this

You want to buy one of the two main new games computers to play multi-player games over the internet.

Write short notes on the factors you should consider when choosing a new games computer.

Use 'spec v price' to give you ideas for your answer. Depending on the specific case you may choose all or just the most appropriate of the spec versus price headings.

Data processing systems

Computer systems can be characterised by, and constructed around, the data they are expected to process.

REFRACTS: features of good data

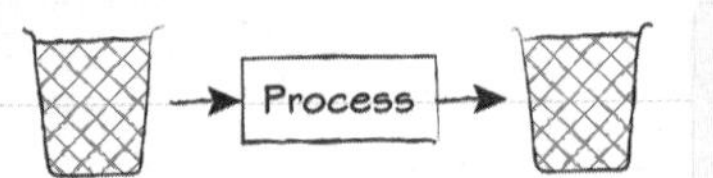

GIGO – garbage in garbage out

Good data is:

- **reliable**: same data give same results
- **economical:** do not cost too much to collect
- **flexible**: can be used in all relevant circumstances
- **relevant**: fit for purpose
- **accurate**: free from error
- **complete**: include all required data
- **time-bound**: can be input as required
- **secure**: handled to only be visible to those that need to see them.

Input for good data

Input may have to be **manual** (e.g. from paper forms, questionnaires, etc.) but wherever possible human error will be eliminated by automating the data entry process.

Computer forms, menus, drop-downs and buttons can be used for direct data entry by humans. This type of entry can be **validated** and **verified** economically as it is input.

Automated data input using specialised input devices may be used to speed up the input process, eliminate as much error as possible, and save money.

Real-time systems will rely heavily on sensor input along with direct human data entry.

Model of data processing system

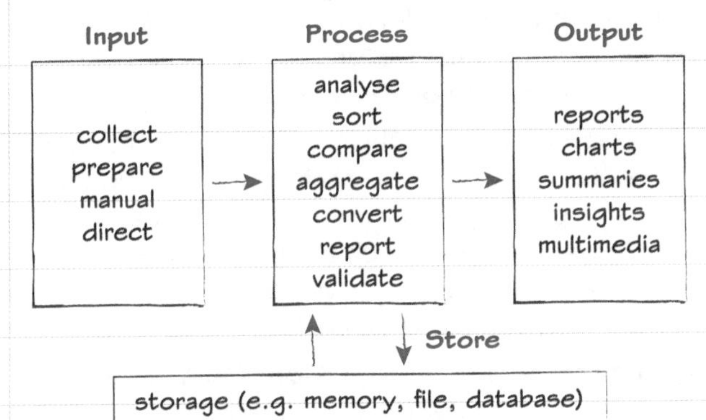

A data processing system can be modelled by a flow chart.

Types of processing

1. **Batch**
   Collections of data such as monthly statements, utility bills or payroll are handled and processed in batches.
2. **Interactive (transaction)**
   Transactions such as hotel or flight bookings, till totals or e-commerce invoices are processed as they occur.
3. **Real-time**
   Events are dealt with as they occur on systems such as car ECUs, computer games, or factory CNCs, ANPR systems.

Design of systems

The system will be designed around the type of output required.

Most large business data processing systems are very flexible and are thus built around database management systems (DBMS) with flexible inputs and reporting so that new forms (**inputs**), queries, functions and procedures (**processes**) and reports, charts, etc, (**outputs**) can be built and stored as required to produce batch or transaction-based (or both) systems.

Real-time systems will usually be designed using more specialised hardware and software.

Now try this

Snow Hotels take bookings for their 200 rooms in their West End Hotel over the internet, using a web-based front end to a database system based in the hotel in London.

1. What type of data processing system is required for this process?
2. What are the main challenges for this type of system?
3. How might these challenges be overcome?

Had a look ☐ Nearly there ☐ Nailed it! ☐

Data processing

Hardware and software play a role in data collection.

Goals of data collection

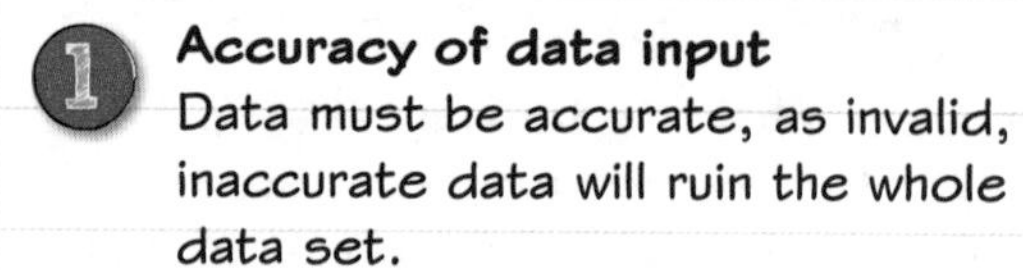

1. **Accuracy of data input**
   Data must be accurate, as invalid, inaccurate data will ruin the whole data set.

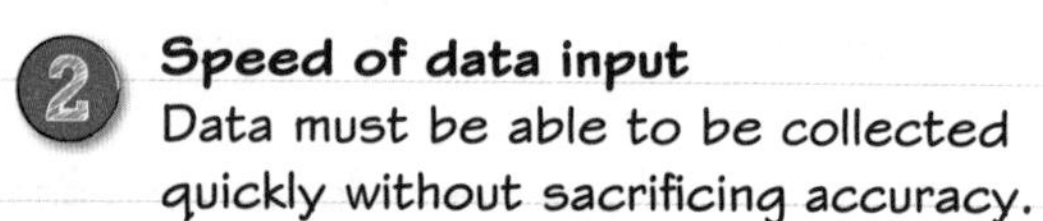

2. **Speed of data input**
   Data must be able to be collected quickly without sacrificing accuracy.
3. **Economy of data input**
   Data must be able to be collected cheaply. More expensive input hardware pays for itself very quickly in mass data processing.

ID recognition

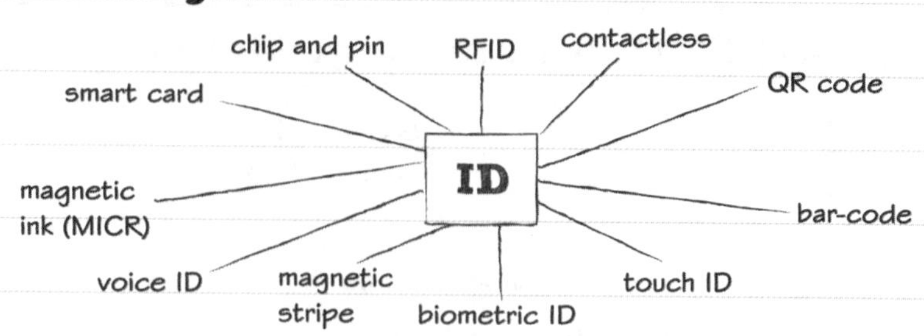

ID systems connect to a database to confirm the ID of a person or object and then autofill as many details as needed.

Forms input

Secure Payment Page
Card details
** Indicates a required field*
**Card number* [ ]
**Security code* [ ]
**Expiry date* [--] [----]
**Cardholder's name* [ ]

A secure payment form.

As far as possible, manual input into data-processing forms will be via **forms**.

As much as possible will be pre-filled so that fewer mistakes are made.

The form will have validated input fields:

- Fields such as the card number will only accept a valid credit card number.
- The date field will only accept a valid date.
- The security code will only accept a three-digit number.

This ensures that the data has integrity and can be processed sensibly. It does not absolutely guarantee that what the user is entering is entirely accurate.

Alternate human input

As computer systems become more powerful it is possible to use more advanced forms of input that do not require a separate keying phase.

Voice recognition software allows banks, building societies and telecommunications companies to answer the phone with a computer and allows the user to answer questions with their voice. The system echoes back the answer to ensure the voice command is not misunderstood.

This works best when the input is very structured and context sensitive so that the voice can be understood within a limited range of parameters. More advanced uses such as Apple SIRI and Amazon Alexa (Echo) and Google Assistant are making this even more powerful.

Optical character recognition (OCR) software allows typed and even handwritten input to be read directly without being rekeyed. It is also digitised through pattern recognition. It again works best when used in a constrained situation.

Optical mark recognition (OMR) software differs in that it does not require pattern recognition algorithms as it is used only to read marked areas of a page such as tick boxes.

Now try this

BioNRG uses an OMR reader to scan in the following forms collected in from its customers every 3 months.

BioNRG Gas meter reading form
Customer number: 1873944
Name = R. Black
Postcode = FT10 9JW ☐ ☐ ☐ ☐

How does this form improve on customers telling operators their reading on the phone? How could you improve it?

Data processing functions

Data processing captures and stores valid (validated) data and then performs functions on it to retrieve information.

Analyse and aggregate

Data analysis applies systematic statistical or logical techniques (IF, >, <, >=, <=, <>) to the data to categorise, compare or evaluate the data. Aggregation is a special case of this in which data are summed, counted, averaged or put into ranges.

Sort

Sorting can often help to understand a data set.

Common sorting techniques include alphabetical by name, ascending (a–z) or descending (z–a), by date, by number, by count.

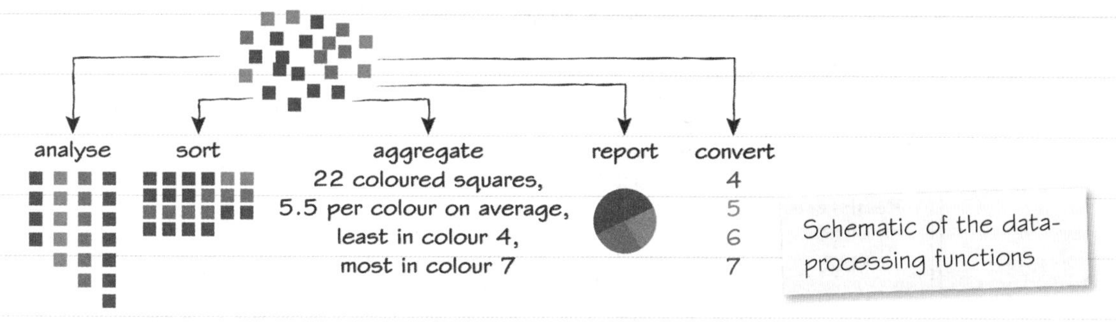

Schematic of the data-processing functions

The data-processing functions perform a variety of actions on data as shown in the schematic.

Convert

Converting is the change of the data from one form to another. This is a particularly useful when aggregating, categorising or comparing items that were originally in different formats.

Web stores use conversion, for example, to display prices in different currencies or shoe sizes in different country standards.

Report

Reports are the standard means of displaying or printing the output of the data-processing system.

Data-processing software allows the user to specify the layout and format of the report in great detail, tailored to its precise usage.

The same basic information could be used, for example, for an order confirmation, an invoice and a delivery note.

Data recovery procedures

The phases of data recovery are outlined below:

1. Repair the storage media:
   - Repair the media so that it can be accessed.

2. Image the storage to a new drive or disk image file:
   - Remove data from the damaged media to new media.

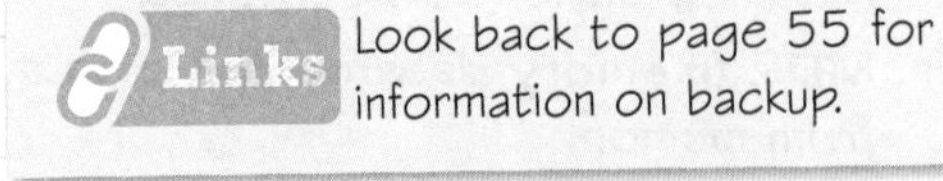

Look back to page 55 for information on backup.

3. Logical recovery:
   - Retrieve files, partitions, MBR or file system structures.

4. Repair damaged files:
   - Once files have been recovered some may need reconstituting or reconstruction.

Now try this

BioNRG is a new clean energy supplier. It has about 100 000 customers from whom it collects gas usage information every month.

Describe an example of how it might use each of the data-processing functions (analyse, aggregate, sort, convert and report) in its monthly cycle.

Had a look ☐ Nearly there ☐ Nailed it! ☐

Approaches to computer architecture

The Von Neumann architecture is a common architecture and the basis of much modern computing.

Von Neumann architecture

The Von Neumann architecture allows a computer program to be stored in and fetched from memory, to be decoded and executed by the CPU rather than having to be all hard wired.

A fundamental part of the architecture is the machine cycle: fetch an instruction; decode it; then execute it.

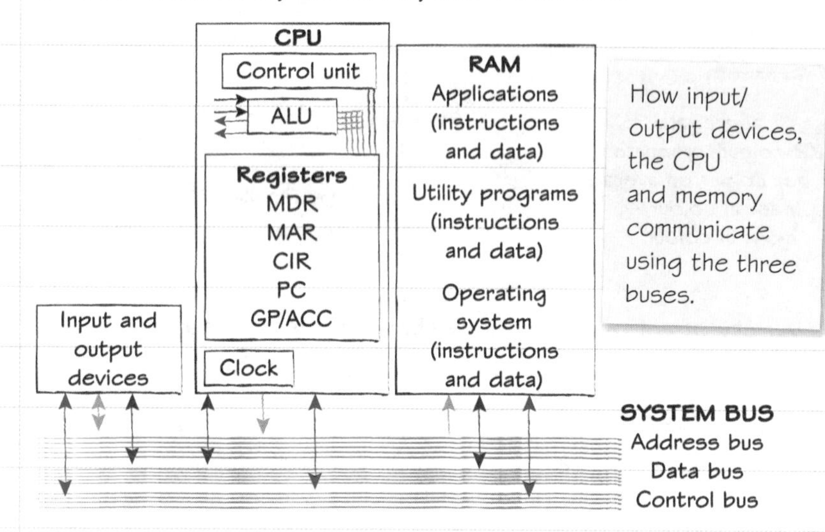

How input/output devices, the CPU and memory communicate using the three buses.

CPU components

Control unit: decodes program instructions into control signals and controls data movements to ALU and memory using control signals.

Arithmetic and logic unit (ALU): performs binary calculations (+−*/) and comparisons (e.g. AND, OR, NOT) on its inputs and puts its results into an **accumulator** (and sets a flag to show its status).

Clock: a device which issues an electronic signal (a tick) to the control bus and fetches one piece of data or decodes it or executes it for each tick. A computer running at 1 GHz can do this 1000 million times a second. One instruction can take >1 tick.

Registers

Registers are super-fast memory on board the CPU used to manage the fetch, decode, execute cycle.

Special purpose registers:

- **accumulator:** name given to register to which ALU sends the result of its operation
- **instruction (CIR):** holds the instruction currently being executed
- **MAR (memory address):** holds the address of the next data/instruction to be fetched
- **MDR (memory data):** holds data as they are moved to and from memory
- **program counter (PC):** holds the address of the next instruction to be fetched – incremented automatically unless a jump instruction is executed, when it is overwritten.

General purpose registers: for general CPU use. When a program is interrupted, for example, the state of the current registers can be saved in general purpose registers.

Choice of architecture model

The computer design engineer will weigh up:

- **performance requirements** – the more speed required the more critical the architecture
- **power and cooling requirements** – act as a constraint on complexity
- **budget** – lower budget will point to a simpler, more standard design
- **programmability** – the more specialised the purpose of the system the more specialised the architecture can be.

The system bus

The system bus is the transport highway for the system. It is a group of wires holding:

- **address bus:** holds address of memory (uni-directional from CPU to memory)
- **control bus:** holds current control signal
- **data bus:** holds data being transferred.

Now try this

Name from memory the five special purpose registers, and three other essential CPU components.

The fetch decode execute cycle

In the Von Neumann scheme there is a strict sequence: at each tick of the clock the CPU cycles round first doing the steps of a fetch, decodes what has been fetched and executes, then starts again.

The fetch decode execute (FDE) cycle

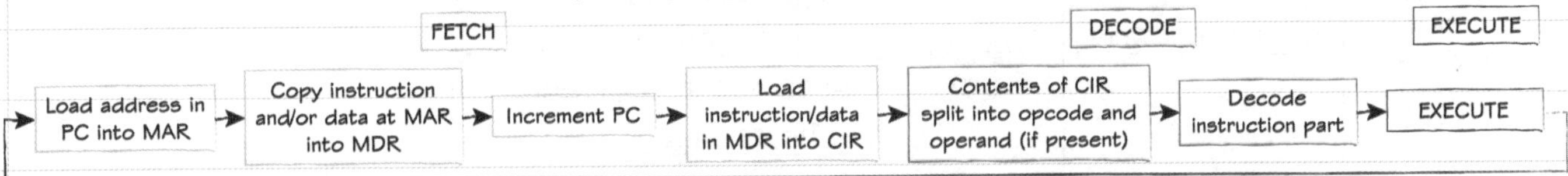

The number of steps in the execute phase depends on the opcode and operands in the CIR:

- If a jump then the address part of CIR is copied to the PC ready for the next cycle.
- If an address is in operand part of CIR it is copied to MAR and then the opcode executed.
- If data is to be moved to or from memory then it is copied into MDR.

Interrupts

An interrupt is an event (e.g. a keypress), exception or error (e.g. a 'printer not ready' flag) whose role it is to interrupt the CPU, to allow execution of a higher priority or critical process. While the system is on the CPU is always performing the fetch decode execute cycle, unless it is interrupted by the interrupt handling system.

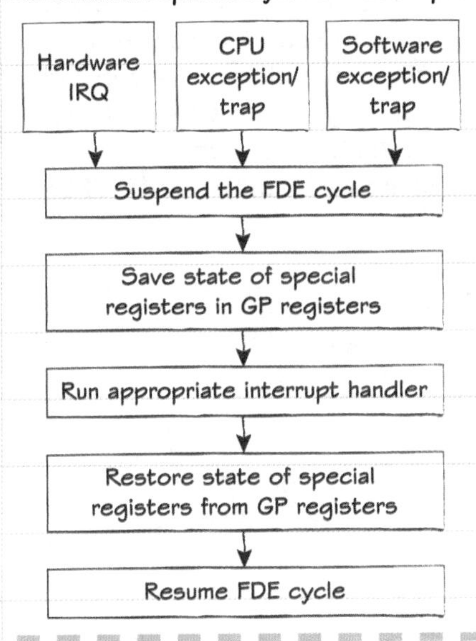

Instruction sets

The CPU instruction set is the complete set of instructions (in binary) that can be given to the CPU. These run in a sequence precisely synchronised with the CPU clock (and thus have a precise breakdown into each step in the FDE cycle). Assembly language is a natural language-like translation of this machine code. Typical instructions (in English) would include instructions such as: LOAD, STORE, ADD, COMPARE, JUMP, JUMP IF, IN and OUT.

An instruction will always include an **opcode**. Depending on the opcode, there will be 0, 1 or more **operands**, for example, '**Load a number**', from an address.

Von Neumann bottleneck

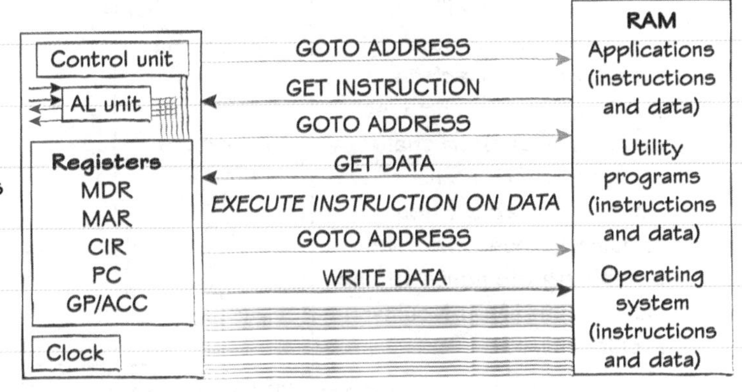

The problem is that for each (machine code) instruction there may be a number of fetches and writes to and from memory for the data. This causes a bottleneck in execution with the faster CPU having to wait as it is dependent on the bus transfer rate. Modern CPUs will therefore go beyond the Von Neumann architecture and include multiple cores, caches and pipelines.

Execution speed

The clock speed determines the time it takes to do one step in the fetch decode execute cycle. The clock can be speeded up (overclocking), but it may make the CPU hotter and more liable to fail. The amount of instructions a computer can perform a second (MIPS) will depend on the number of steps in each phase of the FDE cycle. It will also therefore depend on the size of the system bus (and thus the address bus and data bus). For example, a 32 bit integer can be fetched in one step on a 32 bit bus, but it takes four steps on an 8 bit bus.

1101 1100 0001 0001 1010 1101 0111 0011

Data bus carrying a 32 bit integer

Now try this

In what format would a 16 bit opcode from the instruction set look like to the CPU?

Had a look ☐ Nearly there ☐ Nailed it! ☐

Alternative architectures

There are alternatives to the Von Neumann architecture.

Harvard architecture

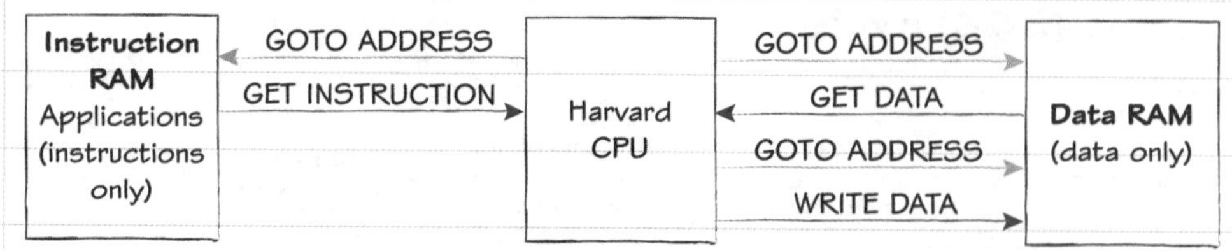

The Harvard architecture splits instructions from data thus avoiding the Von Neumann bottleneck, but at the expense of more difficult coding. Different bus widths can be optimised for data and instructions. In practice it is very useful where there is a heavy processing load on a throughput of data such as for an **embedded CPU**, early mobile phones, a graphics processing unit (GPU) or digital signal processor (DSP).

Hybrid architectures

A modern CPU will pull data and instructions into separate **caches** (on-board small and fast memory areas) so that each instruction and the data is available when required, thus effectively combining elements of the Harvard and Von Neumann architectures.

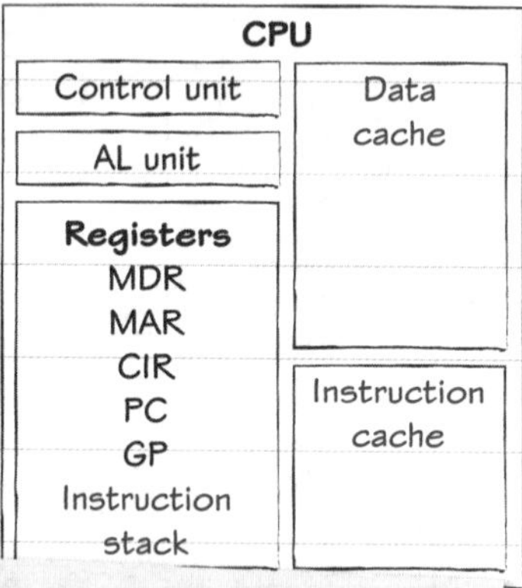

Modern CPU architecture suitable for microcomputer or server

Pipelining

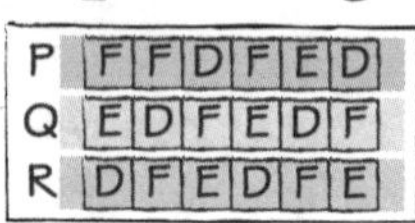

A three-stream pipeline

Instruction cycles are broken down into steps and then, for example, when stream P is fetching an instruction, and the ALU would otherwise be idle, Q will be used to execute and ideally R willl be used for decoding. This ensures that each element of the CPU is being used as fully as possible. This was always an essential part of superscalar computers but now is used by most CPUs.

A PC running a console game

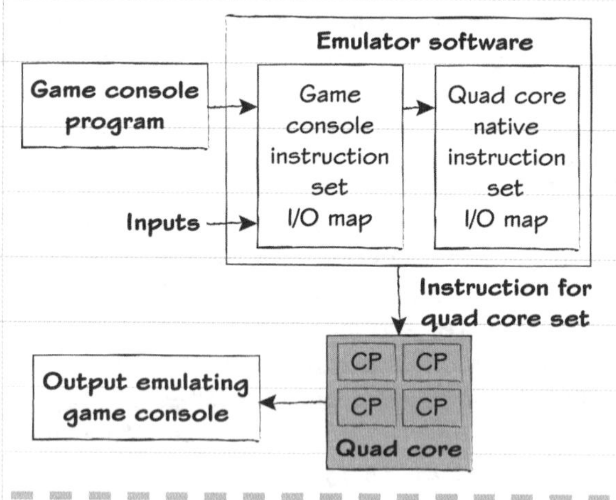

Superscalar CPUs

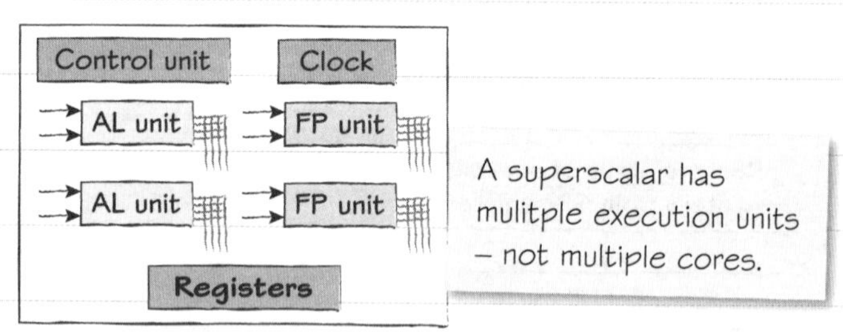

A superscalar has mulitple execution units – not multiple cores.

A superscalar processor is able to execute multiple instructions (from the one instruction stream) per clock cycle by issuing different instructions to different execution units (such as an ALU or FPU) which are used in combination with pipelines to achieve a form of parallelism.

Emulation

CPUs of one type can emulate a CPU of another, using emulator software to translate all instructions and data and I/O requests between the source and target systems. More powerful chips can emulate less powerful ones quite successfully. A perfect emulator, if it existed, would allow all programs and devices used on the one system to be used on the other, albeit more slowly because of the processing overhead for the translation.

Now try this

Virgame is a new start-up that has been asked by a smartphone company if it is possible to write an emulator for a Sony Playstation 4, with its multi-core processor architecture that will run on its phone that uses superscalar architecture.

Describe why this is not feasible, giving two reasons.

Parallel computing

Parallel computing allows a computer system to run multiple tasks at the same time.

Multi-threading

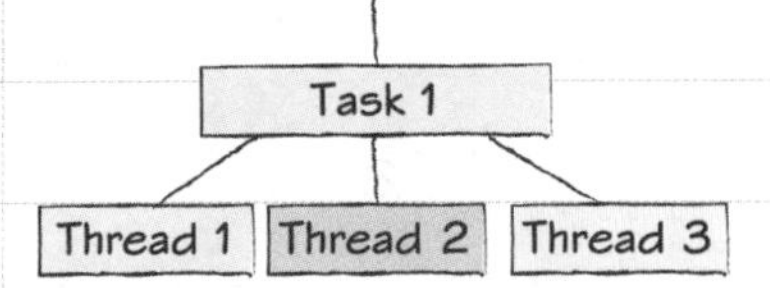

A single application is broken down into multiple operations or threads which can be executed in parallel. If one thread is stalled, for example waiting for input, any threads that are not blocked can carry on. Multi-threading can be implemented in parallel on multiple CPUs or using pipelining on a superscalar single CPU.

Multi-tasking

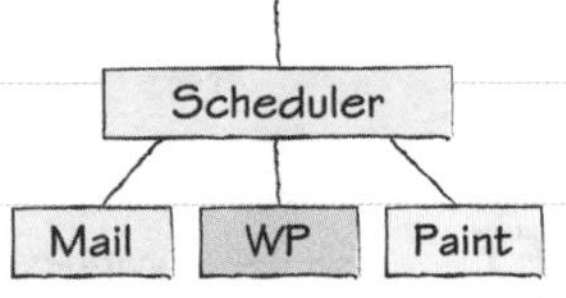

The computer system is running multiple tasks at the same time. In a single core (non-parallel) processor this is achieved by switching between tasks in an efficient and transparent manner. In a multiple CPU or multi-core system the processes can be running in parallel, still controlled by a scheduler.

Distributed computing (non-uniform memory access, NUMA)

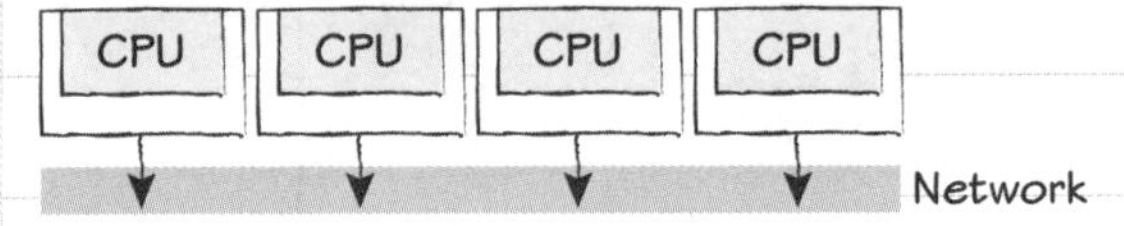

A distributed system comprises a number of computers working together over a network.

Advantages:

- each CPU has access to its own and shared resources (e.g. memory-using NUMA)

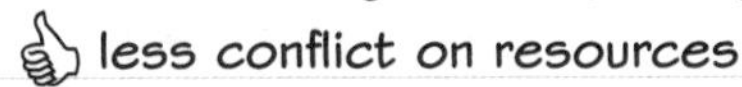

- less conflict on resources
- very scalable – just add new resource.

Disadvantages:

- Using distributed resources requires more coordination and processing power.
- Using remote resources (e.g. memory) is slower than using local resources.

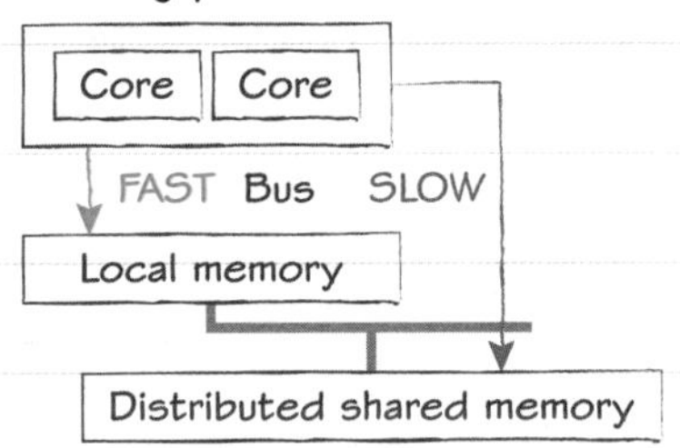

Multi-processing (UMA)

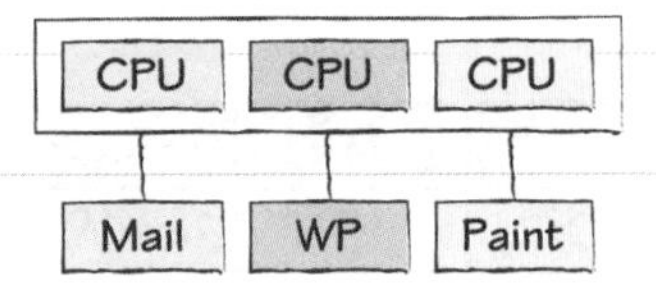

Multi-processing refers to the multiple CPUs which can run multiple applications or services at once and/or multiple threads at once. It can be set up on multiple computers all sharing the same system resources or on a single chip such as, for example, a dual core or quad core processor.

Multi-core CPUs

CPUs such as the Intel Quad Core have multiple processing units on a single chip to enable parallel processing from that one chip.

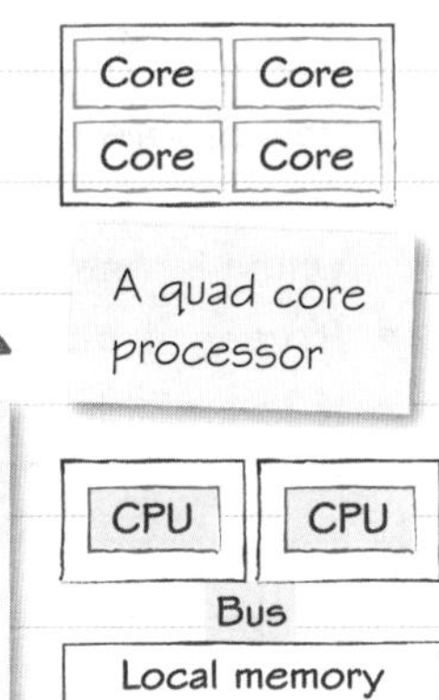

UMA: Fast uniform memory access to all memory, but harder to coordinate and scale than NUMA

Cluster computing (distributed)

A cluster is a group of connected computers all running together to gain the performance advantages of a very large system but with off-the-shelf hardware. Applications include complex simulations and internet search and data warehousing where high performance and scalability are critical. Clusters of captive PCs have also been used to mount major distributed denial of service attacks.

Now try this

State the implications of a large data centre, such as Google's at Berkeley in the USA, using a cluster approach for the computer architecture.

Had a look ☐ Nearly there ☐ Nailed it! ☐

Binary and number systems

Computers work with digital (binary) data.

Binary uses

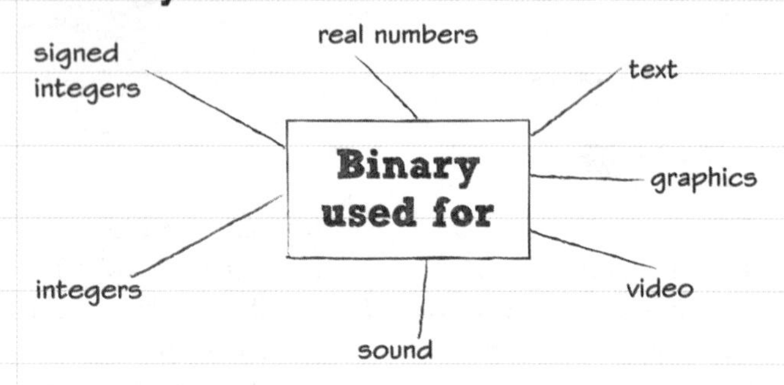

Analogue and digital and binary

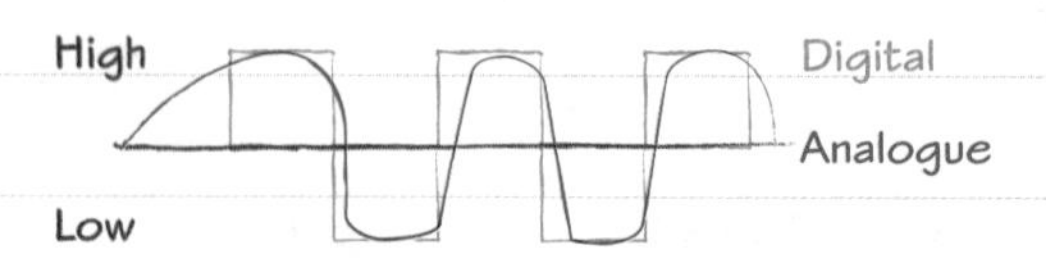

- Analogue data in the real world vary continuously, with an infinite possible number of values.
- Digital data is either high or low, on or off. The binary number models this perfectly (one or zero).

The denary (base 10) system

The number system used everyday is called the denary system. It uses **ten** as its base. It uses digits between 0 and 9 and then moves position by a power of 10.

10000s	1000s	H	T	Units
10^4	10^3	10^2	10^1	10^0
9	9	9	9	9

99999 = 9 * 10000 + 9 * 1000 + 9 * 100 + 9 * 10 + 9

Denary number is 99999.

The binary number system

The number system used by computers is called the binary system. It uses **two** as a base. It uses digits 0 and 1 and then moves up by a power of 2.

8s	4s	2s	Units
2^3	2^2	2^1	2^0
1	1	1	1

1111 = 1 * 8 + 1 * 4 + 1 * 2 + 1

Denary number is 15.

BCD – a hybrid number system

- BCD is used in computer systems for legacy systems and electronic devices such as calculators with LCD displays.
- It uses binary for each individual denary digit, which is easy for humans to follow.
- It uses 4 bits (a nibble) for each digit.
- It is inefficient as the highest digit is 9 (1001).

Tens				Units			
8	4	2	1	8	4	2	1
2^3	2^2	2^1	2^0	2^3	2^2	2^1	2^0
1	0	0	1	0	1	1	1

Take the BCD number 1001 0111

Stage 1: 1001 = 9, 0111 = 7

Stage 2: 9 * 10 + 7

The denary number is therefore 97.

Bits and bytes

Name	Bits	Bytes	Notes
bit	1		1 wire
Nibble	4	0.5	1 BCD digit
Byte	8	1	e.g. 2^8 characters
Word	16	2	e.g. 2^{16} integers
Word	24	3	e.g. 2^{24} colours
Word	32	4	2^{32}
Kilobyte (kB)		1024 bytes	or 2^{10}
Megabyte (MB)		one million kB	or 2^{20}
Gigabyte (GB)		one billion kB	or 2^{30}
Terabyte (TB)		one thousand GB	or 2^{40}
Petabyte (PB)		one thousand TB	or 2^{50}

Now try this

1 How many wires are there in a 32 bit address bus?

2 How many different colours can be represented by 24 bit colour?

Converting between number bases

You can convert between binary, denary and BCD numbers.

Binary to denary

Take the binary number: 10111010

Create a table with the same number of bits.

Most significant bit (highest value bit)
Least significant bit (lowest value bit)

128	64	32	16	8	4	2	1
1	0	1	1	1	0	1	0

- Fill in the place values from LSB to MSB. Start at 1 for LSB and multiply next by 2.
- The MSB will be $2^{\text{no of bits} - 1}$
- Enter the number under each place value.
- Where there is a 1 add the denary value.

For 10111010:

There are 8 bits so create an 8 bit table.

MSB will be $2^{8-1} = 2^7 = 128$; the LSB is always 1.

2 + 8 + 16 + 32 + 128 = 186

Any binary number which is all 1s will be $2^{\text{number of 1s}} - 1$.
So 1111 = 16 − 1 or 15
11111111 = 256 − 1 or 255

Denary to binary

- Take the number (*N*)
- Divide by 2; write down the new number (*N*) and the remainder (1 or 0)
- Do this until you have divided 1 by 2.
- Copy the remainders out from last 1 (which is the MSB) to first 1 (LSB).
- Check the binary number is correct.

For example: 170_{10} (170 in denary):

N	*N* ÷ 2	Remainder
170	85	0
85	42	1
42	21	0
21	10	1
10	5	0
5	2	1
2	1	0
1	2	1

$170_{10} = 10101010_2 = 128 + 32 + 8 + 2$ ✓

BCD to denary

Take the BCD number 1001 1000 0101 0011.

Translate each set of 4 bits in turn (from left to right) from binary to denary.

MSB LSB

8	4	2	1	Answer
1	0	0	1	9
1	0	0	0	8
0	1	0	1	5
0	0	1	1	3

The answer in denary is 9853.

Denary to BCD

Take the denary number 1256.

Translate each denary digit into its binary equivalent.

MSB LSB

Denary	8	4	2	1
1	0	0	0	1
2	0	0	1	0
5	0	1	0	1
6	0	1	1	0

1256_{10} = 0001 0010 0101 0110

Now try this

Perform the following conversions, showing your workings:

(a) binary to denary: 1010 0001, 1111 1111
(b) denary to binary: 52, 148
(c) BCD to denary: 1000 0010 0001 0001, 0101 0000
(d) denary to BCD: 92, 255

It is conventional to puts bits into groups of 4 to make bit patterns easy to read, thus 111111 (63) will usually be written as 0011 1111.

Calculating with binary

Binary numbers can be added or subtracted.

Types of number

A computer system will store each number in a fixed number of bytes. This has an impact on the range (minimum to maximum) of the number. In most computer programs, for example, integers are stored in 2 bytes (16 bits) and thus can only store numbers between 0 and 65 535 ($2^{16} - 1$).

Even a 4 byte (32 bit) integer will only be able to store numbers of less than 4.3 billion. If the number could be negative then it must be less than half that.

Typical number types

Type	Bits	Range
Integer (character)	8	0 … 255 ($2^8 - 1$)
Signed integer (signed char)	8	−127 … +128
Integer	16	0 … 65 535 ($2^{16} - 1$)
Signed integer	16	−32 767 … 32 768
Integer	32	0 … 4 294 967 295 ($2^{32} - 1$)
Floating (real)	32	$\pm 3.4 \times 10^{38}$ (~7 dp)
Double (real)	64	$\pm 1.7 \times 10^{308}$ (~16 dp)

Adding binary numbers

Essentially this is exactly the same as adding in denary: Sum: 0 + 0 = 0; 0 + 1 = 1; 1 + 0 = 1; 1 + 1 = 0, carry 1

0	1	0	1	0	1	0	1	85	
0	0	0	1	1	0	0	1	25	+
0	1	1	0	1	1	1	0	110	
		1				1		carry	

NOTE:

0	1	1	1	1	1	1	1	127	
1	0	0	0	0	0	1	0	130	+
0	0	0	0	0	0	0	1	257	
1	1	1	1	1	1			1	
								carry	

The answer is 1 if 1 byte word with an **overflow** of 1. If 2 bytes then 1 = 256

Two's (2s) complement (signed numbers)

Signed numbers are usually stored using a system called two's complement. This uses MSB = 1 to signify a negative number. It has the advantage that if MSB = 0 the rest is a normal binary number. That is, 0011 1111 = 63.

−63= −128 + 65 so 2s complement of 63 is

MSB … LSB

−128	64	32	16	8	4	2	1
1	1	0	0	0	0	0	1

2s complement into denary:

Take the number	1100 0001
As MSB is 1, it is – so	
Convert rest of number	100 0001 = 65
65 – 128	−128 + 65 = 1 – 63

Denary into 2s complement

Take the denary	−55
Ignore the sign	55
Convert to binary	0011 0111
Reverse (NOT) digits	1100 1000
Add 1	1100 1001

Always check back:
1100 1001 = −128 + 73 = −55 ✓

Subtracting binary numbers

To subtract simply use two's complement numbers and add them.

+a – b:

1	1	0	1	0	1	0	1	−43	
0	0	0	1	1	0	0	1	25	+
1	1	1	0	1	1	1	0	−18	
		1				1		carry	

–a – b:

1	1	0	1	0	1	0	1	−43	
1	1	1	0	0	1	1	1	−25	+
1	0	1	1	1	1	0	0	−68	
1		0		1	1	1		carry	

This final 1 in the carry row is an **overflow** bit and can be discarded here.

Now try this

Perform the following sums using two's complement arithmetic, showing your workings:
(a) 24 – 12, (b) 127 – 125, (c) −2 – 1, (d) 8 + 9, (e) 127 + 3, (f) 0000 0010 + 1000 0001

Working with numbers

Multiplication and division calculations can be performed with both binary and floating point numbers.

Binary multiply and divide

Multiplication

Multiplying in binary by hand follows exactly the same method as for denary, except that only 1s and 0s are ever multiplied:

32	16	8	4	2	1		
		0	1	0	1	5	
		0	1	1	0	6	×
	0	1	0	1	0		
0	1	0	1	0	0		
0	1	1	1	1	0	30	+

Division

Longhand binary division uses the identical method to denary division. For example, to divide 1110 by 10 (14/2):

```
        0 1 1 1
1 0 | 1 1 1 0
        1 0
          1 1
          1 0
            1 0
            1 0
```

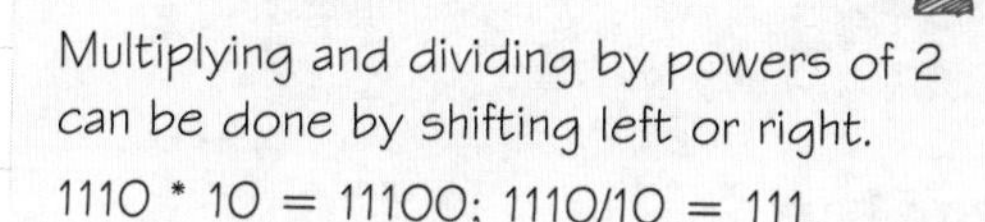

Multiplying and dividing by powers of 2 can be done by shifting left or right.
1110 * 10 = 11100; 1110/10 = 111

Floating point numbers

There are an infinite number of real numbers between any two numbers, for example between 2.0 and 3.0 or between 2.01 and 2.02.

Floating point numbers offer the best compromise between size, speed and accuracy and thus have become standardised on modern computer systems using an IEEE format. This is based on an extended version of standard form.

Standard form

- Very large numbers, for example 72 900 000 000 000 can be written as 7.29×10^{13} (or 7.29E+13).
- Very small numbers, for example 0.000 000 22 can be written as 2.2×10^{-7} (or 2.2E−07).
- Negative numbers such as −123.252345 can be written as $-1.23252345 \times 10^{2}$.

Sign	Mantissa	Base	Sign	Exponent
+	7.29	10	+	13
+	2.2	10	−	7
−	1.23252345	10	+	2

Multiplying using standard form

Multiply mantissa and add exponents

Either: $1.25 \times 10^{3} \times 2.0 \times 10^{2} = (1.25 \times 2) \times 10^{3+2}$
$= 2.5 \times 10^{5}$

or: 1.5E+3 × 2.0E+3 = 3.0E+6

Normalised numbers

$1.234 * 10^{3}$ is the same as $12.34 * 10^{2}$ or $123.4 * 10^{1}$. Normalising involves ensuring there is one number in the mantissa in front of the decimal point.

In binary this number will always be 1.

For example, 1.0010×2^{6} or $1.11111110 \times 2^{-12}$

In IEEE format, therefore, this 1 is assumed to save storage space.

Floating point numbers cannot represent all floating point numbers with total precision (e.g. 10/3).

IEEE 754 Single precision format

+−	Exp	Mantissa	Type
1	8	23	single

Sign bit: 1 = −, 0 = +

Exponent: base 2 known – raised to exp −127;

Note: All 0s or all 1s is used for special cases such as NAN, INF, overflow or underflow.

Mantissa: 1 is assumed so stores bits to right of this and gives the precision of the number.

IEEE format allows for different sizes of floating point number depending on the precision required, for example, single, double extended.

Now try this

(a) Normalise 1200.00 and 80 000 and write the answers in E notation.
(b) Multiply them together in E notation, showing your workings.

Text representation

Text, as with every other type of data, is represented by binary in a computer system as a character set, where each character is represented by its own binary code.

What is ASCII?

ASCII is the American Standard Code for Information Interchange. The original ASCII code used 7 bits for each character with a parity bit to check that the data transmitted was received correctly. 0100 0001 was A in even-parity ASCII. This allowed for 2^7, that is 128, different characters.

It catered essentially for the basic characters found on a tele-typewriter with some additional characters to control the printing, such as to issue a line feed, carriage return or tab.

Extended ASCII

8 bit, or Extended, ASCII replaced 7 bit ASCII for local computer operations and it became possible to add another 128 characters, such as umlaut (ö), circumflex (ô), acute and grave accents. Different sets of 128 could be added in different international areas such as Israel or Greece – in what was known as a code page.

Understanding ASCII

	Char		Character (1–26+) 2^5				
	Number/symbol			Number etc. (0–9 +) 2^4			
8	7	6	5	4	3	2	1
0	1	0	0	0	0	0	1

- 8 = parity
- 7,6 = type of character (5 as well for numbers/symbols)
- 5–1 = character (4–1 for symbols/numbers)

P (parity): 1 bit.
Type: 2 bits (letters) or
3 bits (punctuation, numbers, control codes, etc.)
10 × (65–96) upper case, etc.
11 × (97–127) lower case, etc.

000 (0–31) control
010 (32–47) punctuation
011 (48–64) numbers, operators, ?
10 (64–95) lower case; 11 (96–127) upper case.

Note: Where there are gaps they are filled with punctuation, etc.

Upper case A: 0 10 00001 (1st upper case)
Upper case B: 0 10 00010 (2nd upper case)
Lower case c: 0 11 00011 (3rd lower case)
Number 4 : 0 011 0100 (4th number)

Links See page 71 for converting binary to denary.

Unicode representation

Unicode was devised as a means of representing every character in all the world's alphabets, rather than simply the Western ones in early Western computer systems.

It maps all characters to a number (called a code point). This can use a varied number of bytes (up to 6 at present). It maintains the original 1 byte ASCII within it so that legacy systems still all work, but now can contain almost infinite different characters.

Unlike the original ASCII the way the character number is stored on disk or in memory depends separately on the encoding which specifies the byte order (MSB … LSB or LSB … MSB) and other factors.

UTF-8 encoding

UTF-8 is the most standard means of encoding Unicode characters for transmission and storage on computer systems, used by the vast majority of web developers and internet developers as it encompasses standard ASCII encoding within it.

The statement at the top of most web pages:

Content-Type: text/plain; charset="UTF-8"

is what tells the browser that the characters are in UTF-8 format, and thus how to represent them on the screen.

Encodings options

There are hundreds of possible encodings including UTF7, 8, 16, 32, ANSI, and ISO 8859-1. Look at your browser's **View...Encoding** menu item to see some.

Now try this

The letter A in UTF-8 and ASCII is represented by the denary number 65 (0100 0001) and lower case a by 97 (0110 0001).

What is 'Computer' in denary and binary ASCII?

Image representation

Images can be represented by bitmaps and vectors.

Bitmap (or raster) images

A bit map maps a colour to a pixel on a display or printer.

All images when displayed are displayed as bit maps, though they may be stored as compressed bitmaps or as vector images. Each pixel of a bit map has a colour. When all the pixels are displayed together the clarity of the final image depends on the size of the image versus the resolution and the colour bit depth.

A bit map is stored as the height × width × colour depth. For example, a 100 × 100 bit map using 24 bit colour will take 10000 × 3 (30k) bytes to store without compression. Images stored as bit maps do not scale well, as can be seen from the extract of the photo above.

Vector graphics

Vector graphic of a house design

Vector graphics are stored as a set of instructions that the vector software uses to create the image as a bit map. They are suitable for illustrations and line drawings, but not for photographic type images. For example:

- rectangle (x_1, y_1, x_2 ,y_2, colour)
- triangle (x_1, y_1, h_1, type, colour).

The image is stored very economically as it can be stored as essentially a textual program and can be recreated 100% accurately at larger and larger sizes as the image is remapped every time it is scaled. It can also be plotted very accurately on a high resolution plotter.

Image storage and compression

Images are usually compressed when stored, though RAW images are sometimes stored. **GIF** images are very economical because the colour depth is only 8 bit, and thus compress very well. It is not suitable for complex drawings but can handle transparency and animation. **PNG** can store any image but compresses line drawings best. **JPEGs** are optimal for complex photographic-type drawings and illustrations as the trade-off between compression and quality, and how much metadata is stored is chosen by the user.

Image resolution

Image resolution refers to the density of the pixels in the image. This varies with the purpose of the image. The amount of resolution required or used will depend on the image size needed and the dpi (dots per inch) that can be displayed. To display a 3" × 2" photo on a website at 72 dpi will take 3 × 72 × 2 × 72 (31.1k) pixels. To print a 10" × 8" photo at 600 dpi without upscaling would require 28.8 megapixels. Smartphone displays can now display at a resolution of up to 326 dpi.

Links See page 85 for more on compression.

Sample/bit depth

Bit depth is the number of bits used to specify a colour. 1 is for monochrome. True colour is now expressed in 24 bits (8 bit red, 8 bit green and 8 bit blue). The more bits used the better quality the image will be, but at the expense of storage.

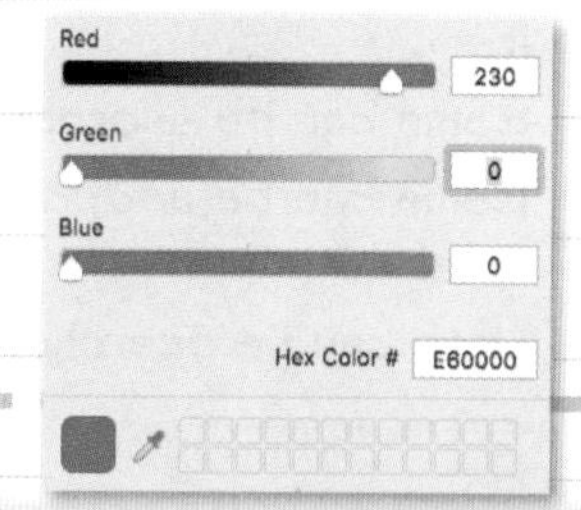

Now try this

JSD has to create a 20" × 20" colour poster at 300 dpi for a new CAD package with a CAD drawing and advertising text overlaid over a photo of a large house and garden

1 How many pixels will the final image require?

2 What file type will be required for the web version?

Had a look ☐ Nearly there ☐ Nailed it! ☐

Data structures (1)

A data structure is a way of organising data so it can be processed efficiently. You need to understand the following data structures.

Stack

A stack is used for storing requests that need to be handled (e.g. a stack of bills that need to be paid).

Characteristics of a stack include:

- A stack is a last in first out structure.
- It grows and shrinks as required.
- Only the top is visible at any time.
- Two operations are possible: **push** and **pop**.

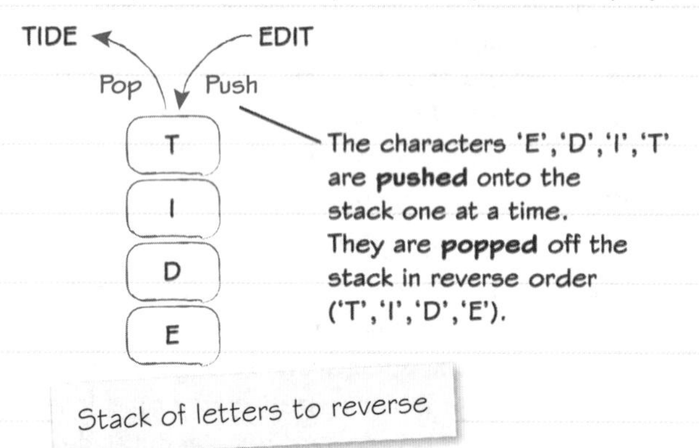

Stack of letters to reverse

Queue

A queue is a list of jobs waiting to be processed (e.g. a printer queue or a queue at a bank).

Characteristics of a queue include:

- A queue is a first in first out structure.
- It grows and shrinks as required.
- The front and back of the queue are visible.
- Two operations are possible: **enqueue** and **dequeue**.

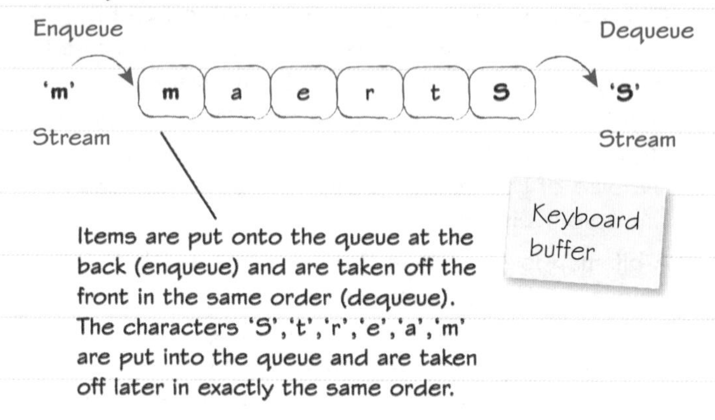

Keyboard buffer

List

A list is a flexible collection of items (e.g. a shopping list).

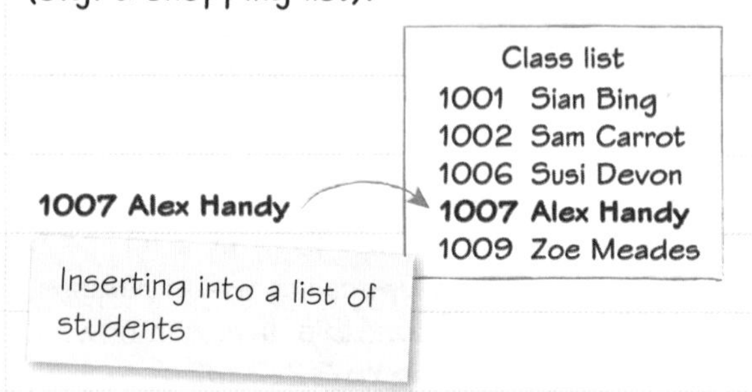

Inserting into a list of students

Characteristics of a list include:

- It can grow and shrink as required.
- It has a first item, next items, and a last item.
- Items can be unordered or ordered.
- Items can be added to or removed from lists.
- Lists can be searched and sorted.

Array

An array is an indexed (numbered normally) sequence of items of the same type.

0	1	2	3	4
Times	Courier	Arial	Palatino	Georia

Font[2] is Arial

Looking up font[2]

Characteristics of an array include:

- Arrays are usually fixed in size.
- Every item is immediately accessible.
- Items can be read using the index number.
- Items can be added using the index number.
- Sorting an array can be complex.

The index in an array

The index is the 'key' to the array

`Print (Font[3])` prints out 'Palatino'.

`Font[2]=Helvetica` changes Arial to Helvetica.

Links See page 58 for more on input/output handling.

Now try this

An operating system, for a single user computer system, will normally send print jobs to the printer to be printed in the order they are requested. Explain which data structure would be best used for the processes.

State which data structure you would use and say why.

Data structures (2)

The way data is structured in a computer's memory can be classified as dynamic or static.

Dynamic data structures

Characteristics of a dynamic data structure:

- size of the structure can vary at run-time
- memory only allocated (and deallocated) as required
- only uses storage space proportional to the data (but requires extra memory to store pointers (links) to the next item in the list)
- fast to sort-only involves pointers.

Contents	H	2056	T	4096	H	0
Address	2048	2049	2056	2057	4096	4097

A list of coin tosses (H or T)

Access to a list, queue and stack is provided in the following ways:

- **list**: access requires traversing the list of pointers from the start
- **queue**: direct access (to front and back)
- **stack**: very fast access (to top); often through a dedicated stack register.

Static data structures (arrays)

Characteristics of static data structures:

- size fixed at compile-time
- can waste storage space if the number of data items stored is less than amount allocated for
- normally stores data in consecutive memory locations
- sorting slow as involves moving data in cells.

An array of five coin tosses (H or T)

Element	toss[0]	toss[1]	toss[2]	toss[3]	toss[4]
Contents	H	T	H		
Address	1024	1025	1026	1027	1028

Access to an array is provided very quickly as data stored sequentially.

`myArray[n] is at myArray + (n*size)`

(if storing an array of 2 byte integers at address 10000, myArray[4] is at address 10008)

Common applications of a stack

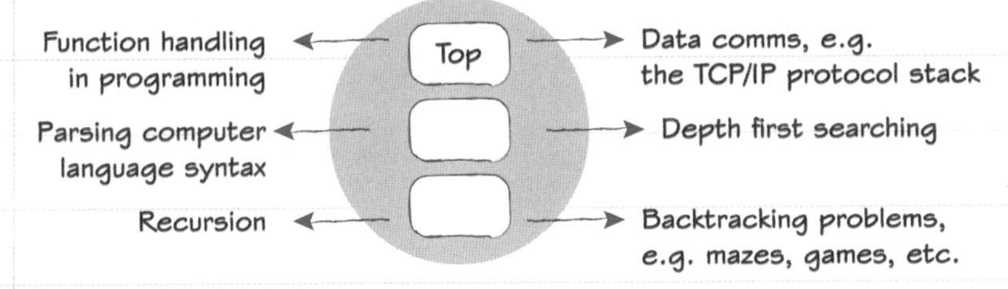

Common applications of a queue

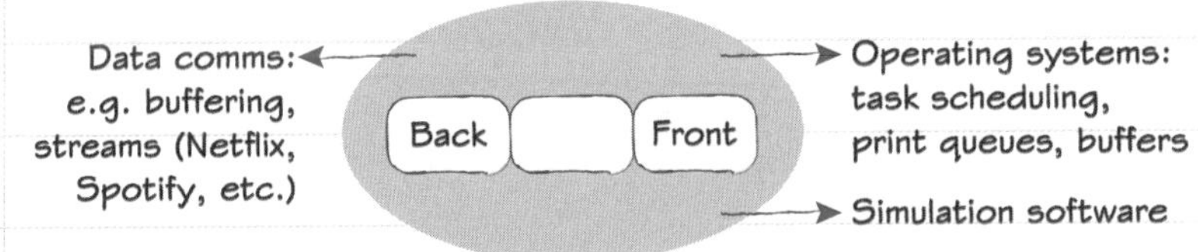

Common applications of a list

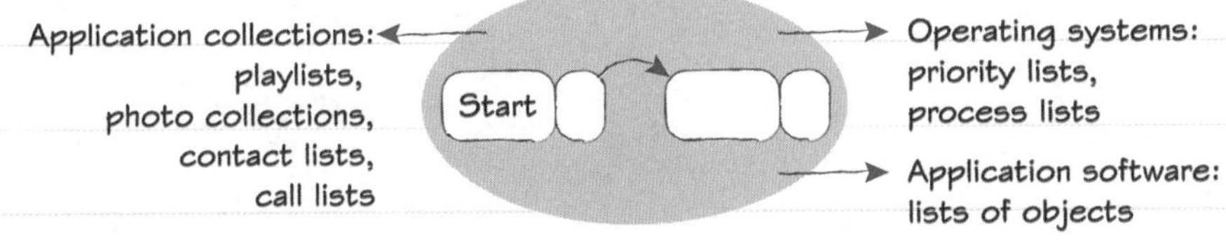

The list is so flexible that it is the basis of a great many collections in programming and systems.

Common applications of an array

An array is a basic collection type implemented in systems and software. Most programming languages offer an array as the standard built-in collection type. They are commonly used to implement **matrices**. Where **dynamic data structures** are not available, an array can also be used to simulate them.

See also page 78 about indices and matrices.

Now try this

Programmers can use lists or arrays to simulate a stack if a stack data structure is not available in the language. Evaluate which would be preferable.

Had a look ☐ Nearly there ☐ Nailed it! ☐

Indices and matrices

A matrix is a mathematical construct for a table of numbers. It is usually represented by an array in computing.

Matrices and arrays

An array is a data structure that represents an indexed collection of data (such as a table or matrix).

An element is an individual item (e.g. a number) within an array or matrix. It can be identified by its index (plural indices).

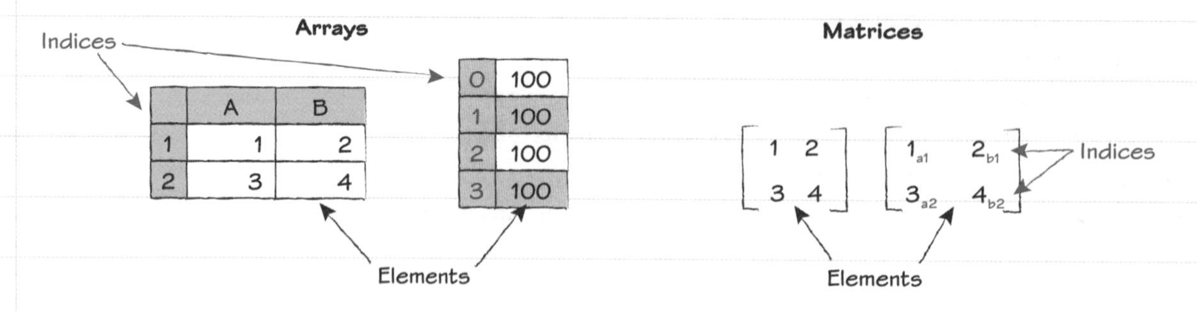

One-, two- and multi-dimensional arrays

A one-dimensional array has one index (*x*) to identify each element. An element within two-dimensional array has indices (*x*, *y*). A three-dimensional array has indices (*x*, *y*, *z*) to identify each element.

0	1
1	4
2	9
3	16

One dimension (*x*)
number [2] = 9

	0	1
0	1	1
1	2	4
2	3	9
3	4	16

Two dimensions (*x*,*y*)
number [2, 0] = 3

z =1	0	1
z=0	0	1
0	1	1
1	2	4
2	3	9
3	4	16

Three dimensions (*x*,*y*,*z*)
number [3, 0, 0] = 4

Now try this

Solve the following:

4	2	1	3	5
7	9	10	7	8
14	13	15	11	12

(a) number [0, 3] =

(b) number [2, 2] =

(c) number [1, 4] × number [2, 1] =

Mathematical operations using matrices

Matrices can be added, transposed and multiplied.

Mathematical operations using matrices

If Jill and Mary are saleswomen in a clothing shop, you can calculate the total number of items they have sold in January, February and March by adding the relevant matrices. To display the items vertically instead of horizontally, you transpose the matrices. Finally, to calculate the total revenue in January, February and March you can multiply the cost of each item by the number of those items sold in the three months, using matrix multiplication.

Matrix operations can be performed using standard mathematical operations as below or by using spreadsheet matrix functions.

	Jill				Mary				Total		
	Number sold										
	Jan	Feb	Mar		Jan	Feb	Mar		Jan	Feb	Mar
T-shirts	12	14	15		8	6	9		20	20	24
Skirts	5	6	6	+	5	5	5	=	10	11	11
Dresses	7	9	8		2	3	4		9	12	12
	Cost in £							T	2		
	T	S	D					S	3		
	2	3	4					D	4		
	Total revenue										
	Jan	Feb	Mar		Jan	Feb	Mar		Jan	Feb	Mar
	67	82	80		39	39	49		106	121	129

Add

$$\begin{bmatrix} 12 & 14 & 15 \\ 5 & 6 & 6 \\ 7 & 9 & 8 \end{bmatrix} + \begin{bmatrix} 8 & 6 & 9 \\ 5 & 5 & 5 \\ 2 & 3 & 4 \end{bmatrix} = \begin{bmatrix} 20 & 20 & 24 \\ 10 & 11 & 11 \\ 9 & 12 & 12 \end{bmatrix}$$

Transpose

$$\begin{bmatrix} 2 \\ 3 \\ 4 \end{bmatrix}^T = \begin{bmatrix} 2 & 3 & 4 \end{bmatrix}$$

Multiply

$$\begin{bmatrix} 2 & 3 & 4 \end{bmatrix} \cdot \begin{bmatrix} 12 & 14 & 15 \\ 5 & 6 & 6 \\ 7 & 9 & 8 \end{bmatrix} = \begin{bmatrix} 67 & 82 & 80 \end{bmatrix}$$

Row-major and column-major order

A 2D array of pixels

	0	1	2
0			
1			
2			
3			
4			

Row-major order $s(x, y)$

	0	1	2
0	1	2	3
1	4	5	6
2	7	8	9
3	10	11	12
4	13	14	15

Column-major order $s(y, x)$

	0	1	2
0	1	6	11
1	2	7	12
2	3	8	13
3	4	9	14
4	5	10	15

It is critical to know whether s(0,5) means s(row = 0, column = 5) (row-major) or means s(column = 0, row = 5) (column major) as both orders are used.

When designing arrays, it is optimal to use the same order for traversing the array as the elements are stored in memory, as traversing an array in sequence (1, 2, 3, 4, 5, 6) is much faster than jumping about the array (1, 6, 11, 2, 7, 12) to get the same information.

Now try this

Calculate:

$$\begin{bmatrix} 1 & 2 & 3 \end{bmatrix} * \begin{bmatrix} 10 & 5 & 20 \\ 20 & 10 & 40 \\ 30 & 15 & 60 \end{bmatrix}$$

Show your workings.

Had a look ☐ Nearly there ☐ Nailed it! ☐

Data communications channels

Devices can be connected to communicate and transmit data in a variety of methods.

Transmission modes

Full duplex

Can communicate in both directions at once

Half duplex

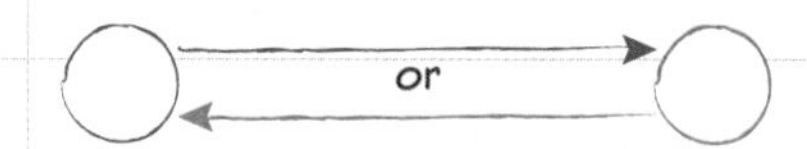

Can communicate in either direction but only in one direction at a time

Simplex

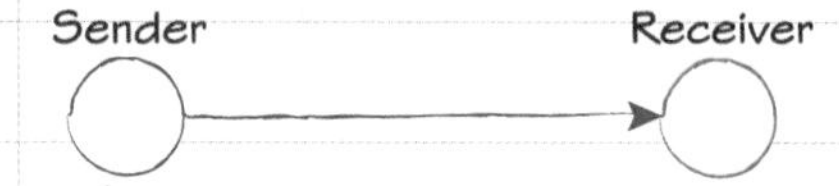

Can only communicate in one direction from a sender to a receiver

Examples of usage

Full duplex devices include:

- mobile phones
- phones
- standard network communications.

Half duplex devices include:

- walkie talkies or CB radios
- push to talk devices.

Simplex devices include:

- baby monitors
- GPS
- satellite TV
- CCTV.

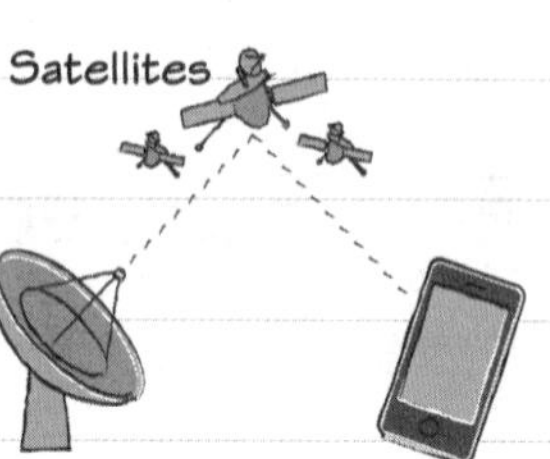

Simplex is from a sender to a receiver only.

Point to point (PTP)

This is a channel between two end points.

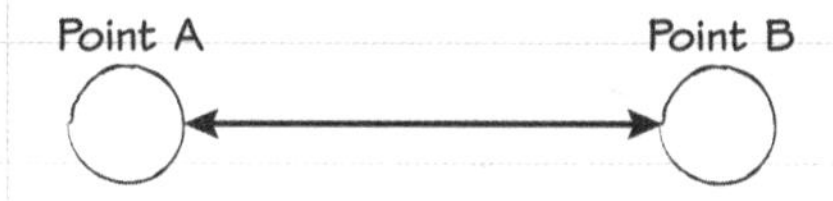

Any communication on a dedicated channel, such as data sent over a telephone line between two computers, or two PCs communicating over an RS232 cable or a PC connecting to an ISP over DSL is point to point. Peripherals such as hard disk controllers using, for example, SATA can also communicate directly over a dedicated PTP channel.

Multi-drop and multi-point

These are communication channels with multiple end points. The term multi-drop channel is usually used for configurations with one master and many slaves such as a mainframe with multiple terminals, and the term multi-point for a standard distributed network channel. Peripheral controllers use multi-drop for PCI and PATA, etc.

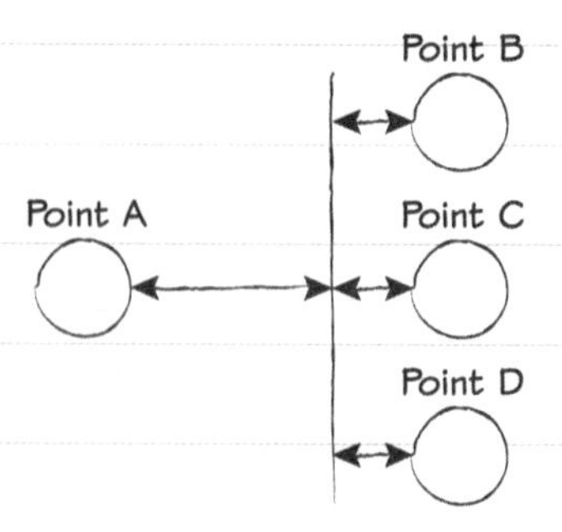

Now try this

General Hospital uses a pager system to call on-call doctors in the event of an emergency. They can use a walkie talkie or mobile phone to ring in.

What types of channels are in use in these cases?

Types of transmission

Data transmission can be parallel or serial, synchronous or asynchronous.

Parallel

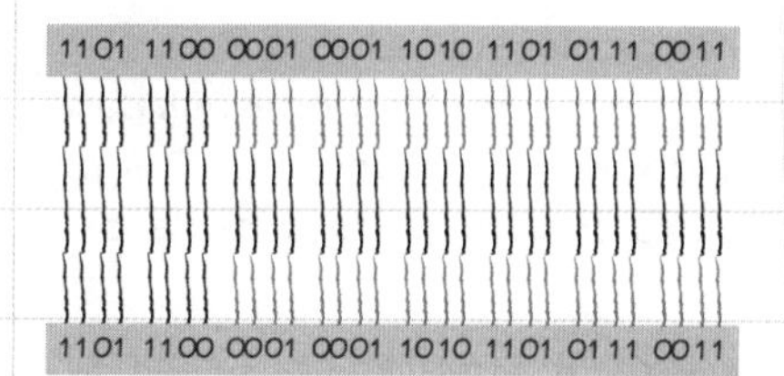

Parallel transmission over 32 lines of a data bus

Parallel transmission is sending data over a number of lines at once. It is very fast but suffers more from noise and it is difficult to synchronise parallel lines over longer distances so is typically only used over very short distances.

Common uses are for:

- computer buses
- computer to display cable
- HDMI cable
- short printer cables.

Serial

Serial transmission over one line

Serial transmission only requires, in theory, one transmission line. The data is sent over 1 bit at a time.

Serial transmission is much more common than parallel over anything but very short distances.

Although serial transmission only transmits data 1 bit at a time rather than 8, 16, 24, 32 or even 64 it is much cheaper to implement than parallel. It is able to be used over much longer runs than parallel transmission without error and thus can be pushed a good deal faster over more than very short distances.

Synchronous

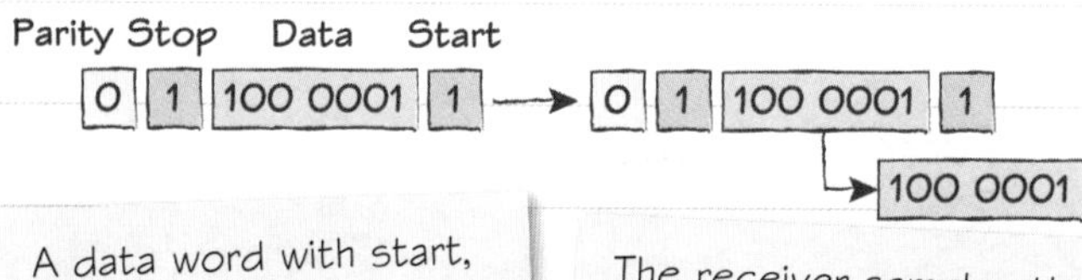

A data word with start, stop and parity bit

The receiver samples the data (on the data bus) at every clock pulse (on the control bus).

For synchronous transmission the speed of transmission is synchronised with a clock signal on a separate wire. Almost all parallel communication is synchronous. It can be very fast.

Asynchronous

Asynchronous communication is more flexible as it only needs to be synched when transmitting. Each word includes a start bit to signal the start, and an end bit to signal the end of the word, and parity if that has been agreed.

Handshaking

Handshaking is the first part of a communication between two devices.

It is the process by which two communication devices agree the protocols they will use to communicate:

- speed they can both work at (bps)
- synchronous or asynchronous
- half duplex or full duplex
- data coding (e.g. ASCII)
- error handling (e.g. parity)
- compression.

Communication speed

Bit rate	The speed at which data is transmitted in bps.
Baud	The number of times a signal changes per second – often intermixed with bps but not quite the same.
Bandwidth	The maximum possible bit rate of the medium – quoted by broadband sellers when average bps can be a good deal lower.
bps	Bits per second.

Now try this

Steve wants to send HDMI (HDMI is a parallel cable) between a TV in the garden shed and a satellite decoder in the front room, about 30 metres away, but his cable does not work.

Explain this.

Had a look ☐ Nearly there ☐ Nailed it! ☐

Data transmission protocols

The internet transmits data in packets, governed by standard protocols such as TCP/IP.

Protocols

A protocol is a set of rules used by two devices to allow them to communicate. On the internet these include:

- **TCP**: controls how data is transmitted
- **FTP**: controls how files are uploaded/downloaded/moved, etc.
- **HTTP**: controls how webpages are handled
- **HTTPS**: controls how secure webpages, such as for e-commerce, are handled.

Physical and logical protocols

Physical protocols ensure that it is possible for two devices to communicate. These include wired v wireless; CAT 6 or Token Ring; microwave; copper cable or fibre optic.

Logical protocols specify the format of the data and control bits, the packet size and format, compression, encryption etc.

Packets

A network packet is the unit of data transmitted in a packet-switched network. It is also sometimes called a datagram. It is typically about 1–2 kilobytes.

It comprises two main parts:

- the user data, or payload (the main part)
- control information.

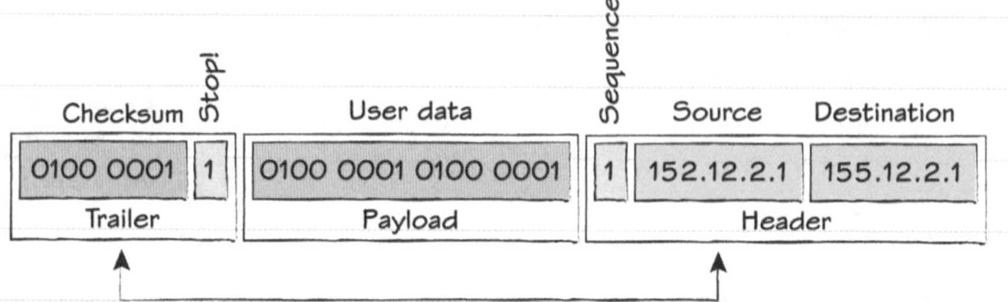

Packet switching

Packets can be sent over the network using whichever route is free. The packets usually contain a sequence number so that the packets can be reassembled in order at the destination.

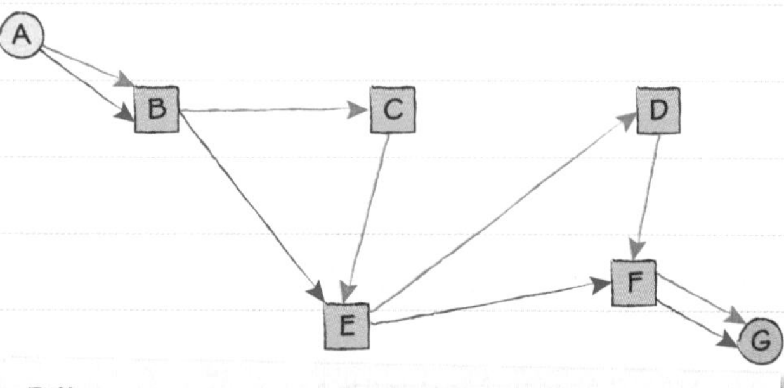

Different packets can take entirely different routes through the network from device A to device G.

Virtual circuit

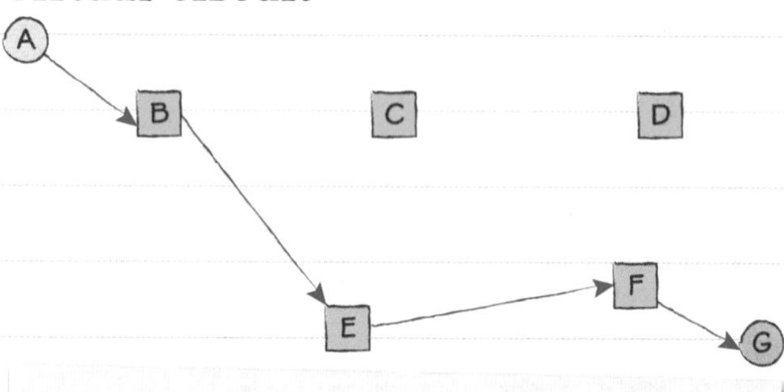

For transmissions where there is packet order and no packet loss a virtual circuit can be established.

See page 86 for more details on checksum handling errors.

Sending and receiving packets

Packets are sent in order, but are received in any order.

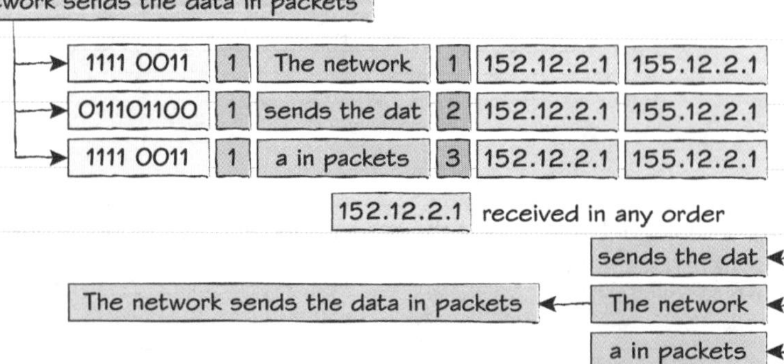

Now try this

What are the advantages and disadvantages of packet switching?

Simple encryption ciphers

Encryption is a vital component of modern computer systems ensuring the security of data on local computer systems and is a vital underpinning for e-commerce applications.

Substitution ciphers

Plaintext	A	B	C	D	E	F	G	H	I	J	K	L	M	N	O	P	Q	R	S	T	U	V	W	X	Y	Z
Offset 🔑	3	3	3	3	3	3	3	3	3	3	3	3	3	3	3	3	3	3	3	3	3	3	3	3	3	3
Ciphertext	D	E	F	G	H	I	J	K	L	M	N	O	P	Q	R	S	T	U	V	W	X	Y	Z	A	B	C

Caesar cipher with a key of 3

Plaintext	S	E	C	R	E	T	M	E	S	S	A	G	E
🔑	T	A	N	K	T	A	N	K	T	A	N	K	T
Offset	18	0	12	9	18	0	12	9	18	0	12	9	18
Ciphertext	L	E	P	B	X	T	Z	O	L	S	N	Q	X

Encryption stages using key 'TANK'

Using the Caesar cipher

Stages when encrypting using a Caesar cipher:

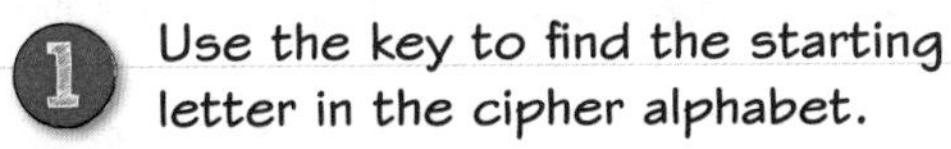

1. Use the key to find the starting letter in the cipher alphabet.

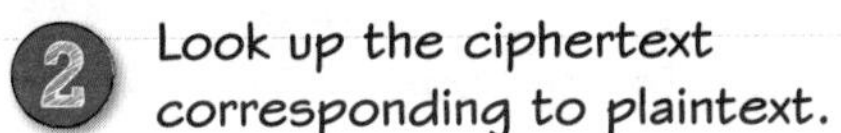

2. Look up the ciphertext corresponding to plaintext.

Features of Caeser cipher encryption:

- 👍 fast and easy to use, even manually
- 👎 easy to crack even manually using frequency analysis or heuristics
- 👎 trivial for a computer to crack using brute force.

Using the Vigenère cipher

Stages when encrypting using a Vigenère cipher:

1. Write the keyword against the message.
2. Use the key to find offset (or find starting letter).
3. Look up the ciphertext corresponding to plaintext.

Features of Vigenère cipher encryption:

- 👍 more secure cipher than Caesar
- 👍 all 26 Caesar cipher alphabets potentially used
- 👍 not immediately crackable using frequency analysis
- 👎 can be cracked by finding patterns to calculate the key length and then using more conventional techniques.

The key

The key may be presented in a number of ways:

1. A letter 'F': the starting letter

2. A denary number '3': the amount to shift by

3. A binary number '0011': the same in number code.

Common cracking methods

- Brute force analysis
- Frequency analysis
- Looking for patterns in the message or key
- Simple heuristics

Now try this

Encrypt the plaintext ANT using a standard Caesar cipher with a binary key of 0000 0011. You are advised to show your working.

Had a look ☐ Nearly there ☐ Nailed it! ☐

Encryption in modern computer systems

Modern computer systems either make use of symmetric key encryption or public key encryption.

Symmetric key encryption

This is the basis for the majority of encryption on modern computer systems including encrypted file storage, wireless network security (WPA/AES), web page encryption and more.

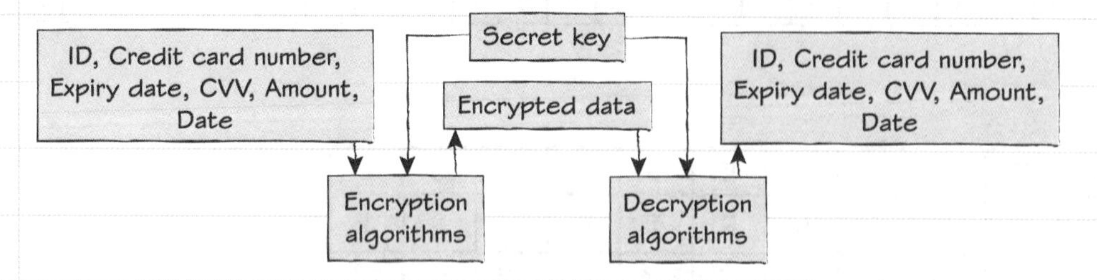

Stages for encrypting data securely using a symmetric private key.

Features of symmetric key encryption

- The key is symmetrical because the same key is used to encrypt and decrypt the message.
- It is fast, powerful and can be extremely secure.
- The ciphertext cannot be decrypted without knowing the private key, even if the encrypting algorithm itself is known.
- The algorithm takes blocks of bits in the message and encodes these. The more bits in the block the more secure it will be.

DES encryption (56 bit) was for many years the US government standard for encryption. This has now been cracked. Now 64 bit, 128 bit and 256 bit encryption are commonly used. The current government standard is AES 256 bit which is regarded as uncrackable given today's technology.

Public key encryption

Public key encryption is used where a different person (or organisation or system) decrypts data from the one that encrypts it. Essentially it solves the problem of how they can share a private key securely over a wide area network such as the internet by using a public–private key pair. Public key encryption is used to transmit data such as a symmetric key safely.

Features of public key encryption:

- The keys are asymmetrical because different keys (public and private) are used to encrypt and decrypt the message.
- Public key encryption is excellent for transmitting data securely between people who trust each other.
- It is relatively slow compared to symmetric key encryption.
- It is used more often for securing small items of data rather than pages of data.

Now try this

Many types of application software allow 'locked' versions of files such as documents to be saved and shared with other users. A password then has to be used to unlock the file before it can be edited or modified.

What form of encryption is this? Why is this not suitable when transmitting the file over a WAN?

Compression

Compression is the process of reducing the number of bytes in a file to make it faster to transmit and/or take less storage space.

Lossless versus lossy compression

No information is lost in the process of compressing and expanding (de-compressing) original data using lossless compression. It works by eliminating statistical redundancy in patterns in the data. The process is totally reversible. Lossy compression, on the other hand, irreversibly compresses the file and the original cannot be restored.

Run length encoding , RLE

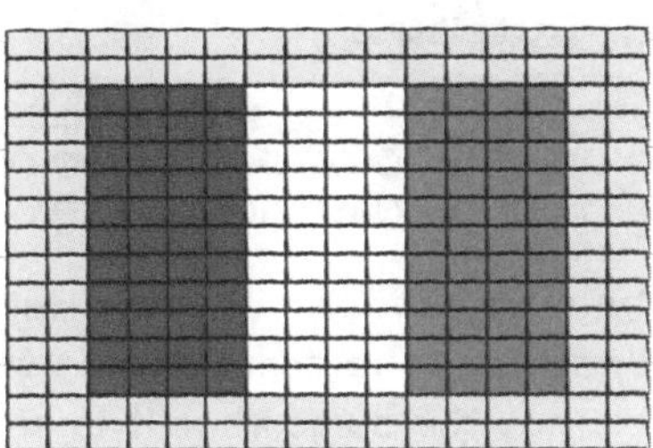

Simple bitmap graphics files (such as 8 bit GIF) can be encoded using run lengths of colours. In this case the 10 bytes B34 R4 W4 G4 B4 would encode the image from the top blue border down to the top line of the flag, which would take 90 bytes as a bitmap.

Dictionary (pattern) encoding

A well-known method of lossless encoding is to pre-scan the input data and create a dictionary of patterns, and then use the dictionary to encode the source data.

For example: analysing this extract of the original poem, *Everywhere*:

Everywhere I go
everywhere I have been
everywhere I know
everywhere I have seen, I know
you have been there for me.

This is the basis of many lossless compression schemes including LZ compression.

Dictionary table

#	Pattern	*n*
1	Everywhere	4
2	I	5
3	go	1
4	have	3
5	been	2
6	know	2
7	seen	1
8	you	1
9	there	1
A	for	1
B	me	1

Simple encoded version:
12312451261247268459 9AB

Original file size 113 bytes
Compressed data size 24 bytes
Dictionary size: 65 bytes
Total 89 bytes

Note: The idea is not actually to compress words but patterns: 'Everywhere I', for example, would be preferred.

Photo and video compression

High-resolution, full-colour (24 bit) colour images do not contain a good amount of repeating pattern. Even adjacent pixels of blue sky are likely to differ a little. Compression is either therefore limited (as in lossless PNG) or lossy (as in JPEG).

JPEG compression removes information by:

- averaging pixel colour values over a block in such a way that humans do not notice a large degradation in quality
- removing metadata such as lens, f-stop, location etc.

The JPEG compression algorithm allows a trade-off between quality and compression. Very high compression is possible with a larger loss in quality.

Audio compression

Audio compression works in the same manner:

- Lossless algorithms such as FLAC look for patterns in the binary data (e.g. silence). Lossless algorithms compress by about 50% from RAW CD format.
- Lossy formats try to lose data that do not make a good deal of difference to humans, though there is some compromise between quality and compression. It is possible to lose very high and very low frequency sound without suffering much loss of quality, as most humans cannot hear these sounds. An MP3 file will store a file in about 8 to 11 times less space than a CD whilst still sounding near identical to the original user.

Now try this

Explain why it is possible generally to compress text more than images or sounds in a lossless manner.

Had a look ☐ Nearly there ☐ Nailed it! ☐

Error detection

Communication channels can be 'noisy', which can cause signals to be altered in transmission. Error detection attempts to deal with this by noticing when an error has occurred. Methods used to detect errors are outlined below.

Repetition

→ data received
0100 0011 0100 0001 0100 0011
0100 0001 0100 0001 0100 0011

The simplest form of error detection relies on repetition. The same data is transmitted twice. If it is not the same then it is an error and it can be requested again. This is the basis of a good deal of form verification.

Redundancy

Raw data	XX

→ Parity bit/word
→ Checksum/check digit
→ Cyclic redundancy check

Other forms of error detection rely on attaching extra information to the raw data which is calculated using an algorithm.

Parity bit

Even parity: parity bit is calculated to make an even number of ones in the word.

1	1	0	0	0	0	1	1	C
0	1	0	0	0	0	0	1	A
0	1	0	0	0	0	1	0	B

Odd parity: parity bit is calculated to make an odd number of ones in the word.

0	1	0	0	0	0	1	1	C
1	1	0	0	0	0	0	1	A
1	1	0	0	0	0	1	0	B

Receipt of 1100 0001 on even parity is definitely an error. It does not trap double errors, however, as these cancel out, so it is possible to have more than one parity bit.

Check digits

Many numbers, such as bar codes (EAN and UPC), ISBN, credit cards and IBAN (international bank account number) have an extra digit(s) which verifies the rest of the number.

Valid ISBN13 code

9	7	8	1	9	0	3	1	3	3	8	0	4

The reader takes the sum of all the odd (blue) digits and adds 3 * the sum of the even (yellow) digits. If this is evenly divisible by 10 (i.e. modulo 10) it is valid. If not it is an error. The code above gives 44 + 3 * 12 = 80, which is valid).

If a digit was transposed or otherwise misread, for example, 9871903133804 then this would be an error.

Checksum

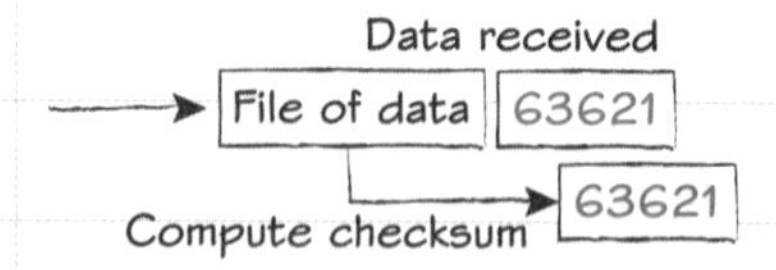

A checksum is a more generalised form of a check digit. It computes a number from the data in a file (usually by summing the digits in some manner) and appends it as a signature. The receiver re-computes the number and if identical, the data has integrity, that is, it is the same as sent. These are commonly used for local or remote data transmission.

Cyclic redundancy check (CRC)

Fixed length block of data	CRC
0100 0011 0100 0001 0100 0011...1101 0001	110100

A CRC is related to a checksum but relies on division rather than summing. To compute a CRC the data are split into fixed-length blocks of binary data. A fast division, hardware-based (shift) algorithm is applied to this data to compute the checksum. This is excellent at detecting accidental errors in transmission and is thus commonly used when storing files to disk and transmitting them over networks. It is also used for writing and checking updateable firmware, solid state drives and other devices.

Now try this

Are 9781903133781 and 9781405868052 valid ISBN13 numbers? Show your workings.

Error correction

When errors are detected when receiving data, error correction is the means of dealing with them. Commonly used error correction systems are outlined below.

Automatic repeat request (ARQ)

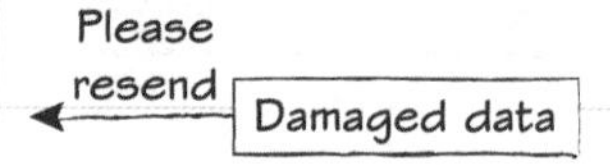

The ARQ is in principle a simple concept. If the errors are detected, then the sender is requested to resend data.

In practice, no actual request is needed, but rather the absence of a positive acknowledgement (an ACK signal) after a certain amount of time has elapsed – a timeout.

ARQ is used a lot on the internet. It does, however, have latency (whilst waiting for time-out signal) and needs a back channel for ACK signal and buffers to hold received data.

Forms of ARQ

Stop-and-wait ARQ

If the sender does not get an ACK within the wait time it resends the packet. The receiver therefore simply drops the damaged packets. It is slow as it sends one frame at a time and waits for ACK.

Go-back-N ARQ

The sender sends frames with a sequence number (frame 1, frame 2, etc.). The receiver discards damaged frames and ones it does not expect (e.g. repeats) and sends an ACK with the last correct one received. The sender will keep sending new sequences of frames starting after that one, dealing with latency but at the expense of many dropped packets.

Selective repeat ARQ

The receiver buffers out-of-order frames and ACKs them, rebuilding the sequence at the end.

Forward error correction (FEC)

Data	ECC
1100 0001 0001	1100

Data frame with error correcting codes

In a FEC scheme, the data is sent with added error-correcting codes (ECC) that will allow errors to be corrected automatically. There is an overhead for the receiver computing the original data from the total information, but this is more than offset by not having to retransmit.

The number of ECC bits must be sufficient to identify the position in the whole data and ecc bits of the error. That is, for 16 bits total of data + ecc, 4 bits (2^4) are needed.

Parity words and RAID systems

RAID 3 and 5 systems are able to rebuild themselves by using parity across drives. In this scheme the data bits are XORed to provide the parity bits.

(1) 10101010 XOR **(2)** 11101010 = **(3)** 01000000

Now any broken drive can be rebuilt by XORing the remaining drive:

(1) 10101010 XOR **(3)** 01000000 = **(2)** 11101010

This scheme works for any number of drives and electronically is easy to implement.

Hybrid ARQ

in hybrid ARQ FEC codes and error detection codes are both added to the data. If the signal conditions are good enough the FEC codes will be good enough to keep the channel running, but if conditions gets too bad then the system can request a repeat. This is very effective but at the expense of a slower throughput.

Now try this

JPS use a RAID system.

The words on the data drives are 0100 0001 and 0110 1100. Compute the word on the parity drive.

Had a look ☐ Nearly there ☐ Nailed it! ☐

Boolean logic

Boolean logic is at the heart of all computers. All circuits are designed using logic and made using some form of logic gates. Boolean algebra can be used to simplify circuits.

The seven main logic gates, algebraic terms and truth table

INPUTS		AND	OR	NOT	NAND	NOR	XOR	XNOR
Inputs to gate								
A	B	A . B	A + B	~A or $\overline{A}$	$\overline{A . B}$	$\overline{A + B}$	$A \oplus B$	$\overline{A \oplus B}$
0	0	0	0	1	1	1	0	1
0	1	0	1	1	1	0	1	0
1	0	0	1	0	1	0	1	0
1	1	1	1	0	0	0	0	1

Creating truth table inputs

Create a table with a header row + $2^{\text{number of inputs}}$ rows below for the possible outputs:

If there are 2 inputs there are 2^2 or 4 outputs
If there are 3 inputs there are 2^3 or 8 outputs

Create the input rows in number order (0, 1, 2, 3 … *n*)
For 2 inputs, in binary: (00, 01, 10, *n*).

A	B
0	0
0	1
1	0
1	1

A	B	C
0	0	0
0	0	1
0	1	0
0	1	1
1	0	0
1	0	1
1	1	0
1	1	1

Creating the truth table outputs

Take each part of the expression and expand each part into a single column – performing one operation at a time and combining:

For example, to create the truth table for **A . B + ~B:**

1. Create A . B by using the AND operator.
2. Create ~B by using the NOT operator.
3. Finally create A . B + ~B by using the OR operator.

A	B	A . B	~B	A . B + ~B
0	0	0	1	1
0	1	0	0	0
1	0	0	1	1
1	1	1	0	1

Creating a circuit diagram

Take each part of the Boolean expression in the same manner as for the truth table.

For example, to create the circuit for **A . B + ~B:**

1. AND gate for A . B

2. NOT gate just for ~B

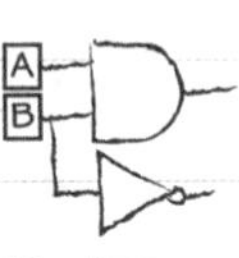

3. Combine the outputs into OR gate

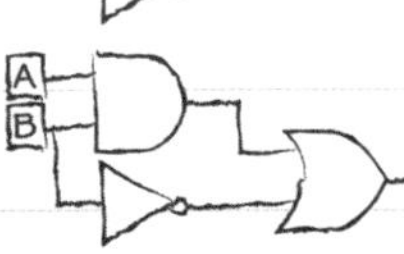

Note: It is possible to simplify this circuit.

Creating an expression from a circuit

Trace from each input to gate to the output.

Put expression at each input or output.

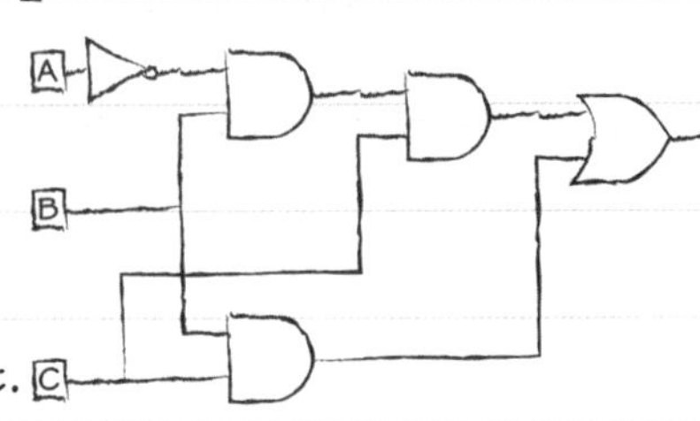

The final expression is ~A . B . C + B . C

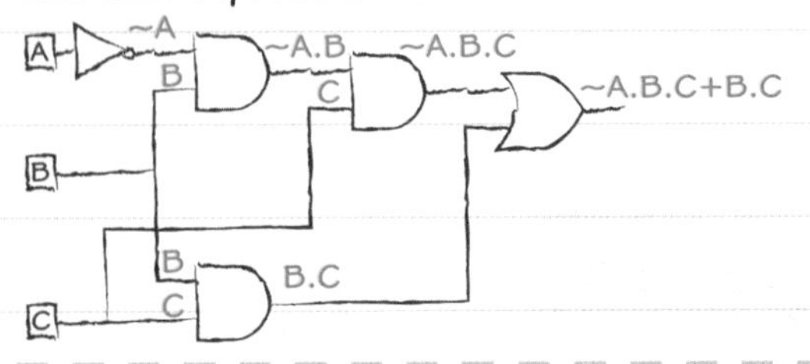

Now try this

Create the circuit and truth table for ~A . B . C + B . ~C

Simplifying expressions

When creating circuits it is often useful to simplify the circuit or change it to use the gates available. Boolean algebra and truth tables can be used to achieve this.

Basic Boolean rules

Precedence rules

1	NOT	2	AND	3	OR

Basic Boolean identities

OR (+)	AND (.)	NOT
A + 0 = A	A . 0 = 0	~~A = A
A + 1 = 1	A . 1 = A	
A + A = A	A . A = A	
A + ~A = 1	A . ~A = 0	

Two very useful identities

A + (A . B) = A

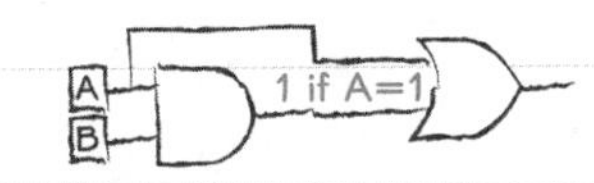

A . (A + B) = A

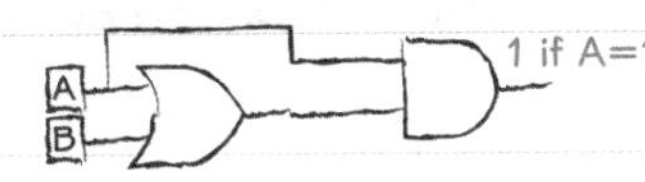

Both the same as: A

De Morgan's theorem

(NOT A) OR (NOT B) = A NAND B

$\overline{A} + \overline{B} = \overline{A . B}$

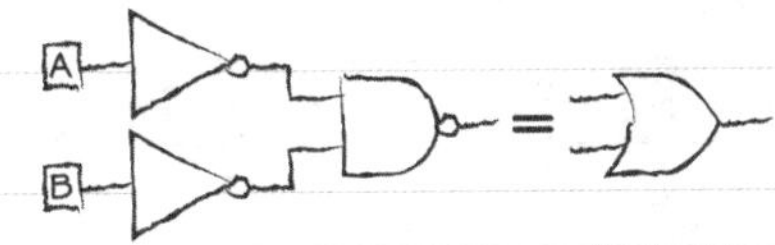

A	B	C	D	C OR D
A	B	NOT A	NOT B	A NAND B
0	0	1	1	1
0	1	1	0	1
1	0	0	1	1
1	1	0	0	0

(NOT A) AND (NOT B) = A NOR B

$\overline{A} . \overline{B} = \overline{A + B}$

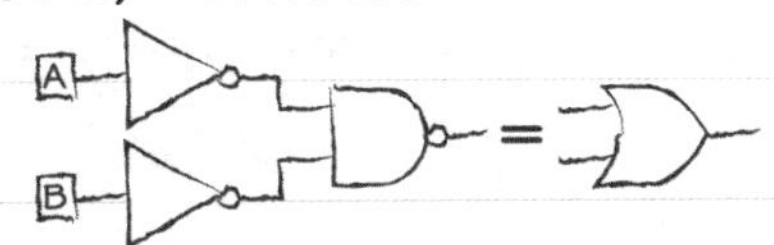

A	B	C	D	C AND D
A	B	NOT A	NOT B	A NOR B
0	0	1	1	1
0	1	1	0	0
1	0	0	1	0
1	1	0	0	0

Applying De Morgan's theorem

Process:

1. Negate whole of expression.

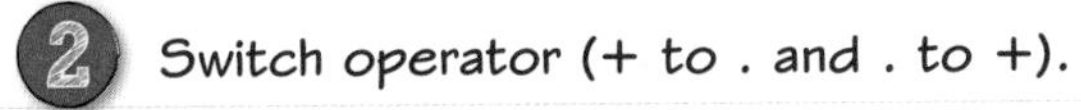
2. Switch operator (+ to . and . to +).

3. Negate each part of expression.

Steps:

A NAND B	Negate	Cancel
$\overline{A . B}$	$\overline{\overline{A . B}}$	A . B
Switch operator	**Negate parts**	**Answer**
A + B	$\overline{A} + \overline{B}$	Not A or Not B

Simplifying using algebra

Apply identities and simplification rules to simplify:

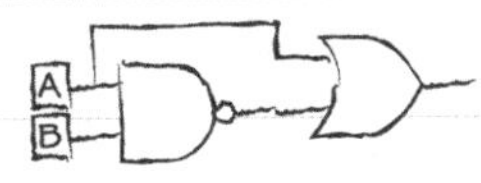

Steps:

$A + \overline{A . B}$

$A + \overline{A} + \overline{B}$ (using De Morgan's theorem)

$1 + \overline{B}$ (using A is $A + \overline{A}$)

1 (using 1 is $\overline{B} + 1$)

$A + \overline{A . B}$ simplifies to 1.

Check using truth table

Truth table for $A + \overline{A . B}$:

A	B	$\overline{A . B}$	$A + \overline{A . B}$
0	0	1	1
0	1	1	1
1	0	1	1
1	1	0	1

That is, whatever the input, the output is 1.

Now try this

Simplify NOT(NOT A OR B), i.e. simplify $\overline{\overline{A} + B}$.

Had a look ☐ Nearly there ☐ Nailed it! ☐

Boolean logic problems

Boolean logic can be used to solve real-world problems.

Breaking down a simple problem

1. Identify conditions.
2. Write the algebra.
3. Simplify, if possible.
4. Draw the circuit.
5. Confirm with truth table.

The following examples show how you can break down problems and processes into distinct steps.

F&N installs a new parking barrier that lifts only when a car approaches when the office is open.

The circuit is shown opposite.

Conditions:

A: car approaches (y or n)
B: office is open (y or n)

Algebra:

Output = A AND B, i.e. A . B

Truth table

A	B	A . B
0	0	0
0	1	0
1	0	0
1	1	1

Circuit:

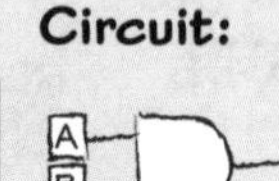

More complex problems

F&N decides the new parking barrier should lift only when a car approaches when the office is open and a valid pass is entered or a valid code entered on the numeric keypad.

Conditions:

A: car approaches B: valid pass entered
C: valid code entered D: office open

Algebra:

Output: (A AND (B OR C)) AND D
i.e. (A. (B + C)). D

Implementing the Circuit

A . (B + C)

Diagram for the inner brackets first:

(B + C)

Adding the outer expression:

A . (B + C)

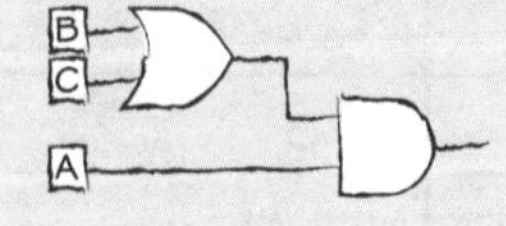

Now try this

A tablet screen will be blank if there is no recent activity, or there is recent activity but the off button is pressed.

Show the circuit.

Show the conditions, algebra, simplifying and truth table.

Flow charts

A flow chart is a flexible diagram that can represent, explain and communicate a workflow, a system, a program, a procedure or process in a logical, unambiguous and concise manner. In computing they can be used to solve problems.

Basic flow chart symbols

Start/end	Input/output	Process	Decision (y/n)	Flow
(rounded rectangle)	(parallelogram)	(rectangle)	(diamond)	(arrow)
Logical start and end	Any input or output data	What is to be done	If (x) then y else z	Directon of flow

There are other useful symbols but these are all that are necessary.

Rules for creating neat flow charts

1. Draw from top down or from left across.
2. Have a logical start and end with one flow.
3. One flow into process and one out.
4. One flow into decision, two (y and n) out.
5. Write yes/no (or e.g. T/F) on out lines.
6. Avoid crossing lines where possible.
7. Use **active verb** for each process.
8. Use a **question** for each decision.

Creating a flow chart

Case study In Mr Nicholson's smart home, if a motion sensor notices movement in front of the front door it will send a message to his smartphone. A porch light will come on if it is dark.

1. Start and end with terminators: Start End

2. Map I/O, processes and condition:

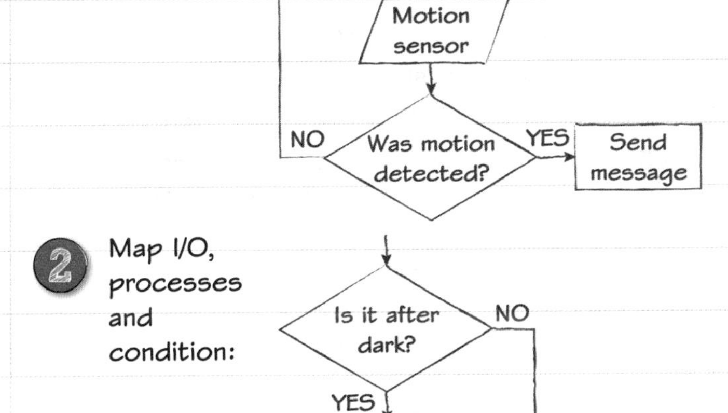

3. Combine and check:

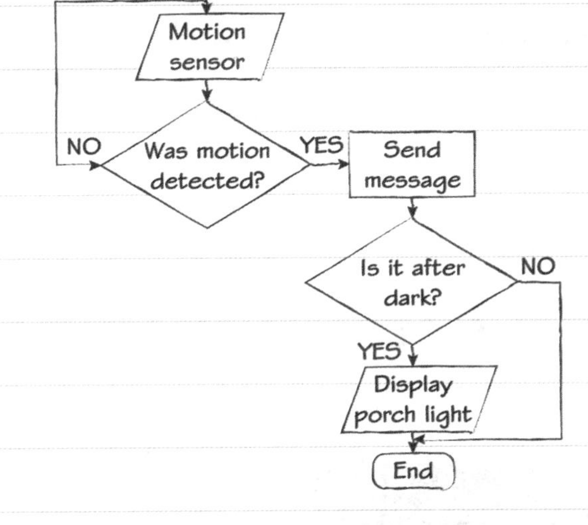

Now try this

An EAN13 barcode has a built-in validation check digit (13th digit). One algorithm for checking that the barcode has been scanned correctly is to read each number from the 1st to 13th. If the number is in an even position, multiply it by three and add to the sum of digits. If in an odd position, then just add it.

Assuming it beeps for an error and looks up the barcode and displays the product if OK, create a flow chart to show this process. Test your flow chart with a 13-digit barcode.

Had a look ☐ Nearly there ☐ Nailed it! ☐

System diagrams

Systems diagrams are a good way to start building or understanding a system and to solve problems. They are usually a fairly high level model of the system and do not require a specific methodology or symbols.

Computer system diagram

A computer system diagram can model hardware, software, processes, data flows and even ideas.

There is no one set diagram to model this range of ideas; rather the models tend to vary according to the detail required and the cirumstances. They tend to be less formal (from pictorial to systematic), but usually attempt to explain a system by showing how the inputs are transformed by processes into outputs and how the data flows between these different parts.

What is crucial is that the model explains the real world by simplifiying it.

Example system diagrams

Generic open system

Input → Process → Output

Actual system

Generic closed system

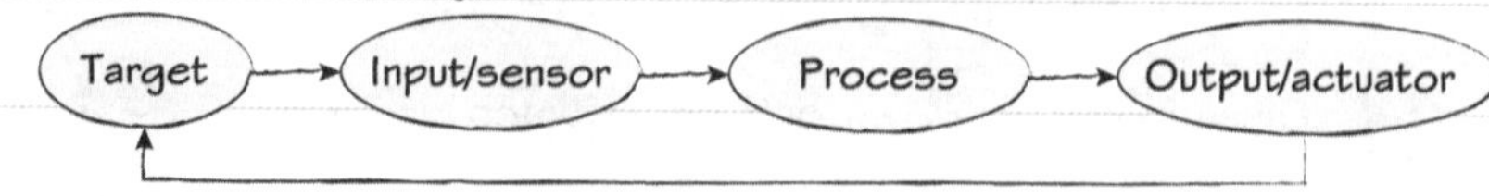

Simple automated heating system

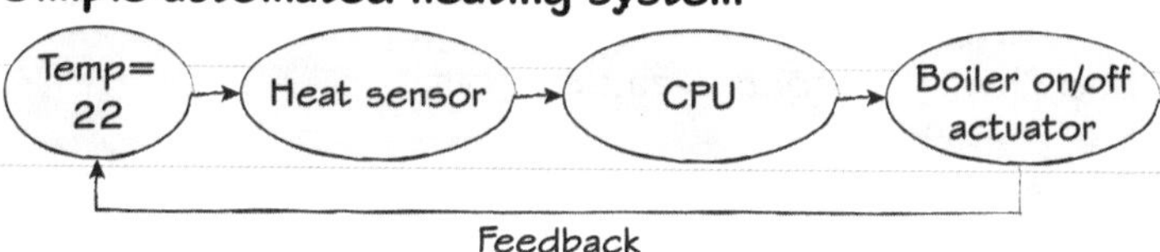

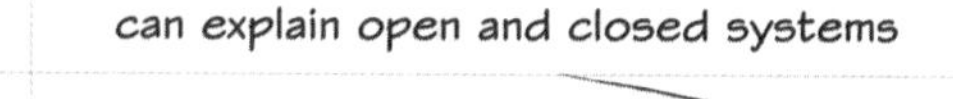

can explain open and closed systems

consider/plan/prototype higher levels of a system

System

model a system using an appropriate level of detail

understand or explain a system in terms of inputs, outputs and processes

Representational model of screen

A capacitive touch screen has the following layers:

- Protective and anti-reflective layers
- Capacitive (x,y) layers (Input)
- Display layer (Output)

Top level model of actions

The following system diagram outlines what happens when a capacitive touch screen is touched.

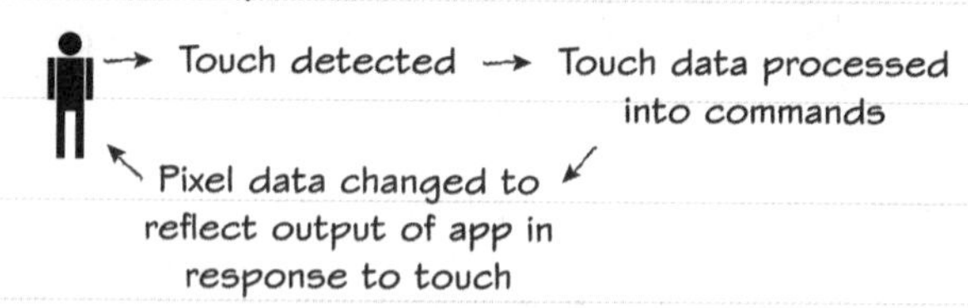

Now try this

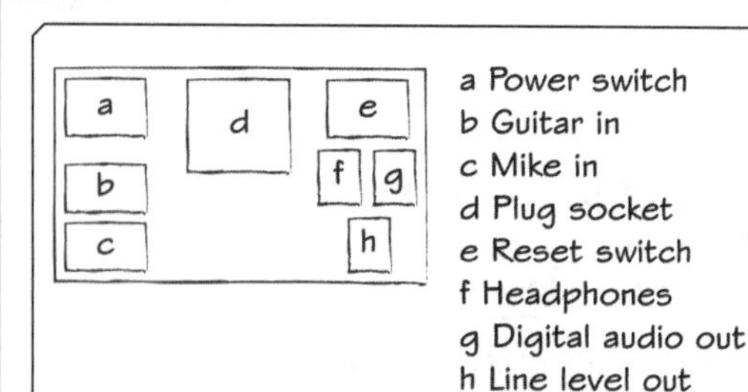

a Power switch
b Guitar in
c Mike in
d Plug socket
e Reset switch
f Headphones
g Digital audio out
h Line level out

Give an advantage of having a simple model of the rear panel of the system rather than a labelled photo:

(a) to the viewer of the model

(b) to the developer of the system.

Your Unit 2 exam

Your Unit 2 exam will be set by Pearson and could cover any of the essential content in the unit. You can revise the unit content in this Revision Guide. This skills section is designed to **revise skills** that might be needed in your exam. The section uses selected content and outcomes to provide examples of ways of applying your skills.

Question types

Command words are the key terms used in questions, for example 'identify', 'explain', 'draw'. They identify the approach you should take to answering the question.

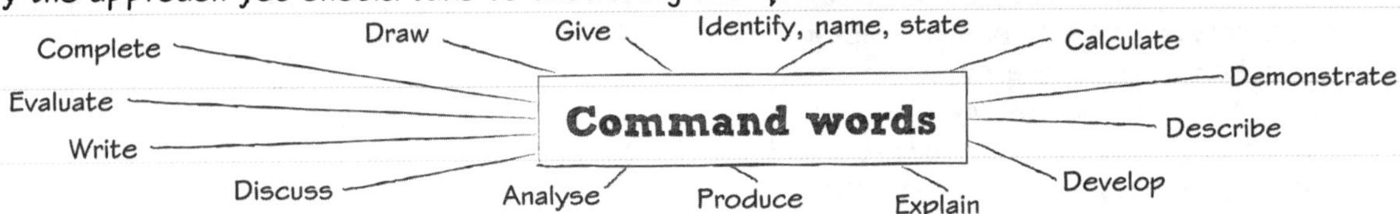

Check the Pearson website

The questions and sample response extracts in this section are provided to help you to revise content and skills. Ask your tutor or check the Pearson website for the most up-to-date **Sample Assessment Material** and **Mark Scheme** to get an indication of the structure of your actual paper and what this requires of you. The details of the actual exam may change so always make sure you are up to date.

Exam checklist

Before your exam, make sure you have:

- ✓ a black pen you like and a spare
- ✓ a pencil, sharpener and eraser for drawing diagrams
- ✓ a calculator in case you are asked to perform calculations
- ✓ double-checked the time and date of your exam.

Worked example

Jane is writing a two-player cross-platform network dice and board type game that has 32 squares to land on, with different actions possible for each square.

Explain which data structure Jane should use for the board squares. **4 marks**

This is an **explain** question. You need to show that you understand the topic and give reasons to support your opinion or argument. Make sure you give enough detail to justify your answer.

Sample response extract

The board has exactly 32 squares that don't grow or shrink. The content can probably be filled at create time and will not change. It will not require inserts or sorts. An array would be ideal as it is a static structure and it is very fast when viewing stored contents.

The size of an array is fixed. Make sure you state the properties of an array **and** explain why they are suitable for this application.

Links Look at pages 76–77 to revise the data structures.

Now try this

Explain why it is important to know whether the memory for the screen display is stored in row-major or column-major order.

This is a short-answer question. You need to give two reasons.

Revise row-major and column-major order on page 79.

Read and understand the questions

Here are some skills you could use to help you read and understand what a question is asking you to do. This will help you to take the right approach to your answer

Worked example

Sally Gaines is a successful singer–songwriter who records and produces her own music on a small computer system based around her laptop, guitar, microphones and a digital mixer and drum machine. She posts it to Youtube, MySpace and her own website where it is possible to stream and buy her tracks. She stores the files on her website in MP3 and AAC lossy formats and WAV and FLAC lossless format and the Youtube videos in MP4.

a) State what MIDI stands for. **1 mark**

Musical Instrument Digital Interface

> **State or name** questions want a short, direct answer.

b) Give a reason why a compressed video format is more suitable for displaying on the web rather than a raw uncompressed format. **2 marks**

Raw uncompressed footage would take a great deal of storage and thus would be very slow to load in an internet browser

> **Give** indicates a fairly simple answer as shown here, rather than a detailed explanation to justify the use of the MP4 format.

c) Describe two ways she could input her guitar audio. **4 marks**

1 Using microphones and an analogue to digital convertor (usually built into the laptop)

2 Using MIDI input from the guitar which would need a MIDI convertor (with ADC) at the guitar end.

> In this **describe** question, the learner has made two points for each of the two parts.

d) Identify two ways she could output her mixed audio. **2 marks**

Headphones
Speakers

> In this case only simple answers – i.e. one word each – are required.

Essential skills

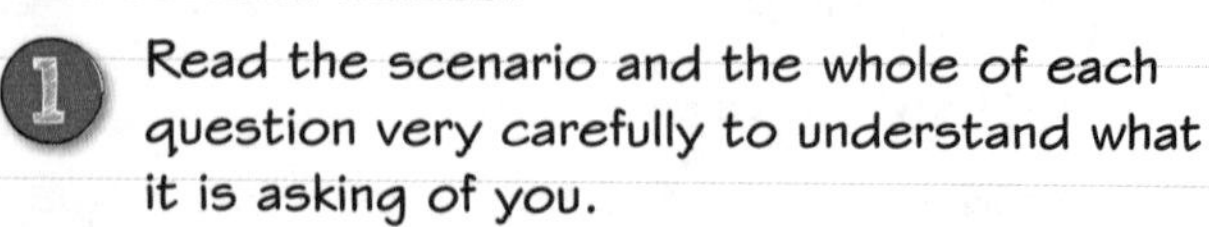

1. Read the scenario and the whole of each question very carefully to understand what it is asking of you.
2. Identify and highlight the command word which will tell you exactly what to do and how to do it.
3. Identify the topic that you are being tested on.
4. Look at the marks available for the question to confirm the level of detail required.

Now try this

Analyse the implications of storing music in lossy formats such as MP3 and AAC rather than in a lossless format such as FLAC (free lossless audio codec) or an uncompressed WAV format.

> When responding to this **analyse** question, identify the elements of the issue, and the relevant topic and discuss pros, cons and issues surrounding these.

> It is important to identify that the topic is compression. Then if you are not sure about FLAC, WAV, AAC use the following techniques:
>
> 1 Discuss the implications of :
> - compressed versus non-compressed
> - lossy versus lossless.
>
> 2 Adapt ideas from another relevant topic such as graphics. The topic is similar and the implications are mostly the same.

Links Revise compression on page 85.

Short-answer questions

With short-answer questions, try to answer as quickly and concisely as possible.

Worked example

Fletcher and Nicholson is building an e-commerce site to sell their designer dresses. This will contain photos of models wearing the dresses and stylised illustrations of the dresses with transparent colours and text over the lines of the garment. Its website designer is storing some of the images as PNG and some as JPEG.

Identify which format is lossy compressed. **1 mark**

Questions that ask you to **state** or **identify** or **give** an answer only require a short, straightforward answer. Do not over-elaborate, nor repeat the question in the answer.

Sample response extract

The JPEG format is lossy.

This question requires one simple statement.

Worked example

Explain which of these two file types you would choose for storing the photographs of models wearing the designer dresses and which the complex illustrations on the website. **4 marks**

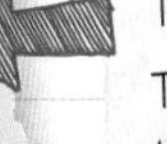

This **explain** question has two parts. This type of explanation question typically requires you to give an answer to each part and then expand the answer.

Sample response extract

The photographs will be best stored in JPEG format. This will allow a high compression rate while maintaining sufficient image quality for a small-sized image.

The illustration should be stored as a PNG as this supports transparency and layers, albeit with less compression. A pure illustration (vector) format may not be compatible with the web browser being used.

Use technical vocabulary and explanations wherever possible, but make sure the explanation is clear.

Worked example

Give two other factors the web designer must take into account when selecting image formats for the web. **2 marks**

This **give** question asks for two factors – only two statements are required, even if there are more possible answers.

Sample response extract

1 Most browsers will only display JPEG, PNG or GIF files, thus these are the most sensible file formats to use.

2 JPEG files are known sometimes to contain viruses and thus some systems with anti-virus software will automatically block them.

Do not give more than two answers nor over-elaborate the answer. Try to use different answers from those for previous questions, however.

Now try this

State one advantage of storing a complex image of a painting as a PNG and one of storing it as a JPEG.

Revise image representation on page 75 and compression on page 85.

Had a look ☐ Nearly there ☐ Nailed it! ☐

Performing calculations

You may need to show that you can perform calculations.

Worked example

Add together the following unsigned binary integers:

```
0100 1000
1010 1000
---------
1111 0000
   1       (carries)
```

Carry out the following subtraction:

```
0112       (borrows)
1000 1100
0011 1100
---------
0101 0000
```

2 marks

Remember to show your workings. Even if your final answer is incorrect, you may get credit for your method. In the case of this type of binary arithmetic this will mean you show the carries.

In most calculation problems it is useful to do a double check. Convert the binary numbers to denary and do the calculation. In the addition example: 72 + 168 = 240. In the subtraction example: 140 – 60 = 80. The double check will confirm you have worked out the calculation correctly.

Worked example

Text can be encrypted using a Caesar cipher. Given a plain text letter 'J' and a binary encryption key of 0000 1100 calculate the encrypted text. 4 marks

Sample response extract

J is the 10th letter of the alphabet.
0000 1100 in binary is 12 in denary.
10 + 12 = 22
V is the 22nd letter of the alphabet.
The encrypted text is V.

In this case the workings are a little more involved so again it is important to spell out each stage.

Spell out the final answer clearly at the end.

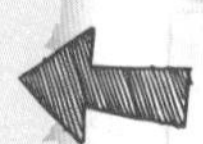

An alternative calculation could be: J is 74 in ASCII, 74 + 12 = 86, 86 in ASCII is V.

Worked example

Calculate: $\begin{bmatrix} 2 & 3 \end{bmatrix} * \begin{bmatrix} 15 & 25 & 15 \\ 4 & 5 & 4 \end{bmatrix}$ 3 marks

Sample response extract

$$= \begin{bmatrix} 15 * 2 & 25 * 2 & 15 * 2 \\ +4 * 3 & +5 * 3 & +4 * 3 \end{bmatrix}$$

$$= \begin{bmatrix} 42 & 65 & 42 \end{bmatrix}$$

The final answer is spelled out clearly.

Each of the stages is spelled out in detail. Even if you make a mistake in your calculations you will gain some marks.

Now try this

A London-based cryptography company uses a simple Caesar code on its website to demonstrate how cryptography works. It displays the cipher HEZK, stating that the key is 0000 0110 and asks students to calculate the plaintext.

Calculate the plaintext.

1. Calculate the offset.
2. Write out the offset cipher alphabet underneath the plaintext alphabet.
3. Read the original word by matching letters to the cipher letters by position.

Drawing diagrams

You may be asked to complete a diagram or draw one from scratch.

Worked example

Look at the partially completed logic diagram for a half adder. Add the correct Boolean gate symbols inside the empty rectangles below. Connect the inputs of the gates to implement the following:

- Inputs x and y are each a binary digit.
- Outputs s and c are given by the truth table below:

4 marks

x	y	s	c
0	0	0	0
0	1	1	0
1	0	1	0
1	1	0	1

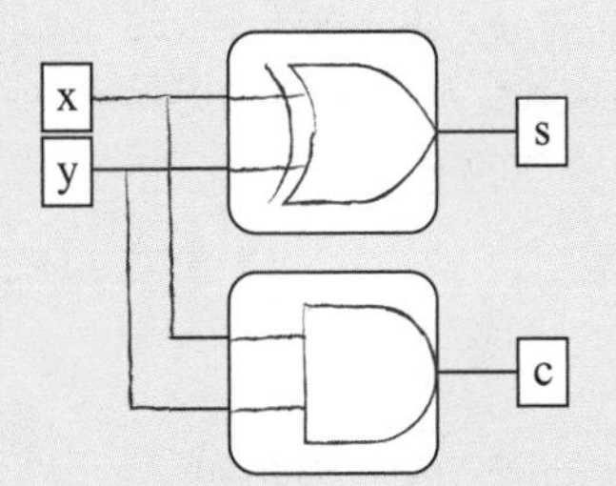

Use a ruler to draw lines.

Use a template for symbols if you have one.

Use a pencil to draft the diagram (or draw in rough elsewhere) and go over the diagram with a black pen.

Circuit lines should where possible be drawn straight. It is clear from the truth table that both gates have the same two inputs. Show the lines branching from each other for neatness.

Worked example

Burwick Estates uses an automated computer system to monitor and record all vehicles entering and leaving its gated communities.

Complete the diagram by adding in the missing words at positions A, B, C, D, E. 5 marks

This question tests your knowledge of concepts and terminology (in this case automated data processing hardware and software). Use appropriate terms in each case.

Start
A Motion sensor
Motion detected?
NO
YES
B CCTV
video
Numberplate image grabbed
C image
D OCR performed on numberplate
E numberplate characters
ANPR database
Match found?
NO
numberplate characters
YES
vehicle details
Create record using details and time and direction
Entry record
Vehicle entry records
End

Always fill in all the missing gaps even if you are not sure.

Now try this

When a proximity sensor senses there is a person in front of the lift it turns on a timer and illuminates the up and down buttons for five seconds, then turns them off and resets the timer.

Draw this as a complete flow chart.

Had a look ☐ Nearly there ☐ Nailed it! ☐

Longer-answer questions

Some questions want longer, more detailed answers. They require a related but slightly different approach.

Worked example

Fletcher and Nicholson is a designer fashion label who uses e-commerce to sell its products, maintain e-commerce databases containing all of its product images, videos, product descriptions and the back-office information such as stock, orders and customer account information.

Explain the need to back up and archive its data and the procedures required to do this. **8 marks**

Read each question very carefully. Longer-answer questions need special care. There are actually four separate parts to this question, to **explain**:

1 need for backup
2 need for archiving (a different thing)
3 procedure for backing up
4 procedure for archiving.

Sample response extract

Fletcher and Nicholson will need to backup its data so that it can be restored if the data is lost or corrupted, through accidental mishap such as a hard disk crash or a malicious act such as sabotage or a virus. If data cannot be restored it could be catastrophic to the firm's trading.

Use technical vocabulary such as corrupted, virus, restored, offline, etc.

Data is archived to keep copies of non-live data (such as previous years' products or accounting data) available for future use. This frees up space on the running or live system whilst maintaining availability if required.

Examples help to reinforce an explanation. Ensure they are relevant and accurate, however.

The procedure for backing up will include a schedule for backing up incremental data such as new products or customers or orders added at least daily and for doing a full backup of all data periodically (perhaps weekly). The data will be backed up to a separate storage medium, with one full copy to be held off site on a removable disk or secure cloud storage.

Try to make about eight points in total spread among four separate parts.

Data are archived to a separate, probably slower and cheaper, storage location, such as an offline disk or tape or DVDR. This can be done periodically but less often, perhaps at a quarter end or year end.

Use a coherent and logical argument which is related back to the case.

Now try this

F.IT, the IT house that manages Fletcher and Nicholson's systems has suggested that the company use a five disk RAID 5 system to complement its backup strategy.

Analyse this use of a RAID 5 system.

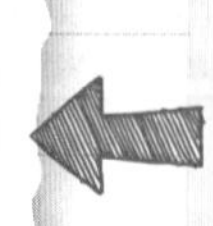

A possible approachis to explain how a RAID 5 system works. Examine the advantages this gives. Examine any problems or relative disadvantages of this system. Come to a balanced conclusion.

Revise RAID on page 55 and error correction on page 87.

'Discuss' questions

You may be asked to discuss a specific topic area or choice. You need to do more than list a number of issues – try to link your points together with a solid chain of reasoning using examples relevant to the case identified.

Worked example

A multi-floor shopping mall intends to add custom-built interactive information kiosks at strategic points in the centre. Discuss the type of user interface it should use. **4 marks**

Sample response extract

The purpose of an interactive information kiosk in a shopping centre is to provide shoppers with information about the centre, and possibly to provide directions and advice. The type of user interface chosen will have to take into account the the diverse range of users, the requirement for system security, and the need for a very fast response in order to answer queries quickly and be compatible with the hardware used for the kiosk.

A command line interface (CLI) would not be at all appropriate as it requires skill and experience to use and potentially exposes the system to accidental error or deliberate hacking. A graphical user interface (GUI) could be considered as it can be easy to use, but a forms-based interface would be the most likely choice as it involves little or no prior experience or skill and can deal with all the required functionality in a very easy to use and secure manner.

A forms UI is fast and easy for the shopper to input choices, such as 'Directions to nearest WC' or 'Jewellers' or 'Coffee' using items such as menu buttons and allows text-based entry in search boxes.

A forms-based interface reduces the possibility of error and of the shoppers' accessing unauthorised parts of the system as it restricts the choices that can be made, which could be a potential problem when using a GUI.

The simplicity of the forms interface means it can be very consistent and efficient to process and a very fast response, thus minimising queues at the kiosk. A GUI may allow further functionality such as, for example, browsing the internet, but this could cause hogging of the kiosk and indeed potential for security breaches.

Finally, a forms-based interface is also fully compatible with a touchscreen which is ideal for use in information kiosks.

To answer this question, start with an introduction that includes a very brief summary of, or restatement of the question and an indication of the range of ideas that you will **discuss**.
This may be in the form of a list of the technical concepts you will discuss or, as here, a list of the factors that will later be matched to the technical issues that will have to be addressed.

Follow through your introduction with a number of points developing your discussion in more detail, using relevant technical terms wherever possible.

You must relate the technical details to the specific case/ content that you are discussing, in this case an information kiosk for a shopping centre. Use concepts such as shopper, shop, café, WC and short examples where possible to illustrate the point you are making.

Now try this

Immersive Source is planning to introduce computer systems to help toddlers with behavioural issues in nurseries.

Discuss the factors it should consider when specifying the hardware for these systems.

Had a look ☐ Nearly there ☐ Nailed it! ☐

'Evaluate' questions

Evaluate questions require you to weigh how effective, correct or worthwhile a decision or judgement is.

Worked example

Fruitful Vegan Restaurant Chain is planning a large expansion across the UK under the direction of new Commercial Director, Bill Fence. It has a single computer system in each branch which runs the whole branch operation. The system uses open source software for all tasks, adapted by a local software house for the company's specific needs, running on a version of the open source BSD operating system. Although this system works effectively, Bill has decided he wants to move to the most popular, proprietary operating system running the standard office software he has always used and that he feels most new recruits will know and understand.

Evaluate Bill Fence's decision. **6 marks**

Sample response extract

Bill Fence's decision to change the operating system and software from an existing working open source system to a proprietary system has a number of implications for Fruitful regarding the compatibility of current hardware, current software, training needs of existing as well as new staff, costs of implementation and handover and the lifetime cost of the new system, including licensing, support costs, etc.

It is useful to have an introduction stating the basis of your argument and the main factors you will weigh.

On the positive side the use of a proprietary system will mean that many new staff will have some familiarity with the basic file operations of the system and may have some experience with the office software already. With a large expansion planned this could be very beneficial. On the other hand, current staff are used to working with the current system.

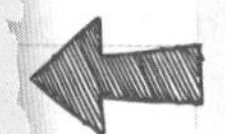

You need to consider all sides of an argument. A scenario is unlikely to be one-sided.

Use your technical knowledge of the area and combine it with details of the specific case to make the points towards your argument.

One of the major issues for Fruitful will be compatibility of their current hardware with the new OS. EPOS tills, contactless card systems, etc. may need to be adapted or indeed changed.

Ideally make a point and then explain it, perhaps using a concise example.

Bill Fence's decision is, on balance, a risky one for Fruitful. It will be changing from an existing, effective system to a new system that will need some development, although it is based on a well-known operating system and software. There will be training needs, development needs and extra costs at each stage of the implementation, handover and during the lifetime of the product. A full feasibility study may be the best option at this stage.

When evaluating a decision it is important to come to a conclusion about the appropriateness of that decision or perhaps make a recommendation. Do note that even when recommending it is best to use academic language rather than say 'I recommend...'

Now try this

Each student at the John Snow School currently has to carry a photo ID card which features a magnetic strip carrying their ID. It is swiped at the entrance to the school and class to register them. It is proposed to replace these with new ID cards that contain RFID chips to automate the class registration system.

Evaluate this decision.

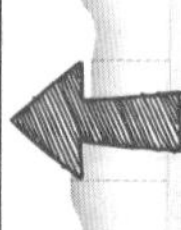

You could explain the basic operation and consider the advantages and disadvantages. As it is an evaluate question, finish with a definite recommendation.

Costs and timescales

A computing project needs to be assessed to ensure it will work as intended. The project budget, milestones, deadlines and interim reviews are all used to determine a project's viability and success.

Project viability

Assessing whether a project is viable involves deciding if it can be achieved within the budget and time available.

The business plan sets out the benefits to the organisation and the feasibility of the project.

Key factors to consider

- Does the project support the **business plan**?
- Can the project be completed within the allocated **time**?
- Can the project be completed within **budget**?

Project budget

The **project budget** is the estimated sum of money required to complete a project. The project manager can measure whether the project is keeping within budget by comparing it against the actual costs.

As you can see from the chart, the actual costs are higher than the budget allocated to the project. This puts the project at risk of not being completed within budget which would mean the project was not viable. Some projects have a contingency fund to cover unexpected costs.

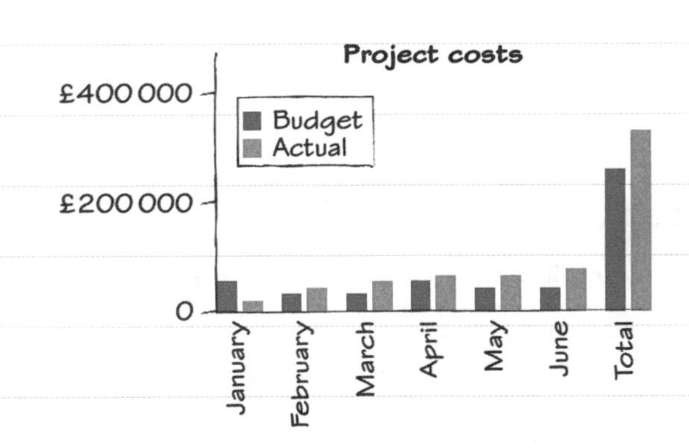

Milestones

Milestones are important events or stages in the project life cycle, such as the end of software design stage, and are a part of the project plan. At the end of the software design stage the project manager will look at the plan to see if all of the software designs have been completed by the required date (milestone). This confirms if the project is on track and can be completed within the allocated time.

Have a look at page 114–115 for examples of how to use milestones.

Deadlines and interim reviews

- A project **deadline** is a set date by which a project task should be completed. Meeting deadlines is important to project success. If a task is not achieved by the deadline, action may be required.
- **Interim reviews** happen at set times throughout the project. They allow the project manager to assess progress and check if the project goals and objectives are being achieved.

Now try this

The project manager has reviewed the project at the milestone date for user requirement. The project was not completed by the required deadline. The interim review shows that the project meets the original business aims and requirements.

What does this mean for the project?

Think about the **key factors** to consider when monitoring projects:
- business plan
- deadline
- budget.

Had a look ☐ Nearly there ☐ Nailed it! ☐

Quality and deliverables

The success of a computing project depends in part on quality management, which defines how the project achieves the outcomes – the deliverables – agreed with the client. You will need to revise how quality standards are applied, customer requirements and the product breakdown structure.

Quality standards

Quality assurance methods ensure that each stage of the project is achieved. The two best recognised **quality standards** are:

ISO/IEC 25010:2011

The product quality model provides a benchmark for software in **eight** key areas:

1. **portability** so that the software can be installed onto the required platform
2. **functional** suitability so that the software delivers the correct result
3. **performance** so that it will process the data as required
4. **compatible** with hardware and other software
5. **usability** to support the user's needs
6. **maintainability** so the software can be modified in the future
7. allowance for a **secure** platform
8. **reliability** to ensure the software is fault free under normal use.

World Wide Web Consortium (W3C®)

This provides four guidelines for website design and functionality to ensure the content is accessible:

1. **perceivable** – relates to tools and functions used to make it easier for the user to hear and see the content
2. **operable** – accessible at all levels, e.g. keyboard or touchscreen
3. **understandable** – accessible and readable content
4. **robust** – can be used on any current and future system.

Customer requirements

Customer satisfaction is an essential requirement of all projects and includes:

- functional requirements – **what** is required for a system to operate
- non-functional requirements – **how** the operation of the system is assessed.

For each functional and non-functional requirement to be achieved **SMART** targets are required to ensure customer satisfaction.

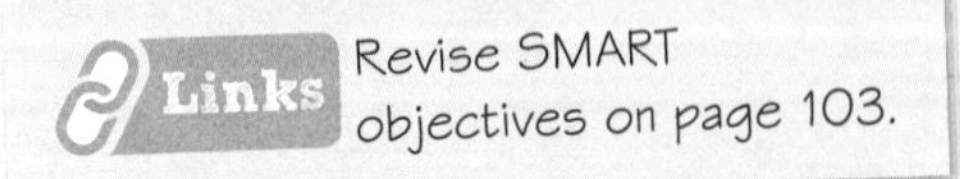
Links Revise SMART objectives on page 103.

Product breakdown structure (PBS)

A PBS is a visual map that shows the relationship between components and activities.

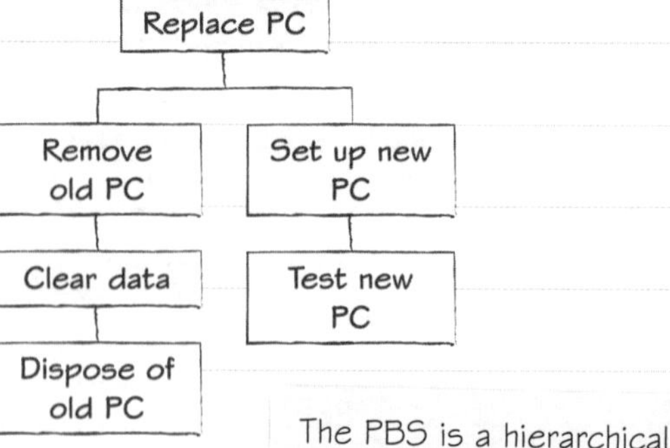

The PBS is a hierarchical list of the product and its components.

Now try this

Identify **two** tools or functions that can be used to make a website easier for a user to hear and see the content.

Think about how to make websites more 'perceivable' to visually impaired users or users with hearing impairments.

SMART objectives

A computing project needs to have SMART objectives so stakeholders can clearly understand what's required from the start. SMART objectives are identified after the project manager has defined the project success criteria.

SMART objectives

Specific
Are you clear about what you want to achieve?
Who will be responsible for achieving the target?
When you are going to achieve it?
How you are going to achieve it?
Where you are going to achieve the target?
Example: 'I will back up my coursework at home to cloud storage every Friday evening.'

Measurable
Can the target be measured?
Example: 'I will create an 8-page website by Friday evening.'

Achievable
Can the target actually be achieved?
Can the target be achieved with the resources available?
Does the project have clearly defined steps?
Example: 'I will achieve a game development qualification next year and apply for jobs towards the end of my course.'

Realistic
Is the target realistic?
Is it meaningful?
Is it too hard to achieve?
Example: 'I am going to spend every Monday and Wednesday evening developing a page for the interactive website.'

Time bound
Is there a timescale for the objective?
Is it realistic?
Is it specific and clear?
Example: 'I will create a computer game by 5 February 20--.'

Now try this

Sage will attend a game programming class at the local college every Thursday night 6–8pm and take the exam on 5/2/17 to improve his computer games development skills and enable him to apply for game developer jobs.

Create **SMART** targets for this project. For each target identify **one measure** that shows that the target has been achieved.

Specific – what does Sage want to achieve?
Measurable – must it happen by a certain time?
Achievable – is it clear how it will happen?
Realistic – is the goal realistic?
Time bound – when should it happen by?

Had a look ☐ Nearly there ☐ Nailed it! ☐

Project risks (1)

All projects involve risks. Risks need to be identified at the start of a project. You will need to develop a risk management strategy for your project using the risk management cycle below. On this page, you will revise the types of risk and how to assess the severity of a risk.

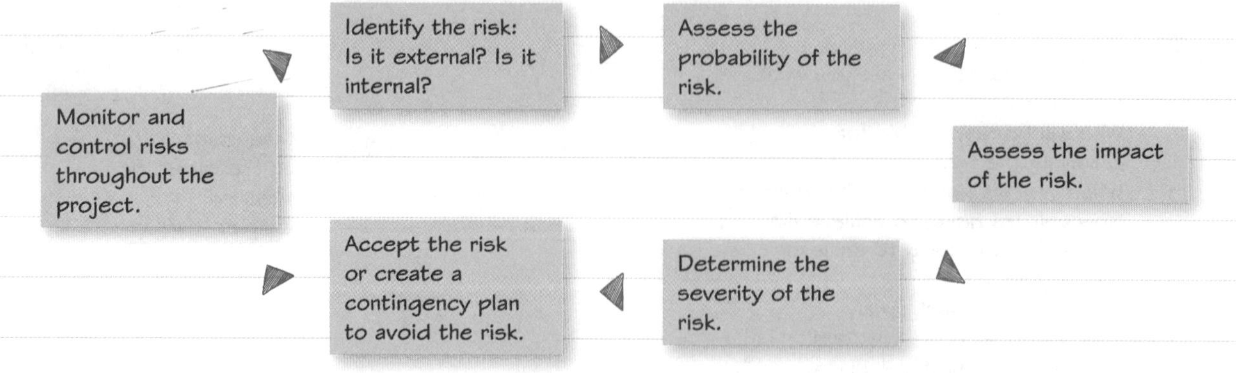

External risks	Internal risks
Malware attacks through email messages, Trojan horses, phishing, hackers Firewalls, antivirus software and security patches not updated	Staff error Laptop theft Data theft by disgruntled staff Password types/sharing, policies not followed Staff use of computer system not monitored

Three-point scale for impact and probability

Probability is the likelihood of a risk occurring in the project. The three-point scale for probability is categorised as high/medium/low. Probability is also referred to as a percentage.

Probability of risk occurring		Impact on project (scale)
Scale	Likelihood	
Low = 1	1%–33%	Minimal impact – easily managed (= 1)
Medium = 2	34%–67%	Significant impact if not managed (= 2)
High = 3	68%–99%	Termination of project (= 3)

Impact multiplied by probability

Once the probability of a risk has been assessed, its impact – the extent to which it may cause disruption to the project – can be measured using the impact multiplied by probability formula:

risk = probability (of risk occurring) × loss/impact (connected to the loss/impact occurring)

For example:

low probability (1) × significant impact (2) = 2
medium probability (2) × significant impact (2) = 4
high probability (3) × minimal impact (1) = 3

Identifying the probability of a risk will not lessen it but it helps the project manager to manage the risk.

Links The outcome is presented as a risk matrix – see page 117.

Now try this

You are upgrading a computer system at a local charity office.
(a) Identify one external risk.
(b) Identify one internal risk.
For each risk describe its probability.

One internal risk is that a member of staff deletes all of the files: low probability 10%.

Project risks (2)

Once a risk to the project has been identified, you will need to either accept the risk, avoid the risk, or create a contingency plan to reduce the impact of the risk.

Types of impact – examples

- Project over budget
- Poor communication between the members of the project team
- Project planning did not take account of all of the requirements
- Project running over the time allowance
- Insufficient resources to carry out the project successfully
- Natural disaster such as a fire or flood

Severity

A risk might be low, but its impact on the project should it occur may be severe. The severity of the risk is categorised as:

Severity	Example
Catastrophic	Trojan horse that made irreparable damage to the hard drive
Critical	Supplier going bankrupt
Marginal	One member of staff sick
Negligible	Room decorated the wrong colour

Planning

During the project planning, risks need to be identified and decisions taken on how to deal with them. It depends on the level of the risk whether plans are put in place to mitigate it. For example, if the impact is likely to be low, then the risk may either be accepted or avoided. If the impact is likely to be high, then a contingency plan will be required.

Contingency plan

A contingency plan identifies situations outside the organisation's control and sets out possible ways to accept, avoid or respond to the risk.

The plan should consider:

- how to solve the problem or how the problem was solved in past projects
- how you are going to deal with the risk
- how to prioritise the risk.

Monitoring and controlling risk

Risks are monitored throughout the project as the level of impact may change and action will need to be taken. The contingency plan should be updated at regular intervals as new risks may need to be planned for.

This will allow for the project to solve the risk quicker as it identifies:

- the risk
- the severity of the risk
- action to resolve the risk
- who is responsible for resolving the risk.

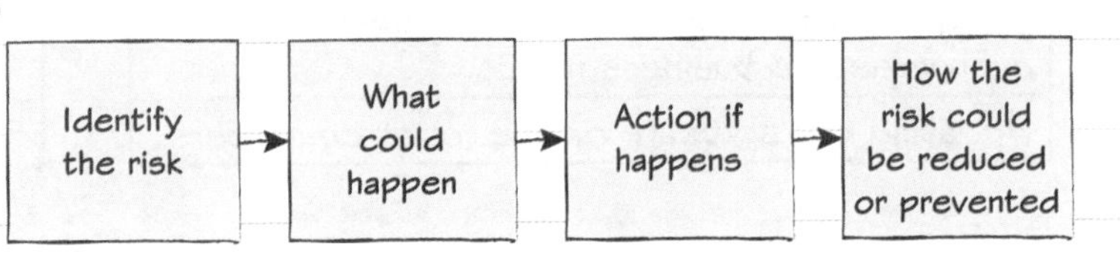

Handling and dealing with risks

Now try this

You are upgrading a computer system at a local charity office.

Identify **one** possible risk. Describe its probability, impact and severity, and devise a contingency plan.

Fire damage is an example of a risk that has **low probability** but **high impact** and **high severity**. A contingency plan could involve data backup, or fire safety.

Links Look at project risks on page 104.

Had a look ☐ Nearly there ☐ Nailed it! ☐

Project benefits

On this page, you will revise the main benefits of a computing project for the organisation and its stakeholders and how to measure a project's success.

Business benefits

Remember – if there are no benefits to the organisation, then the project does not have a business case.

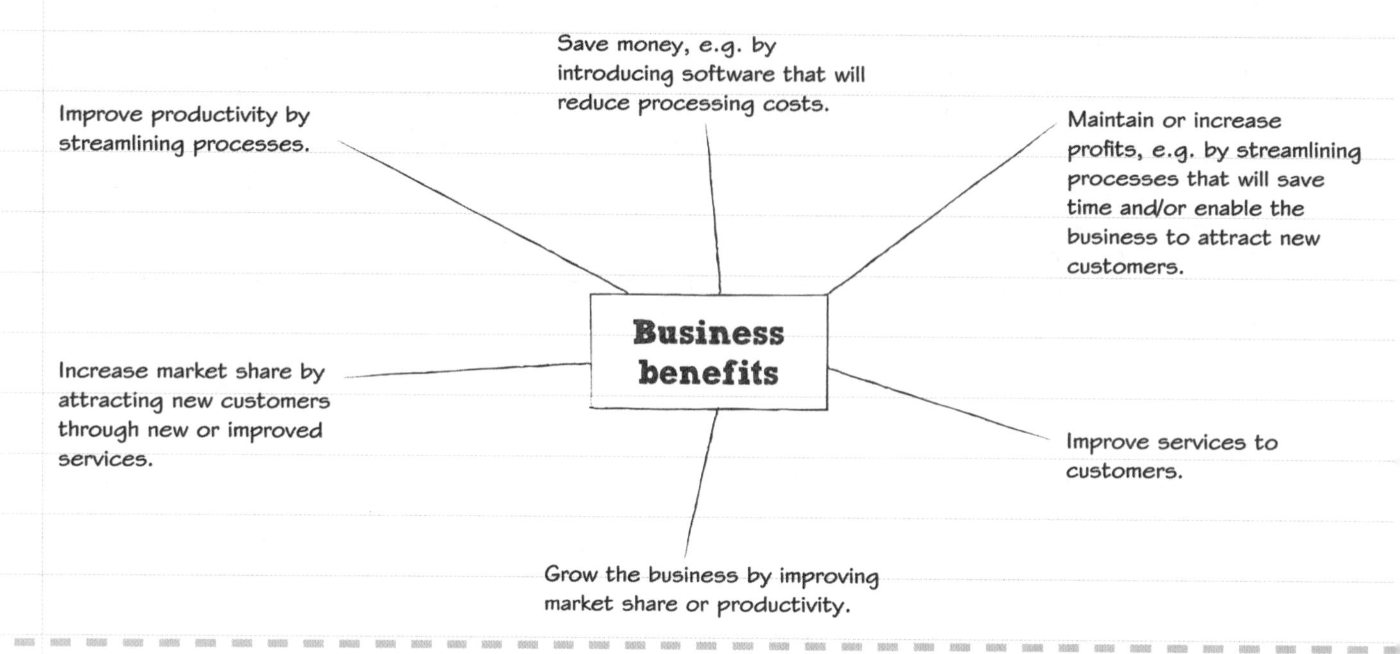

Return on investment

When an organisation invests in a computing project, it expects to benefit from its investment, which will allow it to justify the project.

Examples of business benefit	Expected return on investment
Improved customer data input screens customised to business needs	Improved customer service
Updating the software on the robot computers	Reduced processing costs

How do you measure success?

- ✓ The benefit should be measured at the end of each stage of the project as well as after the implementation stage. Measure the entire system.
- ✓ Does the system deliver its intended benefits?
- ✓ Record what went well and what could improve the next project.
- ✓ Monitor the users to ensure that the benefits have been achieved and what further action is required.

Now try this

One benefit to an organisation and its customers of implementing an online shop is that goods are available 24/7.

(a) Identify two other benefits to the organisation and customers.

(b) Identify two expected returns on investment of the implementation.

(c) How would you measure if the outcome was a success?

Think about the benefits to the owner, organisation and the customers.

What do you think the returns on investment would be to the owner and customer?

First identify an outcome and then how it could be measured.

Project life cycle

The project life cycle identifies every stage of a project from the initial idea through to handover of the product and to evaluation of the project's success. You need to revise every aspect of the project life cycle.

1 Concept and start-up

Every project starts with an idea or a concept. The concept is then evaluated in terms of its benefits to the business. At this stage, the **project mandate**, which asks important questions about the project, is produced, the clients are asked about their requirements and the feasibility of the project is assessed to determine if it is viable.

The project mandate

- What is the project's purpose?
- What is its scope? What will it cover?
- What are the client requirements?
- Is there sufficient finance?
- What is the timeframe?
- Is there anything that might prevent the project happening?

2 Define the project

Once the mandate has been agreed, the project can be defined. This involves:

- setting up the project team
- creating the Project Initiation Document (PID).

Revise the Project Initiation Document on pages 112–114.

3 Plan the project

At the planning stage:

- Timescales and key milestones are agreed.
- Costs are estimated and a budget is agreed.
- Quality management processes to monitor production of the product are identified.
- Risk management and controls are put in place to anticipate and deal with risks.

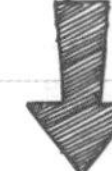

4 Launch and execute the project

During this stage developers carry out the plan and develop the product or service. The project manager will monitor all the activities closely, checking progress using a variety of project management tools such a 33 Project Checkpoint Reports.

Revise how to complete a checkpoint report on page 121.

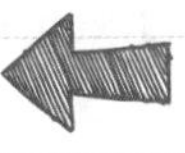

5 Closure of project

After the product has been developed it is handed over to the client, who will test the product – user acceptance testing – to ensure it meets their requirements. The project team is then disbanded.

6 Evaluate the project

The project is evaluated against success criteria. This will highlight areas that could be repeated in other projects and aspects that need changing.

Now try this

What are your project stages?

Write down every step or action since you got out of bed this morning to when you arrived at school.

Can you put them into the project stages, as above?

At the conception and start-up stage you thought about how to get out of bed and then got out of bed.

What happened next?

What was the project mandate?

Can you define the project?

What was your plan?

How did you launch and execute the project?

What time did you close the project?

Had a look ☐ Nearly there ☐ Nailed it! ☐

Professionalism

At work, you will be expected to behave in a professional and ethical manner. You will need to revise how the codes of conduct of professional bodies affect the way a project is planned and managed. On this page, you will also revise how to communicate project activities in a professional way.

Codes of conduct

Codes of conduct have been developed by professional bodies to ensure that their members meet high ethical and professional standards in their working life. The main professional bodies for project planning and management are:

- Association for Project Management (APM)
- British Computer Society (BCS)
- Project Management Institute (PMI).

Characteristics of a professional

As a project manager, you will need to:

- be honest
- respect your clients and colleagues
- behave ethically
- behave with fairness
- carry out your role and responsibilities to the highest standards.

Communicating project planning and management activities

As a project manager, you will need to be able to communicate clearly and effectively how you intend to plan and manage the activities within your computing project.

When communicating and presenting information, the project manager needs to:

- ensure the content and method of communication is appropriate for the target audience depending on the communication requirement, e.g. email, report, newsletter.
- clearly convey what you mean, e.g. an email should be short and to the point, a report should have a detailed account of project progress, the newsletter can summarise the project progress with use of images and bullet lists.
- use the right tone in project documentation so that the meaning is clear and professional.
- use suitable graphics to help the audience understand what you are saying, e.g. the finance report can be supported by graphs to visually convey the differences between project expenditure and project budget.
- use fluent English and appropriate technical language for every type of communication.

Now try this

The finance manager has asked for a monthly budget report.
What would be the appropriate information to send to the finance manager.
How would you ensure that the monthly budget report is presented professionally?

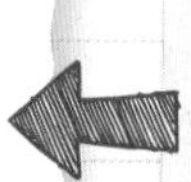

You should consider the method of communication first.

The business case

Before a computing project can go ahead, a business case must be made for it. On this page, you will revise how a business case is put together.

Purpose of project

The first part of the business case sets out:

- why the project is required
- the **options** to be considered and all of the **positive** and **negative** effects of implementing the project considered.

Business benefits

This section evaluates the benefits to the business of implementing the project.

Project manager will create a cost–benefit analysis at a later stage.

Graphs and charts can be used to show the financial benefits.

Business case for project

1 Reasons for project
2 Options
3 Expected business benefits
4 Timescale and major milestones
5 Budget available
6 Major risks

Timescale

This section identifies the time lines and major milestones of the project.

The project manager will use a Gantt chart to communicate the tasks and record them on a timeline.

Examples of how to create a Gantt chart are on page 115.

Budget

This section focuses on the budget available, cost–benefit analysis and forecast. The start-up costs, assets and cash that are needed will be calculated.

Major risks

Major risks need to be identified at the start of the project so that the stakeholders have enough information to proceed with the project. This will inform the risk assessment which will be created later in the project.

Links

For more on risk assessment, see pages 104 and 105.

Now try this

Financial benefit is one benefit set out in the business case.

Identify two other benefits.

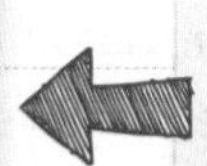

Think about what would benefit an organisation's:

- customers
- users
- finance
- legal requirements.

Had a look ☐ Nearly there ☐ Nailed it! ☐

Stakeholders

A stakeholder is anyone who has an interest in the project or who is responsible for any of the project's activities. A successful project will take account of all stakeholder's needs throughout the life of the project. On this page, you will revise the responsibilities of the key stakeholders.

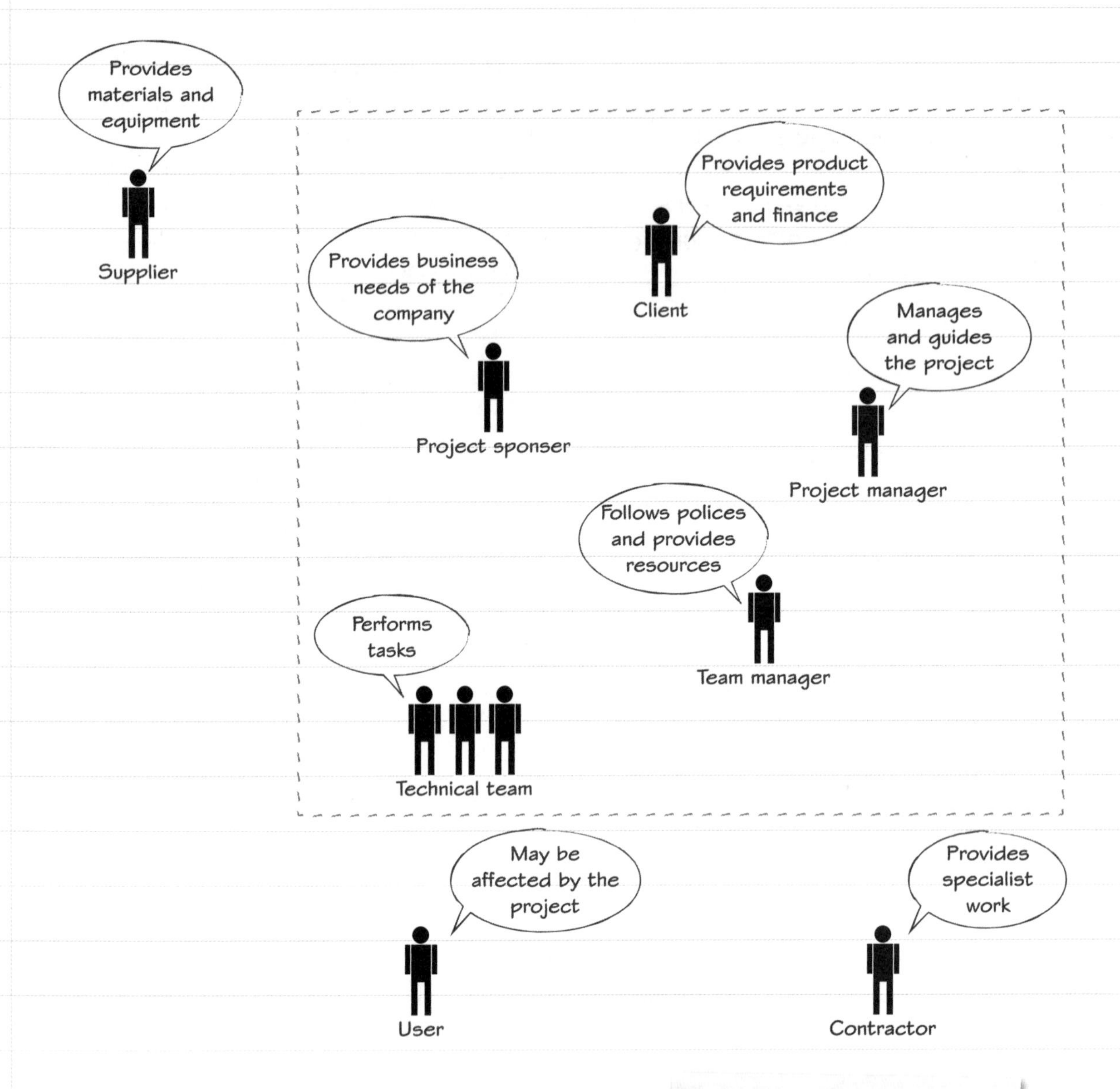

Key stakeholders and their project responsibilities

Now try this

The client initiates the project requirements and provides the budget.
What influence do the project manager and contractor have on the project?

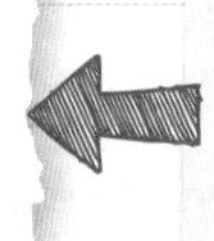

Think about the project manager's role and responsibilities.
Does the contractor provide specific services?

Assumptions and constraints

During the early stages of the project, the project manager must make some assumptions about possible unanticipated risks and constraints that might affect its success. On this page, you will revise the types of assumptions and constraints.

Assumptions

The project manager needs to assess whether there are any factors that might affect the successful outcome of the project. This involves making assumptions. These are classified as low-level risks and are included in the contingency plan.

Testing assumptions

The project manager may make an assumption that testing will remove all of the software bugs.

The contingency plan will identify possible actions that can be taken and by whom, if the software bugs are not removed.

Links See contingency plan on page 105.

Constraints

These are limiting factors that may impact on the success of the project.

Constraints

- **Deadlines** – not completing the project within the time available could impact on the success of the project.
- **Finance** – overspending on the budget and contingency fund would have a detrimental effect on the project as there would be no money to finish it.
- **Staff** – key staff not available to carry out the project when required could delay the completion of the project within the timeframe.
- **Technology** – technology not advanced enough to complete the project might result in having to buy new technology which could impact on the project budget and time.
- **Technical expertise** – staff not able to complete the task because of the lack of technical skills could delay the completion of the project or cost money to train staff.
- **Resources** – specialist equipment not available or out of service could delay the completion of the project within the timeframe or budget if the purchase of new resources is required.

Links Revise how to record assumptions and constraints in the Project Initiation Document on page 113.

Now try this

Compliance with health and safety legislation is a constraint outside the control of the project **and has to be followed**.

Describe **two assumptions** that the project manager should consider.

When identifying assumptions, consider what might go wrong.

Had a look ☐ Nearly there ☐ Nailed it! ☐

Project Initiation Document (1)

The Project Initiation Document (PID) shows stakeholders all the key management information required to get the project underway. On this and the following pages, you will revise what information to include in the PID.

Section	Information required
Project details	This is the first section of the PID. In it, you need to identify: • the project title • the names of the project sponsor, client and manager • the start and completion date of the project • the estimated costs.
Document details	This section records the modifications carried out in the PID. The first PID created will be version 1. The version number and a summary of the modifications made by the author are recorded and dated.
Approvals	In this section you need to record the name and role of the stakeholders who approved the document. It should also clearly record the version number and the date of the approval.
Distribution	This section records who the document has been distributed to. It should clearly identify the name and role of the stakeholder and date of issue. The version of the document is also recorded as it is important to identify which stakeholders have the current version of the PID.
Purpose of the PID	In this section the project aims are summarised to provide a quick reference to the project requirements. The project management control techniques to be used in the project are identified with a detailed background to the proposed work.
Objectives and scope	The objectives measure the success of the project using SMART objectives. It is important that you identify the scope of the project and the relevant objectives, and record them by defining success criteria and using SMART objectives to define project outcomes and date achieved. The **scope** statement should clearly identify what **is** and what is **not** included in the project.
Business case	The business case is set out.
Assumptions and constraints	In this section, assumptions, constraints and their status should be identified. The status of the risk occurring may be categorised as: catastrophic, critical, marginal, negligible.
Risk management strategy	In this section you must show that you have considered what risks might arise, the effect of each risk on the project and create a contingency plan to deal with the risk. The risks have to be assessed for probability, impact and severity on the project outcomes.
Deliverables	In this section you should clearly list the project deliverables by item and component. A full description of the item and component is also required.

Links There is more about SMART objectives on page 103.

Links There is more about assumptions and constraints on page 111.

Links Have a look at page 104 to see how to complete the risk management strategy.

Now try this

The finance manager has reviewed the project requirements, contacted the company's suppliers and agreed a budget of £16 000 for the implementation of a new EPOS system installation arranged for 20 January 20--.

Create SMART objectives for the project.

Remember SMART objectives are:
- specific
- measurable
- achievable
- realistic
- time bound.

Project Initiation Document (2)

The final section of the PID focuses on the project quality strategy. Everyone involved in the project needs to be kept informed and this will ensure that information is delivered to the correct stakeholders in a structured way.

Stakeholders

In this section, you will need to record:

- the key stakeholders
- their responsibilities
- the project management team structure
- the communication plan.

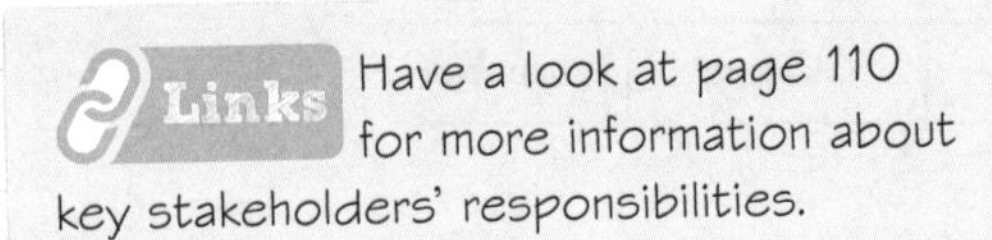

Project management team structure

The project manager will create a team structure chart of the project team.

The team structure shows:

- who's in charge
- roles and responsibilities
- the internal project team
- the external project team.

Communication plan

The communication plan shows:

- what information is sent to the stakeholder
- how often
- the purpose of the information.

Information required by key stakeholders

The managing director and finance director may require weekly progress updates including an updated Gantt chart and a financial report.

Now try this

The project manager wants to plan for the communication of the testing strategy.

What information would the communication plan show?

Think about the communication requirements.

- Who needs the information?
- What or type of information do they require?
- How often do they need the communication?
- What is the purpose of the communication?

Had a look ☐ Nearly there ☐ Nailed it! ☐

Task scheduling

For a project to be delivered successfully, the project manager needs to produce a plan which sets out all the tasks involved, the schedule for each task and milestones to monitor progress. On this page, you will revise work breakdown structure, task scheduling and critical path analysis.

Work breakdown structure (WBS)

This gives stakeholders a visual hierarchical representation of the deliverables and tasks required to complete the project objectives. Each element of the project plan is broken down into work packages, including either a single task or collection of tasks.

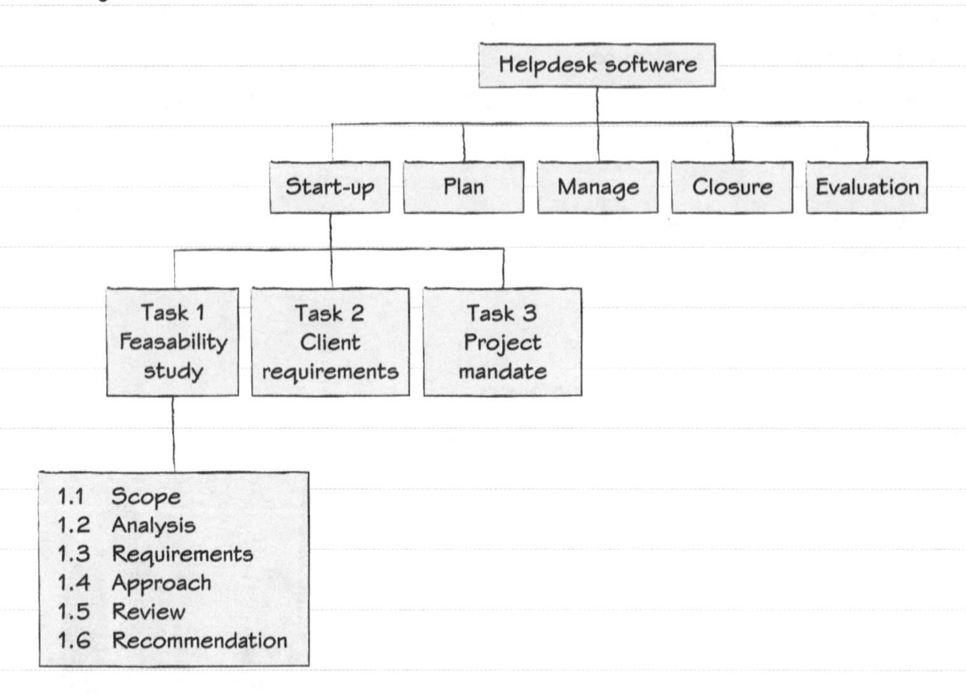

Task scheduling and precedence

Once the work breakdown structure has been created the project manager can schedule each of the project tasks and include milestones. Some tasks are dependent on others and are classified as:

- precedence – must happen first
- serial – must happen after each other
- parallel – must run simultaneously.

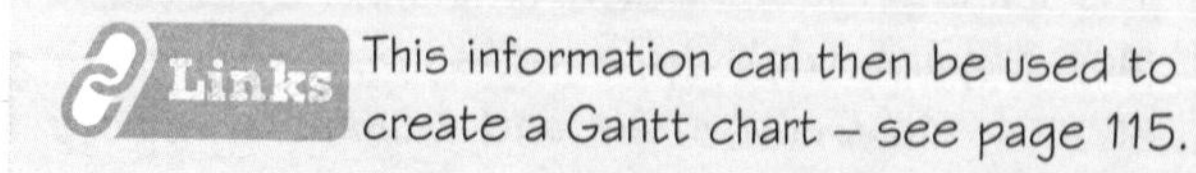

This information can then be used to create a Gantt chart – see page 115.

Critical path analysis

This is a management tool used to work out the earliest and latest start and finish dates of each task in the work breakdown structure. The method is based on calculating the duration of each task and analysing how it relates to other tasks. From this, the project manager can identify the quickest path to complete the project and pinpoint any spare capacity.

Now try this

Create a work breakdown structure for a computer game.

Start at the top of the WBS and work downwards. Identify every work packet. What are the sequences?

Gantt charts

A Gantt chart is a management tool used to plan and track the progress of a project. A variety of software applications can be used to monitor progress.

Gantt chart

A Gantt chart displays all the project tasks and their duration. It provides stakeholders with a visual interpretation of the schedule and helps with time management. The chart allows the project team to schedule task or activity timelines, relationships between tasks, tasks that depend on each other and task progress.

It can also be used to:

- allocate resources to each task
- identify project start and end dates
- set milestones
- establish task start and end dates and the duration of the tasks.

Gantt chart software is one of the most popular software tools used in project management and makes the process of task adjustments manageable and flexible.

Project management software

Benefits	Limitations
Schedules tasks Identifies dependent tasks Tracks and manages project Controls costs Monitors project time Allocates resources Shares documentation and information Encourages collaboration Improves communication Makes calendar entries Shares contacts	Specialist software may be expensive Difficult to use advanced features Can make project more complex Can cause problems when relaying of alerts/features is set up incorrectly

You can use project management software to:

- create and allocate resources
- allocate and track tasks and deadlines
- visualise the plan
- collaborate within a team
- generate reports
- manage resource.

Number	Task	Start	End	Duration (days)	1/8/17	2/8/17	3/8/17	4/8/17	5/8/17	6/8/17
1	Task 1	1/8/17	2/8/17	2						
2	Task 2	2/8/17	4/8/17	3						
3	Task 3	5/8/17	6/8/17	2						

A Gantt chart.

Now try this

Create a Gantt chart for the following project stages:

- conception and start-up on 02/11/17
- definition of the project 2 days
- planning 12 days
- planning milestone
- launch and execution 33 days
- closure 4 days
- project review milestone
- post-project evaluation 2 days.

Use appropriate software to create the Gantt chart.

Start at the beginning of the project list.

Create an event for conception and start-up on 02/11/17.

The first activity is definition of the project, which has a task duration of 2 days.

Remember to include the milestones.

Had a look ☐ Nearly there ☐ Nailed it! ☐

Resources and budgeting

For a project to be successful the project manager must efficiently allocate all resources – staff, equipment and materials – and calculate and then monitor costs. On this page, you will revise estimation techniques and budget planning.

Allocating resources

The project manager is responsible for ensuring:

- work is allocated across the project team
- staff are given materials and equipment to carry out their work.

The project manager will use a variety of software tools to manage the project, such as spreadsheets and project management software.

Pro rata costing

The project manager works out the cost of resources (staff, equipment and materials) for each task, and then calculates a pro rata cost across the task. For example, the cost of hiring a high-specification PC would be £70 a week. The pro rata cost per day would be £10. A team member uses the PC for 3 days at a pro rata cost of £30.

Estimation techniques

Different types of estimation techniques are used to forecast project duration and costs.

Estimation technique	Benefits	Limitations
Bottom-up Starts with defining the tasks then work packet	Organised/detailed tasks/ budgets identified by project team/experts	Time consuming
Parametric testing using function point analysis Breaks the system into small tasks/function points	Provides an accurate estimation of time/cost taken for software input/output/storage	Requires expert input and the user requirements may not be clearly defined
Top-down Starts with the project goal or deliverable	Tasks or work packets are defined by the project manager with no additional costs or time	Project team not consulted in task requirements and relies on the project manager's skills/ experience

A function point is a measurement of time or cost required to complete a part of a software system. For example, it might take 8 developer hours to implement. This is calculated from previous projects.

Budget planning and cash flow

The project manager will be given a budget for the project which they will allocate to the resources according to the estimated costs. The budget and cash flow must then be monitored carefully to ensure that the project does not run out of money. The incorrect allocation of budget or overspending might affect the overall budget and the cash flow.

Now try this

One advantage of using a top-down estimation technique is that the project manager can carry out the task quickly.

Identify one disadvantage of using top-down estimation technique.

Remember to consider the:

- project tasks
- project manager's skills
- project assumptions, constraints and risks.

Risk matrix and issue log

The project manager will use various risk management strategies to ensure that the project risks are managed effectively. On this page, you will revise the risk matrix and recording issues.

Risk matrix

As part of the risk analysis process, the project manager will calculate the severity of each risk and classify whether it is high, medium or low, requiring either controlling, monitoring or no action. This is shown in a risk matrix which allows each risk to be continuously monitored and managed.

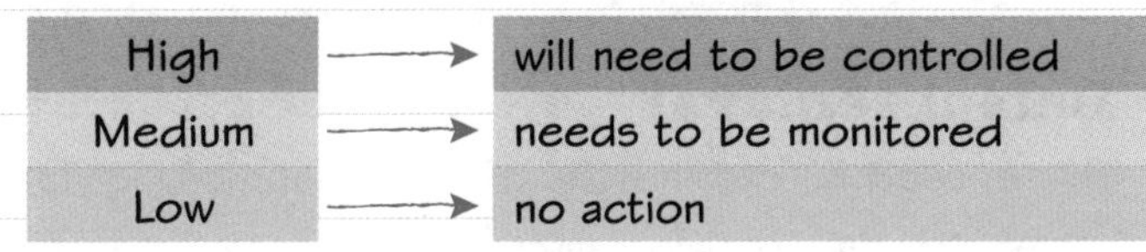

High →	will need to be controlled
Medium →	needs to be monitored
Low →	no action

The risk matrix is colour coded so the project manager can see at a glance the severity of each risk.

Revise the use of impact and probability to calculate the severity of a risk on page 104.

Revise contingency planning for major risks on page 105.

Risk log

A risk log records the **risk status** and is reviewed by the project manager at regular intervals. The log includes:

- risk ID and risk type
- author and date identified
- risk description
- probability, impact and status
- owner.

Cross-referencing to the risk matrix

The probability of a risk occurring can be cross-referenced to the risk matrix to identify the level of severity.

Risk score 16–25	can be critical
Risk score 9–15	moderate harm
Risk score 1–8	low risk

Impact scale	LOW		Occurrence scale	HIGH
HIGH	Scope creep (12)	Hardware not delivered on time (15)	Hardware failure (20)	Testing not completed on schedule (22)
	Virus (8)	Testing strategy insufficient (10)	Software developer sickness (15)	Software not compatible (20)
	Fire (4)	Power failure (6)	Budget exceeded (10)	Software not delivered on time (15)
LOW	Natural disaster (1)	Legislation and standards (3)	Flood (7)	Technician sickness (12)

A cross-referenced risk matrix, showing both the level of risk and its severity.

Now try this

You are creating a new appointment system for a local gym. The current system runs on an old Windows 3.1 system. You have been asked to upgrade the hardware and operating system.

Create a risk matrix for this project.

Remember to consider the probability of occurrence and the impact of the disruption. Colour code your risk matrix so that the risks are clear.

Had a look ☐ Nearly there ☐ Nailed it! ☐

Quality management

The project manager must ensure that the project meets the needs of the stakeholders. This is achieved through quality management processes, techniques and procedures. On this page, you will revise defect removal, testing strategy and using quality standards as a benchmark.

Defect removal

This is used to examine the effectiveness of individual processes.

Defect removal methods

- **Desk checking** – manually enter data to test if the code performs as required
- **Proof-reading** – read the code to ensure correct grammar, spelling and punctuation and contextually correct
- **Inspection** – a planned and formal test arranged and carried out by a software tester. The code is tested, any bugs removed and outcomes officially documented
- **Peer review** – an experienced/peer programmer tests if the code works as expected and offers suggestions for improvements
- **Walkthrough** – an informal test by a peer

Testing strategy

The most common testing strategies used by the software tester are:

Unit testing	• tests code • automatic • at each stage against specification
Integration testing	• tests interactions between modules against design
Systems testing	• tests system against requirements

User acceptance testing

User acceptance testing (UAT) is an essential part of the quality and review process and improves the quality of the software and results in increases customer satisfaction.

- It is carried out at the last stage of the testing process.
- Users/stakeholders test the system to see if it is functional, complete and easy to use.

Quality standards

The project manager also uses external benchmarks to see if the internal quality standards meet external benchmark best practice.

Where they are = Where they need to be

Links Revise quality standards on page 102.

Regression testing

Regression testing is the testing of a system after changes have been made. It is required after any software changes, for example fixing performance issues, or adding new features or code.

Now try this

The software developer has been working with another developer to test the system and the system is now error free.

Before the software is passed for user testing it must be formally tested. What defect removal testing would you recommend?

You should consider all of the defect removal.

Does the testing process need to be recorded?

Communicating with stakeholders

A range of communication methods are used to keep stakeholders informed of the project's progress. There should also be a communications plan.

Communication methods

- **Meetings and one-to-one discussions** – discuss issues face to face, focused agenda, develop relationships, share information, immediate feedback and decisions made
- **Memos and notices** – short written record, permanent record that clarifies an event or issue. Can be easily shared and used to support a legal issue
- **Telephone conversations** – used to communicate directly with stakeholders in different locations, information and ideas can be shared instantly, decision can be agreed
- **Video conferences** – used to communicate interactively with stakeholders in different locations, information and ideas can be shared instantly. Has a personal touch, decision can be made instantly
- **Emails** – emails can be sent electronically and read at any time, documents can be attached to emails
- **Instant messaging** – instant messaging used for real-time chat and discussing small issues
- **Online forums, discussion groups and news groups** – specific discussion topics. Stakeholders can have a continuous dialogues about project issues. Discussion groups can be set up for specific information and discussions with invited group members
- **Collaborative working tools** – software used on any device at any location allows for faster and easier feedback

Devising a communication plan

The communication plan provides a structure for the communications so that the information is delivered to the right person at the right time.

When devising a plan Identify:

- the target audience, for example individual stakeholders
- frequency of communication, for example weekly/ milestones
- type of communication, for example agendas, minutes
- purpose of the communication, for example to keep the stakeholder informed of progress.

Special requests

The stakeholder, such as the project sponsor, might also ask for **specific presentation requirements.** It is important to communicate the documents in the format requested by the stakeholder.

Revise communication plans on page 113.

Now try this

One advantage of collaborative working tools is that information can be stored and accessed in a central workspace.

Can you identify any **other** uses of collaborative working tools?

Specialist collaborative working tools are available to help the project team manage the project. Think about shared:

- digital resources
- collaborative working
- tasks
- time.

Had a look ☐ Nearly there ☐ Nailed it! ☐

Waterfall software development life cycle model

The waterfall software development life cycle model shows the five project stages. Each stage is completed independently and in sequence, and the output of one stage feeds into the next.

Requirements analysis

Identifies stakeholder requirement, system data, system requirement, functional specification, technical limitations and constraints.

Design

Specifies the hardware and software features designed to support the business needs of the organisation.

Construction and testing

Software code is written and tested to ensure that the system is fully functional.

Acceptance testing

The system is tested by its users in the business environment.

Implementation and delivery

Software installed onto the system and configured.
Users trained on the new system.

Advantages of model

- Simple to use and understand
- Easy to manage as each process has its own deliverables
- Works well for small projects
- Works well for project with clear requirements.

Disadvantages of a model

- It can be a long process, as each stage must be completed before the next stage begins.
- If the program is found not to meet all of the functional requirements during the testing stage (because the requirements were not clearly defined), it may be difficult to change the functionality of the program.
- The prototype is developed late in the life cycle process.
- It may have high risk and uncertainty.

Now try this

One advantage of using this model is that it is flexible and stages can be merged.
Identify a **disadvantage** of using this model.

Look at each stage in turn. Each stage has to be completed before the next stage can begin.

Tracking progress

Each task in a project needs to be monitored and recorded to ensure it is going to plan and on schedule. A Project Checkpoint Report (PCR) monitors the work packages/product status at milestones throughout the project.

Project baseline

A project baseline is a set of values such as project plan, budget, scope that the project manager uses to measure the status or performance of the project. They can also be used to inform future project planning.

Variance

Variance is the difference between what is planned and what has been completed.

A work package is a deliverable that is broken down into a single task or collection of manageable tasks.

Project Checkpoint Report

A PCR is used to monitor risk, manage issues and record quality management activity.

Time	Date of checkpoint Period covered
Document	Version number Modifications made Author Date
Approvals	Name of person giving approval Their role in the project Signature Date Document version number
Distribution	Name of person receiving document Their role Date of issue Document version number
Products	Product name Work undertaken Date completed
Quality management	Activities undertaken
Work package tolerance status	Reports on the status of the package, including: • time • cost • quality
Issue log	Date raised Name of person raising issue Description of issue Action taken Date closed
Lessons learned	Identifying the lessons learned from issues that have arisen to ensure more efficient planning of similar projects in the future

Now try this

The data input screen requirements are missing for the online data entry form.

What action is required to ensure that it does not happen again?

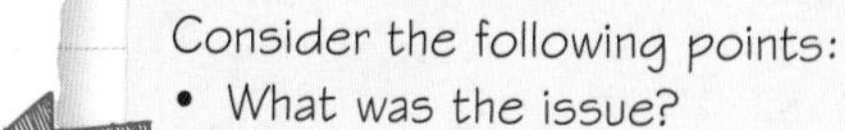

Consider the following points:
- What was the issue?
- Who raised the issue?
- What was the impact of the issue?

Had a look ☐ Nearly there ☐ Nailed it! ☐

Categorising issues

In the life of the project, issues may arise that haven't been planned for. As part of the risk management process, the project manager needs to categorise each issue, take action to deal with it and record the activities.

Issue categories

The project manager will identify the unforeseen issue and place it into one of three categories. This will allow them to determine how urgent it is to find a solution.

Issue category

Request for change – a change requested by the customer that was not originally agreed at the beginning of the project
Example: Customer requests additional functionality in the software.

Off-specification – notification of a new delivery date from the supplier that was not in the original specification
Example: There is an unforeseen delay in delivery resulting from server configuration problems.

Problem or concern – an unforced issue or event that is outside the control of the project but impacts on it
Example: The testing process requires more time as one of the testers is off sick.

Management by exception

The project manager should report major or unforeseen issues and their potential impact on the project to the project sponsor. They should also advise them on strategies for dealing with the issue.

Lessons learned

By recording lessons learned you:

- ✓ identify best practices
- ✓ share issues with the organisation and future projects and ensure they are not repeated
- ✓ identify solutions or recommendations.

Now try this

The network manager reports a delay in the hardware installation process.

Identify the issue category.

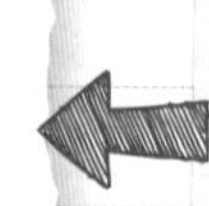

Which category best fits the issue:

- request for change
- problem or concern
- off-specification?

Change management

Issues arising during the life of the project may require changes to its scope and development. The project manager needs to assess to what extent a change may impact on the project and manage the change accordingly.

Impact on the project

The project manager will need to assess whether the change required will affect the whole of the project or just one stage. Even if the change affects only one stage, it may have a wider impact on the project, and the project manager should take account of this. For example, during software development: changes may affect not only that stage but also the entire project outcome.

Change of scope

Changes in the project requirements will affect the scope of the project and could:

- increase the project's costs
- lengthen the timescale required to complete the project
- require alterations to the quality management process.

Development change

The project manager might identify a problem that requires a development change and this may result in a modification to the design of the product.

Input screen design has errors	+	New input screen design	=	Additional time and costs

Impact of a design change on the project

When faults can occur

Fault	Example
Defects in the system analysis	The requirements of the new system are not fully understood or recorded.
Defects in the design documentation	The design documentation does not accurately record the new system requirements.
Software errors	Software errors are identified during the testing process.

How to deal with faults

- ✓ Ensure stakeholder understands their role.
- ✓ Use project management tools and strategies effectively.
- ✓ Manage each stage of the process.
- ✓ Focus on business processes and needs.
- ✓ Communicate clearly at all levels.
- ✓ Allocate experienced staff to manage resources and process.
- ✓ Accurately assess risk.

Now try this

The quality manager has asked for additional user acceptance testing.

Would this impact on the project stage or the entire project?

You should consider at what stage the additional user acceptance testing is required.

Is additional user acceptance testing:

- a change of scope
- a development change
- a process?

Had a look ☐ Nearly there ☐ Nailed it! ☐

Change management process

The project manager requires skills to manage the change process.

Managing the change process

Stage	Example
1 Project manager submits change request	1 The project manager requests a change to the implementation date of the project due to issues with a contractor.
2 Management team reviews change request	2 The management team reviews the implementation schedule and proposes an alternative implementation plan.
3 Management team assesses feasibility of the change of project scope	3 The management team assesses the impact of the change to the project scope to ensure implementation and delivery remain achievable.
4 Management team approves or rejects change	4 The management team approves the alternative implementation plan.
5 Project team implements change	5 The project team implements the revised plan.

Now try this

A request by the user to change the screen layouts can have an impact on the project.

What effect would this change have on the **scope** of the project?

You should consider the following points:

- requirements and effects on quality
- costs
- timescales.

For more on change of scope, see page 123 .

Implementation strategy

At the planning stage, the project manager will agree an implementation strategy with the client. The product may be delivered in one of three ways – direct changeover, parallel running or pilot changeover. During this stage, user acceptance testing, where customers test the product to identify defects, also takes place.

Delivery method	Advantages	Disadvantages
Direct changeover The old system is stopped and the new system becomes operational. OLD system → NEW system HIGH RISK	The new system is up and running quickly. No extra costs are incurred for running the old system. One set of data is required.	If the new system fails, the data is lost and will have to be re-inputted into the old system which takes time and money. There is disruption of services when the old system is turned off and the new system turned on.
Parallel running The old and new systems are both used to process data at the same time for a short period. OLD system NEW system → NEW system LOW RISK	The old system and new system are available at the same time. Staff feel more secure as they can get used to the new system slowly. Outputs from the new system can be compared to the old system to ensure its functionality.	Data must be inputted into the old and new system which takes time. It takes time and money to run two systems at the same time.
Pilot changeover The new system is used in one department/function to process data as well as the old system. OLD system → NEW system OLD system → OLD system LOW RISK	The system is implemented in one department or location. It is easier to manage implementation in one department or location. Issues are resolved before the new system is fully implemented across the organisation. Staff trained on the pilot changeover can support the full implementation.	Staff have to use the old and new system at the same time. Data must be inputted into the old and new system which takes time. It takes time and money to run two systems at the same time.

Now try this

When you need to implement a system quickly direct changeover will be the most appropriate method to use.

When would you use:

(a) parallel running

(b) pilot changeover?

Look at the advantages and disadvantages for parallel running and pilot changeover.

Provide an example of when they could be used.

Had a look ☐ Nearly there ☐ Nailed it! ☐

Closing a live project

The project manager has been planning for this stage throughout the project life cycle. It is time to close the project and move into the operation and maintenance phase.

Project closure checklist

The project needs to be closed in an organised and controlled way.

- ✓ All stages or milestones achieved
- ✓ Project team disbanded
- ✓ Deliverables/outputs tested and meet specification requirements
- ✓ Financial closure
- ✓ Lessons learned
- ✓ Sign off
- ✓ Documentation completed and archived

Operation and maintenance phase

Once the new system is operational, the system processes are monitored closely and supported for functional and non-functional issues, including:

- technical support
- user training and user guides/manuals
- help desk
- data validation
- backup
- security/user access.

The project manager will assess each area of the project to make sure it is fully operational, and will also monitor the system to see if it can be made more effective, secure and efficient.

Assessing the benefits delivered

The benefits of the project will differ at each stage of the software development life cycle model. An evaluation of the benefits of the project should be carried out and reported to the client. Once all the data from the project has been gathered, the benefits can be reviewed again later.

Revise the software development life cycle on page 120.

Closing down risk log, issue log and quality log

Ongoing risks and issues are moved to 'follow-on action' and passed to the project team for further action. The quality log will be updated to record the effects of quality procedures on the project.

Reviewing lessons learned

The risks, issues and quality logs will be analysed to see what lessons can be learned from the project life cycle that can be applied to future projects to improve delivery. This evaluation should summarise, review and record:

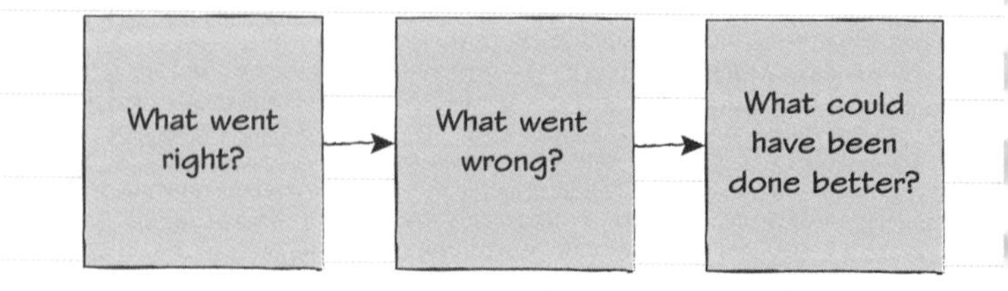

Now try this

What went wrong?

The software testing process overran as both testers were testing the same module.

Identify **one** lesson learned and how it could be resolved.

Review of project success

The project manager's final task is to carry out a review of project success.

Post-project review

The review considers the views of key stakeholders and project success in terms of:

- key factors
- SMART objectives
- lessons learned
- project performance against baseline and project objectives
- final costs, delivery date
- quality of product.

Stakeholders and feedback

Recommendations for future actions are based on the outcome of the post-project review and should be communicated to all key stakeholders such as the sponsor, the client(s), end users and the development team.

Links Look at page 110 for further information on stakeholders. For more on communication and presentation, see page 119.

Methods used to obtain feedback from stakeholders

Interviews		Observations	
Advantages	**Disadvantages**	**Advantages**	**Disadvantages**
Face to face with a personal touch	Difficult to analyse due to limited sample size	Accurate specific observation of event or behaviour	Difficult to plan and organise and time consuming
Less structured	Time consuming and costly	Accurate interpretation of event	Uncooperative observer and untrained observer
Guided response/more accurate/investigate issues in depth	Quality of responses vary by interviewer	Direct method of collecting information	Does not capture quantitative data for analysis
Questionnaires		**Surveys**	
Advantages	**Disadvantages**	**Advantages**	**Disadvantages**
Practical and easy to administer	Scope of the questions limited	Large-scale data collection	Scope of the questions limited
Collects large amounts of data	Validation/views of respondents	Numerous questions can be asked	Data errors/unclear questions
Structured, easy to analyse	Accuracy of completed questionnaire	Flexible format	Response rates low

Now try this

You have been asked to find out about what data and system requirements are in a food warehouse. There are two data input staff working in the office.

What method would you use to capture the information, system data and system requirements?

Consider all of the methods:

- interviews
- observations
- questionnaires
- surveys.

It is important that the responses are accurate as the sample of the data will help you identify the system requirements.

Had a look ☐ Nearly there ☐ Nailed it! ☐

Your Unit 3 set task

Unit 3 will be assessed through a task, which will be set by Pearson. In this assessed task you will need to use your project planning and management understanding and skills to complete project documentation to initiate and launch a computing project, and then monitor and control the project's progress to its completion and closure.

Set task skills

Your assessed task could cover any of the essential content in the unit. You can revise the unit content in this Revision Guide. This skills section is designed to **revise skills** that might be needed in your assessed task. The section uses selected content and outcomes to provide an example of ways of applying your skills.

Set task skills

Project Initiation Document
Revise the skills needed to produce a PID on pages 129–132

Gantt chart
Revise how to set up a chart on page 133

Resource list and cost plan
Have a look at the skills needed to produce these documents on page 134

Project Checkpoint Report
Revise the skills you could use to write a report on pages 135 and 136

Project closure email
See pages 137 and 138 for the skills required to review and evaluate a project

Documentation

To initiate and launch a project you will need to produce:

- a Project Initiation Document (PID)
- a Gantt chart
- a resource list
- a cost plan.

To monitor and control a project's progress to completion and closure, you will need to write:

- a Project Checkpoint Report (PCR)
- an email to the project sponsor.

Check the Pearson website

The activities and sample response extracts in this section are provided to help you to revise content and skills. Ask your tutor or check the Pearson website for the most up-to-date **Sample Assessment Material** and **Mark Scheme** to get an indication of the structure of your actual assessed task and what this requires of you. The details of the actual assessed task may change so always make sure you are up to date.

Now try this

Visit the Pearson website and find the page containing the course materials for BTEC National Computing. Look at the latest Unit 3 Sample Assessment Material for an indication of:

- the structure of your set task, and whether it is divided into separate parts
- how much time you are allowed for each section of the task
- what briefing or stimulus material might be provided to you
- the activities you are required to complete, what documents you may be given and how to format your responses.

Project Initiation Document (1)

Over the next few pages, you will look at how to apply management and planning techniques to a Project Initiation Document (PID), which you will need to produce when initiating and launching a computing project. This page focuses on the skills you could use to complete project and document details.

Links For more on the Project Initiation Document, see pages 112–113.

Worked example

Task brief

You are the project manager in a large organisation. Piper Lsyoige, the IT Director, has received complaints from staff about IT system support. Your manager Carl John, the IT Manager, will be the client for the project and has asked that ISO/IEC 25010:2011 be used as a benchmark for software development and is concerned about software compatibility issues with existing system.

In this task, the **project scenario** gives you an overview of the whole project – you should read it carefully before moving on to the information that follows.

Information (extract)

The project start date will be 16/11/17 and the scheduled launch date 16/03/18. The estimated cost for the project is £16 000. The web-based IT Help Desk System will only be available in house and will not be accessed from outside the organisation. The system is planned to increase productivity and revenue by at least 10% and user satisfaction to 90% by 16/08/18.

On 18/11/17 Piper Lsyoige notified you of new legislation that will impact on the system requirement and on 11/01/18 of a new hardware delivery date.

This task brief provides a wide range of information to enable you to complete the PID. Highlight or make a note of important points – this will help you quickly and accurately identify the information you need.

Sample response extract

Project Initiation Document

Project details

Project title	IT Help Desk System	
Project sponsor name	IT Director	Piper Lsyoige
Project client name	IT System Support Manager	Carl John
Project manager name	A. Learner	
Start date	16/11/17	
Completion date	16/03/18	
Estimated cost	£16 000	

Make sure you enter the information from the task brief accurately, and ensure all parts of the PID are fully completed with relevant information.

Now try this

Complete the document details for this project.

Document details

Version	Modifications	Author	Date
2			
3			

Review the document details to ensure you have completed every section.

Is the information:

- relevant?
- completed in full and detailed?
- accurate?

Had a look ☐ Nearly there ☐ Nailed it! ☐

Project Initiation Document (2)

Here are some of the skills involved in completing sections of the PID relating to approvals, distribution, purpose, background to the proposed work and objectives.

Sample response extract

Approvals

This document requires the following approvals:

Name	Role	Signature	Date	Version
Piper Lsyoige	IT Director	Piper Lsyoige	19/11/17	2
			12/01/18	3

The PID was authorised by the sponsor on 19/11/17. Consider who else will need to approve the PID.

Distribution

This document has been distributed to:

Name	Role	Date of issue	Version
Carl John	IT System Support Manager	19/11/17	2
		12/01/18	3

Make sure you produce an accurate record so you know who the document has been distributed to. Remember, each new document will have the next version number.

Purpose of the Project Initiation Document

Project aims:

The system is planned to increase productivity and revenue by at least 10%.

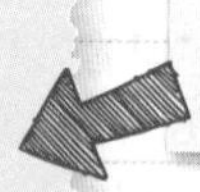

The project aims must be entered accurately.

Project management and control:

ISO/IEC 25010:2011 will be used as it is a benchmark for software development.

Make sure you enter information in full. Always check that the information you include is relevant to the section you are completing.

Background to the proposed work

Piper Lsyoige, the IT Director, has had complaints from staff about IT system support. He has decided to implement a web-based IT Help Desk System.

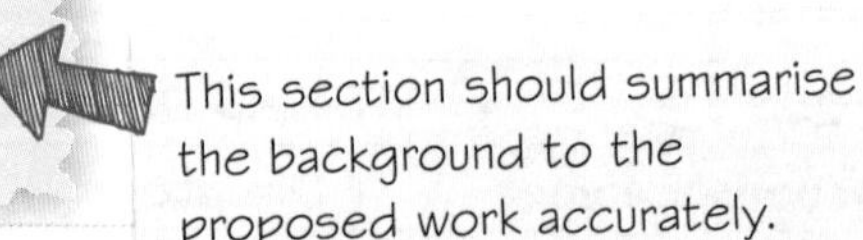

This section should summarise the background to the proposed work accurately.

Objectives

SMART objective	Achieved?	Date and comments
IT Helpdesk System launch date 16/03/18	Yes	16/03/18 successful launch
Budget for the project £16 000		

Remember to write the project objectives as SMART targets.

Revise SMART objectives on page 103.

Now try this

Look back at the revision scenario and information for this project on page 129. Two of the project aims have been identified above. Identify another aim.

Read the scenario carefully. Can you identify any other targets?

Do you have a budget and project end date?

Project Initiation Document (3)

Here are some of the skills involved in completing sections of the PID relating to scope, assumptions and constraints. You will need to refer to the business case.

Sample response extract

Scope

The web-based IT Help Desk System will be available in house and will not be accessed from outside the organisation.

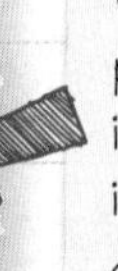

When writing about the scope of the project, make sure that you clearly identify what is and what is **not** included in the project. You need to identify the deliverables, constraints and assumptions.

Find out more about the scope of a project on page 112.

When deciding the status of the assumption, look to see if it is still an issue ('open') – is more information required to confirm it? – or whether there is enough information to confirm the assumption.

Assumptions

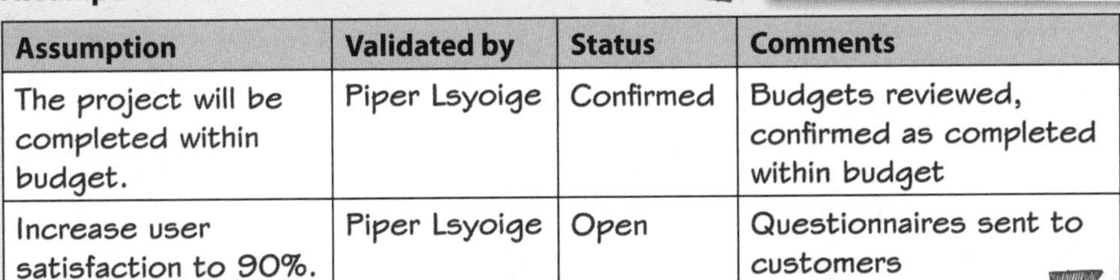

Assumption	Validated by	Status	Comments
The project will be completed within budget.	Piper Lsyoige	Confirmed	Budgets reviewed, confirmed as completed within budget
Increase user satisfaction to 90%.	Piper Lsyoige	Open	Questionnaires sent to customers

Links Have a look at page 111 for examples of assumptions.

Read the business case carefully and note down any assumptions you identify.

The assumptions are validated by the project team.

Look again at the assumptions you have noted in the business case. What information do you have about each one? Add this to the 'comments' column.

Constraints

Constraints	Validated by	Status	Comments
Software compatibility issues with existing system	Carl John	Open	Existing hardware audit required

Look again at the constraints you have noted in the business case. Add any information to the 'comments' column.

Read the business case carefully and note down any constraints you identify.

The client validated the constraint.

Have a look at page 111 for examples of constraints.

Now try this

Look at the project information on page 129 again. Identify another project constraint.

Consider the project management and controls and any specific requests by Carl John, the IT System Support Manager.

Had a look ☐ Nearly there ☐ Nailed it! ☐

Project Initiation Document (4)

The PID also covers risk management strategy, project deliverables, stakeholders' responsibilities in the project (project quality strategy) and the communication plan. Here are some skills you could use to help you complete these sections. You will need to refer to the project management team structure.

Sample response extract

Risk management strategy

Risk	Probability	Impact	Severity	Contingency plan
Not completing project within time	Low 15%	Manageable	Marginal	Monitor progress at key milestones Make more staff available

Use the information you are given to assess the probability, impact and severity of each risk. Then develop a suitable contingency plan.

Use the risk management cycle to help you develop your risk management strategy.

Links Revise the risk management cycle and impact and probability on page 104. For more information on severity of risk and contingency planning, see page 105.

Sample response extract

Deliverables

Item	Components	Description
IT Helpdesk System	User records Asset records Help desk records User guides IT technician records	integrated system that can generate reports and schedule routine maintenance schedule

When writing the project description, include as many details as you can.

Sample response extract

Communication plan

Stakeholder(s)	Frequency	Type	Purpose
Piper Lsyoige IT Director	Weekly	Email	Project update
Carl John IT Manager			

Before developing your communication plan, first identify the stakeholders and their responsibilities. Then consider each key stakeholder's communication requirements. Remember to explain the purpose of each type of communication.

Now try this

Complete the communication plan above for Carl John's communication requirements.

Think about
- what type of information he requires
- frequency and purpose of the communication.

Gantt chart

A Gantt chart is one of a series of documents that you may need to produce, in order to initiate and launch a computing project. Here are some skills you could use to create a Gantt chart. You may find it easier to set up your chart using specialist software.

Links For more on Gantt charts, see page 115.

Sample response extract

Before you set up your chart, identify all the key tasks and dates. Work out the most efficient order in which to do the tasks.

The time for each task has been allocated to show the task **start date** and task **end date.** The software will use these dates to calculate the duration of the task – you must insert correct start and end dates so the duration of the task is recorded accurately.

Make sure your chart shows the correct **milestones** for the completion of each stage.

Project planner		PERIODS											
Task	Task name	Start date	End date	Duration	1/10	2/10	3/10	4/10	5/10	6/10	7/10	8/10	
Task 1	User requirements	01/10/2018	02/10/2018	2			◇						
Task 2	Software design and development	03/10/2018	05/10/2018	3						◇			
Task 3	Prototype testing	06/10/2018	06/10/2018	1							◇		
Task 4	Software installation and training	07/10/2018	08/10/2018	2									◇
Task 5	Hardware purchase and installation	03/10/2018	06/10/2018	4							◇		

Number each task in sequence. Record each task name **accurately** and in the most **efficient sequence**.

The duration of the stage is represented in a **duration bar.** This provides a visual representation of the duration of the task.

Now try this

The project start date will be 05/02/18 and the scheduled launch date is 17/02/18. The User requirements will take 2 days. On 07/02/18, the software design and development will start for 4 days. On 11/02/18, the system will go through prototype testing. The hardware purchase and installation will start on 12/02/18 and last for 3 days. The software installation and training will start on 15/02/18 and last for 2 days.

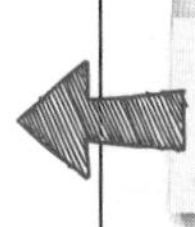

Using project management software is the best way to create Gantt charts.

Create a Gantt chart for this project.

Had a look ☐ Nearly there ☐ Nailed it! ☐

Resource list and cost plan

You may need to produce a resource list and a cost plan when initiating and launching a computing project. Here are some examples of skills involved in preparing these documents.

Sample response extract

Resource list

Description	Notes
PC/keyboard/mouse	2 required
34″ HD monitor	Senior development workstation
21″ monitor	Software tester workstation
Laptop	For prototype testing only
Server	1 required
Helpdesk software	3 years' support included
Operating system	For all systems
Printer	1 required
Network equipment	Covers installation

Identify the resources required for the project. Remember to include all the resources that will be needed. This will help to ensure the accuracy of your cost plan.

Include some notes on each of the resources as this will also help you to prepare an accurate estimation for the cost plan.

Links Have look at page 116 for more information on resources and budgeting.

Sample response extract

Check to make sure you haven't omitted anything from your cost plan – it needs to be complete and accurate.

Cost plan

Description	Qty	Unit Price	Total
PC / keyboard / mouse	2	£459.00	£918.00
34″ HD monitor	1	£249.00	£249.00
21″ monitor	1	£84.00	£84.00
Laptop	1	£299.00	£299.00
Server	1	£946.00	£946.00
Helpdesk software	1	£4500.00	£4500.00
Operating system	4	£792.00	£3168.00
Printer	1	£299.00	£299.00
Network equipment	1	£368.00	£368.00
		£7996.00	£10831.00

Costs must be correctly attributed to provide an accurate estimate of the total project cost.

You must provide:

- a description of the resource
- quantity required
- unit price and total cost.

If possible, use a calculator to work out the total costs.

Now try this

The project manager has agreed a fee of £340 to oversee the project. The system design and development costs will be £1590. Two programme testers have been allocated to the testing process at a cost of £120 per tester. The installation and user testing will cost £400 with an additional cost of £50 for a training manual. 30-day telephone support £120 has also been agreed.

Create a cost plan for the following project.

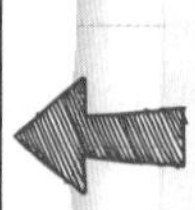

Read this scenario carefully and highlight all of the key information required for the cost plan.

You could use a spreadsheet application to help you calculate the total project costs accurately.

Project Checkpoint Report (1)

A Project Checkpoint Report (PCR) is completed at a specific stage of a project. You may need to refer to the PID, Gantt chart, resource list and cost plan to enable you to produce your report. This page and the next covers some of the skills you could use to write an accurate report.

Links For more information on the Project Checkpoint Report, see page 121.

Worked example

Task brief

Information

Abe Web, the Managing Director, has authorised the project start date 08/01/17, and launch date 01/04/17. The software design and development stage was completed successfully on 30/03/17. On 23/03/17 the Quality Manager reported that ISO/IEC 25010:2011 and the use of flow charts allowed the testing process to be completed before the deadline date 27/03/17. Dora Wix, the Finance Manager, reported that this reduced the budget from £95 000 to £87 500. The Technical Manager reported on 25/03/17 that the EPOS manufacturer has not been able to deliver the systems due to production problems and that delivery is now scheduled for 10/04/17. The installation company has moved to another project and proposed a new installation date 11/04/17.

Sample response extract

Project Checkpoint Report

Report details

Date of checkpoint:	27/03/17
Period covered:	04/03/17 – 27/03/17

Make sure you fill in the dates accurately. This PCR covers the testing process.

Sample response extract

Document details

Version	Modifications	Author	Date
2	Reduced budget due to early completion of testing process	Finance Manager	23/03/17
3	New delivery date 10/04/17 and installation date 01/04/17	Technical Manager	25/03/17

Make sure you complete all parts of the PCR. If there are any empty cells in a table, then check to see what's missing.

Approvals

Name	Role	Signature	Date	Version
Abe Web	Managing Director	Abe Web	25/03/17	3
Dora Wix	Finance Manager	Dora Wix	25/03/17	3

If the project requirements have changed, update the approvals table.

Now try this

Complete the distribution table for the project.

Name	Role	Date of issue	Version

Which stakeholders need to have a copy of the PCR? Enter this information into the distribution table.

Had a look ☐ Nearly there ☐ Nailed it! ☐

Project Checkpoint Report (2)

Sample response extract

Products

Product name	Work undertaken	Date completed
EPOS system	Design and development stage completed	03/03/17

Clearly state the product name, the work undertaken and completion date.

Sample response extract

Quality management

ISO/IEC 25010:2011 benchmark used for the software testing process.

Remember to list all the activities undertaken during the period of the PCR.

For more information on aspects of the PCR, see page 121.

Sample response extract

Work package tolerance status

Time	04/03/17–27/03/17
Cost	£87 500
Quality	ISO/IEC 25010:2011

Enter the information accurately.

Sample response extract

Lessons learned

The EPOS manufacturer was not able to deliver the systems due to production problems, new delivery date 10/04/17. The installation company have moved to another project and proposed a new installation date 11/04/17. The impact could have been a delay in the installation process and project overrun.

When identifying the lessons learned, your comments should relate directly to the project scenario and apply the principles of project management.

Consider:

- what the issue was
- the impact of the issue
- how the issue was resolved.

This needs to be an accurate record of the issues. Identify the date the issue was raised and by whom, then provide a full description of the issue and the action taken to it and date closed.

Sample response extract

Issue log

Date raised	Raised by	Description	Action taken	Date closed
25/03/17	Technical Manager	EPOS manufacturer delivery problem	Delivery re-scheduled 10/04/17 New installation date 11/04/17	25/03/17

Now try this

The lessons learned have been identified above. Identify another impact to the project.

When considering impact to the project, think about:

- deadlines
- finance
- staff
- resources
- technical expertise.

Project closure email (1)

At the end of the project you may be asked to write an email to the project sponsor in which you review how well the project has performed against three main success criteria, evaluate the success of the project management process throughout the project life cycle and summarise the lessons learned and how these can be applied to other projects.

Sample response extract

Email	
From	
To	Abe Web Managing Director
Subject	Project closure

Dear...

Success criteria

The success criteria are ....

Review of project management

The project management ....

Summary of the lessons learned

Lessons learned are ....

Focus on the **key success areas** of the project. You should refer to the following documents to help you write your email:

- Project Initiation Document, including the SMART objectives
- Project Checkpoint Report, including work package tolerance status and lessons learned.

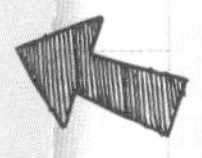

Structure your email into **sub-headings** to make it easier for you to complete. The success criteria should show how quality criteria were met and that you understand the scenario. Start from the beginning of the project.

Links For more information on how to review a project's success, see page 127.

Review of project management

Sample response extract

Email	
From	
To	Abe Web Managing Director
Subject	Project closure

Review of project management

- Conception and start-up – the project management and scope of the project was clearly defined during this stage. The project mandate was detailed and the client requirements captured through focus groups and questionnaires.
- Definition of the project
- Planning
- Launch and execution
- Closure
- Post-project evaluation

Make sure your review is balanced and has a wide-ranging evaluation of **all** relevant aspects of the project life cycle.

You should use clear, logical reasoning and show that you are aware of the project's life cycle, and your summary should have a clear link to the project and any project documents.

Links Have a look at page 107 for more information about the project life cycle.

Now try this

Using the information on page 103, how would you identify if a SMART objective has been met?

EPOS system launch date 01/04/17

Identify the objective first. Consider the information given carefully to identify if the objective was achieved.

Had a look ☐ Nearly there ☐ Nailed it! ☐

Project closure email (2)

Summary of lessons learned

Sample response extract

Email	
From	
To	Abe Web Managing Director
Subject	Project closure

Summary of the lessons learned

Lessons learned are that the testing process was completed before schedule 03/03/17 because ISO/IEC 25010:2011 was used as a benchmark for the software testing process.

Next time use ISO/IEC 25010:2011 for the software testing process. The use of flow charts allowed the testing process to be completed before the deadline date.

What went wrong

EPOS manufacturer has not been able to deliver the systems due to production problems.

Next time monitor the manufacturer's production closely.

Consider the lessons learned from **each stage** of the project life cycle identified:
- what went well and what you would do next time and why
- what went wrong and how would you ensure it did not happen again in new projects.

All of the lessons learned should be specific to relevant areas of the project and should indicate how those lessons could be applied to new projects.

Provide as much **additional information** as possible.

The Project Checkpoint Report also reviews the lessons learned – see page 122.

Look at page 126 for examples of lessons learned.

Check your email

- ✓ Open and close your email using professional language, e.g. Dear X, Yours sincerely, Kind regards.
- ✓ Use appropriate language to convey the lessons learned for the project.
- ✓ Use **accurate** technical vocabulary.
- ✓ Be aware of the intended audience.
- ✓ Check all sections are completed accurately.

Now try this

Create an email template with all of the key headings.

You could use this headings template:
FROM: Your name
TO: senior stakeholder
Subject: identify the project name and content, project closure.

Stages of software development

To solve the problem at the heart of your software development project you will need to match your purpose and actions to each of the stages of the software development life cycle (SDLC).

1 **Conception** – understand the project and what is being asked for

2 **Analysis** – investigate the project's need in greater detail

3 **Design** – produce pseudocode, flow charts, wireframes, data structures and algorithms that solve the problem

4 **Implementation** – translate the design into a working software solution and its deployment to its target environment

5 **Testing** – check to see if the software solution is working as required

6 **Evaluation** – assess the software solution from design, through implementation and testing to a comparison with the client's needs

Software development cycle. There is no standard model of the cycle – although stage names may change, the order generally remains the same.

Key questions

The questions below will help you identify the purpose and actions for each stage of the project life cycle.

Conception	Analysis	Design	Implementation	Testing	Evaluation
Why does this project need to be completed?	What are the client expectations?	What are the inputs, processes and outputs?	Which programming language is being targeted (and why)?	What types of testing are required?	Does the completed software solution meet the client expectations?
What are the stakeholder goals and objectives of the project, and their size?	What are the functional and operational requirements?	What data needs to be stored?	Which hardware and software development tools are required?	What types of test data need to be collected?	Are the design and program robust, accurate, efficient and reliable?
What is the timescale and is it feasible?	What resource and design constraints are present?	How should the user interact with the solution?	Is there any data to convert or training to provide?	Do actual and expected results match?	Is the software solution intuitive?
Who needs to provide project input?	What are the scope and boundaries of the project?	Which algorithms and logic are required?	How will the project be deployed?	What is working, and can identified faults be fixed?	Is the software easy to maintain and can it be improved?

Now try this

The list of key questions above is not exhaustive. Identify any additional questions that would be beneficial to ask at any stage of the SDLC's six stages.

When preparing to solve this problem think about:

- What is needed to investigate the problem?
- What is needed to design and implement a working solution?
- How do you know if the solution meets the client's needs?

Flow charts

You will need to revise the flow chart symbols and their correct usage in order to describe a system or solution for your software development project.

British Computer Society (BCS) flow chart symbols

BCS symbols	Shape name = flow chart name	Purpose
	Ellipse = terminator	Marks the **start** or **end** of the flow chart
	Diamond = decision	Used for making **decisions**
	Parallelogram = input/output	Used for **inputting** data or **outputting** information
	Circle = connector	Used to **connect** parts of the flow chart together without needing to cross lines
	Rectangle = process	Used to show a **process**, e.g. a calculation or action
	Arrow = logical flow	Used to demonstrate the **logical flow** to follow when reading

Advantages and disadvantages of using flow charts

Advantages	Disadvantages
Forms part of the solution's formal design documentation Aids the debugging process Illustrates the logical flow of the solution Provides a visual representation which can be easier to follow than structured English (pseudocode) Can be used to trace specific use cases.	Flow charts can get visually confusing as their logic becomes more complex, making them hard to read Minor modifications can mean time-consuming redrawing It's difficult to see the overall structure of the program, especially if the flow chart covers multiple pages.

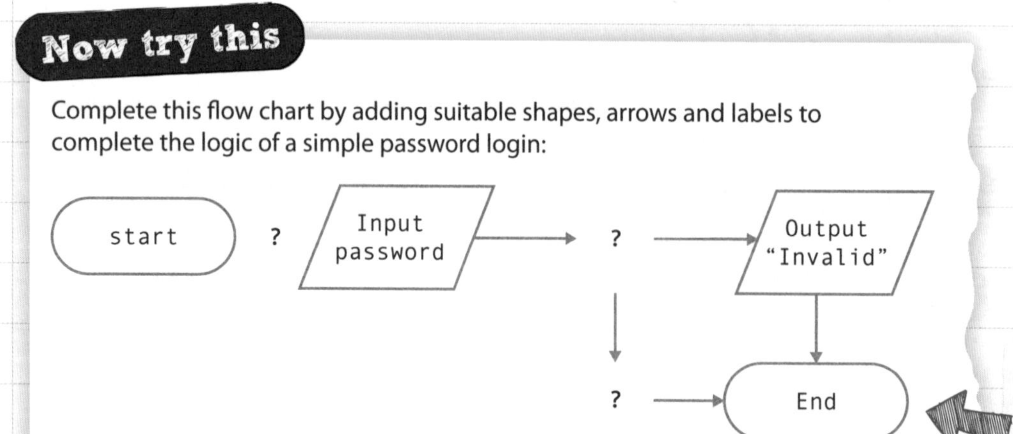

Using simple mnemonics (memory aids) can help you recall which shape performs which function, for example, (D)ecision =(D)iamond.

Pseudocode

You will probably use pseudocode to design an algorithm to solve a set problem before converting it to a specific programming language.

Links For more on pseudocode, see pages 9 and 10.

Pseudocode categories

Category	Concept	Examples
Sequence	A list of pseudocode instructions following one after another	**INPUT** age age = age + 1 **OUTPUT** "Next year you will be " age
Operations	Special keywords used to perform essential tasks in a pseudocode algorithm	**BEGIN** – start a section of pseudocode **END** – end a section of pseudocode **INPUT** – accept a value from the user and store it in an identifier **OUTPUT** – output a value, message or both on-screen **PRINT** – output a value or message, possibly to a printer **READ** – input values from a data file **WRITE** – write values to a data file

Decisions	Make selected pseudocode operations **optional** based on certain conditions	**IF** age < 18
		  OUTPUT "You are a minor"
		ELSE
		  OUTPUT "You are an adult"
		ENDIF

Repetitions	Make selected pseudocode operations **repeat** zero or more times	**INPUT** message **INPUT** times **FOR** counter = 1 to times **OUTPUT** message **END** FOR

Structure	A way of visually highlighting the structural logic of pseudocode, typically using indentation to distinguish decisions and repetitions	**FOR** counter = 1 to 10
		  IF counter **MOD** 2 = 0
		    OUTPUT counter " is an even number"
		  ELSE
		    OUTPUT counter " is an odd number"
		  ENDIF
		END FOR

Links For more on repetitions, see page 165.

Now try this

Look at the pseudocode. Read the algorithm carefully and answer the following questions:

(a) **Describe** the purpose of the algorithm.

(b) **Identify** and **fix** the **three** errors in the pseudocode.

```
INPUT rows
INPUT mytable

rowCount = 0
result = 0

REPEAT
    result = rowCount * table
    OUTPUT rowCount "X" table "=" result
    rowCount = rowCount - 1
UNTIL rowCount < rows
```

Had a look ☐ Nearly there ☐ Nailed it! ☐

Test data

Testing forms the penultimate part of the software development life cycle. A key aspect of proving the functionality of your programmed solution and, eventually, evaluating it is the selection and planning of appropriate tests.

What do you test?

Type of test	What it tests	Things to remember
Functionality	Do the workings of the program match user requirements?	• Functionality testing requires no understanding of the underlying program code. • Black-box testing focuses on this type of testing.
Stability	How reliably does the program perform under difficult conditions?	• Issues such as high data volumes or excessive number of users can place stress on a programmed solution, affecting its stability. • Tests for stability often deliberately go beyond the expected performance limits of a program.
Usability	How easy is the program to operate?	• Best performed by target users who have no involvement in the development process so are unlikely to be biased. • Users are typically observed, to document the issues and confusion that they may encounter whilst using the software, or they may be interviewed or complete questionnaires.

Test data choices

Normal test data	Data which is commonly entered and is within normal use and expected ranges
Extreme test data	Data which is uncommon or at the edges of expected ranges but is not invalid
Abnormal test data	Data which is invalid but could be entered by a user in error

What does test data do?

- ✓ Checks inputs
- ✓ Checks data storage, especially appropriateness of selected variable data types and structures
- ✓ Checks calculations are correct
- ✓ Checks program logic including selections and iterations
- ✓ Checks that validation methods are working correctly (especially for extreme and abnormal test data)
- ✓ Checks outputs
- ✓ Checks that functionality works as required

Now try this

As part of an educational software development project a program is required that simulates a bank's automatic teller machine (ATM), offering the user typical banking facilities such as:

1 enter PIN
2 deposit cash
3 withdraw funds
4 change personal identification number (PIN)
5 print a statement
6 exit ATM.

Anticipated inputs include:

- existing PIN
- new PIN
- menu option
- withdrawal cash amount (pounds only)
- deposit cash amount (pounds and pence).

Determine the different inputs required for the ATM simulator program.

For each input you have identified make suggestions for potential normal, extreme and abnormal test data.

Think about:
- the program's functionality
- the program's inputs
- normal test data
- extreme test data
- abnormal test data.

Design concepts

One key target for your software development project is to ensure the solution is **accurate**, **efficient** and **effective**. Always try to apply the principles of good practice design concepts across the overall solution, program code or actual user interface.

Good design concepts

Goals can be associated with the overall solution, the program code or the actual user interface, although there may be some natural cross-over between them.

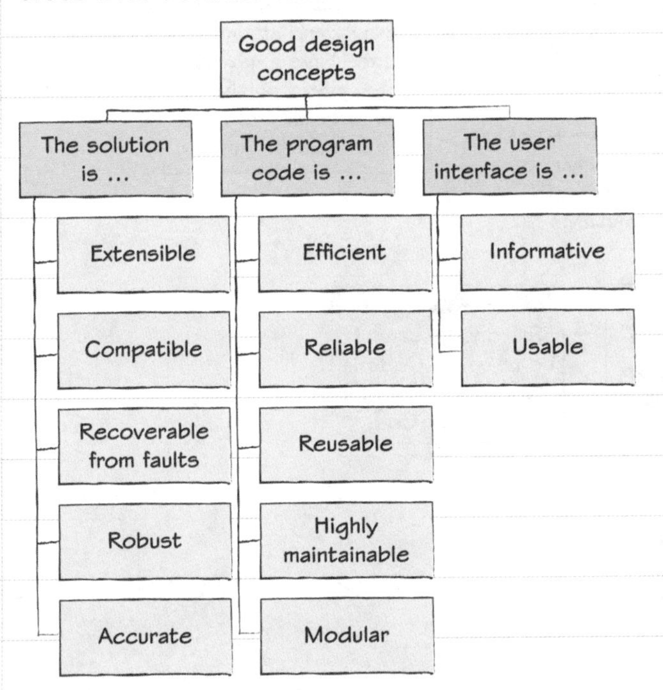

Always try to follow the principles of good design concepts in order to produce a worthwhile software development project for the client.

Goal	How to achieve it
Extensible	Would your program code be easy to modify if the client wanted new functionality or features?
Compatible	Does the solution work well on different platforms (hardware and operating systems)?
Recoverable from faults	If the solution goes wrong is it easy to fix and recover user data?
Robust	Does the solution handle bad data or incorrect key presses without breaking?
Accurate	Does your solution product correct outputs? Are calculations output as expected? Thorough testing should prove this is true.
Efficient	Is the program responsive, producing results quickly?
Reliable	Does your program work as expected every time? Is its behaviour predictable without having occasional unexpected errors?
Re-usable	Can elements of the program code (functions, etc.) be re-used?
Highly maintainable	Modular, well-commented program code is much easier to adapt, debug and expand upon. How professionally written is your program?
Modular	Is the program code split into separate functions rather than exists as one monolithic block?
Informative	Is the information supplied by the program useful to its user?
Usable	Is your program's interface easy to operate – even for new users?

Now try this

Which stage of the software development life cycle (SDLC) can help you to achieve the following good practice goals for your design:

- reliability
- robustness
- accuracy
- usability?
- informative

Think about the six different stages of the SDLC. Work through each stage sequentially until you find the one which has activities that should help you identify and iron out problems associated with achieving these goals.

For more on the SDLC, see page 139.

Had a look ☐ Nearly there ☐ Nailed it! ☐

Design pitfalls

It is quite easy to build solutions which suffer from poor design decisions. Knowing which pitfalls to avoid when designing a solution is critical to a successful software development project.

Key areas to avoid

Poorly designed solutions

Rigidity
The design is difficult to modify, typically because any change made has a 'knock-on' effect for aspects of the design which are highly interdependent.

Fragility
The design is not robust. It can be broken very easily and attempted fixes have a negative effect on the functionality of other parts of the design.

Dissatified users
The impact on user is clear: they become dissatisfied with using designs which challenge them and prove overly difficult to use, even though their functionality and features may be very rich.

Inconsistency
Designs may use different words for the same things or have different layouts or workflows which confuse the user and slow their progress. Designs are more intuitive to use when they are consistently planned.

Immobility
The design cannot be re-used. Code is too specific and single-purpose.

Ways to avoid creating a poorly designed solution

- Ensure you **understand** the nature and scope of the problem you are trying to solve.
- **Always** ask questions if you are not sure or need more information.
- Follow the conception, analysis and design stages of the software development life cycle **carefully**.
- **Decompose** complex problems into smaller chunks – they will be easier to solve.
- Where possible, design solutions in a **modular** fashion (using functions), as this will make it less rigid, easier to modify and not so fragile.
- Always plan to include **validation** as it helps make your code more robust.
- Pay attention to the **user interface aspects** of the solution, attempting to keep a **consistent** look and feel, layout, features and functionality.

Links To revise validation check techniques, see pages 160–164.

Now try this

You are about to start working on the design for your software development project and are anxious not to make silly mistakes.

Create a personal checklist of dos and don'ts that will help you create a good design that solves the problem satisfactorily.

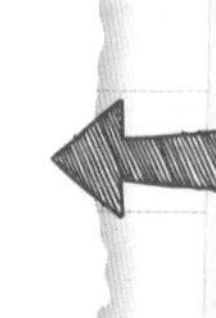

You must make sure that you can create links between the key areas of weakness found in poor designs and the strategies which can prevent these.

Code readability

Your software development project's solution will contain many lines of program code. The solution needs to meet the client's brief while the code should demonstrate your understanding of the underlying development strategy being used and be well written. Good code readability plays a vital role in this.

Links For more on programming development strategies, see page 139.

How to improve code readability

Technique	How it works	Practical example
Maintainability	Writing the program code in small modules ensures that the code is easy to read, understand and modify. Learn to decompose your solutions into these smaller parts to improve its maintainability.	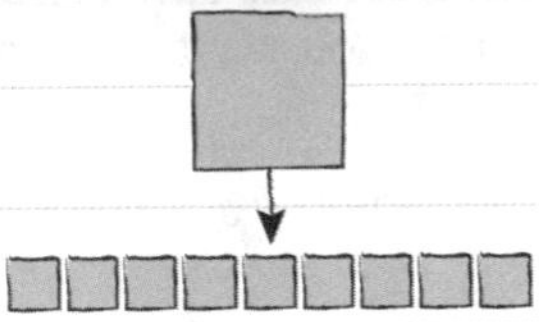

Naming conventions	Use consistent ways of naming identifiers in a program. Common standards include Hungarian notation, snake case and camel case. Above all, make sure all names are meaningful.	`//variable names using different`
		`//techniques`
		`int userAge;            //camel case`
		`float product_price; //snake case`
		`string SuserName;      //Hungarian`
		`int ImaxQty;           //Hungarian`

Indentation	Improve code layout by using white space. Blank lines can be used to separate key sections of code and its logical structure can be highlighted using indentation to align code inside repetitions and selections.	`//code being repeated is indented`
		
		`for (count=1; count<10; count++) {`
		`  cout << "Counter is " << count;`
		`  cout << endl;`
		`}`

Commenting/ code annotation	Most programming languages support the use of single or multiple line comments which are ignored by the computer when the program is translated.
	Remember, comments should explain the 'real-world' purpose of the code, not what the code's syntax actually means.
		`//calculate circle circumference`
		`circum = 2 * 3.14 * radiusCircle;`
		
		`/* This function is designed to`
		`   calculate a customer's order`
		`   discount.`
		
		`   Returns float (discount)`
		`*/`
		`float calcDiscount() {`
		`}`

Factors that contribute to the quality of code

Quality of code

Efficiency – solving the problem using the most processing-efficient manner

Readability – ensuring your code can be understood improves its maintainability

Robustness – writing code which is unlikely to crash makes your solution more reliable to use

Usability – adding features in the solution which improve the user's experience

Portability – how easy it will be to run your solution on another operating system or convert to a different programming language if required

Now try this

This section of C++ program code performs a fairly common arithmetic task but it is poorly written.

```
void myfunc (float n) {
int z; z = n * n * n;
cout << z;
}
```

Examine the code and make changes to improve its readability and overall quality.

Search for:

- missed opportunities for comments and code annotation
- lack of white space (blank lines or indentation)
- lack of meaningful identifiers
- potential bad choices which could affect the program's robustness.

Had a look ☐ Nearly there ☐ Nailed it! ☐

Simple data types

It is inevitable that you will need to declare different constants and variables as part of your software development project's program code for storing inputs, calculations and outputs. In order to store data accurately you have to be able to identify the correct data type to use.

When and how to use simple data types

Unlike C++, some programming languages such as Python determine a variable's data type from its initialisation.

Data type	When to use it	How to use it

Integer	When you want to store a **whole number**, i.e. one that has no decimal part.
	Examples: age, number of children, quantities.
		`Declaration in C++`
		`int userAge;          //user's age`
		
		`Declaration/Initialisation in Python 3.X`
		`userAge = 0           # user's age`

Floating point	When you want to store a number which **may** have a decimal part.
	Examples: monetary sums, discount percentage, prices, accurate measurements, etc.
		`Declaration in C++`
		`float productPrice; //product price`
		
		`Declaration/Initialisation in Python 3.X`
		`productPrice = 0.0  # product price`

Character	When you want to store a **single** character – may be any valid character for the operating system, for example digit, letter, symbol, etc.
	Examples: initial, grade, key press, gender.
		`Declaration in C++`
		`char gender;          //M or F`
		
		`Declaration/Initialisation in Python 3.X`
		`gender = "?"          # M or F`

String	When you want to store a **combination** of different **characters**.
	Examples: names, addresses, postcodes, serial numbers, telephone numbers.
		`Declaration in C++`
		`String lastName;     //last name`
		
		`Declaration/Initialisation in Python 3.X`
		`lastName = "Unknown" # last name`

Boolean	A logical data type which can only store TRUE or FALSE, usually to act as a 'flag'.
	Examples: isInstalled, isValid, isOpen, passwordOK.
		`Declaration in C++`
		`Bool isValid;        //valid flag`
		
		`Declaration/Initialisation in Python 3.X`
		`isValid = False      # set false`

Things to consider when selecting the most appropriate data type

- ✓ **Suitability** – does the chosen type store the value fully with no data loss?
- ✓ **Range** – what is the effective value range for a specific data type, for example, an integer can vary between languages?
- ✓ **Data type name** – some data types vary in name between programming languages, for example, Pascal's 'real' data type is similar to C/C++'s 'float'.
- ✓ **Portability** – does a similar data type exist in other programming languages?

Now try this

A project needs to calculate a student's subject completion by their average grade (F, P, M or D), calculated from averaging three different subject exam percentages in a year. Write either the correct variable declarations in C++ or initialisations in Python.

- Think about the values that need storing.
- Think about what data types are needed.
- Think about using meaningful names for each variable.

Arrays in Python

On this page, you will revise how to handle data in a program using the Python programming language. If your software development project needs to store a great quantity of data which requires to be processed in a similar way, then you will use arrays.

Types of array and how to use them

An array is a data structure which may be fixed in size and typically stores elements of the same data type. Array elements can be accessed in **any order** using their positional (or '**index**') number. Although Python doesn't have a native array data structure, the use of **lists** is a good substitute.

Array type	When to use it	How to use it

One-dimensional (1D)	Storing a sequence of values of the same type, for example temperatures recorded across **a week.**
	7 floating point elements are required.
	The first element typically starts at index 0.
		Declaration and initialisation in Python
		`#1 week temps`
		`tempWeeks = [12.9,13.2,14.2,17.1,16.0,17,15]`
		
		Storing in Python
		`tempWeeks[2]=14.3`
		
		Accessing in Python
		`print(tempWeeks[0],' deg C')`

Two-dimensional (2D)	Storing a sequence of values of the same type, for example temperatures recorded across **two weeks.**
	2 x 7 floating point elements are required.
	In Python, multidimensional arrays can be treated as a list of sub-lists, allowing each sub-list to be accessed separately.
		Declaration and initialisation in Python
		`#2 week temps`
		`tempWeeks=[[12.9,13.2,14.2,17.1,16.0,17],[14.1,13,16,15.5,13.2,14.2,10]]`
		
		Storing in Python
		`#week 2, Day 1`
		`tempWeeks[1][0] = 22.4;`
		
		Accessing in Python
		`#print all 1st week`
		`print(tempWeeks[0])`
		
		`#print 2nd week, Day 1`
		`print(tempWeeks[1][0], ' deg C')`

Three-dimensional (3D)	Storing a sequence of values of the same type, for example temperatures recorded across **two weeks** in **three** different locations.
	3 x 2 x 7 floating point elements are required.
		Declaration and initialisation in Python
		`tempWeeksLocs=[[[12.9,13.2,14.2,17.1,16.0,17,15],[14.1,13,16,15.5,` <···>
		`13.2,14.2,10]],`
		`[[22.9,23.2,24.2,27.1,26.0,27,25],[24.1,23,26,25.5,23.2,24.2,20]],`
		`[[32.9,33.2,34.2,37.1,36.0,37,35],[34.1,33,36,35.5,33.2,34.2,30]]]`
		
		Accessing in Python
		`#print 3rd Location, 1st week, Day 7`
		`print(tempWeeksLocs[2][0][6], ' deg C')`

<···> indicates the next line of code is a continuation of the same line.

Now try this

Examine each array required and write its correct declaration (and sample initialisation) in Python:

(a) points scored by a team for 10 English Football Association matches

(b) function state (working/not working) of 20 desktop computers in a classroom.

Before writing the correct array declaration think about:

- a meaningful array name
- the number of dimensions and elements required
- the type of data that needs to be stored.

Had a look ☐ Nearly there ☐ Nailed it! ☐

Arrays in C++

On this page, you will revise how to handle data in a program using the C++ programming language. If your software development project needs to store a great quantity of data which requires to be processed in a similar way, then you will use arrays.

Types of array and how to use them

An array is a data structure which may be fixed in size and typically stores elements of the same data type. Array elements can be accessed in **any order** using their positional (or '**index**') number.

Array type	When to use it	How to use it

One-dimensional (1D)	Storing a sequence of values of the same type, for example temperatures recorded across **a week**.
	7 floating point elements are required.
	The first element typically starts at 0.
		`Declaration in C++`
		`float tempWeek[7];  //1 week temps`
		
		`Storing in C++`
		`tempWeek[0] = 23.5f;`
		
		`Accessing in C++`
		`cout << tempWeek[0] << " deg C";`

Two-dimensional (2D)	Storing a sequence of values of the same type, for example temperatures recorded across **two weeks**.
	2 x 7 floating point elements are required.
		`Declaration in C++`
		`float tempWeeks[2][7];  //2 week temps`
		
		`Storing in C++`
		`tempWeeks[0][0] = 23.5f; //Week 1, Day 1`
		`tempWeeks[1][0] = 22.4f; //week 2, Day 1`
		
		`Accessing in C++`
		`cout << tempWeeks[0][0] << " deg C";`
		`cout << tempWeeks[1][0] << " deg C";`

Three-dimensional (3D)	Storing a sequence of values of the same type, for example temperatures recorded across **two weeks** in **three** different locations.
	3 x 2 x 7 floating point elements are required.
		`Declaration in C++`
		`float tempWeeksLocs[3][2][7];`
		
		`Storing in C++`
		`//Location 3, Week 1, Last day`
		`tempWeeksLocs[2][0][6] = 17.5f;`
		
		`Accessing in C++`
		`cout << tempWeeksLocs[2][0][6] << " deg C";`

Things to consider when using arrays:

- Some languages allow arrays to be resized, making them a dynamic rather than static data structure.
- Some languages allow arrays to contain mixed data types.
- Accessing elements beyond array limits may cause unexpected results or crash your program!

Now try this

Examine each array required and write its correct declaration in C++:

(a) points scored by a team for 10 English Football Association matches
(b) function state (working/not working) of 20 desktop computers in a classroom
(c) heights (in metres) of two flood-risk rivers over the past 30 days.

Think about:

- a **meaningful** array **name**
- the number of **dimensions** required
- the number of elements required in **each** dimension
- the **type of data** that needs to be stored.

Date and time in Python

Many real-world problems involve the processing of dates and times. In software development projects where you may be dealing with bookings, appointments, events, timestamps and so on, you may need to perform various kinds of basic arithmetic on these data types, for example, calculating the date in 7 days time or the time in 30 minutes.

Calculating with dates and times in Python

Python uses a datetime library to assist with the processing of dates and times. This library has four types of objects that you should know: date, time, datetime and timedelta.

To use these, you add the following line of code to your Python script:

```
from datetime import date, time, datetime, timedelta
```

Operation	When to use it	How to use it

Creating a specific date	To create a new date, for example for a calendar	`#set today's date`
		`today = date.today()`
		`#set a specific date`
		`birthday = date(2000, 2, 1)`

Creating a specific time	To create a new time, for example for an appointment event in a diary
	Remember: use a 24-hour clock to specify am or pm
		`#set current time`
		`rightNow = datetime.now().time()`
		`print(rightNow)`
		
		`#set a specific time`
		`appointmentTime = time(hour=9, minute=30, second=10)`
		`print(appointmentTime)`

Calculating with dates	To work out how many days have elapsed between two dates or to project a new date in the future	`#working out age in days`
		`daysOld = today - birthday`
		`print(daysOld)`
		`#set arrival date`
		`arrival = date(2017,1,7)`
		`daysStayed = timedelta(days=7)`
		`#calculate departure date`
		`departure = arrival + daysStayed`
		`print("Your stay is ", arrival," to ", departure)`

Calculating with times	To calculate the number of minutes that have elapsed between two events on the same day, for example the length of a work shift	`#working out work shift length`
		`startShift = time(hour=8, minute=45, second=0)`
		`endShift = time(hour=17, minute=30, second=0)` ↔
		`lengthShift = datetime.combine(date.today(), endShift)`
		`- datetime.combine(date.today(), startShift)`
		`print ("Minutes logged: ", lengthShift)`

Things to consider when using dates and times:

- Remember to import the relevant module and objects needed.
- Different types of objects exist, e.g. date, time, datetime, timedelta, etc.
- There are many ways of achieving the same outcomes when working with dates and times.

Now try this

The following Python code outputs dates in a number of different formats.

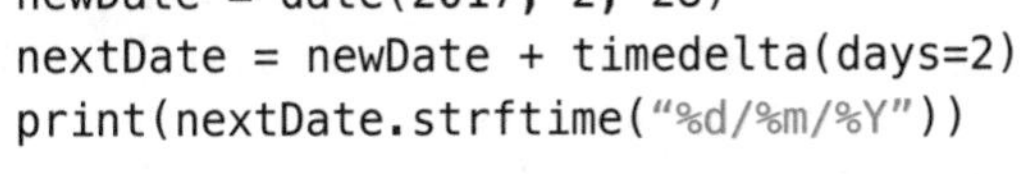

```
newDate = date(2017, 2, 28)
nextDate = newDate + timedelta(days=2)
print(nextDate.strftime("%d/%m/%Y"))
```

Examine each line of Python code and work out what the final output will be.

Think about:
- the way date objects are created
- how date arithmetic works
- how dates are typically formatted.

Classes and objects

Both Python and C++ are object-oriented programming (OOP) languages. You may decide to adopt the OOP paradigm while working on your software development project. To do so successfully you need to revise classes and objects.

Classes and objects

A class consists of encapsulated methods (functions which act on data) and properties (its data). An **object** is a 'concrete' instance of a **class**. Each **instantiated** object has the same methods, but can have unique properties. The interactions between objects define how modern OOP solutions work.

Action	How to use it

C++
Create a class
	`class circle {`
	
	`private:`
	`  float radius;`
	`  float area;`
	
	`public:`
	`  void setRadius(float tempR) {this->radius = tempR;}`
	`  void calcArea();`
	`};`
	
	`void circle::calcArea() {`
	`  this->area = pow(this->radius,2) * 3.14f;`
	`  cout << “Area is ” << this->area << endl;`
	`}`

C++ Declare an object from the class	`circle myCircle;`
C++ Call an object's methods	`myCircle.setRadius(10);` `myCircle.calcArea();`

Python
Create a class
	`class circle:`
	
	`  def setRadius(self, tempR=None):`
	`    self.radius = tempR`
	
	`  def calcArea(self):`
	`    self.area = pow(self.radius,2) * 3.14`
	`    print(“Area is ”, self.area)`

Python Declare an object from the class	`myCircle = circle()`
Python Call an object's method	`myCircle.setRadius(10)` `myCircle.calcArea()`

Things to consider when using classes:

- A class should be self-contained, having all the methods and properties it needs to function.
- An OOP solution may need many different classes.
- Objects are created from classes.
- Objects interact to form the solution.

Now try this

The program is to be modified to also calculate and output the circle's circumference, using the same radius. Examine the problem and modify the provided code to extend the existing OOP solutions in either C++ or Python.

Think about:

- whether any new properties are needed
- whether any new methods are needed
- what actions the new method will perform
- how the new method will be called
- circumference is calculated as 2 × π × radius.

Records

You will need to use record-like data structures if your software development project intends to store mixed data and potentially use data files.

How to use records

A record is a data structure which consists of a number of different elements. Unlike a classic array, each element may be of a different data type. Record elements can be accessed in **any order** using their name. Record structures may have different names depending on the programming language you have chosen; C/C++ uses **struct**, Python can use various techniques including **lists**, **tuples** and **dictionaries**.

Action	How to use it – C/C++	How to use it – Python (dictionaries)

Create a record structure	`struct product {`
	`int productID;`
	`string name;`
	`float price;`
	`int stockQty;`
	`bool discontinued;`
	`};`
		`#No direct equivalent`

Declare a variable of this new type	`product myProduct;`	`#No direct equivalent`

Initialise a new record	`myProduct.productID = 10;`
	`myProduct.name = “Widget”;`
	`myProduct.price = 0.99f;`
	`myProduct.stockQty = 100;`
	`myProduct.discontinued = false;`
		`myProduct = { 1 : {‘productID’: 10, ‘name’:` <⋯>
		`‘Widget’, ‘price’ : 0.99, ‘stockQty’: 100,`
		`‘discontinued’ : False }}`

Output the new record	`cout << myProduct.productID;`
	`cout << myProduct.name;`
	`cout << myProduct.price;`
	`cout << myProduct.stockQty;`
	`cout << myProduct.discontinued;`
		`print (myProduct[1][‘productID’])`
		`print (myProduct[1][‘name’])`
		`print (myProduct[1][‘price’])`
		`print (myProduct[1][‘stockQty’])`
		`print (myProduct[1][‘discontinued’])`

Things to consider when using records:

- Arrays can be used to create multiple records, for example multiple products.
- Records can be written to a data file for non-volatile storage.
- Records can be read from data file.

Now try this

Declare an appropriate record structure to store data required for a comic book fan's collection of 2000 comics. A sample entry is shown below:

ID : 1010
Title: The Incredible Hero-man!
Volume: 1
Issue: 300
Grade: NM
Price: 40.00
Notes: 300th Anniversary Issue

Examine the data required for the record structure and write its correct declaration and initialisation in C++ and Python.

Think about:
- a **meaningful** record **name**
- meaningful name for each record element
- the **type of data** that needs to be stored for each element.

Sets in Python

Practical knowledge of using sets is an essential skill if your software development project needs to perform membership testing and checking for duplicate entries.

Sets and how to use them

A set is a data structure which stores a collection of **non-duplicated values** of the same data type. Members of the multiple sets can be interrogated through the use of mathematical operations.

Union

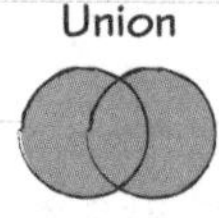

Intersection

Difference

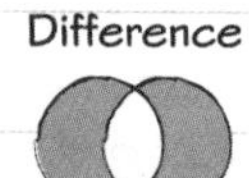

Set operation	When to use it	How to use it

Creating a set	To create a set of non-duplicated values, for example a list of users who have an account
	Remember: Python can create **empty sets** and can **remove** any duplicates
		#create empty set of user names
		usernames = set()
		
		#create set of valid user names
		usernames = {'tom','claire','nisar','odette','tom'}
		
		#list the users (no duplicates)
		print('list of users: ', usernames)

Testing membership of the set	To see if a particular data value is present in the set, for example if a particular user's name is a member of the set	#input a name and check if its valid
		name = input('Enter name: ')
		if (name in usernames):
		  print('Yes, ', name, ' is valid')
		else:
		    print('No, ', name, ' is invalid')

Intersection	To list unique users in the **intersection of both sets**, for example normal users who **also** have an admin account	#creating a second set
		usersadmin = {'tom','odette','chen'}
		
		print (usernames & usersadmin)

Difference	To list unique users in **just one set**, for example admin users who don't have a normal user account	print (usersadmin - usernames)
Union	To list in **either** set, for example any type of user	print (usersadmin | usernames)
Symmetric difference	To list unique users **who are only in one set**, for example admin or normal user, **but not both**	print (usersadmin ^ usernames)

Things to consider when using sets:

- Sets are ideal for storing membership lists.
- Sets can be used to combine and separate similar sets of data.
- Sets can be used for simple validation.

Links For more on validation checks, see pages 160–164.

Now try this

The following Python code could be used to differentiate potential names for babies of either gender.

```
boyNames = {'frank','ron','phil','alex','jo','chris'}
girlNames = {'jess','alex','jo','chris','alex'}
print (boyNames & girlNames)
print (boyNames - girlNames)
print (boyNames | girlNames)
print (boyNames ^ girlNames)
```

Examine each line of Python code and work out what the outputs are from each print function.

Lists in Python

One of the most basic aspects of problem solving is the ability to manage lists of data. If your software development project needs to store and process lists of data, you will need to revise Python's versatile list data structure.

Lists and how to use them

A list is a data structure which stores a collection of data items. In Python these values can be of **mixed** data types, for example, characters, strings and integers.

List operation	When to use it	How to use it

Creating a set	To create a list of values which can be used to store mixed or single-type data items	`#create list of valid user names`
		`usernames = ['tom','claire','nisar','odette']`
		
		`#create list of mixed values`
		`myValues = ['Quincy',1.24,1983,"a"]`
		
		`#create list of products, quantities and prices`
		`customerBasket = ['Widget',2,2.40,'Doohickey',3,1.20]`

Accessing values in the list	To output a particular value or subset of values	`#outputting data at index position 2`
		`print(usernames[2])`
		
		`#outputting data in index positions 1 to up to 4`
		`print (usernames[1:4])`

Updating and deleting values in the list	To change specific values in the list or remove them	`#changing the customer's Doohickey quantity to 9`
		`customerBasket[4] = 9`
		
		`#removing the 'Widget' item from the basket`
		`del customerBasket[0:3]`

Performing basic functions on a list	To get the number of items in a list, join lists together or check if a value is present	`#outputting the number of items in the list`
		`print(len(myValues))`
		
		`#joining two lists (appending)`
		`newusers = ['matt','bek','jo','chris']`
		`usernames = usernames + newusers`
		
		`#checking customer's basket for a particular product`
		`print('Flange' in customerBasket)`

Things to consider when using lists:

- They are ideal for validating a list of permissible values.
- They can store mixed data types.
- They are created using a simple comma-separated notation.

Now try this

The following Python code processes a simple list of month names.

```
months = ['Jan','Feb','Mar','Apr','May']
months = months + ['June']
del months[3]
months[3] = months[4]
print('May' in months)
```

Examine each line of Python code and work out what the final output will be.

Think about:
- the data stored in the list and each item's position
- which list operations are being performed
- how the list will be changed by each operation.

Had a look ☐ Nearly there ☐ Nailed it! ☐

Local and global variables

It is almost impossible to write a program for a software development project without having to create variables. A variable, which is a type of identifier that represents a value stored in the computer's RAM, may be declared either locally or globally. This choice has an impact on how the rest of the program is written.

Local versus global variables

<table>
<tr><th>Type</th><th>Strengths and weaknesses</th><th>How to declare them</th></tr>
<tr><td>Local</td><td>👍 Declared within a function or block of code
👍 RAM used by local variables is normally de-allocated when function ends (short 'lifetime')
👎 Can only be seen and used within that function or block (called its scope)
👎 Local variables have to be passed 'in' to functions as parameters to be processed
👍 Can assist debugging as variable errors can be tracked to their specific functions</td><td rowspan="2">In Python
<code>def calcWages():</code>
<code>   wages = hours * rate</code>
<code>   print("Wages are £",wages)</code>

<code>hours = int(input("Enter hours worked: "))</code>

<code>rate = int(input("Enter hourly rate (£) : "))</code>

<code>calcWages()</code>

In this example:
• hours and rate are global (declared outside the calcWages function)
• wages is local (declared inside the calcWages function)
• wages cannot be accessed outside the function as it would be outside its scope and not visible
• hours and rate are global so can be accessed anywhere in the program (even in the calcWages function).</td></tr>
<tr><td>Global</td><td>👍 Declared outside a function or block of code
👍 Can be used anywhere (have global scope)
👍 Have a long lifetime
👎 More difficult to debug as errors changing their values could be anywhere in the program</td></tr>
</table>

Things to consider when declaring variables:

- It is generally easier to code using global variables.
- Global variables can make debugging more difficult.
- Local variables can have the same names as global variables (and would take precedence within their scope) but this can be confusing.
- Use of local variables is usually preferred.
- Some programming languages have different ways of declaring local and global variables.

Now try this

The following Python code has an error which needs to be debugged:

```
def calcGrades():
    totalMarks = mark1 + mark2 + mark3
    average = totalMarks / 3
mark1 = int(input("Enter marks for exam 1: "))
mark2 = int(input("Enter marks for exam 2: "))
mark3 = int(input("Enter marks for exam 3: "))
calcGrades()
print("Exam average is: ", average)
```

Examine the Python code, locate the error and correct it to produce a working program. Explain your debugging rationale.

Think about:
- the purpose of the program
- which variables are global
- which variables are local
- the scope of each variable and its visibility.

Naming conventions

The key to creating identifiers, particularly variables, is having a good understanding of the problem you are trying to solve. Although choosing correct data types is critical, the selection and consistent application of naming conventions will help your software development project to look more professional.

Different naming conventions

There are many naming conventions used in commercial development and almost all are usable in the most popular programming languages. Some languages such as Java recommend different naming conventions for different types of identifier (variables, constants, classes, methods, etc.).

Type	Features	C++ examples

PascalCase	• Sometimes called 'UpperCamelCase'.
	• First letter of every word is capitalised.
	• The capital letters recall the humps of a camel's back.
		`string UserName;`
		`int QuantityOfItems;`
		`float OrderPrice;`
		`bool CustomerFound;`

Snake_case	• Each word is written in lower case.
	• Each word is separated by an underscore
	• A study has reported improved identifier recognition speeds when using this style.
		`string user_name;`
		`int quantity_of_items;`
		`float order_price;`
		`bool customer_found;`

camelCase	• Sometimes called 'lowerCamelCase' or medial capitals.
	• Each word is capitalised **apart** from the first one.
		`string userName;`
		`int quantityOfItems;`
		`float orderPrice;`
		`bool customerFound;`

Hungarian notation	• Named after the Hungarian custom of names being presented 'surname' then 'first name'.
	• Each identifier has a lower case prefix which describes the **data type** or **purpose** of the variable, for example, fnCheckLogin is a function, fpWages is a floating point number.
	• There are two forms: system and apps.
	• Was popularly used by Microsoft.
		`string strUserName;`
		`int iQuantityOfItems;`
		`float fpOrderPrice;`
		`bool bCustomerFound;`

Why do we use naming conventions?

- ✓ To improve the program's readability
- ✓ To meet standards and expectations of an organisation or customer
- ✓ To avoid ambiguity
- ✓ To help connect the program to the real-world problem
- ✓ To self-document identifiers, for example, add additional information (metadata) as part of their names
- ✓ To assist future maintenance, especially after developer changeover
- ✓ To provide a professional look and feel
- ✓ To assist Integrate Development Environments, which can re-factor (split and re-organise) code automatically if names are used consistently.

Now try this

A C++ program is required which asks users about their household internet connection. It will allow the user to input:

- their postcode
- the monthly cost of their broadband connection
- whether their broadband connection includes cable television
- the number of devices typically connected to the internet in the house at any given time.

Write C++ program code to declare the required variables using Hungarian notation.

Think about:
- which data types are being used
- the purpose of each variable
- how the chosen naming convention is applied for each data type.

Arithmetic operations

Arithmetic operations are likely to play an important part in building the calculations, decisions and repetitions required to complete your software development project.

Links For more on date and time, see page 149.

Arithmetic symbols and their meanings

Category	Concept	Examples
Mathematical	Symbols used to perform basic and advanced operations on numerical data	**+** add **−** subtract **/** divide (forward slash symbol) ***** multiply (asterisk symbol) **%** or **MOD** (get the remainder from integer division)
Relational	Symbols used to compare two different values (of comparable data type), for example numeric, string, date	**=** or **==** the test for equality (same) **< >** or **!=** the test for inequality (not the same) **<** less than **>** greater than **<=** less than or equal to **>=** greater than or equal to
Boolean	Operators which perform logical operations on data	**NOT** – inverting true to false, false to true **AND** – all things must be true **OR** – one or the other (or both) must be true

When to use the different types of operator

✓ Arithmetic – when performing mathematical calculations on data, for example, calculating a result

✓ Relational – when comparing two different values, often in the condition in a decision or repetition

✓ Boolean – when joining multiple conditions together in a decision or repetition

Building conditions using different operators

Remember that **relational** and **Boolean** operators may be combined to form **compound conditions** that control decisions or repetitions, for example:

- for a simple decision

```
IF quantity < 1 OR quantity > 100
  OUTPUT "Quantity in basket must be between 1 and 100."
ELSE
  OUTPUT quantity " item(s) added to your basket."
END IF
```

- for a simple repetition.

```
REPEAT
  OUTPUT "Seats to book? (max 3 per customer):"
  INPUT seats
UNTIL seats >= 1 AND seats <= 3
```

Now try this

Evaluate each of the expressions and determine these correct screen outputs by identifying the operator and using it correctly to process its associated data.

```
OUTPUT 2 - 7
OUTPUT "Hello" + " World!"
OUTPUT 10 > 99
OUTPUT "a" == "b"
OUTPUT 13 % 2
OUTPUT 10 > 20 OR 15 < 30
OUTPUT 32/2 == 4 * 4
OUTPUT "A" < "B"
```

Each expression will evaluate to a single text, numeric or Boolean value.

Arithmetic functions

In addition to the common arithmetic operators (+, /, − and *), most programming languages have built-in functions which offer opportunities to develop your software development project's program more efficiently.

Random

Python has a pseudo-random number generator which can be accessed by importing its random module, for example:

```
import random

#random number between 0and1
print(random.random())
```

This **could** output:

0.0908436062120459

It is also possible to request a random integer in a **specific range**, for example:

```
print(random.randint(1,20))
```

Round

You could use this function to round floating point numbers to a specific number of decimal places, for example:

```
myNumber = 10.528
myRounded = round(myNumber,2)
print(myRounded)
```

This **would** output:

10.53

Arithmetic functions

Range

You can use this function to generate a sequence of numbers (such as when pre-filling data), for example:

```
for counter in range(0,5):
  print(counter)
```

This **would** output:

0
1
2
3
4

Truncate

Python has many mathematical functions that can be accessed by importing its math module, usually for approximation, for example to truncate a float and just leave the integer part:

```
import math
myNumber = 2.985
print (math.trunc(myNumber))
```

This **would** output:

2

Now try this

A statistics program is being developed for a client as a software development project. Part of the solution requires the random roll of two dice. As in the real world, each dice can only show numbers 1 to 6 inclusive.

Write appropriate Python code to generate and output the two dice roll values.

Test this code repeatedly to ensure the dice behave normally.

Identify the correct arithmetic function to use.

Had a look ☐ Nearly there ☐ Nailed it! ☐

String-handling functions

Strings are an important component of any program written as part of a software development project. On this page, you will revise the built-in functions which exist to handle these strings in your chosen programming language.

String-handling techniques and how to use them

Technique	How to use it – C/C++	How to use it – Python
Concatenation ('joining together')	string part1 = “Hello”; string part2 = “ World!”; string part3 = part1 + part2; cout << part3;	string1 = “Hello” string2 = “ World!” string3 = string1 + string2 print (string3)
Obtaining string length	string sample = “Pearson”; int length; length = sample.length(); cout << sample << “ is ” << length << <--> character(s) long”;	sample = “Pearson” length = len(sample) print (sample, “ is ”, length, “ <--> character(s) long”)
Extracting characters (position)	string sample = “Pearson”; char char3 = sample[2]; cout << char3;	sample = “Pearson” char3 = sample[2] print (char3)

Conversion to string	//Integer to string
	int iTelephone = 123456;
	string sTelephone = to_string(iTelephone);
	cout << sTelephone;
	
	//Float to string
	float fPrice = 12.95;
	string sPrice = to_string(fPrice);
	cout << sPrice;
		#Integer to string
		iTelephone = 123456
		sTelephone = str(iTelephone)
		print (iTelephone)
		
		#Float to string
		fPrice = 12.95
		sPrice = str(fPrice)
		print (sPrice)

Conversion from string	//String to integer
	string sTelephone = “123456”;
	int iTelephone = stoi(sTelephone);
	cout << iTelephone;
	
	//String to float
	string sPrice = “12.95”;
	float fPrice = stof(sPrice);
	cout << fPrice;
		#String to integer
		sTelephone = “123456”
		iTelephone = int(sTelephone)
		print (iTelephone)
		
		#String to float
		sPrice = “12.95”
		fPrice = float(sPrice)
		print (fPrice)

Things to consider when working with strings:

- In most languages it is not possible to perform arithmetic on a string, even if its value 'looks' like a number; you will need to convert it first.
- In most programming languages the first character position (or index) is 0.
- Strings can be empty.

Now try this

A program requires a new product's stock code to be calculated from the initial letter of its category and the length of its name multiplied by 9. The product is called a 'Widget99' and it is a 'Miscellaneous' item. Process and output the new stock code.

Read through the problem extract carefully and solve it using both C++ and Python.

Think about:
- how the data is initially stored
- the names of the variables being used
- the built-in functions which you will need to use in both programming languages.

General functions

On this page, you will revise common functions that exist within a programming language.

General functions

Print

Python uses the print function as its primary technique for outputting messages and values on the screen or file, for example:

```
number = 10.5

print("hello")
print(number)
print("Number is ", number)
```

It can also be used in conjunction with other functions, for example, displaying today's date:

```
import time
print(time.strftime("%d/%m/%y"))
```

Input

This function is the preferred way to pause a Python script and accept key presses from the user, storing it in a variable for later use, for example:

```
name = input("What is your name?")
print("Hello, ", name)
```

This would display:

What is your name? Mark
Hello, Mark

Range

Range is a flexible function and has many varied uses, for example, to populate a list of values.

```
myList = list(range(1,10))
print(myList)
```

This would display:

[1, 2, 3, 4, 5, 6, 7, 8, 9]

Open

This powerful function opens files for **reading** and **writing** data more permanently, for example to disk:

```
myfile = open("myFile.txt","r")

for eachLine in myfile:
    print(eachLine,end='')

myfile.close()
```

This would read and output the contents of named text file to screen.

Now try this

Using appropriate software, type and execute this code to determine what it does and how it works.

```
myMax = int(input ("Enter max. value:"))

myData = list(range(1, myMax))

myNewFile = open("myNewFile.txt","w")

for eachNumber in myData:
    print(eachNumber, file=myNewFile)

myNewFile.close()
```

The short Python code extract contains a number of general functions.

Had a look ☐ Nearly there ☐ Nailed it! ☐

Validation check: Data type

Validation is the process of checking whether a user's inputs make sense. Including effective validation in your program will improve its quality by making it much more robust.

Validating by data type

One of the most common types of error occurs when a user enters data of the wrong type, for example inputting text when a number is expected. Implementing validation by data type in your software development project is easily achieved in programming languages such as Python.

Data types that can be validated

- Numeric types, for example integers and floating point numbers
- Strings
- Dates

Example – validating an integer

To validate an input as an integer the best technique is to use a programmer-defined function to attempt to convert the inputted string to an integer in a try...except block, returning a Boolean true if it succeeds and a Boolean false if the conversion fails.

Place this inside a pre-conditioned while loop to keep repeating until an integer is input.

Python code.

```
def is_int(n):
  try:
    int(n)
    return True
  except ValueError:
    return False

myInput = input("Enter a new integer")
while (not is_int(myInput)):
    print("Sorry, you must input an integer")
    myInput = input("Enter a new integer: ")

print("Thank you for entering a valid integer")
```

Example – validating a date

Inputting and validating dates is an important part of any software development project where the solution needs to track bookings, events, attendances, diary entries, etc.

The code is largely the same as the integer validation version, but specifically requires dates to be entered in a dd/mm/yyyy format, for example 10/1/2017 for 10 January 2017. Unlike the integer solution, the code needs to include the appropriate module and classes.

Python code

```
from datetime import datetime

def is_date(d):
  try:
    datetime.strptime(d,'%d/%m/%Y')
    return True
  except ValueError:
    return False

myInput = input("Enter a new date (dd/mm/yyyy): ")
while (not is_date(myInput)):
    print("Sorry, you must input a date (dd/mm/yyyy): ")
    myInput = input("Enter a new date (dd/mm/yyyy): ")

print("Thank you for entering a valid date")
```

Now try this

Part of a software development project involves the input of prices for purchased goods. Each item has a price that may be expressed as a floating point number, for example 1.36.

Modify the integer validation to perform suitable validation for an inputted product price. Integer inputs should also be allowed.

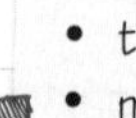

Think about:

- the data type required
- modifications to function names
- modifications to input prompts to fit the given scenario.

Validation check: Range

You need to revise how to perform range-based validation as this is a very common programming requirement.

What is a range?

A range is a continuous set of values that occur between a set of inclusive lower and upper limits, for example a range 1 to 5 would incorporate the values 1, 2, 3, 4 and 5. In some programming languages, ranges can also be alphabetic, for example, an inclusive range of 'A' to 'E' would include 'A', 'B', 'C', 'D' and 'E'. Range validation may also include specifying the number of characters in a string, using its minimum and maximum length.

Working with non-contiguous ranges

Sometimes you may wish to check a range of values that **aren't** adjacent to each other. In Python this can be achieved using a **list**:

```
menuChoice = ' '
while menuChoice not in ['D','W','S']:
    print("Welcome to Python Bank!")
    print("(D) Deposit money")
    print("(W) Withdraw money")
    print("(S) Show balance")
    menuChoice = input("Choose D, W or S: ")
```

How to perform range checking in Python

Range validation	Python code

Validating a number between 1 and 5, for example a valid number of seats allowed for a cinema booking	`#validation range check – method 1`
	`numberSeats = int(input("Enter number of seats required: "))`
	`validRange = range(1,6)`
	`while numberSeats not in validRange:`
	`    print ("Sorry, seats must be between 1 and 5")`
	`    numberSeats = int(input("Enter number of seats required: "))`

	`#validation range check – method 2`
	`numberSeats = int(input("Enter number of seats required: "))`
	`while 1 >= numberSeats <= 5:`
	`    print ("Sorry, seats must be between 1 and 5")`
	`    numberSeats = int(input("Enter number of seats required: "))`

	`#validation range check – method 3`
	`numberSeats = int(input("Enter number of seats required: "))`
	`while numberSeats <1 or numberSeats >5:`
	`    print ("Sorry, seats must be between 1 and 5")`
	`    numberSeats = int(input("Enter number of seats required: "))`

Checking the length of an inputted string, for example ensuring a user's password is at least six characters long	`#while loop for length check validation`
	`password = input("Enter password (min 6 chars): ")`
	`while len(password) < 6:`
	`    print ("Sorry, password must be at least 6 characters")`
	`    password = input("Enter password (min 6 chars): ")`

Now try this

You have been asked to create a simple calculator that can process two integers using common arithmetic operations. Modify and extend the example shown above so that the required solution displays menu options to Add, Multiply, Divide or Subtract. Incorporate appropriate code to limit the user inputs to the valid range of options.

Consider:

- what type of data needs to be input, for example string, integer, etc.
- the minimum allowed value
- the maximum allowed value
- how to include appropriate help for the user in the input prompt.

Had a look ☐ Nearly there ☐ Nailed it! ☐

Validation check: Constraints

One of the most common types of error occurs when a user enters a string which doesn't contain the correct type of data, for example entering letters in a telephone number. Python has various string methods which can be used to perform constraint-style validation.

Validating using constraints

Some key examples are shown below:

Type of constraint	Practical example	Python code

Alphabetic only	Validating a username	`userInput = input("Enter your username: ")`
		`if (userInput.isalpha()==False):`
		`    print("Sorry, only alphabetical letters allowed")`

Alphanumeric	For example: validating a product code or postcode	`userInput = input("Enter a product code: ")`
		`if (userInput.isalnum()==False):`
		`    print("Sorry, only alphanumeric characters allowed")`

Numeric digits only	Validating a telephone number	`userInput = input("Enter your telephone number: ")`
		`if (userInput.isdigit()==False):`
		`    print("Sorry, only digits allowed")`

Lowercase only	Ensuring input is fully lowercase (or not)	`userInput = input("Enter passphrase (lowercase): ")`
		`if (userInput.islower()==False):`
		`    print("Sorry, only lowercase characters allowed")`

Uppercase only	Ensuring input is fully uppercase (or not)	`userInput = input("Enter passphrase (uppercase): ")`
		`if (userInput.isupper()==False):`
		`    print("Sorry, only uppercase characters allowed")`

Titlecase only e.g. Canada, Tom, Ford, Barack Obama	Validating a person's first or last name	`userInput = input("Enter first name: ")`
		`if (userInput.istitle()==False):`
		`    print("Sorry, input should be titlecase, e.g. Omar")`

Alternatives to validation

Most strings will be entered via the keyboard and typing mistakes are very likely to occur. Although it is possible to detect uppercase, lowercase or titlecase strings using constraint methods, you can also 'force' strings to a target letter case using different string methods.

```
fullName = input("Enter full name: ")
print("Welcome, ", fullName.title(),"!")
```

Forcing different cases

Now try this

The **len()** string method can be used to discover the number of characters present in a string.

Modify an existing example to validate a user's password input as alphanumeric and six characters or longer.

If you are feeling confident, you may expand your answer by repeating the input until it is valid.

Think about:

- the type of data being input
- the correct constraint method which needs to be used
- how the error message should be expressed.

Validation check: Case statements in Python

A **case statement** is a structured alternative to using nested IF statements in your software development project. Not all programming languages refer to them as case statements; Python uses a combination of **if** and **elif** statements to perform the same job.

How case statements work

They work by providing a list of options that can be matched to determine the correct action to execute.

Working with case statements

One of the advantages of using case statements is that they are easy to modify, making it relatively painless to expand upon the program's original functionality to add new options.

How to perform/use a case statement (or equivalent) for validation

In this example, Python uses **if** and **elif** to check different menu options. Any option not matching these will 'fall' into the final **else** part, triggering a suitable 'that option is not valid' style error message.

```
#input the two integers
number1 = int(input("Enter 1st number: "))
number2 = int(input("Enter 2nd number: "))

#repeat the menu until menu option in valid range
menuChoice = ' '
while menuChoice not in ['A','M','D','S']:
    print("My Python Calculator!")
    print("(A) Add")
    print("(M) Multiply")
    print("(D) Divide")
    print("(S) Subtract")

    menuChoice = print("Choose A, M, D or S: ")

    #check menu option, perform calculation and output answer
    if menuChoice == 'A':
        answer = number1 + number2
        print ("The answer is: ", answer)
    elif menuChoice == 'M':
        answer = number1 * number2
        print ("The answer is: ", answer)
    elif menuChoice == 'D':
        answer = number1 / number2
        print ("The answer is: ", answer)
    else:
       print ("Sorry, that option is not valid.")
```

Now try this

Make appropriate changes to the Python code to complete the process of adding a 'subtract' option to the calculator.

When thinking about how to validate a user input using a case statement or equivalent consider:

- which options are required
- how to structure the case statement or equivalent
- what should happen in the final part.

Had a look ☐ Nearly there ☐ Nailed it! ☐

Validation check: Case statements in C++

A case statement in C++ is referred to as a **switch statement**.

How to use a case statement (or equivalent) for validation

C++ uses a **switch statement** to check different menu options. Any option not matching these will 'fall' into the final **default** part, triggering a suitable 'that option is not valid' style error message.

```
#include <iostream>
#include <cstring>
using namespace std;

int main()
{
    int number1;
    int number2;
    int answer;
    char menuChoice;
    //input the two integers
    cout << "Enter 1st number: ";
    cin >> number1;
    cout << "Enter 2nd number: ";
    cin >> number2;
    //repeat the menu until menu option in valid range
    menuChoice = ' ';
    while (!strchr("AMD",menuChoice)) {
      cout << "My Python Calculator!" << endl;
      cout << "(A) Add" << endl;
      cout << "(M) Multiply" << endl;
      cout << "(D) Divide" << endl;
      cout << "Choose A, M or D:  " << endl;
      cin.ignore(1);
      cin.get(menuChoice);
      //check menu option, perform calculation and output answer
      switch (menuChoice) {
        case 'A': answer = number1 + number2;
                cout << "The answer is: " << answer << endl;
                break;
        case 'M': answer = number1 * number2;
                cout << "The answer is: " << answer << endl;
                break;
        case 'D': answer = number1 / number2;
                cout << "The answer is: " << answer << endl;
                break;
        default : cout << "Sorry, that option is not valid." <<
endl;
      }
  }
  return 0;
}
```

Now try this

Make appropriate changes to the C++ code to add a subtract option to the calculator.

When thinking about how to validate a user input using a case statement or equivalent consider:
- which options are required
- how to structure the case statement or equivalent
- what should happen in the final part.

Loops

When writing pseudocode, software designs often make use of repetition ('loops') to build complex logic and algorithms. Most programming languages have a variety of loops, each with their own particular uses, strengths and weakness; knowing **when** to use **which type** will greatly improve the effectiveness of your code. Some programming languages, particularly those in the C family, have a slightly richer choice of loop types.

Pre- and post-conditioned loops

A loop is a control structure that allows you to repeat a number of actions. Loops are an essential part of most commercial programming languages although their names and syntax often vary. They can be described as being either **pre**- or **post-conditioned**; this simply means where the **controlling loop condition** ? is placed in relation to the repeating **actions** A .

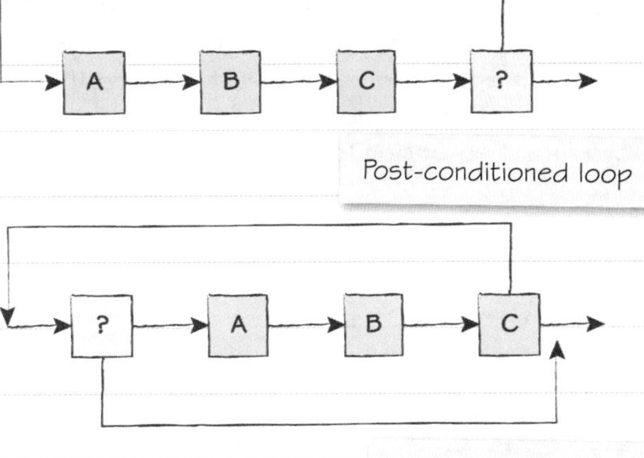

Post-conditioned loop

Pre-conditioned loop

Loop types

<table>
<tr><th>Loop type</th><th>Features</th><th>Code examples (Python)</th></tr>
<tr><td>Repeat</td><td><ul><li>Post-conditioned</li><li>Use when a loop has to work at least once</li><li>Typically loops until a condition is true</li><li>Not always available</li></ul></td><td><pre>#Python doesn't have a Repeat post-conditioned loop,
#but it can be simulated using True and break
while True:
    name = input("Enter your name: ")
    if (len(name)<1):
      print ("Sorry, please try again.")
    else:
      break;
print("Welcome, ",name)</pre></td></tr>
<tr><td>For</td><td><ul><li>Pre-conditioned</li><li>Use when you have a fixed number of iterations to perform</li><li>Very useful for traversing data structures such as arrays and lists</li></ul></td><td><pre>#list of 4 exam results for a student
examScores = [56, 78, 89, 34]

#version 1
for aScore in examScores:
  print ("Exam ", examScores.index(aScore)+1,": ", <···>
  aScore)

#version 2 - using the index
for index in range(len(examScores)):
  print ("Exam ", index+1,": ", examScores[index])</pre></td></tr>
<tr><td>While</td><td><ul><li>Pre-conditioned</li><li>Useful when you might not want a loop to work at all</li></ul></td><td><pre>name = input("Enter your name: ")
while (len(name)<1):
  if (len(name)<1):
    print ("Sorry, please try again.")
    name = input("Enter your name: ")
print("Welcome, ",name)</pre></td></tr>
</table>

Now try this

Write the C++ program code versions of the 'repeat' and 'for' loop examples provided.

Think about:

- the Python loop types being used
- equivalent C++ loop types available
- C++'s do...while post-conditioned loop.

Had a look ☐ Nearly there ☐ Nailed it! ☐

Branches

Making a **choice** is a fundamental requirement of any software design, with most programming languages offering a variety of different branching control structures. Using each type appropriately should improve the effectiveness of your code. Some programming languages, particularly those in the C family, have a slightly richer choice of branches.

Different branches

Branches are an essential part of most commercial programming languages although, as with loops, their names and syntax often vary. The most common branching control structures are IF...ELSE...ENDIF and the SWITCH statement. The 'simple' IF...ELSE...ENDIF is most commonly used to introduce two-option logic into a program using a controlling condition ? .

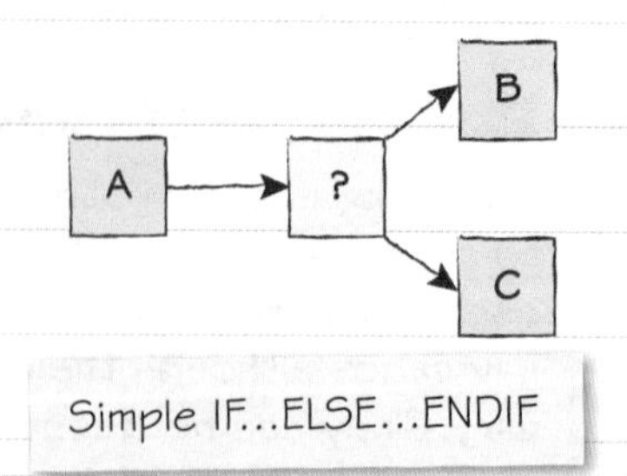

Simple IF...ELSE...ENDIF

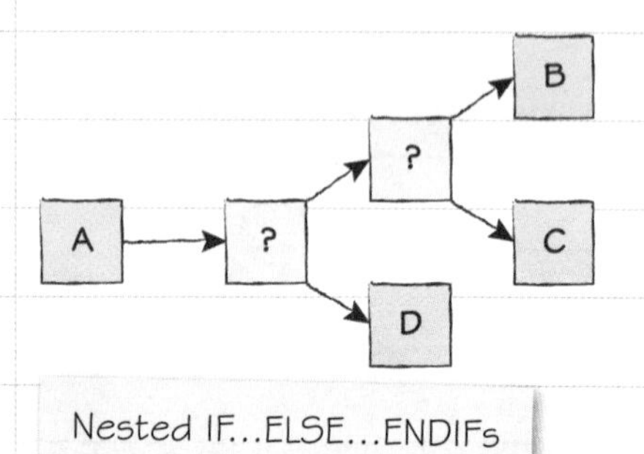

Nested IF...ELSE...ENDIFs

Using a SWITCH statement

If statements can be '**nested**' to check **multiple** options but can make program code difficult to read. A viable alternative is to use a **SWITCH** statement, popular in the C family, but not always found in other programming languages; for example, Python uses **ELIF** (ELSEIF) to check **more** than two options instead.

Coding branches

Selection type	Features	Code examples (Python)

IF...ELSE... ENDIF	• Simplest type of branch, ideal for **two options.**
	• The ELSE may be **optional** if there is no alternate action to perform.
	• IF statements can be **nested** to check multiple options.
	• Not all programming languages use an ENDIF, but it can be added as a comment.
		`#simple 2 option calculator`
		`result = 0`
		`number1 = int(input("Enter 1st number:"))`
		`number2 = int(input("Enter 2nd number:"))`
		`choice = input("Enter operation + or - :")`
		`if choice == "+":`
		`    result = number1 + number2`
		`else:`
		`    result = number1 - number2`
		`#endif`
		`print(number1,choice,number2,"=",result)`

SWITCH (elif in Python)	• Ideal for checking **multiple** (three or more) options, for example for menu system.
	• SWITCH statement does not always exist in a target programming language, although there are usually alternatives, for example ELIF.
	• Visually neater than using nested IF...ELSE...ENDIF statements.
		`#modified 3 option calculator`
		`result = 0`
		`number1 = int(input("Enter 1st number: "))`
		`number2 = int(input("Enter 2nd number: "))`
		`choice = input("Enter operation +, -, * : ")`
		`if choice == "+":`
		`    result = number1 + number2`
		`elif choice == "-":`
		`    result = number1 - number2`
		`elif choice == "*":`
		`    result = number1 * number2`
		`print(number1,choice,number2,"=",result)`

Now try this

Write the C++ program code versions of the IF...ELSE...ENDIF and SWITCH branch examples provided.

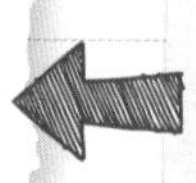

Think about:
- the Python branch types being used
- equivalent C++ branch types available
- C++'s switch statement.

Function calls

You can improve the effectiveness of your program code by analysing the solution and looking for opportunities to include programmer-defined functions in your solution.

Anatomy of a function

A **declaration** is typically a statement which introduces the function to the compiler. A **definition** fleshes out the function by adding **identifiers** and the **processing** that the function performs.

Function calls

A function **'call'** is used to **execute** the function. Some functions may have values (called **'arguments'** or **'parameters'**) passed to them for processing.

Define, declare and call functions

	C++	Python
Defining a function	`float convertDollars (float);`	`#Python has no separate declaration!`

Declaring a function	`//function to convert pounds to dollars`
	`float convertDollars (float pounds) {`
	`  float dollars;`
	`  dollars = pounds * 1.5f;`
	`  return dollars;`
	`}`
		`#function to convert pounds to dollars`
		`def convertDollars(pounds):`
		`    dollars = pounds * 1.5`
		`    return dollars`

Calling a function	`int main()`
	`{`
	`  float holidayMoney;`
	`  float pounds = 300.0f;`
	
	`  //call the function`
	`  holidayMoney = convertDollars(pounds);`
	
	`  cout << "£" << pounds << " converts to ";`
	`  cout << "$" << holidayMoney;`
	`  return 0;`
	`}`
		`holidayMoney = 0.0`
		`pounds = 300.0`
		
		`#call the function`
		`holidayMoney = convertDollars(pounds)`
		`print("£",pounds,"converts to",end="")`
		`print(" $",holidayMoney)`

When to use functions:

- When you find **repeating blocks** of code
- When the same block of code might be needed again
- When blocks of code become **overlong** – splitting code into functions is called **re-factoring**
- For separating calculations, validation, etc.

Why use functions?

- They occur naturally as you **decompose** a problem into smaller parts.
- They make it easier to code your solution in **manageable 'chunks'**.
- They reduce unnecessary duplication of code and are **re-usable**.
- They make the program easier to **read**, **understand** and debug.

Now try this

How could your code be optimised by rewriting this validation as a separate 'validateInput' function? Write the amended C++ code.

The amended function must allow the user to enter a simple integer value, and validate it within a flexible range until it is in an acceptable range. The validated value can then be returned.

```
do {
  cout << "Enter a value between 10 and 20: ";
  cin >> value;
  if (value <10 || value >20) {
    cout << "Sorry, try again." << endl;
  }
} while (value <10 || value >20);
```

Had a look ☐ Nearly there ☐ Nailed it! ☐

Data structures

Data structures store data in an organised fashion and enable solutions to process data more efficiently.

Different data structures

Most programming languages support a range of different data structures. The syntax, features and functionality associated with each data structure can vary between languages.

Matching data structures to a defined need

A core skill is interpreting a scenario and deciding which data structure can most appropriately represent it.

Common data structures

Data structure	Features	Common applications
List	• Linear data structure, accessed sequentially • Used to store a collection of data items, possibly of different data types • Each data item can reoccur • Normally dynamic (can shrink and grow as items added and removed) • Typical operations: add, remove, insert, count elements, test if empty, and access a particular data item	• Validation • Lookups • Searching and sorting • Storing multiple instances of the same variable, for example names in Top 10 high-score table • Reducing length and complexity of program code
Array (single and multi-dimensional)	• Linear data structure, accessed sequentially or directly • Used to store a collection of data items (elements), typically of the same data type • Each data item can reoccur • Depending on the language, may be static (fixed in size) or dynamic • Each array element accessed via its index or associative name • 2D or 3D arrays are common	• Typically more memory efficient than using lists • Searching and sorting • Storing multiple instances of the same variable, for example names in Top 10 scoretable • Reducing length and complexity of program code • Orthogonal coordinates in 3D space (X, Y, Z)
Record	• Formed by a collection of data items • Record data items can be different types • Data items occur in a fixed order per record • Sometimes called a 'struct' • The basis of a database table's record structure	• Storing related data of different data types, for example student information • Creation of record-based tables, for example to store customer, product or flight details • Key component in building table-based database
Set	• A collection of data items • No particular order, but no repeating items • Operations exist to test if empty, test if member, find union, difference and subset	• Validation • Discovering relationships between different data sets • Mathematical operations

Now try this

Examine each of these data needs and suggest a suitable data structure along with a supporting reason for your choice:

(a) storing hourly rates of graded employees
(b) storing branch details about a restaurant in a national chain
(c) storing vertices of 3D objects in a computer game
(d) storing locations of hidden objects in a geocache trail
(e) determining which pupils are members of both the football and swimming teams.

Think about:
- what type of data is being stored
- how much data is being stored
- how the data is organised
- how the data will be accessed
- how the data will be processed.

Evaluation of design

On this page, you will revise ways to carry out an evaluation of your software solution.

Key design questions

To effectively evaluate your project's design you need to focus on the following characteristics, adding and removing these **strengths** (left-hand side) and **weaknesses** (right-hand side) to help balance your judgement:

Strengths

- BCS flow chart symbols and notation used correctly
- Pseudocode sequence, structure and iteration used correctly
- Required functionality covered in your design and list of omissions
- Design's strengths identified and improvements suggested
- Use of flow chart or pseudocode for a specific scenario assessed

Weaknesses

- Incorrect or incomplete pseudocode
- Functionality missing; some required functionality not identified in the design
- Strengths and weaknesses of design not considered; no suggestions for improvement
- How the flow chart or pseudocode may be applied to a specific scenario not assessed

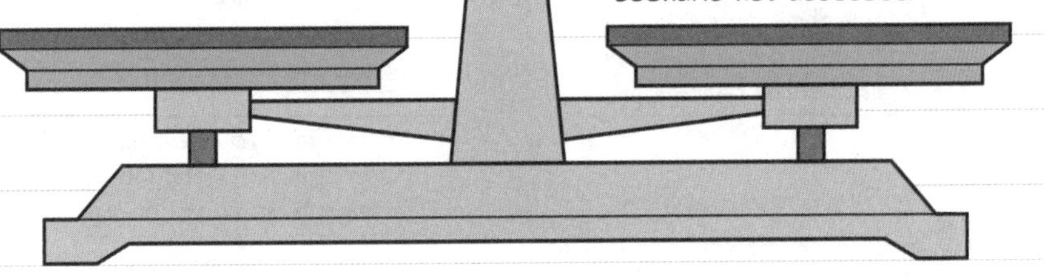

Simply add and remove blocks from each side of the scales to discover how well you have designed your project's solution. If there are more blocks on the left, it is likely that your design approach has been thoughtful and inclusive. If you acknowledge more aspects on the right, these weaknesses point to an incomplete and flawed design.

How to evaluate the design effectively

- Understand the client's brief and its requirements **fully**.
- Identify the aspects where your design is strong.
- Identify the aspect where your design is weak – always be honest as deliberately excluding an obvious weakness suggests that you have failed to spot it.
- Weaknesses lead you to areas of improvement – say how things can be made better.
- Always include the reasoning for your judgements, for example if using research or material from a website, book or journal, cite your sources correctly.

Now try this

Which aspects of the problem should you **minimally** identify to ensure you have covered the basic functionality requirements?

Write down each aspect, including a short description.

Investigation of the scenario during the analysis stage of the software development life cycle typically involves identification of four key aspects needed to solve the problem.

Evaluation of software testing

On this page, you will revise methods of testing.

Software testing flow chart

Use this flow chart to help you assess the effectiveness of your testing. If you miss any steps, it is likely that your testing will be incomplete and unknown and/or unresolved issues may still exist.

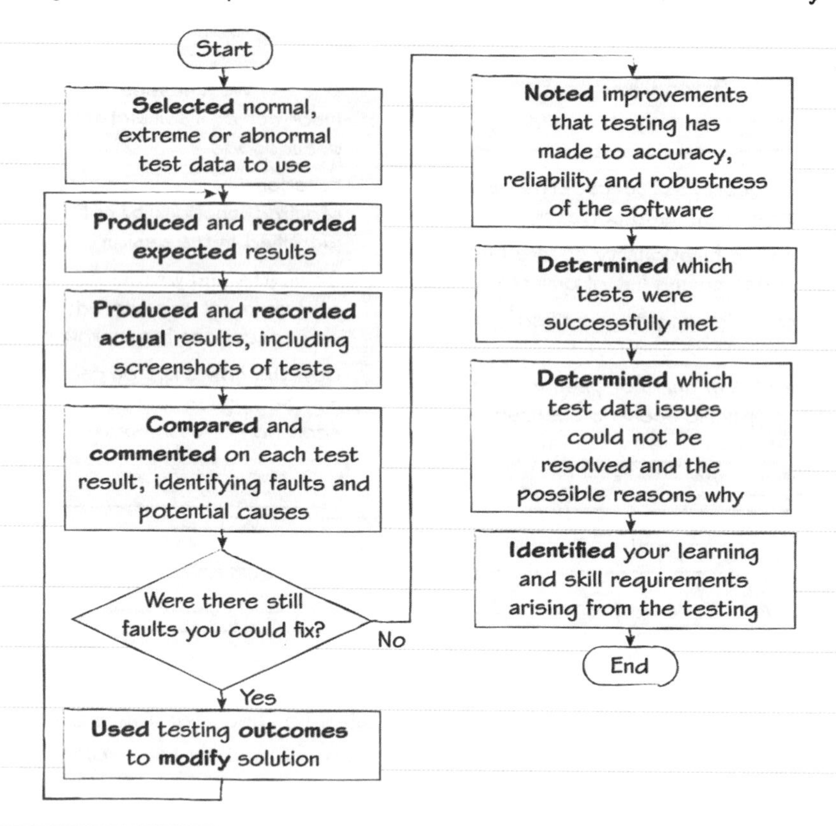

Making use of testing outcomes

If you have tested effectively, the following should be true:

- ✓ The solution will produce accurate results, meeting the requirements of the scenario.
- ✓ The solution will be reliable, producing accurate results every time it is used.
- ✓ The solution should be robust, difficult to break even when the user selects the wrong options or inputs nonsensical data.
- ✓ No expected errors should occur.
- ✓ Unexpected behaviour or errors should be minimal, though not impossible (no solution can be 100%).
- ✓ The client will have confidence in using the solution.

Now try this

There are many mistakes you can make while testing your solution.

Write down the ones you think are most common and their potential impact on the solution.

Think about the key objectives of software testing. What are you trying to prevent or prove by completing this process?

Evaluation of the software

You will need to evaluate your software solution against the requirements of the client's brief. This will involve identifying the strengths and weaknesses of the software.

Identifying strengths and weaknesses

Is the solution fit for purpose?
- Is the solution good enough to do the job it is supposed to do?
- Does it do the job accurately, reliably and efficiently?
- Does the solution feel robust?

Is the software intuitive to use?
- Is the user interface clear?
- Are screen options, instructions and user messages easy to understand?
- Can the user navigate the program's functions and features easily?
- Is help documentation easy to understand?

Was there an impact by the choice of programming language?
- Did the programming language constrain the available solution? If so, why? What was the nature of the impact?
- Were there other programming languages that should have been considered? If so why weren't they?

Is the software maintainable?
- Is the software easy to modify when errors are found?
- Is the software easy to extend when new functions or features are required?
- Has the coding approach helped to make the software maintainable? If so, which techniques and good practice have been used?

Does the software meet the client's brief?
- Does it fully meet the requirements identified in the client's original brief?
- If not, which aspects are missing, incomplete or faulty?
- If not, what are the reasons why the brief has not been satisfactorily met?

Learning and skills requirements

Remember to include in your evaluation:
- what you have learnt whilst completing the software development project: new knowledge, new skills, new thought processes and techniques, etc.
- technical shortcomings in the solution that you can identify as areas to improve skills
- weaknesses you have identified in your problem solving and project management skills.

Now try this

List the three key aspects that need to be evaluated so that you can correctly appraise your software development project. If you can, also try to recall the elements that you should try to cover for each aspect of the project.

Think about what you have created for the software development project and the processes you have performed.

Had a look ☐ Nearly there ☐ Nailed it! ☐

Your Unit 4 set task

Unit 4 will be assessed through a task, which will be set by Pearson. In this assessed task you will need to use your software design, development, testing and evaluation understanding and skills to produce a program that meets a client's requirements. This skills section is designed to **revise skills** that might be needed in your assessed task. The section uses selected content and outcomes to provide an example of ways of applying your skills.

Your software design and development project

- 👍 Before you start, make sure you fully understand the problem.
- 👍 Break the problem down into inputs, processing, storage and outputs.
- 👍 Start programming only once you have designed the solution.
- 👍 Apply good design practices.
- 👍 Make your code as readable as possible.
- 👍 Test your program thoroughly.
- 👍 Evaluate the design, the software, its testing and your own performance and areas to improve.

- 👎 Don't skip any stages of the software development life cycle (see below).
- 👎 Don't forget to solve all the requirements of the set task.
- 👎 Don't neglect opportunities to optimise your solution or improve its accuracy.

Use the software development life cycle as your guide

Remember to use the software development life cycle (SDLC) as a step-by-step guide for completing your software development project. Follow the stages in the correct order and carefully perform all their required actions to progress logically through the set task.

Links You can find the software development life cycle on page 139, where you can also revise the key questions that you should ask at each stage.

Check the Pearson website

The activities and sample response extracts in this section are provided to help you to revise content and skills. Ask your tutor or check the Pearson website for the most up-to-date **Sample Assessment Material** and **Mark Scheme** to get an indication of the structure of your actual assessed task and what this requires of you. The details of the actual assessed task may change so always make sure you are up to date.

Now try this

Visit the Pearson website and find the page containing the course materials for BTEC National Computing. Look at the latest Unit 4 Sample Assessment Material for an indication of:

- the structure of your set task
- how much time you are advised to spend on each section of the task
- what briefing or stimulus material might be provided to you
- the activities you are required to complete and how to format your responses.

Use standard methods and techniques to design a solution

You can use flow charts and structured English (pseudocode) to design solutions to a problem.

Links To revise how to draw flow charts and write pseudocode statements, see on pages 140 and 141.

When to use flow charts and pseudocode

- Flow charts are better for showing the internal logic of the algorithm and can assist testing.
- Pseudocode can be used as a basis for the program code; each line can be converted to a target programming language equivalent, enabling fast creation of workable program code.

Evaluations

When you evaluate your designs, the accuracy of your flow charts, that is, the correct application of BCS (British Computer Society) symbols and using the correct pseudocode keywords are key concerns.

Worked example

A solution requires that a user's password must be at least 8 characters long.

Sample response extract

Pseudocode extract

```
REPEAT
  INPUT password
  if length of password < 8  then
    OUTPUT "Must be at least 8 chars"
  ENDIF
UNTIL length of password > 8
```

Flow chart extract

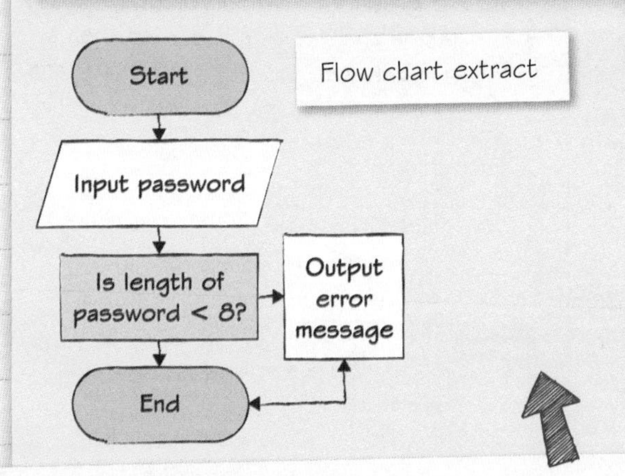

This solution has a number of problems:

- pseudocode IF and THEN keywords not capitalised
- pseudocode UNTIL condition should be >=8
- calculating the password length twice is inefficient
- flow chart uses wrong symbol for a decision
- flow chart arrows are wrong and loop decision missing
- flow chart has no 'Yes' and 'No' labels on its decision.

Improved response extract

Pseudocode extract

```
REPEAT
  INPUT password
  passwordLength = length of password
  IF passwordLength < 8  THEN
    OUTPUT "Must be at least 8 chars"
  ENDIF
UNTIL passwordLength >= 8
```

Flow chart extract

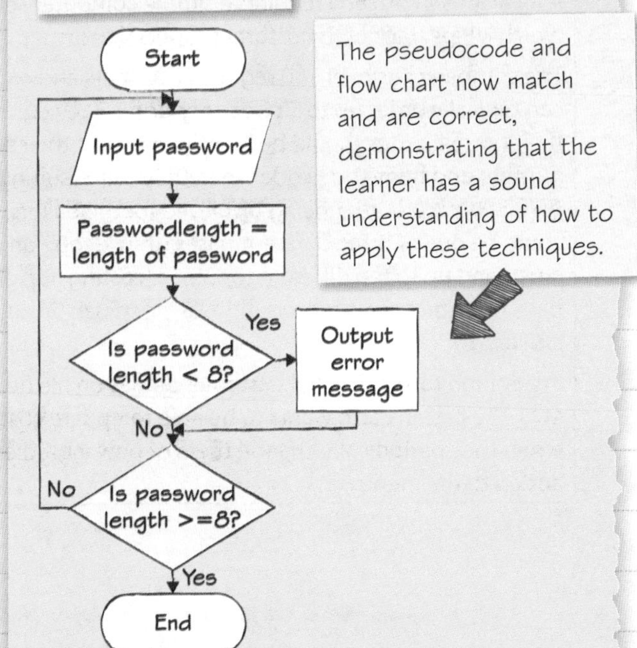

The pseudocode and flow chart now match and are correct, demonstrating that the learner has a sound understanding of how to apply these techniques.

Now try this

Write pseudocode that displays numbers 1 to 10 (inclusive) using a pre-conditioned WHILE loop.

Had a look ☐ Nearly there ☐ Nailed it! ☐

Analyse a task and design a solution

The most important stages of the software development life cycle occur when you analyse a problem and begin to design a workable solution.

Links Revise the key questions that you need to ask during analysis and design on page 139.

Breaking the scenario down

When analysing a problem and attempting to design a solution try to **decompose** the task into four separate – but related – aspects:

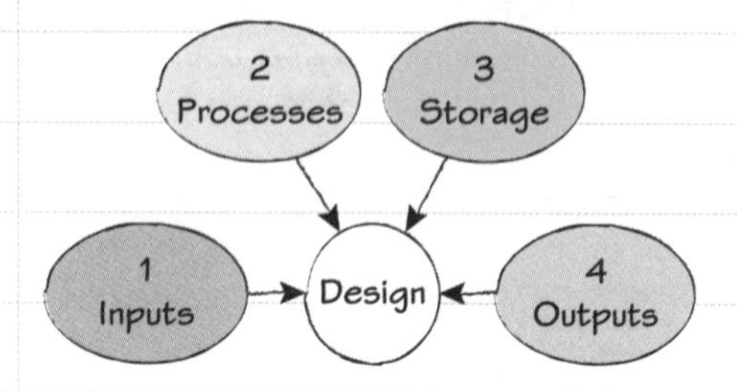

1. **Inputs** define the **values entered** into the program.
2. **Processes** define the **actions** that the program needs to **perform**.
3. **Storage** defines the **data requirements** (in RAM or backing storage, i.e. on disk).
4. **Outputs** define the **information** that the program **must generate** from its processes.

Analysis of scenario

Worked example

A local artisan pizzeria requires a simple computerised solution which keeps track of its customers' speciality orders.

The company has over 100 regular customers and each customer can typically order up to 5 pizzas per order. Each customer and their normal order should be identified by just their telephone number and home postcode when they call, resulting in the correctly priced order being displayed for the bakers. Each pizza could be one of three different bases (thin, deep pan or stuffed crust) and up to ten different toppings (costing 40p each). Each base pizza price is as follows: thin £3, deep pan £4 and stuffed crusted £5.

In addition to keeping full customer details on file (name, address, etc.), the pizzeria also wants to be able to update customer orders when they periodically change them or new ingredients are added to the menu.

When reading through this scenario, you might find it helpful to identify the four key aspects visually. This is best achieved using a highlighter or coloured pens. You could use a different colour for each aspect, for example inputs are red, outputs are green, etc. When you start to design the solution it should then be relatively easy to identify the various components that you need to include.

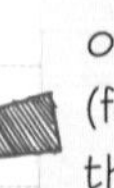

Read the scenario carefully and, by identifying **nouns** (for inputs, outputs and storage) and **verbs** (for processing), correctly highlight the key facts in preparation for solving the problem.

Now try this

A bank customer enters their PIN after being prompted by an on-screen message, the ATM checks if this is correct and either displays a list of options or an 'incorrect PIN' message.

Visually identify the inputs, processes and outputs.

Develop a software solution

Converting algorithms and pseudocode to programming language

Once you have designed a solution and represented the algorithms as flow charts and pseudocode you will need to convert these to your chosen programming language.

A basic technique is to take each line of the pseudocode and find the equivalent statement and/or function that is required, for example input in C++ tends to use 'cin', Python the 'input' function. Work through each line of code until you have converted the algorithm successfully, although be prepared to make some language-specific changes if necessary!

Programming language differences

Python (3.4 or later) and languages in the C family have many similarities but often have very different syntax when dealing with common tasks such as input, output, branches, loops and functions.

Many pages in this unit's revision guide contain examples of both Python and C++ syntax. Revise both to appreciate their differences and similarities.

Worked example

A solution requires that a user's password must be at least 8 characters long.

Sample response extract

Pseudocode extract

```
REPEAT
  INPUT password
  passwordLength = length of password
  IF passwordLength < 8  THEN
    OUTPUT "Must be at least 8 chars"
  ENDIF
UNTIL passwordLength >= 8
```

Flow chart extract

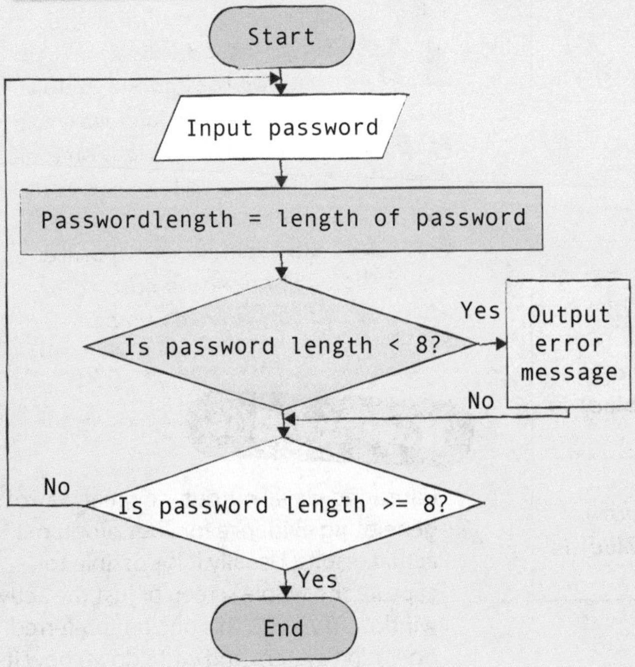

```
Start
  → Input password
  → Passwordlength = length of password
  → Is password length < 8?  —Yes→ Output error message
                             —No→
  → Is password length >= 8?  —No→ (back to Input password)
                              —Yes→ End
```

Sample response extract

Python solution

```
while True:
  password = input("Enter password: ")
  passwordLength = len(password)
  if (passwordLength < 8):
    print("Must be at least 8 chars")
  else:
    break
```

C++ solution

```
int main()
{
  string password;
  int passwordLength;

  do {
    cout << "Enter password: ";
    cin >> password;
    passwordLength=password.length();
    if (passwordLength < 8) {
      cout<<"Must be at least 8 chars";
    }
  } while (passwordLength < 8);

  return 0;
}
```

Now try this

Parallelogram-shaped boxes on a flow chart would typically be converted to what type of statement/function in C++ or Python?

Had a look ☐ Nearly there ☐ Nailed it! ☐

Select test data

In order to test the functionality and stability of an identified solution, for example generating a customer loan repayment schedule, you will need to select suitable test data.

Selecting appropriate data

Start being aware of all the inputs used in the solution. Identify **each input**, its **data type** and **validation methods**.

Input	Data type	Validation
Loan value	Integer	Range check (must be between £500 and £5000)
Repayment period	Integer	Range check (must be between 12 and 60 months)
Annual percentage rate (APR)	Decimal	Range check (must be between 12% and 28%)

Choice of test data

Your selection should include data from each category:

- **normal test data**
- **extreme test data**
- **abnormal test data.**

Links To revise test data, see 142.

Being professional

Your test data should be professionally documented using word-processing or spreadsheet-based tools. Either will allow you to create neat, tabular test data.

Worked example

For each input, select suitable test data values in each category.

Sample response extract

Input	Test data values
Loan value	Normal: 520, 1000, 1200 Extreme: 500, 5000, 4999 Abnormal: John, 500.5, 0
Repayment period	Normal: 50, 14, 30 Extreme: 60, 59, 12 Abnormal: John, 23.5, –10, 0, null
Annual percentage rate (APR)	Normal: 16.0, 12.1, 24.25 Extreme: 28.0, 12.5, 12.0 Abnormal: John, 13%, null, 12.9999

There is no 'magic number' that describes the **ideal quantity** to use when selecting test data. Simply try to cover all input permutations, even the unexpected ones as these will help you assess the **stability** of the solution. **Zero** and **negative values** should always be checked. Identify **each category clearly** and have selected test data which **matches**.

Improved response extract

Input set	Test data values	Notes
1	520, 60, 28.0	Testing **maximum range** for repayment period and APR (both **extreme**), other data (loan value) is **normal**.
2	520, 12, 12.0	Testing **minimum range** for repayment period and APR (both **extreme**), other data (loan value) is **normal**.

When selecting test data for inputs which use **range-based** validation it is important that you test **above**, **below** and **on** both the **minimum** and **maximum** values, as this tests the validation logic most thoroughly. In addition, it is usually advisable to assemble test data into **sets**; each set identifies a **separate run** of the solution. Add a note to say what you are testing each time.

Links For more on validation checks, see pages 160–164.

Now try this

Capturing visual output is a great way of generating evidence for your program's actual results. Usually it is possible to capture the whole screen or just the active window. Try to do this on your preferred operating system and write down how it is achieved.

Code readability

You will need to adopt a number of good practices to improve your program's code readability.

Links: To revise code readability, see page 145.

Help yourself

Improving the readability of your code typically makes it much **easier to read**, **understand** and **debug**. But remember, making a program more readable **doesn't** necessarily mean making it **shorter**, particularly if you are improving its maintainability.

Worked example

Validate two inputted product codes against an available stock list and display their corrected price (or an error message if either of the product codes don't exist).

The three stock items are: A01 (0.25), B02 (0.50) and C03 (0.75).

Sample response extract

C++ solution

```
string c;
float Price;
int times;
for (times=0; times<2; times++) {
cout << "Enter code:";
cin >> c;
if (c=="A01") Price = 0.25f;
else
if (c=="B02") Price = 0.50f;
else
if (c=="C03") Price = 0.75f;
else
cout << "Invalid stock code!" << endl;
cout << "Price for " << c << " <…>
is "<<Price<<endl; }
```

Things that should be improved:

1. Using a **function** makes the code more maintainable and extensible.
2. Use **data structures** rather than long-winded nested IF...ELSE branches to make the code more efficient.
3. Use a **single naming convention**.
4. Use **indentation** to highlight the program logic.
5. **Add comments** that describe the **purpose** of the program code.

Improved response extract

```
//function to look up product code and
//output its price or an error if not
found
void findProductPrice(string tempCode) {
  string prodCodes[3] =
  {"A01", "B02", "C03"};
  float prodPrices[3] =
  {0.25f, 0.50f, 0.75f};
  int loop;
  for (loop = 0; loop < 3;  loop++) {
    //product code found?
    if (tempCode==prodCodes[loop]) {
      cout << "Price for ";
      cout << tempCode << " is ";
      cout << prodPrices[loop] << endl;
      break;
    }
  }
  //product code not found?
  if (loop == 3) {
    cout << "Invalid stock code!" << endl;
  }
}
int main()
{
  //declare variables
  string prodCode;
  int prodLoop;
  //process two stock items
  for (prodLoop=0; prodLoop<2; <…>
  prodLoop++){
    //enter product code
    cout << "Enter code:";
    cin >> prodCode;
    //call function
    findProductPrice(prodCode);
  }
  return 0;
}
```

The improved solution is longer, but all of the identified improvement points have been carried out. As a result, the code is easier to read and should be more maintainable.

Now try this

Why do we add comments to a program?

Had a look ☐ Nearly there ☐ Nailed it! ☐

Define and declare constants and variables

Data, in the form of constants and variables, forms the heart of any software solution and needs to be carefully identified.

Links To revise simple data types, see page 146.

Working with identifiers

Once a simple data item is identified, you need to give it:

- a **meaningful name** (ideally using a consistent naming convention)
- an **appropriate data type**, for example Boolean, character, string, floating point (real), integers and date/time
- an **initial value** (for variables)
- a **fixed value** (for constants)
- a **description** (can be used for comments)
- appropriate **scope**, for example for variables – local or global (if required for functions).

Worked example

Each week a customer orders comics via an online store. They receive a discount based on the value of their order; orders above £30 receive 5% discount and orders above £60 receive 10% discount. Customers have to specify the title, issue number and quantity of each title bought. An option exists to request a variant cover at no additional cost. Orders above £70 automatically receive free postage and packing, otherwise it is 15p per comic.

Sample response extract

Consider what data needs to be stored in each variable or constant and use an appropriate data type.

Identified data

Name	Data type	Variable or constant	Value	Description
comicTitle	String	Variable	“ ”	Comic's title
comicPrice	Float	Variable	0.0	Comic's price
comicQty	Int	Variable	0	Comic's quantity
discountLow	Int	Constant	5	Low discount % applied
discountHigh	Int	Constant	10	High discount % applied
discountAmount	Float	Variable	0.0	Discount given
variantCover	Boolean	Variable	False	Variant cover or not
totalPrice	Float	Variable	0.00	Total price of order
postAndPack	Float	Variable	0.00	Cost of posting and package
orderDate	Date	Variable	Null	Date of customer order

Remember to include a description column.

Draw a data table (or data dictionary) to list the variables and constants identified.

Choose an appropriate type for 'comicPrice' (float rather than int) and create two sensible 'discount' constants. To improve the answer, two more could be created which store the £60 and £70 discount thresholds.

Now try this

What types of data would be needed to store these data values?
10/07/2017, True, 1.2, 10 and 'Saturn'

Process data with mathematical expressions

Many real-world problems and solutions involve complex calculations which you will need to replicate in your chosen programming language.

Links To revise the different arithmetic operations that you can use in your chosen programming language, see page 156. You will also find useful arithmetic functions such as Round and Random on page 157.

Carrying out calculations

When you encounter a real-world calculation you should first identify the data required, the data types needed (typically integer or floating point) and the operators required.

Use BIDMAS to organise the calculation correctly, ensuring that the various parts of the calculation are performed in the correct order. For example:

Converting a temperature between degrees Celsius (°C) and degrees Fahrenheit (°F) is written as:

Multiply by 9, then divide by 5, then add 32.

The required variables are: **degC** and **degF**. The required operations are *, / and **+**.

The resulting C++ would be:

```
degF = degC * 9 / 5 + 32;
```

BIDMAS

Even in software development, the order in which you carry out a calculation is important. BIDMAS ('**b**rackets', '**i**ndices', '**d**ivision', '**m**ultiplication', '**a**ddition' and '**s**ubtraction') still applies when building calculations in a target programming language, for example:

```
result = num1 * (num2 - num3);
```

In this example, the brackets tell the computer to subtract num3 from num2 **first** and **then** multiply the difference by num1 to achieve the correct result. Without brackets, the multiplication would have been performed first, probably generating a very different answer!

Worked example

Write a C++ program to convert an inputted temperature from degrees Celsius to degrees Fahrenheit.

Sample response extract

```
int main()
{
float degC;
float degF;
cout << "Enter temperature (degrees C): " ;
cin >> degC;
degF = ((degC * 9) / 5) + 32;
cout << "Temperature in Fahrenheit is: ";
cout << degF << endl;
return 0;
}
```

The code is sound but has no comments, poor indentation and unnecessary brackets around parts of the calculation.

Improved response extract

```
int main()
{
  //declare variables
  float degC;
  float degF;
  //input temperature
  cout << "Enter temperature (degrees C): " ;
  cin >> degC;
  //perform the conversion
  degF = degC * 9 / 5 + 32;
  //output the result
  cout << "Temperature in Fahrenheit is: ";
  cout << degF << endl;
  return 0;
}
```

The improved version has meaningful comments, correct indentation and demonstrates a better understanding of BIDMAS.

Now try this

Write (and test) an equivalent calculation in Python using best coding practices.

Had a look ☐ Nearly there ☐ Nailed it! ☐

Function calls

The use of programmer-defined functions will improve the effectiveness of your software development project's programming code.

Links To revise function calls, see page 167.

Key function tips

Some programming languages such as Python do not separate function definition and declaration. Always check to see if a built-in function exists that can perform the task you are trying to achieve.

Arguments and return values

A function can accept values for processing which are passed to it as arguments (actual parameters) via the functional call.

Some functions may perform an action; others may calculate a value and return it to the caller.

Worked example

Part of a software project's solution needs a programmer-defined function which can return the number of times a specific character occurs within a given string. The function is to be called 'countChars' and will accept two parameters (the search character and the string) and return the count of matching characters found.

Write a Python program to count the number of times a specific character occurs in a given string.

Sample response extract

```
def countChrs(s, c):
    t = 0
    for e in s:
      if e == c:
        t += 1
    return t

a = countChrs('Hello', 'l')
print('l appears in Hello ',a,' time(s)')
```

Things that should be improved:

1. Although it will still work, the function name is misspelt when defined and called.
2. There are no comments.
3. Variables should be named more meaningfully, using an appropriate naming convention.
4. Ideally the string and search character should be based on a user input.

Improved response extract

```
#countChars function definition
#arguments = string, search char
def countChars(myString, myChar):
    charTotal = 0
    #walk along the string
    for eachChar in myString:
      #does current char match?
      if eachChar == myChar:
        #increment the total
        charTotal += 1
    #return the total to the caller
    return charTotal

#user inputs
inputS = input('Enter string: ')
inputC = input('Enter search char: ')

#call function and store result
myCount = countChars(inputS,inputC)

#output result
print(inputC,' appears in ', <↩>
inputS' ',myCount,' time(s)')
```

The code has been improved by correcting the function name, adding comments which annotate the program code to explain how it works. All variables have been given more meaningful names and consistently use the camelCase naming convention. The function call has been changed to accept values entered from the keyboard.

Now try this

Write (and test) an equivalent function in C++.

Control structures

You may need to select and use the most appropriate control structures to analyse, develop and improve your program code.

Links To revise loops, see page 165.

Selecting appropriate loops

To select the most appropriate type of loop you should think about what you are trying to achieve.

Ask yourself these key questions:

- Am I looping a **fixed number** of times? Yes – use a For loop.
- Do I want to loop **at least once**? Yes – use a Repeat loop.
- Is it possible that my loop **might not need to work even once**? Yes – use a While loop.

Being professional

Most algorithms can be solved by any type of loop. However, your program will be **more effective** and **efficient** if you select the **right type**.

Building a validation loop

Worked example

Part of a software project's solution requires an inputted user's age to be validated between 18 and 65 inclusive. Any incorrect input should output a helpful error message.

Sample response extract

C++ solution

```
int age;
do {
  cout << "\nEnter age (10-65): ";
  cin >> age;
  if (age <10 || age>65) {
    cout << "Age must be between 10 and 65.";
  }
} while (age<10 || age>65);
```

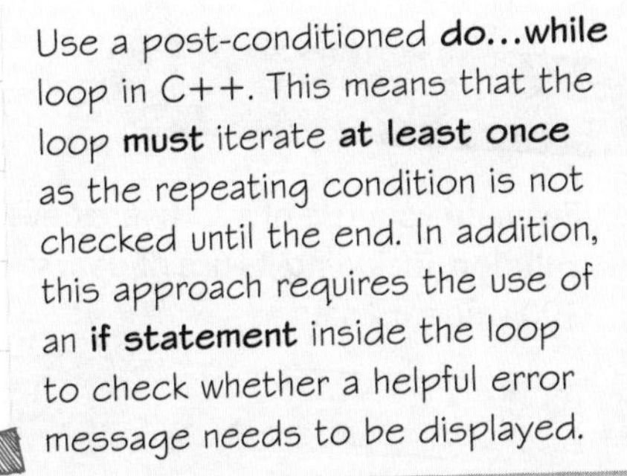

This solution works, but it is more complex and less efficient than it needs to be.

Improved response extract

```
//input and validate age
int age;
cout << "Enter age (10-65): ";
cin >> age;
while (age<10 || age>65) {
  cout << "Sorry, age must be between 10 and 65." << endl;
  cout << "Enter age (10-65): ";
  cin >> age;
}
```

The same solution has been made more efficient by switching to a pre-conditioned **while** loop. This means that the loop **does not have to run** if the original input is **within** the acceptable range. In addition, there is no longer a need for the **if statement**. To improve the code further, the **new line** has been moved to the end of the error message and a suitable **comment** has been added to explain the code's purpose; both changes make the code much more readable. This code is now much improved and demonstrates a better use of control structures to solve a problem.

Now try this

The following Python program code uses a FOR loop control structure; what would be its on-screen output after it executes?

```
mapLocations = [[1,2],[2,4],[5,6],[1,9]]

for aLocation in mapLocations:
    print (mapLocations.index(aLocation)+1,':', aLocation)
```

Data structures

You may be required to select and use common data structures to both store and process data.

Links To revise data structures, see page 168.

Selecting appropriate data structures

Choosing the correct data structures to use in a software development project may not be immediately obvious. Data structures common in Python and the C family:

- lists
- arrays (single and multi-dimensional)
- records
- sets.

Choice of data structures

The type of data structures you select will affect:

- ✓ how easy it is to store and retrieve data
- ✓ how easy it is to organise data
- ✓ how easy it is to search and sort data
- ✓ how efficiently your algorithms will be.

Links To revise lists, arrays, records and sets, see pages 153, 147, 148, 151 and 152.

Worked example

Evaluate your use of a software development solution, including its use of data structures, to store 100 students' data.

Sample response extract

```
string studentName[100];
string courseTitle[100];
int studentAge[100];
bool passedCourse[100];
```

I chose four separate arrays of different data types to store the data i needed for 100 students.

This response correctly identified the data required and the different data types each would need. Creating four separate arrays is efficient, however it would mean looping separately through each array. There is a better solution...

Improved response extract

```
struct studentRecord {
   string studentName;
   string courseTitle;
   int studentAge;
   bool passedCourse;
};
studentRecord students[100];
```

I used a record, which kept together the four data items I needed for one student. This meant I was able to create an array of 100 of these records and could access each more efficiently:

```
students[20].studentName;
```

This response explains the reasons for the improved solution which uses the more appropriate record data structure and provides an example of it being used. Explaining the efficiency using an algorithm example would improve the answer further.

Now try this

Write the Python declaration and initialisation of ten exam results (20, 22, 78, 89, 99, 55, 54, 60, 17, 40) in a one-dimensional array.

Evaluating your software development project

A key aspect of any project is your ability to evaluate evidence to make informed judgements about the success of your software product's design and performance.

Links Revise the key questions and correct processes to follow when evaluating design, software and testing on pages 169–171.

Effective evaluation

Your evaluation should be presented as a well-written reflection on the project as a whole and its key strengths and weaknesses. Remember to:

- evaluate the three key aspects of your project: **design**, **software** and **testing**
- identify **strengths** and **weaknesses**; the latter will give you **areas to improve**
- provide **supporting evidence** for your judgements; your opinion alone isn't enough
- address **key points**, for example whether your solution has met all the **requirements** of the scenario
- **justify** your decisions.

What do you evaluate?

There are **three aspects** that should be examined in order to fully evaluate your software development project:

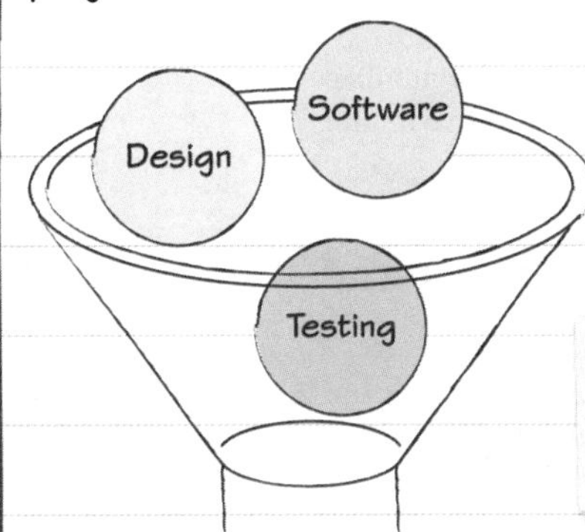

Evaluation of your software development project

Remember to identify your own **learning and skill requirements** that arise from the testing process.

Worked example

Write an evaluation of your project's testing.

Sample response extract

[...] My testing used a mixture of normal, abnormal and extreme data and I recorded the expected and actual results (using screenshots). The extreme data identified errors in my validation code and I had to modify the branches and loops for it to work correctly. The impact of doing so meant that the solution became more robust because it wouldn't allow bad data to be input. Identifying these faults helped me to understand how to use the various control structures more effectively. [...]"

This evaluation identifies (**by name**) the three different types of data the learner has used. It also states that one type of data has helped the learner to locate a problem with their validation, that is, a **specific part** of their solution.

When writing your evaluation, remember to note **which parts** of the solution you have had to fix (loops and branches) and the **overall impact** this has had on your solution (it has become **more robust**).

When writing your conclusion, reflect on **how** this has improved your knowledge of particular control structures.

Now try this

What type of evidence can you use to support your justification of the program's testing?

Answers

Unit 1: Principles of Computer Science

1. Identifying problems and processes

(a) Outputs needed for this app:
- date
- cost of materials
- cost of labour
- builder contact details.

(b) Inputs needed for this app:
- cost of each material item
- quantities of material items
- labour hours
- client contact details.

(c) Actions needed to test for validity:
- cost of each material item – a positive number
- quantities of material items – a positive number
- labour hours – a positive number
- client contact details – text, not blank.

2. Breaking down problems and processes

(a) What's needed to make this practical:
- shelf labels with product names and barcodes
- barcode recognition software
- database of product barcodes.

(b) Steps needed to make such a mobile phone app work:
- scan item
- look up item from database of product barcodes
- show product name
- enter quantity on shelf.

3. Communicating problems and processes

- calculate subtotal
- if last purchase date less than 1 year from current date apply loyalty discount
- if more than 1 item apply 10% discount
- calculate and apply postage rate
- calculate and apply VAT.

4. Pattern recognition

Benefits	Disadvantages
Easier testing	Code may not be exactly what's needed
Reduces cost	May include extra code to fulfil more functionality and so be less efficient
Can reduce development time	Code needs to be fully documented
Can be easier to understand the code due to modules having clearly defined functions	
Helps teams to work together	

The benefits of re-using code within an organisation outweigh the disadvantages.

5. Describing patterns and making predictions

1

	A	B	C	D	E	F	G	H
1	0	1	1	2	3	5	8	13
2	0	1	=B2+A2	=C2+B2	=D2+C2	=E2+D2	=F2+E2	=G2+F2

2

```
SET Num1 = 0
  SET Num2 = 1
  FOR i 0 to n DO
    SET tmp = Num2
    SET Num2 = Num1 + Num2
    SET Num1 = Num2
  END FOR
  RETURN Num1
```

6. Pattern generalisation and abstraction

Key processes:
- calculate total
- calculate shipping cost.

Repeated processes:
- enter password for login
- add item to cart
- continue shopping.

7. Representing the new system

Members

Field names	Data types
MemberRef	text
MemberType	text
Firstname	text
Surname	text
DateOfBirth	date/time
Address1	text
Address2	text
Postcode	text
Email	text
Phone	text

Payments

Field names	Data types
PaymentRef	text
MemberRef	text
PaymentDate	text
Amount	currency

Activities

Field names	Data types
ActivityRef	text
Description	text

Bookings

Field names	Data types
BookingRef	text
MemberRef	text
ActivityRef	text
Time	date/time
Date	date/time

8. Algorithm design

```
REPEAT
  IF engine is labouring
    Change gear downwards
  ELSEIF engine is racing
    Change gear upwards
  INPUT Speed
  IF Speed > SatNav
    OUTPUT apply brake
  ELSEIF Speed < TargetSpeed
    OUTPUT apply accelerator
UNTIL brake pedal is used
```

9. Structured English (pseudocode)

```
OPEN DataWorksheet
CurrentCell = FirstCell
GOTO CurrentCell
REPEAT
  COPY current row
  IF CurrentCell = Worksheet#1
    OPEN Worksheet#1
  ELSEIF CurrentCell = Worksheet#2
    OPEN Worksheet#2
  ELSEIF CurrentCell = Worksheet#3
    OPEN Worksheet#3
  ELSEIF
    OPEN Worksheet#4
  Jump down to first blank row
  PASTE row
  OPEN DataWorksheet
  Set CurrentCell to cell below CurrentCell
UNTIL CurrentCell is blank
```

10. Interpreting pseudocode

Loop six times. During this loop, if the current dice is '1' then the score increases by 100 and the number of dice left is reduced by 1. If the current dice is '5' then the score increases by 50 and the number of dice left is reduced by 1. After the loop completes, the score is shown on the form.

11. Flow charts

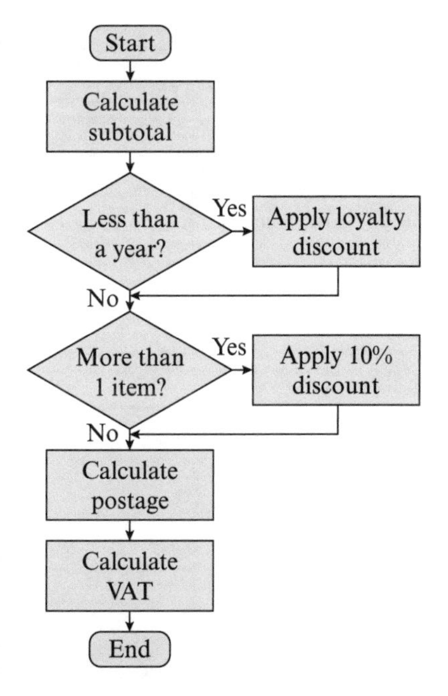

12. Handling data within a program

```
Dim Item1, Item2 As String
FileOpen(1, "Original data.csv", OpenMode.Input)
FileOpen(2, "New data.csv", OpenMode.Output)
While Not EOF(1)
  Input(1, Item1)
  Input(1, Item2)
  Print(2, "REF" & Item1)
  Print(2, ",")
  PrintLine(2, Item2)

End While
FileClose(1)
FileClose(2)
```

13. Constants and variables

Possible solution:

```
If chkAgree.Checked = True Then
  lblResult1.Text = UCase(txtString.Text)
Else
  lblResult1.Text = LCase(txtString.Text)
End If
lblResult2.Text = Format(txtInteger.Text * txtCurrency. <⋯>
Text, "£0")
lblResult3.Text = DateDiff(DateInterval.Day, Now(), <⋯>
dtpDate.Value)
lblResult4.Text = Format(txtReal.Text * txtCurrency. <⋯>
Text, "£0.00")
lblResult5.Text = Chr(txtByte.Text)
```

14. Managing variables

Possible response:

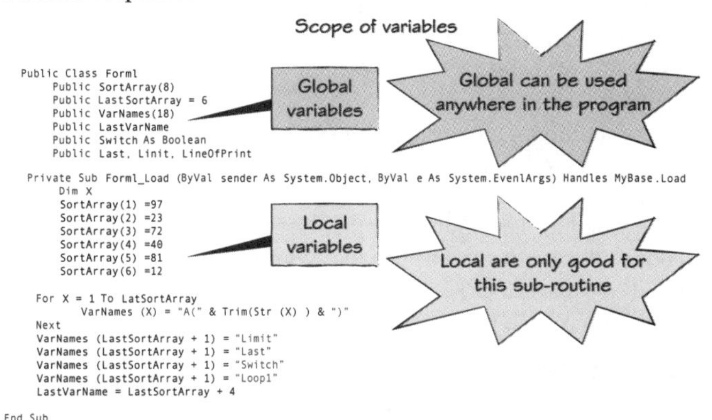

15. Arithmetic operations

	A	B	C	D	E
1	=D3*E1+D4	1525		13	38
2	=D3/D4	8		18	25/12/2019
3	=MOD(D3,E4)	40		40	12
4	=D3<=E1	FALSE		5	75
5	=NOT(D3<D1)	TRUE			
6	=E2-D4	20/12/2019			
7	=AND(D3>E3,D4<E4)	TRUE			
8	=OR(D1>E1,D4>E4)	FALSE			

16. Arithmetic functions

	A	B	C
1	.=RANDBETWEEN(3,50)	=NOW()-RANDBETWEEN(1,365)	=CHAR(RANDBETWEEN(65,90))
2	38	09 May 2016	J
3	26	12 February 2016	P
4	28	28 December 2015	R
5	4	21 March 2016	O
6	14	11 April 2016	Z
7	37	01 December 2015	F
8	30	04 March 2016	L
9	42	06 July 2016	L

17. String handling and general functions

```
Dim DoRpos, MonthLen As Integer
Dim DoR As Date
Dim strDoR As String
Dim DoRmonth, MsgText As String
```

```
DoR = "9/5/2017"
strDoR = CStr(Format(DoR, "long date"))
MonthLen = Len(strDoR) - 8
DoRpos = strDoR.IndexOf(" ") + 2
DoRmonth = Mid(strDoR, DoRpos, MonthLen)

MsgText = "This was received in "
MsgText = MsgText & DoRmonth

MsgBox(MsgText)
```

18. Validating data

A postcode validation from a simple check of two letters, two numbers, two letters would not be useful as there are exceptions to this format as well as issues around whether a space is present or not.
Entering an address can be validated using the postcode looked up from a data set provided by the Royal Mail.
Many website forms ask the user to type in their postcode, then provide a list of the addresses for that postcode for the user to click on and to confirm as correct.

19. Loops

FOR…NEXT
This is an unconditional loop as it will iterate the number of times defined in the FOR line. A loop variable is used to keep count of the iterations. The default is to increment the loop variable by one each time through the loop, but this can be changed using STEP. The loop can end early using an EXIT FOR line of code.
REPEAT UNTIL
This conditional loop will run through the code at least once and keep iterating UNTIL the condition is TRUE.
WHILE
This loop has the condition at the start in the WHILE line of code and will not run through the code at all if the WHILE condition starts as FALSE. It will keep iterating WHILE the condition is TRUE.

20. Branches

```
Dim Points
Points = txtPoints.Text
If Not IsNumeric(Points) Then
  MsgBox("Invalid input")
  txtPoints.Text = ""
  txtPoints.Select()
  Exit Sub
End If
If Points < 0 Or Points > 48 Then
  MsgBox("Invalid number")
  txtPoints.Text = ""
  txtPoints.Select()
  Exit Sub
End If
Select Case Points
  Case Is < 18
    lblGrade.Text = "Fail"
  Case Is < 26
    lblGrade.Text = "Pass"
  Case Is < 42
    lblGrade.Text = "Merit"
  Case Is < 48
    lblGrade.Text = "Distinction"
  Case Else
    lblGrade.Text = "Distinction*"
End Select
```

21. Function calls

Code

```
Function RefNumber(ByVal FN, ByVal LN, ByVal DoB)
  RefNumber = Mid(FN, 1, 2) & Mid(LN, 1, 2) & Mid(DoB, 1, 2)
End Function
```

Spreadsheet

	A	B
1	20 January 2001	
2	Richard	
3	Wyatt	
4	RiWy20	=LEFT(A2,2) & LEFT(A3,2) & LEFT(TEXT(A1,"dd-mmm-yyyy"),2)

22. Lists

	0	1	2	3	4	5	6	7	8	9	A	B	C	D	E	F
0	15	20	A	B	D	U	L	L	A	H	1F	16	A	L	E	X
1	A	N	D	E	R	2E	27	R	O	S	E	M	A	R	Y	26
2	2F	S	A	R	A	H	-1	-1	T	A	N	G	E	L	-1	-1
3	T	E	R	R	E	N	C	E								

00 Birmingham (B)   0A London (L)   01 Driver (D)   0B No licence (N)

B	D	Abdullah
L	N	Alexander
B	N	Rosemary
L	D	Sarah
L	N	Tangel
B	D	Terrence

23. Arrays

```
Dim PostageRates(3, 6)
Dim Insurance, Weight, WeightRange

PostageRates(1, 0) = "£500"
PostageRates(2, 0) = "£1000"
PostageRates(3, 0) = "£2500"
PostageRates(0, 1) = 100
PostageRates(1, 1) = "£6.45"
PostageRates(2, 1) = "£7.45"
PostageRates(3, 1) = "£9.45"
PostageRates(0, 2) = 500
PostageRates(1, 2) = "£7.25"
PostageRates(2, 2) = "£8.25"
PostageRates(3, 2) = "£10.25"
PostageRates(0, 3) = 1000
PostageRates(1, 3) = "£8.55"
PostageRates(2, 3) = "£9.55"
PostageRates(3, 3) = "£11.55"
PostageRates(0, 4) = 2000
PostageRates(1, 4) = "£11.00"
PostageRates(2, 4) = "£12.00"
PostageRates(3, 4) = "£14.00"
PostageRates(0, 5) = 10000
PostageRates(1, 5) = "£26.60"
PostageRates(2, 5) = "£27.60"
PostageRates(3, 5) = "£29.60"
PostageRates(0, 6) = 20000
PostageRates(1, 6) = "£41.20"
PostageRates(2, 6) = "£42.20"
PostageRates(3, 6) = "£44.20"

Insurance = 0
If rdo500.Checked = True Then Insurance = 1
If rdo1000.Checked = True Then Insurance = 2
If rdo2500.Checked = True Then Insurance = 3

Weight = Val(txtWeight.Text)
Select Case Weight
  Case Is <= 100
    WeightRange = 1
  Case Is <= 500
    WeightRange = 2
  Case Is <= 1000
    WeightRange = 3
  Case Is <= 2000
    WeightRange = 4
  Case Is <= 10000
    WeightRange = 5
  Case Is <= 20000
    WeightRange = 6
  Case Else
    MsgBox("Weight too heavy")
    Exit Sub
End Select

lblPostage.Text = PostageRates(Insurance, WeightRange)
```

24. Records

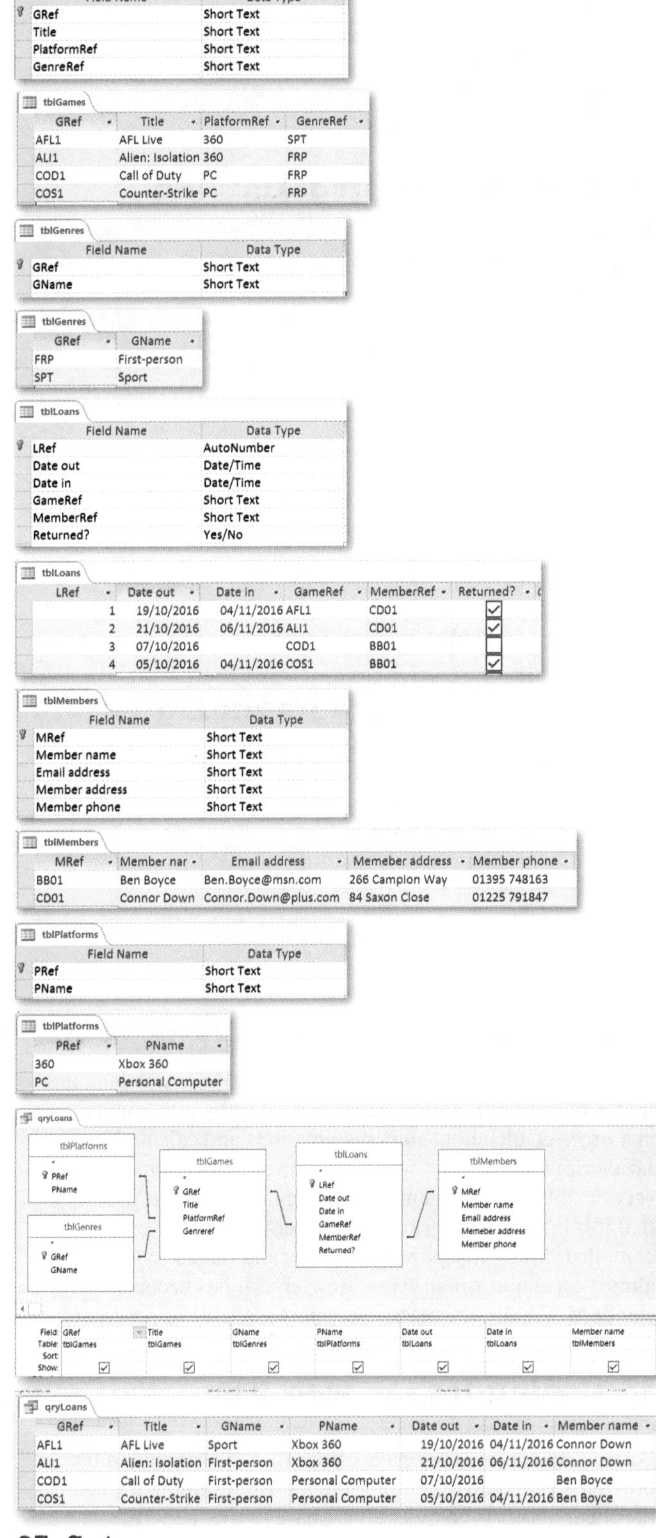

tblGames

Field Name	Data Type
GRef	Short Text
Title	Short Text
PlatformRef	Short Text
GenreRef	Short Text

tblGames

GRef	Title	PlatformRef	GenreRef
AFL1	AFL Live	360	SPT
ALI1	Alien: Isolation	360	FRP
COD1	Call of Duty	PC	FRP
COS1	Counter-Strike	PC	FRP

tblGenres

Field Name	Data Type
GRef	Short Text
GName	Short Text

tblGenres

GRef	GName
FRP	First-person
SPT	Sport

tblLoans

Field Name	Data Type
LRef	AutoNumber
Date out	Date/Time
Date in	Date/Time
GameRef	Short Text
MemberRef	Short Text
Returned?	Yes/No

tblLoans

LRef	Date out	Date in	GameRef	MemberRef	Returned?
1	19/10/2016	04/11/2016	AFL1	CD01	☑
2	21/10/2016	06/11/2016	ALI1	CD01	☑
3	07/10/2016		COD1	BB01	☐
4	05/10/2016	04/11/2016	COS1	BB01	☑

tblMembers

Field Name	Data Type
MRef	Short Text
Member name	Short Text
Email address	Short Text
Member address	Short Text
Member phone	Short Text

tblMembers

MRef	Member nar	Email address	Memeber address	Member phone
BB01	Ben Boyce	Ben.Boyce@msn.com	266 Campion Way	01395 748163
CD01	Connor Down	Connor.Down@plus.com	84 Saxon Close	01225 791847

tblPlatforms

Field Name	Data Type
PRef	Short Text
PName	Short Text

tblPlatforms

PRef	PName
360	Xbox 360
PC	Personal Computer

qryLoans

Field:	GRef	Title	GName	PName	Date out	Date in	Member name
Table:	tblGames	tblGames	tblGenres	tblPlatforms	tblLoans	tblLoans	tblMembers
Sort:							
Show:	☑	☑	☑	☑	☑	☑	☑

qryLoans

GRef	Title	GName	PName	Date out	Date in	Member name
AFL1	AFL Live	Sport	Xbox 360	19/10/2016	04/11/2016	Connor Down
ALI1	Alien: Isolation	First-person	Xbox 360	21/10/2016	06/11/2016	Connor Down
COD1	Call of Duty	First-person	Personal Computer	07/10/2016		Ben Boyce
COS1	Counter-Strike	First-person	Personal Computer	05/10/2016	04/11/2016	Ben Boyce

25. Sets

applications: students who have applied, but not yet confirmed
courses: students who are on the same course
classes: students who are on the same course and in the same group
tutor groups: students who have the same tutor
supported: students who have an in-class support worker

26. Bubble sort

Bubble sort

A(1)	A(2)	A(3)	A(4)	A(5)	A(6)
52	17	8	98	12	10
17	52	8	98	12	10
17	8	52	98	12	10
17	8	52	12	98	10
17	8	52	12	10	98
8	17	52	12	10	98
8	17	12	52	10	98
8	17	12	10	52	98
8	12	17	10	52	98
8	12	10	17	52	98
8	10	12	17	52	98

27. Quick sort

Quick sort

A(1)	A(2)	A(3)	A(4)	A(5)	A(6)
67	12	13	56	10	21
12	67	13	56	10	21
12	13	67	56	10	21
12	13	10	56	67	21
12	13	10	21	67	56
10	13	12	21	67	56
10	12	13	21	67	56
10	12	13	21	56	67

28. Insertion sort

Insertion sort

A(1)	A(2)	A(3)	A(4)	A(5)	A(6)
78	14	21	67	80	8
14	78	21	67	80	8
14	21	78	67	80	8
14	21	67	78	80	8
8	14	21	67	78	80

29. Searching

1 (a)

	A	B	C	D	E	F	G	H	I
8									
9		1000000	1048576		10000	16384		100	128
10	1	500000	=2^A29	1	5000	=2^D23	1	50	=2^G16
11	2	250000		2	2500		2	25	
12	3	125000		3	1250		3	13	
13	4	62500		4	625		4	7	
14	5	31250		5	313		5	4	
15	6	15625		6	157		6	2	
16	7	7813		7	79		7	1	
17	8	3907		8	40				
18	9	1954		9	20				
19	10	977		10	10				
20	11	489		11	5				
21	12	245		12	3				
22	13	123		13	2				
23	14	62		14	1				
24	15	31							
25	16	16							
26	17	8							
27	18	4							
28	19	2							
29	20	1							

(b)

	Linear			Binary		
	Minimum	Maximum	Average	Minimum	Maximum	Average
100	1	100	51	1	7	4
10000	1	10000	5001	1	14	8
1000000	1	1000000	500001	1	20	11

2 The obvious choice of algorithm for these searches is binary because it needs many fewer comparisons than linear and is therefore a lot faster unless the data set is very small or unordered.

30. Using stacks and queues

- Code is running in original code.
- It starts to execute line of code calling the sub-routine.
- Address of the next line of original code is pushed from program counter onto stack.
- The address of first line of sub-routine is code copied to program counter. Sub-routine code runs.
- When the END SUB line of code is executed, address of previous code popped from stack into the program counter.
- Code continues running from after the sub-routine call in original code.

31. Procedural programming structure

```
Function ReverseLetters(ByVal Rword)
  Dim, AMCount, BMCount As Integer
  Dim ReversedWord As String
  ReversedWord = ""
  For X = 1 To Len(Rword)
    ReversedWord = Mid(Rword, X, 1) & ReversedWord
  Next
  ReverseLetters = ReversedWord
End Function
```

32. Procedural programming control structures

```
Dim NumberArray(10)
Dim X As Integer
Dim NumberMean, MeanAverage, AboveMean, BelowMean As Single

Numbermean = 0
For X = 1 To 10
  NumberArray(X) = InputBox("Enter number " & X)
  NumberMean = NumberMean + NumberArray(X)
Next
MeanAverage = NumberMean / 10
lblMean.Text = MeanAverage

AboveMean = 0
AMcount - 0
BelowMean = 0
BMcount
For X = 1 To 10
  If NumberArray(X) > MeanAverage Then
    AboveMean = AboveMean + NumberArray(X)
    AMcount = AMcount +1
  ElseIf NumberArray(X) < MeanAverage Then
    BelowMean = BelowMean + NumberArray(X)
    BMcount = BMcount +1
  End If
Next
lblAboveMean.Text = AboveMean / AMcount
lblBelowMean.Text = BelowMean / BMcount
```

33. Object-oriented programming structure

```
class Invoice
{
public:
  string customerName;
  float amount;
  string invoiceDate;
  string description;

  void outputInvoice();
}
```

34. Object-orientated programming features

```
Public Class DrawShape
  Public Sub Shape(sender, X, Y, ShL, ShH)
    Dim myBrush As New System.Drawing.SolidBrush(System. <…>
    Drawing.Color.Red)
    Dim formGraphics As System.Drawing.Graphics
    formGraphics = sender.CreateGraphics()
    formGraphics.FillRectangle(myBrush, New Rectangle <…>
    (X, Y, ShL, ShH))
    myBrush.Dispose()
    formGraphics.Dispose()
  End Sub
End Class

Public Class OverloadedDrawShape
  Inherits DrawShape
  Public Overloads Sub Shape(sender, X, Y, ShL)
    Dim myBrush As New System.Drawing.SolidBrush(System. <…>
    Drawing.Color.Blue)
    Dim formGraphics As System.Drawing.Graphics
    formGraphics = sender.CreateGraphics()
    formGraphics.FillRectangle(myBrush, New Rectangle <…>
    (X, Y, ShL, ShL))
    myBrush.Dispose()
    formGraphics.Dispose()
  End Sub
```

35. Event-driven programming structure

```
Private Sub pctEvents_MouseEnter(sender, e) Handles <…>
pctEvents.MouseEnter
  pctEvents.BackColor = Color.Aqua
End Sub

Private Sub pctEvents_MouseHover(sender, e) Handles <…>
pctEvents.MouseHover
  Static HoverCount As Integer
  HoverCount = HoverCount + 1
  lblHoverCount.Text = HoverCount
End Sub

Private Sub pctEvents_MouseLeave(sender, e) Handles <…>
pctEvents.MouseLeave
  pctEvents.BackColor = Color.Beige
End Sub
```

36. Event-driven programming features

```
Private Sub tmrClock_Tick(sender, e) Handles tmrClock.Tick
  Static SecondsCount, MinutesCount As Integer
  SecondsCount = SecondsCount + 1
  If SecondsCount Mod 60 = 0 Then
    MinutesCount = MinutesCount + 1
    SecondsCount = 0
  End If
  lblSeconds.Text = SecondsCount
  lblMinutes.Text = MinutesCount
End Sub
```

37. Coding for the web: Characteristics

Possible response: JavaScript is the most popular web language that can be used to program just about anything to happen in a browser, including games, animations and calculations. JavaScript code can run without internet connection, making it very flexible. It is a dynamic programming language, meaning that it is interpreted at run-time, rather than needing to be compiled. JavaScript provides capable and reliable code that is almost certain to run in every browser as it has become a strong standard. Finally, the massive support available to programmers has contributed to its global success.

38. Coding for the web: Uses

Client-side processing:
Possible response: A webpage could use code running in the browser to validate user input into a form. Running the code in the client makes for a quicker response to user actions.
Server-side processing:
Possible response: A website could use server-side processing to query a database, returning a dataset for the user to see containing matching records. Running the query on the server makes the search a lot quicker as the data is held on the server and there is no need to transfer the whole database to the user, just the matching records.

39. Translation issues

Possible response: There has to be a strong reason to translate code between programming languages to justify the effort required, debugging and time taken. Usually, there will be a change such as new hardware or software that means an existing programmed solution cannot run any more or no longer interacts with other systems in the organisation. Even so, it is often easier to simply re-write an app, rather than translate it into a new environment as this is an opportunity to improve the app and also to have control over the source code. Therefore, the main reason for translating, rather than re-writing, is usually a need to produce a quick fix to the problem.

40. Translation alternatives

Student's own advert.

41. Your Unit 1 exam

Student's own revision timetable.

42. Understanding the question

```
INPUT Materials, Hours, Distance
Set HoursCost to Hours * HourlyRate
OUTPUT HoursCost
Set TravelCost to Distance * TravelRate
OUTPUT TravelCost
Set JobCost to Materials + HoursCost + TravelCost
OUTPUT JobCost
```

43. Short-answer questions

(a) date/time – any data involving a date or time, such as order date, birthday, delivery time.
(b) integer – any data involving a whole number, such as number of items ordered, exam mark.
(c) Boolean – any data involving one of two possibilities, such as delivered or not, passed or failed.

44. Performing calculations

50 steps in level 1 = (50 * 10) + 50 = 500 + 50 = 550
48 steps in level 2 = (48 * 15) + 100 = 720 + 100 = 820
58 steps in level 3 = (58 * 20) + 200 = 1160 + 200 = 1360
52 steps in level 4 = (52 * 25) + 400 = 1300 + 400 = 1700
12 steps in level 5 = (12 * 30) + 800 = 360 + 800 = 1160
Total score = 5590

45. Drawing diagrams or flow charts

```
Set ArrayItem to 0
Set Found to FALSE
REPEAT UNTIL Found or end of array
  IF Array(ArrayItem) = SearchItem THEN
    Set Found to TRUE
  ELSE
    Increment ArrayItem
IF end of array THEN
If Found THEN
  OUTPUT "Item found"
ELSE
  OUTPUT "Item not found"
```

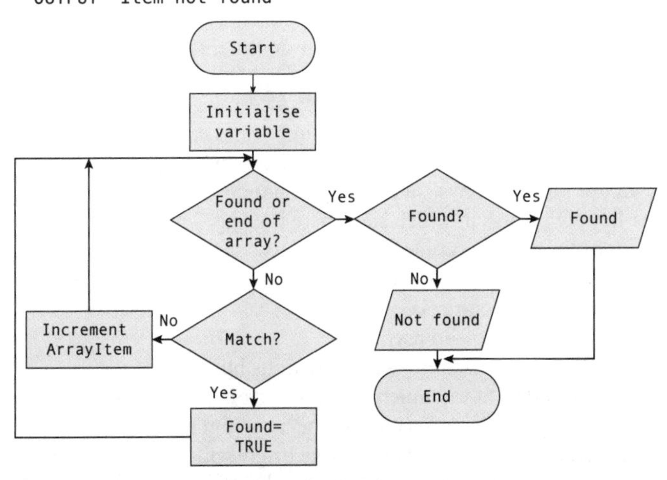

46. Longer-answer questions

A function is written into a program in a similar way to a sub-routine. The name of the function is defined with any arguments declared, for example, Function Password(UserName), with the workings of the function inside this code module. The value returned by the function will be set by a line of code inside the module, such as Password=PWvar, where PWvar is a variable containing this value. Calling the function will be from a line of code elsewhere in the program, using the function name where the value is needed, for example, lblPassword Text = Password(txtUser.Text).

47. Analyse data and information

Translating code between programming languages needs to be carried out if there is a change in the organisational systems, such as disposing of an old incompatible system which is to be replaced by current technologies.
The benefits of translating code between programming languages are outweighed by the drawbacks because there are often more benefits to re-visiting the design and algorithms, rather than simply porting to the new platform.
Benefits can include:

- can save time if the translation works and testing does not identify any issues in the new system
- can save cost from not needing much programmer involvement if there is no need to re-write sections of problematic code
- may be able to use a lot of the original documentation from the original app
- may be able to re-use previous test plan and data.

Drawbacks can include:

- time needed to test the new translations work correctly
- thorough testing required to ensure everything works as intended and that no logic or processing error has occurred
- distancing of translated version from original program design and implementation
- readability of code reduced because humans usually write code that makes sense, using names of variables in such a way that the source code is understandable and self-documented
- translated code may need a lot of editing to make it understandable for future maintenance
- original code results from a lot of thinking and planning, may use structures too subtle for a software utility to recognise, leading to errors from a simple translation.

48. Predicting outcomes

	A	B	C	D	E
1	= tNumber1 + tNumber2 * tNumber3	=E1+E2*E3	415	tNumber1	23
2	= (tNumber1 + tNumber2) * tNumber3	=(E1+E2)*E3	553	tNumber2	56
3	= tNumber2 / tNumber3	=E2/E3	8	tNumber3	7
4	= tNumber1 + tNumber2 Mod tNumber3	=E1+MOD(E2,E3)	23		
5	= tNumber1 < tNumber3 Mod tNumber2	=E1<MOD(E3,E2)	FALSE		
6	= tNumber2 > tNumber1 * tNumber3	=E2>E1*E3	FALSE		
7	= tNumber1 < tNumber2 Or tNumber2 < tNumber3	=OR(E1<E2,E2<E3)	TRUE		
8	= tNumber2 >= 60 And tNumber3 = 7	=AND(E2>=60,E3=7)	FALSE		
9	= Not tNumber2 > tNumber3	=NOT(E2>E3)	FALSE		
10	= tNumber1 <> tNumber2 Or tNumber3 = 7	=OR(E1<>E2,E3=7)	TRUE		

49. 'Evaluate' questions

- Define arrays: An array can be defined as a variable able to hold more than one value. The name of the array ends with a pair of brackets which are used to hold the subscript(s), numbers that indicate which item of the array is to be used.
- Describe one- and multi-dimensional arrays: A one-dimensional array has one subscript, and is conceptually like a simple list of items. A multi-dimensional array has more than one subscript. The number of subscripts is often used to refer to the type of array, with a 2D (two-dimensional) array having two subscripts, a 3D array having three subscripts and so on. A 2D array is conceptually like a table of items, like a simple range in a spreadsheet. A 3D array is conceptually like a collection of 2D arrays, like the worksheets in a spreadsheet or the pages in a book.
- Evaluation of one- and multi-dimensional arrays: A one-dimensional array could be used for a simple list such as temperatures measured by a sensor. Uses of 2D arrays include lookup tables where one dimension could be ranges of weights and the other price ranges. A 3D array could be used to hold appointments where one dimension could be days in the

week, another dimension could be slots in each day and the third dimension week numbers or months. Although all of the above could be implemented in a one-dimensional array, it would be easier to understand and manage using the 2D and 3D examples in multi-dimensional structures. However, there may be a point at which an array structure becomes too complex to conceptualise. For example, how would you model a 10-dimensional array? Programming languages can handle any number of dimensions in an array, but most of us would struggle to follow much over 3D or 4D arrays. It is necessary to consider the purpose for your array and decide which would be best for your program before it is implemented in code.

Unit 2: Fundamentals of Computer Systems

50. Types of computer system

Mobile devices

small, portable, suited to mobile tasks, general purpose computing and communication tasks

Personal computers

general purpose computers, small number of users, suited to general purpose computing and communication tasks

Servers

large, interact with many users and other computers, suited to general-purpose computing and communication tasks and tasks involving large-scale data handling and communications.

51. Internal components

lots of possible answers, for example:

fan – cools the computer, RAM – stores software when the computer is on, ROM – contains boot code permanently, CPU – central processing unit controls the whole computer, ports – connect to peripherals

52. Input and output devices (1)

- a faster speed of response: less time with eyes off the road
- a more accurate response/resolution: easier to find exact track/station
- more controllability/smoothness: easier to find exact track/station
- more feedback/feel: more can be achieved without looking at output
- automation/accuracy: defaults can take user to exact station/last track in one press, etc.
- improved ease of use through ergonomics form factor: good knobs/buttons/scrolls in the right place to minimise hand and eye movement
- making it configurable: setting up own defaults and preferences, saving time and making everything much easier, for example, Radio 1 on button 1
- using the most appropriate interface/connector: using standards to enable swapping to better system when available.

53. Input and output devices (2)

Example notes on upgrade:

- possibly 3D ultrasound
- full colour imaging
- higher resolution
- faster image processing and printing
- automatic display of fetal heartbeat
- higher resolution colour printing with choice of photo sizes for clients to purchase.

54. Storage

An SSD would be the ideal choice. It would be small and light as required by the cyclist. The small form factor would allow it to be packaged well to be marketed with the system. It would be relatively shockproof if the system was dropped or otherwise bumped. It is fast enough to retrieve data as necessary.

55. Data storage and recovery

The RAID 5 system would give an improved performance to some extent over a RAID 1 system. The RAID 1 system ensures a degree of fault tolerance because it creates a mirror image of the original disk as it writes the data. It is more efficient than a scheduled backup as it is maintained automatically as the data are written. If one of the disks fails then it is possible to put a new one in and copy the data back onto it. On the other hand, it takes twice as much storage space as the data that have to be saved, as there is a mirror image.

The RAID 5 system works by writing the data in stripes across a matched number of disks, and then parity information that allows any of the other disks to be rebuilt automatically if one fails. The parity information is distributed across all the disks. If any one disk fails, it can be swapped out and a new one put in and it can be rebuilt from the remaining parity information on the other disks. To this extent it is easier to use and more secure than a mirror system and more efficient as it does not maintain a 1:1 backup against the original data. If, however a second disk fails whilst a rebuild is going on the system will fail completely.

56. Operating systems (1)

A device driver.

The driver:

- communicates between the CPU and mouse using the system bus
- provides the commands that control the hardware
- provides the interrupt handling information
- provides the software interface between the mouse and the controlling software.

57. Operating systems (2)

The printer task is created and put into a waiting state.

When the CPU is ready it puts the printing task into the running state.

- The printer initiates and whilst waiting to print it blocks the printer task.
- The next task starts running.
- When the printer is ready it informs the scheduler and this changes the state of the printer task from blocked to waiting.
- When the CPU becomes free next it carries on printing.
- When the printing is complete the task is terminated.

58 The kernel: Managing the system

- The operating system manages the filesystem so that the physical details are irrelevant to the user.
- File access becomes simple and consistent for the user at the expense of the complexity in the operating system.
- The operating system is free to fragment the data, move the data, etc. without worrying about the user.

59. Operating systems (3)

The user interface should be very simple and easy for the guitarist to use as the guitarist will be using it either whilst playing and so will not have the physical capacity to handle complex operations or between songs in which case there is a very limited time to deal with outputs and accomplish the inputs.

As it will be used in the dark it would help if it had large, bright and very simple controls.

A CLI would be of no use.

A GUI could be used for some functions but really it is too complex and with too much scope for error.

The ideal type of interface would be a custom forms interface with large, bright controls and large bright, obvious outputs (such as pictures of the different amps being modelled) that could be used within the small screen.

Voice input would not be useful in such an audio rich environment, but foot-driven switches and pedals could also be provided so that the guitarist can continue playing whilst choosing a new effect.

60. Utility and application software

Applications – any three sensible choices including point 1, for example:

1 integrated office software – word processor to write letters to donors, recipients and other people and institutions; spreadsheets to simulate effects of different campaigns; presentation software to create presentations for potential donor organisations
2 DBMS – to maintain a database of potential donors and donations for mailshots, analysis, etc; to keep records of PCs in, built and sent
3 accounting – to maintain accounts for charity commissioners, etc.
4 web authoring software – to create web pages for the charity website.
5 payroll – to pay staff.

Utilities – any three sensible choices with an explanation, for example:

1 anti-virus – to ensure systems are virus free
2 screensaver/theme handlers – to put charity logo and/or charity theme on desktop
3 system monitor – to check the system once built.

61. Open source software

The design studio must consider:

- The cost of buying and maintaining the system will potentially be a good deal cheaper.
- Upgrading licences every year or so to latest version on proprietary system can be very expensive.
- It is a transparent development system so a lot is known about it, bugs openly reported and a good deal of support is available.
- The software will be available even when the proprietary system's might be dropped because of lack of economic viability.
- If the software house is able to train and support them then the transition can be reasonable.

62. Choosing hardware and software

S: What security features/issues does each have ? (viruses, secure payments, identity)
P: Which has the better performance? (CPU HG, internet speed, camera resolution, etc.)
E: Are there any efficiency issues playing over the net? (How easy is each to set up/manage, etc?)
C: Compatibility with existing games? (with friends' games machines)

P: Does either have any features that will allow better productivity?
R: Which meets all the specific requirements better?
I: When are each available? How soon can each be up and running?
C: What is the cost of each and are they affordable?
E: Which is easier to use? Any previous experience?

63. Data processing systems

1 Interactive (transaction) system
2 Ensuring the same room/period is not booked more than once; ensuring the users' identities and payment information are correctly captured.
3 Room only confirmed after booking made on database – first to book is only one who is confirmed; all fields validated and verified in detail.

64. Data processing

The customer account is recognised through the barcode so the whole process can be semi-automated. The digits, if they fill the space, can be read reasonably accurately by OCR. The two together can be verified against each other. BioNRG only needs to manually process the ones that are not verified.

It could be improved by using voice recognition software over the phone to ask the questions instead of having to scan the forms, which is still relatively labour intensive. The form could also include dials, whose position could be read reasonably accurately by OCR. Better still is to have direct entry into the computer system against the customer's account which eliminates operator input altogether for BioNRG, and so is both cheaper and more accurate.

65. Data processing functions

Examples include:

Analyse:

- fuel usage between electricity and gas
- between renewable source and non-renewable source
- usage of electricity between daylight and night savings rates
- when fuel usage is particularly high or low.

Aggregate:

- totals on bills
- total revenues from customers
- total and average usage of fuel.

Sort:

- customers by postcode for meter reading
- customers by surname for printing bills to send on each of first 26 days of month.

Convert:

- usage in units to usage in kWh for pricing.

Report:

- electricity statement
- gas statement
- energy report.

66. Approaches to computer architecture

- accumulator
- instruction (CIR)
- MAR (memory address)
- MDR (memory data)
- program counter (PC)
- arithmetic and logic unit (ALU)
- control unit
- clock.

67. The fetch decode execute cycle

It would be simply binary code. A 16 bit binary number would be, for example, 1111 0000 1010 1000.

68. Alternative architectures

It is not sensible to attempt to emulate an advanced system like the Playstation with a less advanced system such as a superscal-based mobile phone. The instruction set would be too difficult or even impossible to emulate on the phone.
The I/O on the phone is so different from the Playstation that it is unlikely that the experience on the phone could even begin to match that for the PS4; even it were possible to attach the Playstation 4 controllers, etc, it is unlikely that the operating system for the phone would be able to support the necessary I/O.

69. Parallel computing

A cluster computing architecture involves having a distributed set of computers all acting together to form the task, such as doing an internet search.
The main positive implications of this approach are that:

- It is highly scalable as it is easy to add new resources, such as memory, switches or even CPUs as these can be simple commodity items and the architecture allows for adding to the network.
- Each CPU has access to its own resources, including memory, as well as shared resources. A computer can be scheduled to search a particular area and store its results locally and then when the local task is complete share these remotely to build the complete picture.

- The networked architecture means that there is less likely to be conflicts for resources than a shared memory architecture.
- It is a relatively cheap method of achieving massive power as a number of simple commodity items are aggregated to a powerful whole.

On the other hand:

- Using distributed resources does require more processing power overall to manage the distributed nature of the processing and needs to be programmed specially for this type of parallelism.
- Access to shared resources, especially memory, can be slower, although this is managed within the scheduling as much as possible. Non-uniform memory access can be managed by caching and by programming to be very efficient.

70. Binary and number systems

1 32 wires
2 2^{24} or 16 777 216 different colours.

71. Converting between number bases

(a) 1010 0001 = 161
1111 1111 = 255
(b) 52 = 0011 0100
148 = 1001 0100
(c) 1000 0010 0001 0001 = 8211
0101 0000 = 50
(d) 92 = 1001 0010
255 = 0010 0101 0101

72. Calculating with binary

(a) 0001 1000 24
1111 0100 − 12
0000 1100 12
111 carry (overflow = 1)
(b) 0111 1111 127
1000 0011 − 125
0000 0010 2
11111 carry (overflow = 1)
(c) 1111 1110 − 2
1111 1111 − 1
1111 1101 − 3
111111 carry (overflow = 1)
(d) 0000 1000 8
0000 1001 9
0001 0001 17
1 carry
(e) 0111 1111 127
0000 0011 3
1000 0010 2
1111111 carry (overflow = 1)
(f) 0000 0010 2
1000 0001 − 127
1000 0011 − 125
no carry

73. Working with numbers

(a) 1.20 E+03
8.00 E+04
(b) (1.2 × 8.0) E+4+3 = 9.6 E+7

74. Text representation

C	3rd letter	67	010	00011
o	15th letter	111	011	01111
m	13th letter	109	011	01101
p	16th letter	112	011	10000
u	21st letter	117	011	10101
t	20th letter	116	011	10100
e	5th letter	101	011	00101
r	18th letter	114	011	10010

75. Image representation

1 20 × 300 × 20 × 300 = 6000 × 6000 = 36 Mp
2 A JPEG image will be best for the web version, where speed of data transmission and loading must be traded off against the quality of the image.

76. Data structures (1)

The most appropriate data structure is a queue. The first print job to be taken off the queue will be the first one to be put on the queue (FIFO). This will allow the printer to print the jobs in the order they are invoked.

77. Data structures (2)

A list is a dynamic structure, like a stack. The size and memory allocated can be varied at run time. It is easy to adapt a list to work like a stack by storing a link to the first item entered so it can be accessed quickly.
An array is a static structure and is more useful for collections of a fixed maximum size. If the required stack has a fixed maximum size an array can be used quite simply to model a stack. However, it will be inefficient in comparison to a list.
A list is the preferred option.

78. Indices and matrices

(a) number [0, 3] = 3
(b) number [2, 2] = 15
(c) number [1, 4] × number [2, 1] = 8 × 13 = 104

79. Mathematical operations using matrices

$$\begin{bmatrix} 1 & 2 & 3 \end{bmatrix} * \begin{bmatrix} 10 & 5 & 20 \\ 20 & 10 & 40 \\ 30 & 15 & 60 \end{bmatrix}$$

= [1 * 10 + 2 * 20 + 3 * 30, 1 * 5 + 2 * 10 + 3 * 15,
1 * 20 + 2 * 40 + 3 * 60]
= [140, 70, 280]

80. Data communications channels

pager: simplex
walkie talkie: half duplex
mobile phone: duplex

81. Types of transmission

HDMI is a parallel form of communciation. Parallel communication is fast and useful for sending huge streams of data as is required for high definition TV. However, parallel cables are subject to noise problems, especially if travelling through an electrically dense situation such as a house and then into a garden. Also the longer the cable the more chance of skew in the data received – i.e. the more difficult it is to synchronise over all the different wires of the cable.
In order to transmit the data, a very high quality cable, shielded from noise, may work; alternately the signal can be deconstructed, translated and sent over shielded ethernet using TCP/IP and rebuilt at the other end.

82. Data transmission protocols

Advantages:

- Packet switching enables transmission to continue even on a very noisy network.
- Lost packets are resent.
- Only the individual packets that are lost need be resent, not the whole message.
- The system does not slow down whilst waiting for a lost packet.
- It is reasonably secure everywhere except at the sender and receiver so it can be difficult to intercept a whole message.

Disadvantages:

- A noisy network will still slow down transmission.

- There is a good deal of processing overhead at sending and receiving ends as packets are broken down and headers and trailer information dealt with.

83. Simple encryption ciphers

Stage 1: 00000011 = 2 + 1 = 3. The offset is 3 so the encrypted alphabet starts with D.

A	B	C	D	E	F	G	H	I	J	K	L	M	N	O	P	Q	R	S	T	U	V	W	X	Y	Z
D	E	F	G	H	I	J	K	L	M	N	O	P	Q	R	S	T	U	V	W	X	Y	Z	A	B	C

Stage 2: ANT = DQW

84. Encryption in modern computer systems

This is symmetric key encryption.
It is not suitable for transmission as the key would have to be swapped openly across the WAN whereas on a private system the key is kept private.

85. Compression

All compression is done on binary patterns (though the computer is able to know what type of data it is dealing with through its operating system). As there are only limited numbers of characters in text (e.g. 127 in ASCII) but 65 535 different possible sound samples and 16 777 215 possible different colours, it is inevitable that there will be many more patterns even in random characters than in images or sounds. Additionally, text tends to come in patterns of repeating words, whereas images tend to be almost infinitely varied.

86. Error detection

9781903133781
= 9 + 8 + 9 + 3 + 3 + 7 + 1 + (7 + 1 + 0 + 1 + 3 + 8) * 3
= 40 + 60 = 100
100 Mod10 = 0; valid.
9781405868052
= 9 + 8 + 4 + 5 + 6 + 0 + 2 + (7 + 1 + 0 + 8 + 8 + 5) * 3
= 34 + 87 = 121
121 Mod10 = 1; invalid

87. Error correction

0100 0001
0110 1100 XOR
0010 1101 parity word

88. Boolean logic

~A . B . C + B . ~C

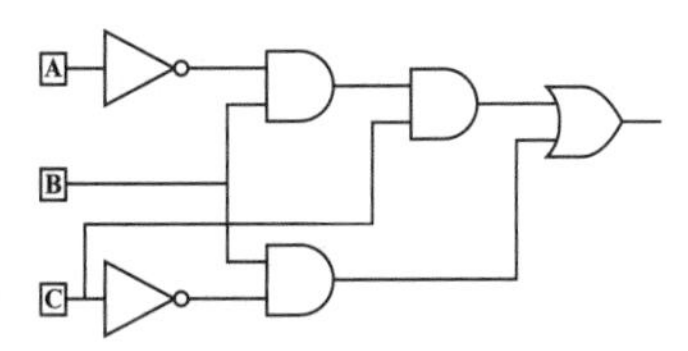

A	B	C	~A	~A.B	~A.B.C	~C	B.~C	~A.B.C+B.~C
0	0	0	1	0	0	1	0	0
0	0	1	1	0	0	0	0	0
0	1	0	1	1	0	1	1	1
0	1	1	1	1	1	0	0	1
1	0	0	0	0	0	1	0	0
1	0	1	0	0	0	0	0	0
1	1	0	0	0	0	1	1	1
1	1	1	0	0	0	0	0	0

89. Simplifying expressions

Steps:
$= A+\overline{B}$
$A.\overline{B}$

90. Boolean logic problems

Circuit:
draw circuit as shown in red box to the right
start **Conditions** on new line

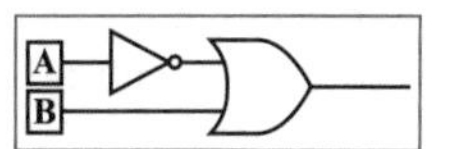

Conditions:
A: recent activity
B: Off button pressed
Algebra
Output: (A. B) OR NOT(A)
Simpifying:
$A . B + \overline{A}$
$\overline{A} + \overline{A} . B + \overline{A}$
$1 . B + \overline{A}$
$B \text{ OR } \overline{A}$

Truth table

A	B	A . B	$\overline{A}$	$\overline{A}$. B	A + $\overline{A}$. B
0	0	0	1	0	0
0	1	0	1	1	1
1	0	0	0	0	1
1	1	1	0	0	1

Check this makes sense in the real world: No recent activity or button off.

91. Flow charts

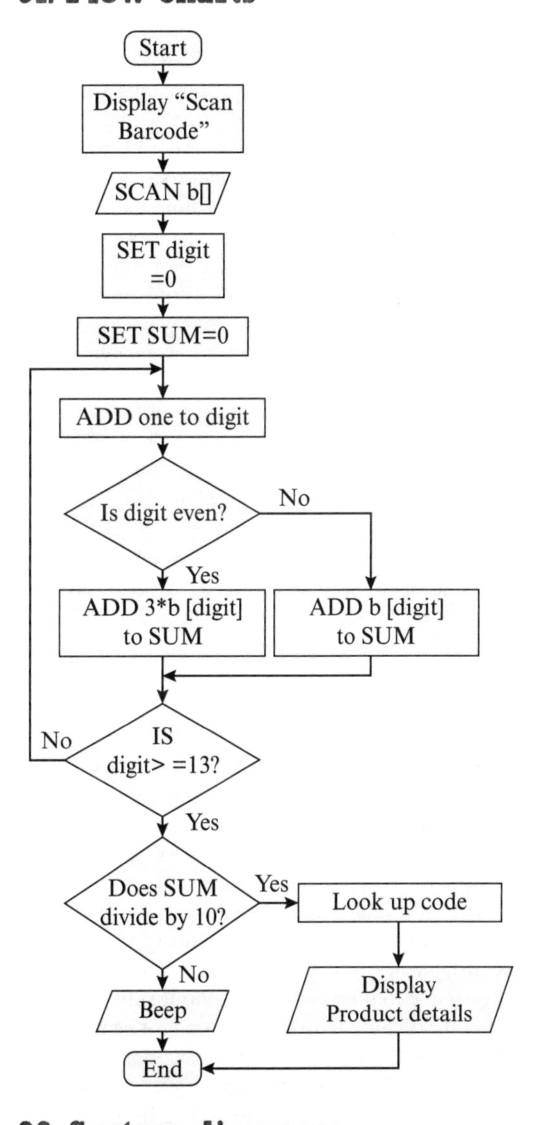

92. System diagrams

(a) The model allows for a very clear, accurate view of the system with no extraneous detail to distract that is easy to follow and easy to use.
(b) It is very easy to update and amend when the system is updated.

93. Your Unit 2 exam

When designing arrays it is optimal to use the same order for traversing a multi-dimensional array as the elements are actually stored in memory. Accessing an array in sequence is much more efficient than jumping about the array to access the same information.

94. Read and understand the questions

Music is an analogue medium, so it has to be encoded to digital to be stored or transmitted on a computer or disk or CD, DVD audio, BluRay disk or similar.

Audio to digital encoding and resolution:

A standard CD takes samples of the original audio 44 100 times a second (44. 1kHz). It stores each sample in a 16 bit word (2 bytes). This takes a lot of storage and original CD audio format (CDA or CDDA) would not be a useful format for storing on a website.

Note also that whilst most people believe that CD music is a very high quality medium some audiophiles suggest that it reduces the quality from the analogue and that even more information should be stored for each sample (e.g. 24 bit or higher) and that it should be sampled more often.

Compressed formats attempt to reduce the amount of space required and thus also the transmission time required.

The digital file can therefore be held in a number of formats of three main types, each with their own implications:

- Uncompressed: The raw digital data is held as it is first encoded, exactly the same as it is on a CD (CDA, compact disk audio). There may actually be slightly more data than the original, as in a WAV file, as there may be some header data attached to the raw encoded data. To play these back simply requires an application that can send the data to a digital-to-audio convertor (DAC) and that this be connected to an analogue playback system. However much the file is stored, retrieved, transmitted, etc, there will be no loss of quality from the original encoding of the recording at the output of the DAC, though obviously the playback quality will depend, as with all formats, on the quality of the analogue playback system (e.g. amplifier and speakers).
- Lossless compressed: The data are compressed, but in such a way that the original data can be reconstructed when playing the music back using an algorithm. This might be achieved, by noticing patterns in the audio and coding these. (For example, 1 second of silence in a file or 0.001 seconds of silence may be stored as a number (length of time) and a code for silence. This way 1 second and .001 second, or indeed 10 seconds of the song will both take the same amount of storage.) Typically lossless compressed formats will take half as much space as uncompressed formats with no loss of quality from that of the original CD. It does require some processing power to handle the extra processing of the decompression algorithms whilst streaming the music to the DAC, but most modern processors are able to handle this with ease. The files are still quite large and thus take up a good deal more storage space than lossy compressed files, and when streamed from the web there could possibly be an issue if there is a slow connection.
- Lossy compressed: The data are compressed to retain as much quality as desired but when decompressed some of the original quality will be lost. Typically, for example, it is possible to lose very high and very low frequency sound without suffering much loss of quality because most humans cannot hear these sounds. An MP3 file will typically store a file in about 8 to 11 times less space than a CD whilst still sounding near identical the original to most users. There is a trade-off to be made between the quality and the compression. The file can be compressed more, but at some point there will be a noticeable loss of quality. This point will vary according to the hearing acuity of each user. Of course, the user may be prepared to accept some loss of quality to store more music files if, for example, their mobile device has a low amount of storage. This is especially true if the analogue output hardware is not of a very high quality, for example a small Bluetooth speaker.

In summary, all three types of file have their uses. For most consumers of Sally's music the lossy compressed formats will be the ideal file type as they offer very high compression rates, but still a very high quality listening experience. They are ideal for storing large volumes of files on mobile devices with expensive storage. They are just as good where the analogue output facilities are not very hi-fi. For the audiophile however FLAC may offer a better compromise as, although it takes a lot more storage space, it retains all of the original digital quality.

95. Short-answer questions

A PNG is a lossless format and thus all the image information can be retained (though metadata may not be).

A JPEG will allow the user to trade off between quality and compression percentage and give some control over the retention of any metadata.

96. Performing calculations

cipher: HEZK

key: 0000 0110

Offset is 6 in denary giving:

ABCDEFGHIJKLMNOPQRSTUVWXYZ plaintext

GHIJKLMNOPQRSTUVWXYZABCDEF cipher

plaintext: BYTE

97. Drawing diagrams

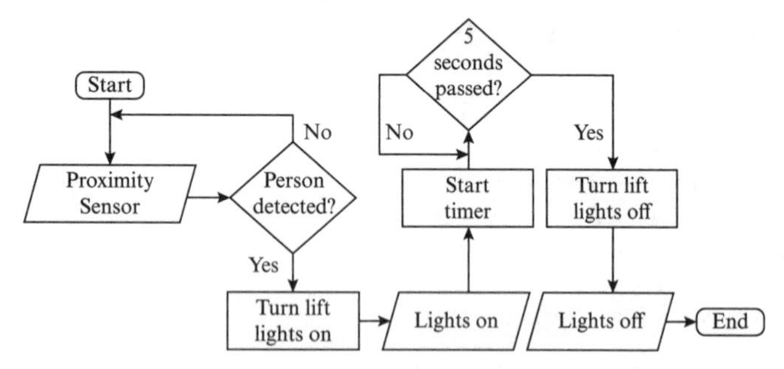

98. Longer-answer questions

A RAID 5 system uses striping and distributed parity across a number of independent and possibly inexpensive disks to maintain a backup of the data as they are written to the storage device.

A five-disk system will write data to four disks and then a parity word on the fifth disk of the set. Each write across the five disks will place the parity information on a different drive so that the parity information is distributed across the disks and not all put onto one disk where it might possibly be more vulnerable.

If one of the five disks fails then it can be rebuilt by using the other four. It uses a simple XOR parity scheme to do this which can be implemented in hardware and is therefore very fast.

This means that it offers a good compromise between security of data, processing overhead and memory overhead.

A five-disk system will have about a 20% overhead in storage space for the parity data which is reasonable for a backup.

The fast parity scheme is very efficient and fast.

It will give added automatic protection albeit at a cost.

The drawbacks of the scheme are that the system will fail completely (original data and backup) if more than one disk fails or a second disk fails whilst repairing the first failure. If the disks are bought at the same time this is not impossible.

Also, and crucially, if the wrong disk is swapped out to rebuild the whole data will be corrupted, so great care must be taken in the event of a system failure.

Overall a RAID 5 system is a good backup system for Fletcher and Nicholson but strict procedures must be put in place in the event of failure of a disk.

99. 'Discuss' questions

The hardware should be robust enough to withstand rough usage by users who may exhibit behavioural issues. If a toddler throws a hand controller about it would be best if it could withstand such 'play'.
The system connections should be as tamper proof and rip proof as possible. Power connections like the magnetic connections on a Macbook would be ideal. Wireless/Bluetooth/IR I/O connections would be ideal so that there are as few physical connections as possible for the toddlers to damage or hurt themselves on.
The systems should be extremely easy to use to deal with from very young and inexperienced users who will not be capable of dealing with detailed or complex instructions.
The software should be capable of being prodded and played with in very random ways without complaining or giving very negative feedback to the users.
The systems should be as easy to set up and use as possible for the helpers whose main job is pedagogical – i.e. helping the toddlers – rather than computing.

100. 'Evaluate' questions

Explanation:
The RFID system will register each student as the card carried by the student approaches the RFID reader. The student will not actively have to log in to the class.

Advantages:
- The registration will be automatic, so the student can't 'forget' to swipe. Entry to the school and each class can be recorded automatically as the pupil enters and updated when the pupil leaves as the ID is transmitted using RF to the receiver.
- It will be a good deal faster entering as no queues need build up as they can when students use the magnetic swipe reader.
- If a card is lost it can be disabled automatically so no other student can use it.

Disadvantages:
- The system will be relatively expensive to change to and expensive to maintain, though this will be offset by the time saved.
- If the student loses the card registration will still have to be manual until the card is replaced.

Recommendations:
Provided the new system is affordable the school should adopt it.

Unit 3: Planning and Management of Computing Projects

101. Costs and timescales

Although the project manager reviewed the project at specific milestones the project was not completed within the allocated time and this may result in additional staffing or resource costs. The interim review shows that the project is on course to achieve its business aims and objectives.

102. Quality and deliverables

Any two from the following:
- alternative text for images to make sure that the webpage content is accessible for all; allow for keyboard input as some users cannot use a mouse
- text transcript of podcasts for visually impaired users
- add captions to all videos with sound for the hearing impaired
- resize text to ensure that the page content is accessible if changed to a larger font
- consistent navigation to ensure that all icons and buttons are in the same place on each webpage
- low reading level to ensure that all users can read the webpage content
- help function to provide guidance on using and navigating the website.

103. SMART objectives

- Sage will attend a game programming class at the local college every Thursday to improve his computer games development skills and apply for game developer jobs.
- Sage will attend a game programming class at the local college every Thursday night 6–8pm.
- Passing the exam on the 5/2/17 is a time-bound SMART target.

104. Project risks (1)

(a) Any one of the following:
- malware attacks through email messages: medium probability 50% = all staff to be made aware of the threat of opening email from unknown links
- trojan horses: medium probability 30% = all firewalls and virus software to be kept up to date
- phishing: medium probability 30% = all firewalls and virus software to be kept up to date
- hackers: medium probability 30% = all firewalls and virus software to be kept up to date.

(b) Any one of the following:
- staff error: high probability 80% = all staff to trained on the system
- laptop theft: high probability 80% = all laptops to be kept secure
- data theft by disgruntled staff: medium probability 50% = all staff use of the system to be monitored
- password types/sharing: low probability 20% = all passwords to be changed every month.

105. Project risks (2)

Hardware and software compatibility is a **high probability** risk with **high impact** and **high severity**. A contingency plan could involve establishing the minimum hardware specification required for the software installation.

106. Project benefits

(a) Increased customer satisfaction, convenience as customers could order goods from any location, cheaper prices, larger stock and variety of goods, saves time as customers do not have to visit shop and queue to pay for items.
(b) Allows the business to access new customers, improved customer service, increased market share.
(c) Increase in market share, increased profits, customer satisfaction.

107. Project life cycle

- Conception and start-up stage: initiates while you are in bed.
- Definition stage: how you are going to get to school.
- Planning stage: plan your way to school – risk/benefits/time/cost.
- Launch and execution stage: you went to school.
- Closure stage: you arrive at school.
- Evaluation stage: review how successful the process/journey was.

108. Professionalism

A written report with budget details and graphs.
Each section should clearly show the monthly expenditure against project budget.
Use fluent English, financial terms and a professional tone.

109. The business case

Any two of the following: improved customer service, improved software tools and functions, reduced costs.

110. Stakeholders

The Project Manager will influence all stages of the project, from planning to handover and closure. They can lessen risks significantly by controlling the risks to minimise uncertainty.

They will also coordinate activities, influence schedules and resources to ensure that the project is completed within the defined timescales and to the required quality specification. The contractor will carry out specialist work to the required specification, within the time allowance and budget. They will also keep the Project Manager updated on progress.

111. Assumptions and constraints

Any two of the following:
- hardware purchase – on budget
- testing completed between 2 December and 8 December
- training completed after the testing stage 9 December
- software bugs removed after testing
- supplier delivers hardware on time.

112. The Project Initiation Document (1)

specific – implement a new EPOS
measurable – EPOS system to be installed 20 January 20--
achievable and realistic – the installation is achievable as it replaced the old EPOS system and suppliers have been contacted; £16 000 budget agreed
time bound – installation arranged for the 20 January 20--

113. The Project Initiation Document (2)

stakeholders = quality manager and testers
frequency = after the software design and development stage
type = report on the testing strategy and testing perimeters with high level specific technical content
purpose = to ensure that the testing covers the requirements

114. Task scheduling

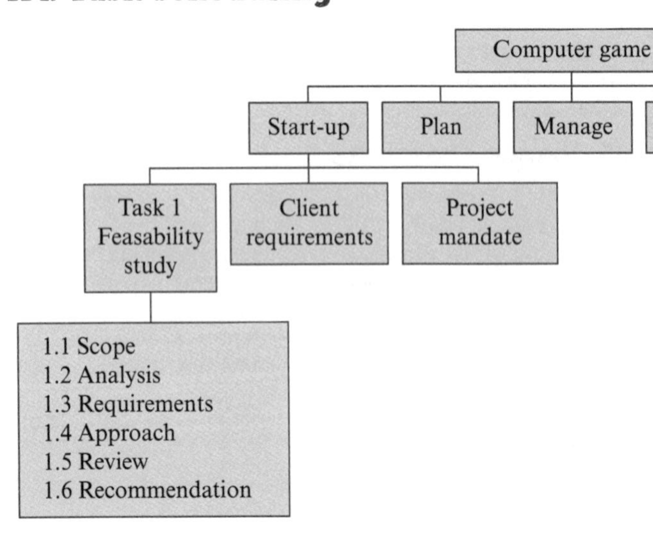

115. Gantt charts

Whichever version of software is used, the Gantt chart should show the list of tasks required, with milestones after each activity.

116. Resources and budgeting

Any one of the following:
- project team are not involved or consulted in the process of task allocation
- the project manager might not have the skills or the experience required to carry out the task
- the technique is high risk as the project manager might not identify all of the project assumptions, constraints and risks.

117. Risk matrix and issue log

Scope creep	Hardware not delivered on time	Hardware compatibility	Testing not completed on schedule
Virus	Hardware failure	Operating system compatibility	Software compatability
Fire	Budget	Testing strategy	Operating system not delivered on time
Natural disaster	Legislation and standards	Power failure	Technician sickness

118. Quality management

Inspection as it must be a planned and formal test arranged and carried out by a software tester. The code is tested, any bugs removed and outcomes officially documented so that it is ready for user testing.

119. Communicating with stakeholders

Any one of the following:
- documents and information stored on a single workspace, users invited to join via email; users allowed different access permissions to folders and documents
- project members working collaboratively on document to update progress/identify completed tasks
- Gantt chart used to track and update duration/time of project tasks.

120. Waterfall software development life cycle model

Any one of the following:
- high risk, for example difficult at the testing stage to resolve design issues
- not suitable for projects where user requirements are not clearly defined
- not suitable for large project as each stage must be completed before the next stage can begin.

121. Tracking progress

Action taken:
1. Observe data entry and record the process.
2. Research similar data entry forms.
3. Interview users to clarify the input requirements.

122. Categorising issues

problem or concern

123. Change management

Additional user acceptance testing is an additional process, not a change of scope or development change.
It may affect the testing stage and have an additional cost. It may not affect the project time as more users could be asked to test the system at the same time.

124. Change management process

Modifications to the designs are required that would impact on:
- the project requirements and effects on quality outputs
- costs of the additional design and software development
- timescales, as they would have to be increased due to additional software development.

125. Implementation strategy

(a) Can be used for an account system so that the outputs from the new system can be compared to the old system to ensure functionality.

(b) Where the new system can be installed in the payroll department first; large organisations can reduce risk into one department.

126. Closing a live project

- recommend testing strategy be documented and clearly communicated with testers
- testing recorded in a central location.

127. Review of project success

Observation is the most appropriate method:

- accurate specific observation of data input staff behaviour
- accurate interpretation of event
- direct method of collecting information, system data and system requirements.

128. Your Unit 3 set task

Own research.

129. Project Initiation Document (1)

Version	Modifications	Author	Date
2	updated for legislation requirements	Piper Lsyoige	18/11/17
3	hardware delivery date update	Piper Lsyoige	11/01/18

130. Project Initiation Document (2)

Any one of the following:

- increase productivity and revenue by at least 10% by 16/08/18
- user satisfaction of 90% by 16/08/18
- scheduled launch and project end date 16/03/18.

131. Project Initiation Document (3)

Carl John, the IT Manager has asked that ISO/IEC 25010:2011 be used as a benchmark for software development.

132. Project Initiation Document (4)

Stakeholder(s)	Frequency	Type	Purpose
Carl John IT System Support Manager	Daily	Email	Project update

134. Resource list and cost plan

Description	Qty	Unit price	Total
Project manager	1	£340.00	£340.00
System design and development	1	£1590.00	£1590.00
Tester	2	£120.00	£240.00
Installation and user testing	1	£400.00	£400.00
Training manual	1	£50.00	£50.00
Telephone support	1	£120.00	£120.00
		£2620.00	**£2740.00**

135. Project Checkpoint Report (1)

Name	Role	Date of issue	Version
Abe Web	Managing Director	25/03/17	3

136. Project Checkpoint Report (2)

Any one of the following:

- additional cost of the delay in the delivery of the EPOS system
- key staff not available on the delivery date
- delayed project delivery date due to the re scheduling of installation
- key staff not available on the installation date.

137. Project closure email (1)

EPOS system launch date 01/04/17 was not achieved.

The EPOS manufacturer has not been able to deliver the systems due to production problems and that delivery is now scheduled for 10/04/17.

The installation company have moved to another project and proposed a new installation date 11/04/17.

The project has been delayed by 10 days.

138. Project closure email (2)

Email	
From	
To	Abe Web Managing Director
Subject	Project closure

Hello

Success criteria

The success criteria are ....

Review of project management

The project management ....

Summary of the lessons learned

Lessons learned are ....

133. Gantt chart

Project planner

Task	Task name	Start date	End date	Duration	05/02/18	06/02/18	07/02/18	08/02/18	09/02/18	10/02/18	11/02/18	12/02/18	13/02/18	14/02/18	15/02/18	16/02/18	17/02/18
Task 1	User requirements	05/02/18	06/02/18	2	■	■											
Task 2	Software design and development	07/02/18	10/02/18	4			■	■	■	■							
Task 3	Prototype testing	11/02/18	11/02/18	1							■						
Task 4	Hardware purchase and installation	12/02/18	14/02/18	3								■	■	■			
Task 5	Software installation and training	15/02/18	16/02/18	2											■	■	
Task 6	Launch date	17/02/18	17/02/18	1													■

Unit 4: Software Design and Development Project

139. Stages of software development

Possible key questions could include (SDLC stages are shown in parenthesis):

- (conception) Is this project replacing an existing computerised solution or manual process?
- (analysis) Are there any existing documents which show inputs, outputs, etc.?
- (design) Which input values need to be validated? And how?
- (implementation) Why is a particular programming language preferred?
- (testing) Is testing thorough enough to help with evaluation?
- (evaluation) How could I improve my approach to solving this problem and managing this software development project?

140. Flow charts

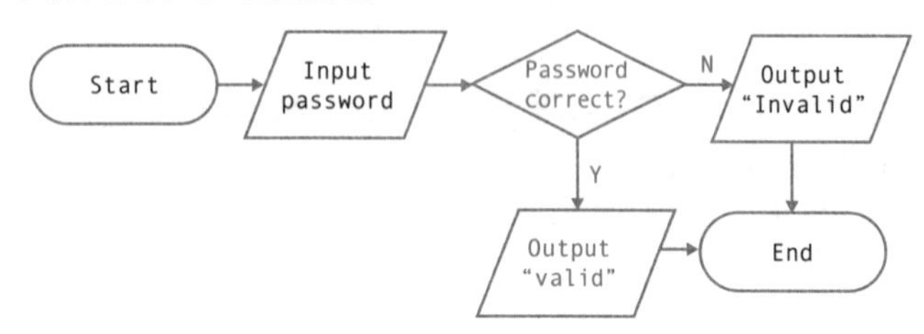

141. Pseudocode

(a) The algorithm uses a post-conditioned loop to calculate and output a times table, based on the user's inputted preferences for the table number and rows required.

(b) corrected pseudocode with commentary:

```
INPUT rows
INPUT table

rowCount = 0
result = 0

REPEAT
    result = rowCount * table
    OUTPUT rowCount "X" table "=" result
    rowCount = rowCount + 1
UNTIL rowCount > rows
```

Fixed errors:

- The wrong variable was being input. This is changed from 'mytable' to 'table'.
- The rowCount variable was being decremented rather than incremented.
- The controlling loop condition used a '<' (less than) operator rather than a '>' (greater than) operator.

142. Test data

suggested test data could include:

	Test data type		
Input	**Normal**	**Extreme**	**Abnormal**
Existing PIN	1234, 2456, 4563	0000, 1111, 9999	A123, ABCD, £$%^
New PIN	1234, 2456, 4563	0000, 1111, 9999	A123, ABCD, £$%^
Deposit cash amount	100.00, 1200.34, 0.12	0.01, 9999999.99, 0	A, z, *, 1.2A
Withdrawal cash amount	5, 10, 50	6, 100, 1000, 0	–10, ABC, 12
Menu option	1, 2, 6	0, 7, 11	A, z, *

Normal data should include values that the user might be expected to input in everyday usage, for example a withdrawal of £10.

Extreme data should include values which are unusual but not impossible, for example a repeating digit being used for a PIN (1111) or attempting to withdraw very large sums of money. Abnormal data should include values which are invalid for a particular input, for example trying to press a menu option which doesn't actually exist (A) or entering a denomination which doesn't exist, for example a £12 note.

143. Design concepts

Testing: comprehensive testing of the program code, especially in an iterative fashion, should identify issues with its performance, outputs, on-screen displays and user dialogues.

144. Design pitfalls

Possible dos and don'ts for a personal checklist could include:

- Do ask questions if you are not sure.
- Do ask for feedback from the client.
- Do plan the design thoroughly before thinking about its implementation.
- Do make sure you have identified all the key inputs.
- Do make sure you understand all the key processes.
- Do make sure you have identified all the required outputs.
- Do check your work for silly mistakes.
- Do try to design for the client not yourself.
- Don't make any assumptions!

145. Code readability

```
/*  function to calculate the cube of a given number

    parameters: float number
    returns: none

*/
void cubeNumber (int number) {

  int cubedValue;                                  //store <···>
  cubed value
  cubedValue = number * number * number;           <···>
  //calculate cube
  cout << number << " cubed is " << cubedValue; <···>
  //output answer

}
```

Improvements to code readability could include:

- making name of function more meaningful
- using white space to add blank lines and indent code
- making variable names more meaningful
- changing parameter data type to int to avoid truncation
- improving the output message
- adding multi-line comments which describe the function
- adding single line comments which describe each line's purpose.

146. Simple data types

C++ answers provided using camelCase:

```
string studentName;
string subjectName;
int examResult1;
int examResult2;
int examResult2;
string year;      or   int year;
float meanAverage;
char grade;
bool unitComplete;
```

Python answers provided using camelCase:

```
studentName = "Jones"
subjectName = "English"
examResult1 = 0
examResult2 = 0
examResult2 = 0
year = "2017"      or   year = 2017
meanAverage = 0.0
grade = "F"
unitComplete = False
```

147. Arrays in Python

(a) `EFATeamResults = [3,0,1,3,3,3,0,0,3,3]`

(b) `desktopWorking = [False, True, True, True, True, True, True, True, True, True, True, True, True, False, False, True, True, True, True, False]`

148. Arrays in C++

(a) `int EFATeamResults[10];`

(b) `bool desktopWorking[20];`

(c) `float riversHeights[2][30];` or `float riversHeights[30][2];`

149. Date and time in Python

Final output: 02/03/2017
Rationale: February is not a leap year in 2017, so adding 2 days would increment the current date to 2nd March 2017. The strftime("%d/%m/%Y") code will change the date object to a string, formatted in a dd/mm/yyyy format.

150. Classes and objects

Highlighted code indicates suggested modifications.
(C++ answers provided using explicit 'this'):

```
#include <iostream>
#include <cmath>

using namespace std;

class circle {

private:
  float radius;
  float area;
  float circumference;

public:
  void setRadius(float tempR)  {this->radius = tempR;}
  void calcArea();
  void calcCircumference();

};

void circle::calcArea() {
  this->area = pow(this->radius,2) * 3.14f;
  cout << "Area is " << this->area << endl;
}

void circle::calcCircumference() {
  this->circumference = 2 * 3.14f * this->radius;
  cout << "Circumference is " << this->circumference << endl;
}

int main()
{
  circle myCircle;

  myCircle.setRadius(10);
  myCircle.calcArea();
  myCircle.calcCircumference();

  return 0;
}
```

Python:

```
class circle:

  def setRadius(self, tempR=None):
    self.radius = tempR

  def calcArea(self):
    self.area = pow(self.radius,2) * 3.14
    print("Area is ", self.area)

  def calcCircumference(self):
    self.circumference = 2 * 3.14 * self.radius
    print("Circumference is" self.circumference)

myCircle = circle()

myCircle.setRadius(10)
myCircle.calcArea()
myCircle.calcCircumference()
```

151. Records

C++:

```
struct comic {

  int comicID;
  string title;
  int volume;
  int issue;
  string grade;
  float price;
  string notes;
};

comic myComics[2000];

myComics[0].comicID = 1010;
myComics[0].title = "The Incredible Hero-man!";
myComics[0].volume = 1;
myComics[0].issue = 300;
myComics[0].grade = "NM";
myComics[0].price = 40.00;
myComics[0].notes = "300th Anniversary Issue";
```

Python:

```
myComics = {  1 : {'comicID': 1010, 'title': 'The Incredible Hero-man!', 'volume' : 1, 'issue': 300, 'grade' : 'NM', 'price':40.0, 'notes' :'300th Anniversary Issue' }}
```

152. Sets in Python

```
Names suitable for boys or girls (intersection)
{'alex', 'chris', 'jo'}

Names for boys, not used for girls (difference)
{'phil', 'frank', 'ron'}

Names for either boys or girls, no duplicates (union)
{'frank', 'alex', 'ron', 'jo', 'chris', 'phil', 'jess'}

Names only used for boys or girls (not both)
{'frank', 'ron', 'phil', 'jess'}
```

153. Lists in Python

False

Python code	Effect on the list
`months=['Jan','Feb','Mar','Apr','May']`	['Jan','Feb','Mar','Apr','May']
`months = months + ['June']`	['Jan','Feb','Mar','Apr','May', 'June']
`del months[3]`	['Jan', 'Feb', 'Mar', 'May', 'June']
`months[3] = months[4]`	['Jan', 'Feb', 'Mar', 'June', 'June']
`print('May' in months)`	False

154. Local and global variables

Corrected code (highlighted code indicates correction):

```
def calcGrades():
    totalMarks = mark1 + mark2 + mark3
    average = totalMarks / 3
    print("Exam average is: " , average)

mark1 = int(input("Enter marks for exam 1: "))
mark2 = int(input("Enter marks for exam 2: "))
mark3 = int(input("Enter marks for exam 3: "))
calcGrades()
```

Debugging rationale:
'average' is declared within the calcGrades function. This makes it a local variable and its scope is limited to this function and so its value cannot be output in the main section of the code. One simple solution is to move the output to the function.

Alternative solution: (highlighted code indicates correction)

```
def calcGrades():
    totalMarks = mark1 + mark2 + mark3
    return totalMarks / 3

mark1 = int(input("Enter marks for exam 1: "))
mark2 = int(input("Enter marks for exam 2: "))
mark3 = int(input("Enter marks for exam 3: "))
average = calcGrades()
print("Exam average is: ", average)
```

Debugging rationale:
An alternative solution could return the average calculated in the calcGrades function and store it in a global variable which is then output.

155. Naming conventions

```
string strPostcode;
float fpConnectionPrice;
bool bIncludesCableTv;
int iNumberOfDevices;
```

The actual variable names should be meaningful in the context given and each variable should use an appropriate Hungarian notation-style prefix which reflects its data type.

156. Arithmetic operations

OUTPUT 2 – 7	–5
OUTPUT "Hello" + " World!"	Hello World!
OUTPUT 10 > 99	FALSE
OUTPUT "a" == "b"	FALSE
OUTPUT 13 % 2	1
OUTPUT 10 > 20 OR 15 < 30	TRUE
OUTPUT 32/2 == 4 * 4	TRUE
OUTPUT "A" < "B"	TRUE (based on ASCII values of 65 and 66 respectively)

157. Arithmetic functions

```
import random

firstDie = random.randint(1,6)
secondDie = random.randint(1,6)

print ("Dice rolled are ", firstDie, " and ", secondDie)
```

158. String-handling functions

C++:

```
string productName = "Widget99";
string category = "Miscellaneous";
int productLength = productName.length();
string stockCode = category[0]+to_string(productLength*9);
cout << "Stock code is " << stockCode;
```

Python:

```
productName = "Widget99"
category = "Miscellaneous"
productLength = len(productName)
stockCode = category[0]+str(productLength * 9)
print ("Stock code is ", stockCode)
```

159. General functions

The Python code will create a text file called 'myNewFile.txt'. The contents of this text file will be a simple list of integers, one per line, starting at 1 and ending at '*n*–1', where '*n*' is the maximum value entered by the user at the keyboard.

160. Validation check: Data type

```
def is_price(n):
  try:
    float(n)
    return True
  except ValueError:
    return False

myInput = input("Enter price of item:")
while (not is_price(myInput)):
    print("Sorry, you must enter a valid price:")
    myInput = input("Enter price of item:")


print("Thank you for entering a valid price.")
```

161. Validation check: Range

```
#input the two integers
number1 = int(input("Enter 1st number: "))
number2 = int(input("Enter 2nd number: "))

#repeat the menu until menu option in valid range
menuChoice = ' '
while menuChoice not in ['A','M','D','S']:
    print("My Python Calculator!")
    print("(A) Add")
    print("(M) Multiply")
    print("(D) Divide")
    print("(S) Subtract")

    menuChoice = input("Choose A, M, D or S: ")

#check menu option and perform calculation
if menuChoice == 'A':
    answer = number1 + number2
elif menuChoice == 'M':
    answer = number1 * number2
elif menuChoice == 'D':
    answer = number1 / number2
else: answer = number1 - number2

#output the answer
print ("The answer is: ", answer)
```

162. Validation check: Constraints

Basic solution:

```
myPassword = input("Enter password: ")
if (len(myPassword) <6 or myPassword.isalnum()==False):
  print("Sorry, password must be 6 alphanumeric characters
(or longer)!")
```

Expanded solution:

```
myPassword = input("Enter password: ")
while (len(myPassword) <6 or myPassword.isalnum()==False):
  print("Sorry, password must be 6 alphanumeric characters
  (or longer)!")
  myPassword = input("Enter password: ")
```

163. Validation check: Case statements in Python

Highlighted code indicates suggested modifications.

```
#input the two integers
number1 = int(input("Enter 1st number: "))
number2 = int(input("Enter 2nd number: "))
#repeat the menu until menu option in valid range
menuChoice = ' '
```

```
while menuChoice not in ['A','M','D','S']:
    print("My Python Calculator!")
    print("(A) Add")
    print("(M) Multiply")
    print("(D) Divide")
    print("(S) Subtract")

    menuChoice = input("Choose A, M, D or S: ")

    #check menu option, perform calculation and output
answer
    if menuChoice == 'A':
        answer = number1 + number2
        print ("The answer is : ", answer)
    elif menuChoice == 'M':
        answer = number1 * number2
        print ("The answer is : ", answer)
    elif menuChoice == 'D':
        answer = number1 / number2
        print ("The answer is : ", answer)
    elif menuChoice == 'S':
       answer = number1 - number2
       print ("The answer is : ", answer)
    else:
       print ("Sorry, that option is not valid.")
```

164. Validation check: Case statements in C++

Highlighted code indicates suggested modifications.

```
#include <iostream>
#include <cstring>

using namespace std;

int main()
{
  int number1;
  int number2;
  int answer;
  char menuChoice;

  //input the two integers
  cout << "Enter 1st number: ";
  cin >> number1;
  cout << "Enter 2nd number: ";
  cin >> number2;

  //repeat the menu until menu option in valid range
  menuChoice = ' ';
  while (!strchr("AMDS",menuChoice)) {
    cout << "My Python Calculator!" << endl;
    cout << "(A) Add" << endl;
    cout << "(M) Multiply" << endl;
    cout << "(D) Divide" << endl;
    cout << "(S) Subtract" << endl;
    cout << "Choose A, M, D or S: " << endl;
    cin.ignore(1);
    cin.get(menuChoice);

    //check menu option, perform calculation and output
    answer
    switch (menuChoice) {
      case 'A': answer = number1 + number2;
                cout << "The answer is : " << answer << endl;
                break;
      case 'M': answer = number1 * number2;
                cout << "The answer is : " << answer << endl;
                break;
      case 'D': answer = number1 / number2;
                cout << "The answer is : " << answer << endl;
                break;
      case 'S': answer = number1 - number2;
                cout << "The answer is : " << answer << endl;
                break;
      default : cout << "Sorry, that option is not <->
      valid." << endl;
    }
  }
  return 0;
}
```

165. Loops

Repeat:

```
#include <iostream>
#include <string>

using namespace std;

int main()
{
  string name;

  //C++ doesn't have a Repeat post-conditioned loop,
  //but we can use a do...while loop instead
  do {
    cout << "Enter your name: ";
    getline(cin, name);
    if (name.length()<1) {
      cout << "Sorry, please try again." << endl;
    }
  } while (name.length()<1);

  cout << "Welcome, " << name << endl;

  return 0;
}
```

For:

```
#include <iostream>

using namespace std;

int main()
{
  //array of 4 exam results for a student
  int examScores[4] = {56, 78, 89, 34};

  //version 1 - using the index
  for (int index=0; index < 4; index++) {
    cout << "Exam " << index+1 << ": " << examScores[index]
<< endl;
  }

  return 0;
}
```

166. Branches

IF...ELSE...ENDIF:

```
#include <iostream>

using namespace std;

int main()
{
  //simple 2 option calculator
  int result;
  int number1;
  int number2;
  char choice;

  cout << "Enter 1st number: ";
  cin >> number1;
  cout << "Enter 2nd number: ";
  cin >> number2;
  cout << "Enter operation + or - :";
  cin >> choice;
  if (choice == '+') {
    result = number1 + number2;
  } else {
    if (choice == '-') {
```

```
      result = number1 - number2;
    }
  }
  //endif
  cout << number1 << choice << number2 << "=" << result <→>
  << endl;

  return 0;
}
```

SWITCH:

```
#include <iostream>

using namespace std;

int main()
{
  //simple 2 option calculator
  int result;
  int number1;
  int number2;
  char choice;

  cout << "Enter 1st number: ";
  cin >> number1;
  cout << "Enter 2nd number: ";
  cin >> number2;
  cout << "Enter operation + , - or *:";
  cin >> choice;
  switch (choice) {
    case '+': result = number1 + number2;
          break;
    case '-': result = number1 - number2;
          break;
    case '*': result = number1 * number2;
          break;
  }

  cout << number1 << choice << number2 << "=" << result <→>
  << endl;

  return 0;
}
```

167. Function calls

```
#include <iostream>

using namespace std;

//validation function; between min and max
int validateInput(int, int);

int main()
{
  int value1;
  int value2;

  value1 = validateInput(10,20);
  value2 = validateInput(1,10);

  return 0;
}

//validation function; between min and max
int validateInput(int min, int max) {

  int value;
  do {
    cout << "Enter a value between ";
    cout << min << " and " << max << ": ";
    cin >> value;
    if (value <min || value >max) {
        cout << "Sorry, try again." << endl;
    }
  } while (value <min || value >max);

  return value;
}
```

168. Data structures

Suggested data structures which could be appropriately used for each data need:

(a) list or single dimension array (simple values of the same data type, for example floating point numbers)
(b) record (different data items, different data types – but all data related to each other)
(c) multi-dimensional array (3D) (*x*, *y* and *z*-coordinates needed)
(d) multi-dimensional array (2D) (*x* and *y*-coordinates needed)
(e) set (specific set operations such as finding the intersect required).

169. Evaluation of design

There are many aspects which should be identified to ensure that the basic functionality is fully covered by your design. However, the four key ones are:

- inputs – values which the user will enter into the design
- processes – key actions that the design must perform, for example validation, calculations, sorting, searching, etc.
- storage – data that needs to be stored, particularly in data files for future read and writing
- outputs – information that needs to be generated by the design and how it is organised.

170. Evaluation of software testing

Common testing mistakes:

- Test data is not representative – the mix or quantity of normal, extreme or abnormal data selected is insufficient and will not test the solution effectively.
- The coverage of the program's logic (for example, different branches) has not been fully tested.
- Actual results are not screen-captured to prove outcomes.
- Obvious differences between expected and actual results are not identified.
- Identified issues are not used to modify the solution, but no reason is given.
- Testing records are not complete.

Common impacts:

- Code is incomplete – not all functionality required is delivered.
- Code is inaccurate – results are wrong or not to the required degree of accuracy, for example two decimal places.
- Code is unreliable – the software solution doesn't always work correctly.
- Code is fragile – the software solution crashes or locks when the user inputs 'bad' data.
- The software solution is flawed and does not meet the client's expectations.

171. Evaluation of the software

- design (pseudocode, flow chart, functionality, algorithms, etc.)
- testing of the software (test data selection, expected vs actual test results, bugs found and improvements made)
- software solution.

172. Your Unit 4 set task

Own answer.

173. Use standard methods and techniques to design a solution

```
counter = 0
WHILE counter <= 10
    OUTPUT counter
    counter = counter + 1
ENDWHILE
```

174. Analyse a task and design a solution

inputs: red
processes: blue
outputs: green

A bank customer enters their INP after being prompted by an onscreen message, the ATM checks if this is correct and either displays a list of options or an 'incorrect PIN' message.

175. Develop a software solution

Parallelograms are typically used for input or output, for example:

Python:

```
password = input('Enter password:')
```

C++:

```
cout << "Enter password:";
cin >> password;
```

Note: it is generally acceptable to convert a parallelogram into two lines of code, separating the user prompt and the input.

176. Select test data

Windows PC:
Print Screen will capture the whole screen.
ALT+Print Screen will capture the active window.

Apple Max OS X:
Command (⌘)+Shift+3 will capture the whole screen.
Command (⌘)+Shift+4, move pointer to the desired window, highlight it, click the mouse will capture the active window.

177. Code readability

To explain the real-world purpose of the program code **not** how the syntax actually works. For example:
Appropriate use:

```
#stores X,Y map locations for 4 hidden objects in our educational game
mapLocations = [[1,2],[2,4],[5,6],[1,9]]
```

Inappropriate use:

```
#this creates a two dimension array of integers
mapLocations = [[1,2],[2,4],[5,6],[1,9]]
```

178. Define and declare constants and variables

date, Boolean, floating point, integer (preferably or floating point) and string.

179. Process data with mathematical expressions

```
#input temperature
degC = float(input('Enter temperature (degrees C): '))

#perform the conversion
degF = degC * 9 / 5 + 32

#output the result
print ('Temperature in Fahrenheit is: ', degF)
```

180. Function calls

```
#include <iostream>

using namespace std;

//function definition
int countChars(string, char);

int main()
{
  //variable declarations
  string inputS;
  char inputC;
  int myCount;

  //user inputs
  cout << "Enter string: ";
  cin >> inputS;
  cout << "Enter search char: ";
  cin >> inputC;

  //call function and store result
  myCount = countChars(inputS,inputC);

  //output result
  cout <<inputC<<" appears in "<<inputS<<" "<<myCount<<" ↩
  time(s)";

  return 0;
}

//countChars function declaration
//arguments = string, search char
int countChars(string myString, char myChar) {

  int charTotal = 0;

  //walk along the string
  for (int pos=0; pos < myString.size(); pos++) {
    //does current char match?
    if (myString[pos] == myChar) {
      //increment the total
      charTotal++;
    }
  }
}
```

Note: depending on the C++ compiler being used and available libraries, it is possible that a built-in function may be used instead.

181. Control structures

```
1 : [1, 2]
2 : [2, 4]
3 : [5, 6]
4 : [1, 9]
```

182. Data structures

```
#10 exam results
examResults = [20, 22, 78, 89, 99, 55, 54, 60, 17, 40]
```

183. Evaluating your software development project

Permanent evidence such as:

- screenshots of the program working
- independent feedback from peers or the client, for example witness statements
- video captures of the program working.

Published by Pearson Education Limited, 80 Strand, London, WC2R 0RL.

www.pearsonschoolsandfecolleges.co.uk

Copies of official specifications for all Pearson qualifications may be found on the website: qualifications.pearson.com

Typeset and illustrated by Kamae Design, Oxford
Produced by Out of House Publishing
Cover illustration by Miriam Sturdee

First published 2017

20 19 18

10 9 8 7 6 5 4 3

British Library Cataloguing in Publication Data
A catalogue record for this book is available from the British Library

ISBN 978 1 292 15020 8

Printed in Italy by L.E.G.O. S.p.A.

Acknowledgements
The author and publisher would like to thank the following individuals and organisations for permission to reproduce photographs:

Fotolia.com: fidelio 86, Viacheslav Iakobchuk 118, perlphoto 75;
Getty Images: BigRedCurlyGuy 10; **Shutterstock.com**: 113, Digital Storm 60, Mjgraphics 59, Monkey Business Images 7, Scanrail1 50

All other images © Pearson Education

Notes from the publisher
1. In order to ensure that this resource offers high-quality support for the associated Pearson qualification, it has been through a review process by the awarding body. This process confirms that this resource fully covers the teaching and learning content of the specification or part of a specification at which it is aimed. It also confirms that it demonstrates an appropriate balance between the development of subject skills, knowledge and understanding, in addition to preparation for assessment.
Endorsement does not cover any guidance on assessment activities or processes (e.g. practice questions or advice on how to answer assessment questions), included in the resource nor does it prescribe any particular approach to the teaching or delivery of a related course.

While the publishers have made every attempt to ensure that advice on the qualification and its assessment is accurate, the official specification and associated assessment guidance materials are the only authoritative source of information and should always be referred to for definitive guidance.

Pearson examiners have not contributed to any sections in this resource relevant to examination papers for which they have responsibility.

Examiners will not use endorsed resources as a source of material for any assessment set by Pearson.

Endorsement of a resource does not mean that the resource is required to achieve this Pearson qualification, nor does it mean that it is the only suitable material available to support the qualification, and any resource lists produced by the awarding body shall include this and other appropriate resources.

2. Pearson has robust editorial processes, including answer and fact checks, to ensure the accuracy of the content in this publication, and every effort is made to ensure this publication is free of errors. We are, however, only human, and occasionally errors do occur. Pearson is not liable for any misunderstandings that arise as a result of errors in this publication, but it is our priority to ensure that the content is accurate. If you spot an error, please do contact us at resourcescorrections@pearson.com so we can make sure it is corrected.

Websites
Pearson Education Limited is not responsible for the content of any external internet sites. It is essential for tutors to preview each website before using it in class so as to ensure that the URL is still accurate, relevant and appropriate. We suggest that tutors bookmark useful websites and consider enabling students to access them through the school/college intranet.